Communications in Computer and Information Science 1207

Commenced Publication in 2007
Founding and Former Series Editors:
Simone Diniz Junqueira Barbosa, Phoebe Chen, Alfredo Cuzzocrea,
Xiaoyong Du, Orhun Kara, Ting Liu, Krishna M. Sivalingam,
Dominik Ślęzak, Takashi Washio, Xiaokang Yang, and Junsong Yuan

Editorial Board Members

More information about this series at http://www.springer.com/series/7899

Mohamed Hamlich · Ladjel Bellatreche ·
Anirban Mondal · Carlos Ordonez (Eds.)

Smart Applications and Data Analysis

Third International Conference, SADASC 2020
Marrakesh, Morocco, June 25–26, 2020
Proceedings

 Springer

Editors
Mohamed Hamlich
ENSAM
Hassan II University
Casablanca, Morocco

Anirban Mondal
Ashoka University
Sonipat, India

Ladjel Bellatreche
ISAE-ENSMA
Poitiers, France

Carlos Ordonez
University of Houston
Houston, TX, USA

ISSN 1865-0929   ISSN 1865-0937 (electronic)
Communications in Computer and Information Science
ISBN 978-3-030-45182-0   ISBN 978-3-030-45183-7 (eBook)
https://doi.org/10.1007/978-3-030-45183-7

This Springer imprint is published by the registered company Springer Nature Switzerland AG
The registered company address is: Gewerbestrasse 11, 6330 Cham, Switzerland

Preface

With a track record of three editions, the International Conference on Smart Applications and Data Analysis for Smart Cyber-Physical Systems (SADASC 2020) has established itself as a high-quality forum for researchers, practitioners, and developers in the field of Cyber-Physical Systems. SADASC 2020 topics cover the main layers of data-enabled systems/applications: source layer, network layer, data layer, learning layer, and reporting layers. This year's conference (SADASC 2020) builds on this tradition, facilitating the interdisciplinary exchange of ideas, theory, techniques, experiences, and future research directions.

Our call for papers attracted 44 papers, from which the Program Committee finally selected 17 full papers and 8 short papers, yielding an acceptance rate of 39%. Each paper was reviewed by an average of three reviewers and in some cases up to four. Accepted papers cover a number of broad research areas on both theoretical and practical aspects. Some trends found in accepted papers include the following: Ontologies, Modeling, and Meta Modeling; Cyber-Physical Systems and Block-Chains, Machine Learning, Recommender Systems, Combinatorial Optimization, and Simulations and Deep Learning.

One workshop was associated with SADASC 2020 on Data Enrichment in Smart Applications (DESA 2020), co-chaired by Imane Hilal and Najima Daoudi, both from ESI, Morocco. This workshop received six papers and its Program Committee finally selected two papers that are included in the SADASC 2020 proceedings as short papers. Each paper was reviewed by three reviewers.

Due to the reputation and topics, novelty of SADASC 2020, editors of well-known journals have agreed to receive extended versions of best papers selected from our program. This year, we are pleased to have a special issue in: the *IEEE/CAA Journal of Automatica Sinica*, the *International Journal of Reasoning-based Intelligent Systems* (IJRIS, Scopus indexed journal), and the *Journal of Systems Architecture* (Scopus indexed journal).

We would like to thank all authors for submitting their papers to SADASC 2020 and we hope they submit again in the future. On the other hand, we express our gratitude to all the Program Committee members who provided high-quality reviews. We want to acknowledge the ease of use and flexibility of the EasyChair system to manage papers. Finally, we would like to thank the support of local organizers.

For conference attendants, we hope the technical program, informal meetings, and interaction with colleagues from all over the world was most enjoyable. For readers of these proceedings, we hope these papers are interesting and they give you ideas for future research.

SADASC 2020 was postponed to June due to the COVID-19 pandemic. The committee and local organizers have done a great job managing the review process and the conference, despite this pandemic.

February 2020

Mohamed Hamlich
Ladjel Bellatreche
Anirban Mondal
Carlos Ordonez

Organization

Program Committee

Abdessadek Aaroud	UCD University, Morocco
Elfazziki Abdelaziz	Cadi Ayyad University, Morocco
El Hassan Abdelwahed	Cadi Ayyad University, Morocco
Wilfried Yves Hamilton Adoni	Hassan II University of Casablanca, Morocco
Abdelhafid Ait Elmahjoub	ENSAM Casablanca, Morocco
Mohammed Al Sarem	Taibah University, Saudi Arabia
Ahmed Azouaoui	ENSIAS, Mohammed V University in Rabat, Morocco
Ayoub Bahnasse	Hassan II University of Casablanca, Morocco
Abderrazak Bannari	Arabian Gulf University, Bahrain
Karim Baïna	ENSIAS, Mohammed V University in Rabat, Morocco
Amin Beheshti	Macquarie University, Australia
Abdelkrim Bekkhoucha	Hassan II University of Casablanca, Morocco
Chourouk Belheouane	Poitiers University, France
Mostafa Bellafkih	INPT, Morocco
Ladjel Bellatreche	ENSMA Poitiers, France
Sadok Ben Yahia	University of Tunis, Morocco
Faouzia Benabbou	Hassan II University of Casablanca, Morocco
Abdelhamid Benaini	Normandie Université, France
Djamal Benslimane	Université Lyon 1, France
Kamel Boukhalfa	USTHB University, Algeria
Mourad Bouneffa	LISIC, ULCO, France
Juan M. Carrillo De Gea	Universidad de Murcia, Spain
Salmi Cheikh	University of Boumerdès, Algeria
Ibrahim Dellal	LIAS, ENSMA, France
Abdeslam En-Nouaary	INPT, Morocco
Bouchaib Falah	Al Akhawayn University, Morocco
João M. Fernandes	University of Minho, Portugal
Alexandra Sofia Ferreira Mendes	University of Beira, Portugal
Philippe Fournier-Viger	Harbin Institute of Technology, China
Dufrenois Franck	LISIC, France
Jaafar Gaber	Université de Technologie de Belfort-Montbéliard, France
Denis Hamad	LISIC, ULCO, France
Mohamed Hamlich	ENSAM, Hassan II University of Casablanca, Morocco
Imane Hilal	ESI Rabat, Morocco
Mirjana Ivanovic	University of Novi Sad, Serbia

Uday Kiran	University of Tokyo, Japan
Mohamed Kissi	Hassan II University of Casablanca, Morocco
Frédéric Kratz	INSA Centre Val de Loire, France
Mohamed Lahby	ENS, Hassan II University of Casablanca, Morocco
Wookey Lee	Inha University, South Korea
Pascal Lorenz	University of Haute Alsace, France
Wojciech Macyna	Wrocław University of Technology, Poland
Simão Melo de Sousa	Release, LISP & LIACC, Universidade da Beira Interior, Portugal
Anirban Mondal	Ashoka University, India
Mustapha Nourelfath	Laval University, Canada
Carlos Ordonez	University of Houston, USA
Samir Ouchani	École d'Ingénieur en Informatique, CESI eXia, France
Yassine Ouhammou	LIAS, ENSMA, France
Krishna Reddy Polepalli	IIIT-H, India
Benkrid Soumia	ESI Rabat, Morocco
El-Ghazali Talbi	Inria, France
Sebastián Ventura	University of Cordoba, Spain

Additional Reviewers

Ait Wakrime, Abderrahim
Amina Taouli, Amina
Bazhar, Youness
Galicia Auyon, Jorge
Ghodratnama, Samira
Haddache, Mohamed
Mondal, Anirban
Mouakher, Amira
Ouchani, Samir
Rahma, Djiroun
Sabiri, Khadija
Yakhchi, Shahpar

Abstracts of Keynotes

Recommending POIs in LBSNs with Deep Learning

Yannis Manolopoulos

Open University of Cyprus, Cyprus
yannis.manolopoulos@ouc.ac.cy

Abstract. In recent years, the representation of real-life problems into k-partite graphs introduced a new era in Machine Learning. The combination of virtual and physical layers through Location Based Social Networks (LBSNs) offered a different meaning to the constructed graphs. As a consequence, multiple diverse models have been introduced in the literature that aim to support users with personalized recommendations. These approaches represent the mathematical models that aim to understand users? behavior by detecting patterns in users? check-ins, reviews, ratings, and friendships. In this talk, we will discuss state-of-the-art methods for POI recommendations based on deep learning techniques. First, we categorize these methods based on data factors or features they use, the data representation, the methodologies applied, and the recommendation types they support. By briefly representing recent key approaches, we highlight the limitations and trends. The future of the area is illustrated.

Keywords: Recommenders · Points of interest · Location based services · Deep learning

Natural Language Based Augmentation of Information, Conversations and Software: Issues, Applications and Directions

Boualem Benatallah

University of New South Wales (UNSW), Australia
b.benatallah@unsw.edu.au

As economies undergo significant structural change, digital strategies and innovation must provide industries across the spectrum with tools to create a competitive edge and build more value into their services. With the advent of widely available data capture and management technologies, coupled with intensifying global competition, fluid business, and social requirements, organizations are rapidly shifting to data-fication of their processes. Accordingly, they are embracing the radical changes necessary for increased productivity, added value, and insights.

However, while advances in big data analytics and AI enable tremendous automation and scalability opportunities, new productivity and usability challenges have also emerged. A commonly overlooked limitation of current systems is that they do not provide effective integration of analytics, AI enablement, and end user workspace environments (e.g., investigators, analysts user productivity tools). We discuss critical challenges in the effective integration of data and AI driven insights and end user- oriented case management technologies. We will discuss synergies between machine reading, data curation, digital augmentation, and assistance as a step forward to empower end users to effectively use data and AI technologies, while share and collaborate on the fly, in order to generate and evolve insights.

We will also discuss cognitive services and conversational AI to augment and improve productivity and effectiveness of their customers, workers, and stake-holders, automate business processes, and deliver data-driven insights. However, there are significant gaps in the cognitive service-enabled endeavor. We will discuss how integration of cognitive services APIs are unlocking application, data source, and device silos through standardized interaction protocols and access interfaces. To leverage the opportunities that APIs bring, we need cognitive service development to 'scale' in terms of how efficiently and effectively they can integrate with potentially large numbers of evolving APIs. We will discuss some critical challenges to achieve this objective. First, a core challenge is the lack of latent and rich intent and APIs knowledge to effectively and efficiently support dynamic mapping of complex and context-specific user intents to API calls. Second, user intent may be complex and its realization requires composition of multiple APIs (e.g., triggering multiple APIs to control IoT devices using one user utterance). Existing intent composition techniques typically rely on inflexible and costly methods including extensive intent training or development of complex and hard-coded intent recognition rules. We will discuss challenges in API aware training of cognitive services. We will discuss novel latent knowledge-powered middleware techniques and services to accelerate bot development pipelines by: (i) devising novel intent and API element embeddings and matching techniques; (ii) declaratively specifying reusable and configurable conversation models to support complex user intent provisioning; and (iii) dynamically synthesizing API calls instead of the ad hoc, rule-based, and costly development of intent-to-executable-code mappings.

Data Mining in Predictive Maintenance: Overview and Applications

Sebastián Ventura Soto

University of Cordoba, Spain
sventura@uco.es

Abstract. Maintenance costs are a significant part of the total operating costs of all manufacturing or production plants. Depending on the specific industry, they can represent between 15 and 60 percent of the cost of goods produced. Recent surveys of maintenance management effectiveness indicate that one-third of all maintenance costs is wasted as the result of unnecessary or improperly carried out maintenance. It is then clear the enormous impact the maintenance operation plays in productivity.

Modern manufacturing systems use thousands of sensors retrieving information at hundreds to thousands of samples per second. Predictive maintenance makes use of this massive amount of data to predict malfunctioning or failures in the system and recommend a maintenance operation just before the failure happens. The objective of this presentation to show the role that machine learning and big data mining algorithms play in the development of predictive maintenance strategies, illustrating with several successful examples described in the literature. We will finish the speech by illustrating a case study: the predictive maintenance of trucks belonging to the Spanish land army.

Contents

Machine Learning Based Applications

Ontologies and Meta Modeling

LGMD: Optimal Lightweight Metadata Model for Indexing Learning Games

Maho Wielfrid Morie[1]([⊠]) [ID], Iza Marfisi-Schottman[2],
and Bi Tra Goore[1]

[1] Institut National Polytechnique Felix Houphouët-Boigny,
1093 Yamoussoukro, Côte d'Ivoire
{maho.morie, bitra.goore}@inphb.ci
[2] Le Mans Université, EA 4023, LIUM, 72085 Le Mans, France
iza.marfisi@univ-lemans.fr

Abstract. Learning Games (LGs) have proven to be effective in a large variety of academic fields and for all levels; from kindergarten to professional training. They are therefore very valuable learning resources that should be shared and reused. However, the lack of catalogues that allow teachers to find existing LGs is a significant obstacle to their use in class. It is difficult for catalogues, or any type of search engine, to index LGs because they are poorly referenced. Yet, many researches have proposed elaborate metadata models for LGs. However, all these models are extensions of LOM, a metadata model that is widely used for referencing learning resources, but that contains more than 60 fields, of which more than half are irrelevant to LGs. The gap between these models and the information that game designers are willing to provide is huge. In this paper, we analyze the LG metadata models proposed in previous research to detect the fields that are specific to LGs and the fields that are irrelevant to LGs. We then propose LGMD (Learning Games Metadata Definition), an optimal lightweight metadata model that only contains the important information for LG indexing. LGMD reduces by two thirds the number of fields compared to the previous models. We confronted this model with the information actually provided by LG editors, by analyzing 736 LG page descriptions found online. This study shows that LGMD covers all the information provided by the LG editors.

Keywords: Learning Games · LOM · Game description · Metadata model · Learning game indexing · Lightweight model

1 Introduction

The use of Learning Games (LGs) has become more and more popular among teachers who want to change their teaching methods. A wide variety of LGs are developed each year for all levels of teaching. These LGs offer great potential for learning and can be used in many ways. They can be used to introduce new concepts, spice up a lab session or even as homework. Unfortunately, these learning resources are not easily accessible. The existing LG catalogues are not well adapted to the teacher's needs: either they are too specialized (only LGs for a specific field and level) or they are too general. Indeed, most of these catalogues offer all types of games, educational and non-education, and

M. Hamlich et al. (Eds.): SADASC 2020, CCIS 1207, pp. 3–16, 2020.
https://doi.org/10.1007/978-3-030-45183-7_1

are not always up to date [1–3]. Teachers who are looking for LGs therefore have to find these catalogues and browse several of them before finding the appropriate LG. Table 1 presents the three up-to-date catalogues with the most LGs, that can be found in the literature [1, 4].

Table 1. List of biggest Learning Games catalogues

Catalogue	All games	LGs
SeriousGameClassification [5]	3,300	402
MobyGames [6]	110,558	260
Serious Games Fr [7]	183	74

The problem with these catalogues is that they do not offer filtering or indexing systems that facilitate the selection of LGs that are adapted to specific teaching needs. The *SeriousGameClassification* [5] catalog, for example, offers to filter the list of games depending on their purpose (e.g. educational message, subjective message, storytelling), the target market (e.g. entertainment, corporate, media), and the public (e.g. general public, 3–6 years). The *MobyGames* [6] catalog, on the other hand, proposes to search for games by platform (e.g. PC, Android, Nintendo), the production year (e.g. 2008, 2019), the game theme (e.g. shooter, visual novel, board game) and the rating system (e.g. PEGI rating, ESRB rating). Finally, *Serious Game Fr* [7] only allows searching by title and keywords. These search filters are inadequate for teachers. Not only do they not propose basic research criteria such as the educational field, the age or grade level of the students, but they do not make it easy to pick out the LGs from the non-educational games, that are much more numerous.

Yet, several elaborate LG indexing models have been proposed. These early models are based on standards established for learning resources such as the *Learning Object Metadata* (LOM). This standard was used for the *Learning Object Repositories* (LOR) project [8] and the ARIADNE project [9]. It is composed of 68 fields that cover all aspects of learning resources. In order to inventory LGs, several researchers proposed extensions of LOM by modifying the meaning of some fields and by adding extra fields to cover the gaming aspects. These metadata models are therefore very heavy, and more than half of the fields are irrelevant to LGs. Even if we consider only the appropriate fields, many appear too complex and specific for LG editors, who are simply not willing to spend time providing such detailed information [1]. In addition, LG editors do not come from the academic world and are not familiar with this standard or its vocabulary. They are more accustomed to indexing systems used in the video gaming industry.

As a result, LGs are completely absent from learning resource platforms and find themselves indexed on specialized game platforms, hidden among many non-educational games. Not only is it not very likely for teachers to find these platforms but, even if they do, the filtering systems on these platforms are of little use to find LGs that could fit their educational needs.

In this paper, our objective is to propose an optimal metadata model for LGs, that contains only the important information to reference LGs. First, we provide an analysis of the LG metadata models proposed in previous research to detect the fields that are specific to LGs and the fields that are not relevant to LGs. We then propose LGMD (Learning Games Metadata Definition), an optimal lightweight metadata model for LGs. Finally, we test the proposed model by comparing it with the data provided by LG editors.

2 Analysis of Metadata Models for Learning Games

2.1 Characterization of Learning Resources

As any other type of learning resource, sharing and reusing LGs makes complete sense. Even more so given the fact that the development of LGs requires a lot of financial investment and a high level of skills in design, programming and scriptwriting [10, 11]. Furthermore, in the context of the constant improvement of teaching methods, the demand for these innovative pedagogical tools is high. In order to help teachers find LGs that meet their needs quickly, these resources need to be categorized with the relevant type of information [12]. Early research on LG inventories propose the use of the LOM model, widely used for describing learning resources [13, 14] and one of the key foundations to Learning Management Systems. LOM has 68 fields, organized in nine categories, that describe all aspects of learning resources [15, 16]:

- General - Main characteristics of the learning resource (title, description, etc.).
- Lifecycle - Information about the design of the learning resource (version, etc.).
- Meta-Metadata - Information about the metadata models used to describe the learning resource.
- Technical - Technical characteristics (format, size, installation mode, etc.).
- Educational - Pedagogical functions of the resource and its context of use (type of audience, age, language of the learner, etc.).
- Rights - Legal conditions for using the resource (costs, copyright, etc.).
- Relation - Relationships that may exist between resources.
- Annotation - Comments on the pedagogical use of the resource.
- Classification - Define the resource with classification system such as taxonomies.

LOM can be used to characterize the educational aspect of LGs, but it does not cover their gaming aspects. Important characteristics such as the platform on which the game is played (computer, console, online), the gameplay, the graphical style of the game (2D, isometric, 3D) or the type of game, are not found in LOM, initially intended for learning resources such as books, images, audio and video [11]. How can these characteristics be considered in a metadata model? In the following section we analyze several LOM extensions that aims to solve this problem.

2.2 Metadata Models for Learning Games

In this section, we focus on the metadata models proposed to describe LGs. Indeed, LGs have specific characteristics that are not found in other learning resources [17] and therefore require the modification of LOM [18, 19].

One of the first LG metadata models, proposed in 2011, is LOMFR-SG, an extension of the French version of LOM for Serious Games [20]. The authors add seven extra fields in the Educational category. Some of these are required or recommended such as "5.2 Learning Resource Type" and "5.14. Game Type" and others optional such as "5.12 resulting activity", "5.13 knowledge validation", "5.15 tutor assistance", "5.16 re-playability" and "5.17 game objectives". They also added an extra category 10. Course integration with 4 fields that provide information on how the LG can be used on the learning platform. In particular, the field "10.4 progress indicator" indicates the information that can be used by teachers to evaluate the progress of their students (e.g. scores, gaming time, % of completion).

Another model, called G/P/S, identifies several important fields for the description of LGs [21]. For example, in the Gameplay section of this model, we can see the importance of defining the message of the game and to distinguish the student's player profile from the student's learner profile. Hendrix et al. [22] propose to expand the existing technical category by adding information on the operating systems required to play the LGs, in addition to the platform (i.e. PC, Nintendo, Tablet, etc.). They also add a field related the game's scoring based on systems such as the PEGI (*Pan European Game Information*) [22, 23]. Similarly, the contributions of the SG-LOM model [24] add several fields: "8.5 game rating", "8.4 gaming experience required" and "5.18 multiplayer value". They also add the recommended field "9.5 gameplay" which provides information about the graphical style of the LG (e.g. 2D, isometric, 3D). Table 2 combines the above proposals, in which we find 60 fields (20 required or recommended and 40 optional). Most of the additions (marked with a *) or modifications are in the Educational categories and in the new category 10 *Course integration*.

Table 2. LOM field extensions to match the characteristics of Learning Games

Categories	Main fields	Quality	Authors
1. General	1.1 Identifier	Req	
	1.2 Title	Req	
	1.3 Language	Rec	
	1.4 Description	Rec	
	1.5 Keywords	Rec	
	1.6 Coverage	Opt	
	1.7 Structure	Opt	
	1.8 Aggregation Level	Opt	
	1.9 Documentary Type*	Rec	LOMFR-SG
2. Lifecycle	2.1 Version	Rec	
	2.2 Status	Rec	
	2.3 Contribution	Rec	
3. Meta-Metadata	3.1 Identifier	Opt	
	3.2 Contribution	Opt	
	3.3 Metadata Schema	Opt	
	3.4 Language	Opt	

(*continued*)

Table 2. (*continued*)

Categories	Main fields	Quality	Authors
4. Technical	4.1 Format	Rec	LOMFR-SG
	4.2 Size	Opt	
	4.3 Location	Rec	LOMFR-SG
	4.4 Platform Requirements*	Opt	LOMFR-SG, SG-LOM
	4.5 Installation Remarks	Opt	
	4.6 Other Platform Requirements	Opt	
	4.7 Duration	Opt	
5. Educational	5.1 Interactivity Type	Opt	
	5.2 Learning Resource Type*	Rec	LOMFR-SG
	5.3 Interaction Level	Opt	
	5.4 Semantic Density	Opt	
	5.5 Public	Rec	
	5.6 Context	Rec	
	5.7 Typical Age Range	Opt	
	5.8 Difficulty	Opt	
	5.9 Typical Learning Time	Opt	
	5.10 Description	Opt	
	5.11 Language	Opt	
	5.12 Resulting Activity*	Opt	LOMFR-SG
	5.13 Knowledge validation*	Opt	LOMFR-SG
	5.14 Game Type*	Rec	LOMFR-SG
	5.15 Tutors assistance*	Opt	LOMFR-SG
	5.16 Re-Playability*	Opt	LOMFR-SG, SG-LOM
	5.17 Game objectives*	Opt	LOMFR-SG
	5.18 Multiplayer Value*	Opt	SG-LOM
6. Rights	6.1 Cost	Opt	
	6.2 Copyright	Rec	
	6.3 Description	Rec	
7. Relation	7.1 Kind of relation	Opt	
	7.2 Resource	Opt	
8. Annotation	8.1 Entity	Opt	
	8.2 Date	Opt	
	8.3 Description	Opt	
	8.4 Gaming Experience Required*	Opt	SG-LOM, [20, 24]
	8.5 Game Rating*	Opt	SG-LOM, [22]

(*continued*)

Table 2. (*continued*)

Categories	Main fields	Quality	Authors
9. Classification	9.1 Purpose	Rec	SG-LOM, G/P/S, [22]
	9.2 Taxon Path	Opt	
	9.3 Description	Opt	
	9.4 Keywords	Opt	
	9.5 Gameplay*	Rec	SG-LOM, G/P/S
10. Course Integration*	10.1 Component Type*	Rec	LOMFR-SG
	10.2 Available settings*	Opt	LOMFR-SG
	10.3 Observables*	Opt	LOMFR-SG
	10.4 Progress indicators*	Opt	LOMFR-SG, SG-LOM

* Categories and field added in LOM extension
Req = Required, Rec = Recommended, Opt = Optional

There are several similarities between the model proposals that show the importance of the added fields. Apart from LOMFR-SG, which removes three fields from the Educational category, the other metadata schemas keep all the LOM fields, probably to stay compatible with existing learning resource repositories. However, in reality, only 20 fields are actually used in most of the learning repositories [25]. The authors of this study also estimate that the LOM fields are not used correctly in 68% of the cases. Furthermore, it is very rare to find learning repositories that simultaneously reference textual documents, audiovisual materials and LGs. Is it therefore relevant to keep so many fields that will certainly not be used?

It is difficult for the LG editors and catalogue designers to reference LGs according to metadata models with so many fields and several ambiguities [20]. For example, the field "language", which is found in several categories (General, Pedagogical and Metadata) with different values for each of them, can create confusion in its interpretation. The same applies to the fields "description", "contribution" and "platform requirements". Therefore, we may wonder whether the proposed LOM extensions do not add more weight to the already complex metadata schema? We therefore propose, in the following section, a lightweight metadata model, that will contain only the fields that are relevant to LG characteristics.

3　Learning Game Metadata Definition (LGMD)

3.1　LGMD Description

The analysis of LG metadata models shows that previous research has resulted in extensions that make LOM even more complex. The challenge is to propose an optimal metadata model, that contains only the fields necessary for describing LGs in all their complexity. Our hypothesis is that this optimal model can be found by keeping all the fields that were identified as important in the previous LG metadata models and removing all the fields that are not relevant to LGs.

General Category

In this category, we keep all the fields with the quality "required" or "recommended" (see Table 3). We also remove the field "document type", since all the LGs would have the same value "Learning Game" for this field. We also remove the field "1.1 identifier" because this information is provided by the catalog rather than the LG editors.

Table 3. Fields in the General category of the LGMD model

Fields	Explanation	Quality
Title	Title or name of the LG	Req
Language	LG language	Rec
Description	Complete description of the LG and its environment	Req
Keywords	Set of keywords to classify the LG without reading the description	Req

Lifecycle Category

In this category, we remove the field "status" which deals with the availability of the LG, because we do not find useful to index unavailable LGs and this information can be found in the "version" field. In addition, we add the field "date" to describe the date of LGs release.

Technical Category

In addition to the fields qualified as recommended, we keep the fields "size" and "technical requirement" which describe respectively the size and the platform required to run the LG. We believe the last field is essential because it will help teachers select LGs according to the material, they have access to (e.g. tablet, computer, Nintendo).

Educational Category

In this category, we merge the fields "context" and "public" since they describe the same information. We remove the "learning resource type" that would be "application/game" for all LGs. We add the field "domain", which is originally part of values of field "9.1 purpose" in the Classification category. It seems important to include this field in the Educational Category because it describes the educational field for with the LG can be used. Finally, we keep the field "progress indicator", that was in the extra category (10 - Course integration), added by the LG metadata models (see Table 4).

Table 4. Fields in the Educational category of the LGMD model

Fields	Meaning	Examples	Quality
Public	The type of learner for whom the LG is intended	Student, Middle-School	Rec
Age Range	The age required for using the LG	6–10th, 18+, −6	Rec
Game Type	The type of gameplay	Puzzle, Strategy, Adventure	Rec
Domain	The field of study for which the LG can be used	Math, Biology, Environment	Req
Resulting Activity	The pedagogical activities engaged during the LG	Create, exchange, Organize	Opt
Knowledge Validation	The skills and knowledge developed with the LG	The alphabet, quantum physics, ecofriendly attitude	Opt
Multiplayer value	The game mode	Solo, Multiplayer	Opt
Progress Indicator	Information on the learner's progression in the LG	Scoring, percentage of good answers, timer	Opt

Rights Category

The "description" field of this category creates an ambiguity with those in the General and Annotation categories and the information can be provided in the "copyright" field value. Thus, only the "copyright" and "cost" fields are kept.

Category Classification

In this category, we integrate the field "game rating" proposed by the LOM extensions in the category "Annotation", since we consider it is a characteristic of the LG that allows us to classify it. Indeed, the rating systems used as values in this field are considered as classification systems based on the player's profile (e.g. PEGI +3, ESRB +14) [26, 27]. We also keep the field "gameplay" proposed by the LOM extensions. We remove the other fields because they are redundant. Indeed, the "taxon path" field that describes the taxonomy in which the LG is classified represents a different classification model that needs to be dissociated from the metadata model. The same applies to the "description" and its associated "descriptor" fields. The "9.1 purpose" field is in fact a collection of values that can be found in several other fields such as "8.4 gaming experience required", "5.13 knowledge validation" and "5.5 public". Often, in this field, we find a value about the domain of LGs. Yet, this is the essential educational information we need to have about LGs.

3.2 LGMD Model Overview

In summary, the LGMD model keeps most of the fields qualified as required or recommended and deletes the fields qualified as optional, except for some that we consider important for the description of LGs such as the fields "5.12 resulting activity" and "5.13 knowledge validation", "4.2 size" and "4.4 Platform requirements". The categories

Meta-metadata, Relation and Annotation are removed because they do not provide significantly useful information for the description of LGs and result in creating ambiguity.

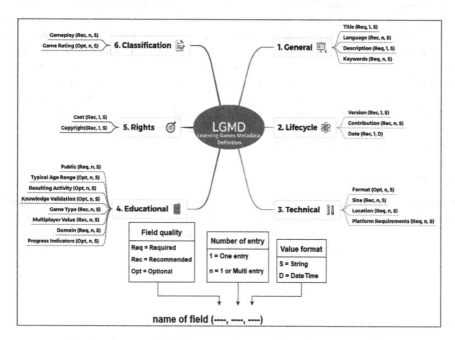

Fig. 1. Overview of the Learning Game Metadata Definition fields

As depicted in Fig. 1, the resulting LGMD model has 23 fields, divided into six categories. It reduces the fields of the metadata models studied previously by two thirds, as it is intended to be concise and simple so that it can be easily used by LG editors. However, the trap to be avoided is removing too many fields. Removing fields that could be relevant for describing LGs. In the next section, we therefore verify if the LGMD metadata model covers all the information currently provided by LG editors.

4 Analysis of Data Provided by Learning Games Editors

4.1 Data Collection

The LGMD model is designed to be lighter and easier to use for LG editors than the existing models based on LOM extensions [20, 25]. We therefore removed all the fields that seemed redundant or irrelevant to LGs. In order to make sure we did not remove too many fields, we need to ensure that the fields in LGMD still cover the information actually provided by LG editors.

To do this, we analyze data from 736 LGs, available in the three major LG catalogues (see Table 1). We limited ourselves to LGs created after 2008 and available on the main platforms (PC, Mac, Smartphone, Tablet) and operating systems (Windows, Linux, iOS, Android) or online.

As LG editors do not follow a specific metadata model, we used the description information of their LGs to find the values for each of the fields of the LOM extension models presented in Table 2 and the fields of the proposed LGMD model. We rely on an automatic extraction model, presented in previous work, that parses and analyzes text on web pages. This extraction model was tested on a sample of 24 LG web pages, with the help of teachers. Even though these pages had very different formats (e.g. simple pages, pages with popups, pages presenting several LGs), the keywords extracted for each of the metadata fields have an average accuracy score of 80% with a minimum of 60%. The extraction of the text for the "description" field is particularly good with an average accuracy level of 85%, and never lower than 80%. This extraction model can therefore be considered as an effective way to extract useful information for each metadata field.

4.2   Result Analysis

The analysis of the data from the 736 LGs shows that only the information for 17 fields is provided (out of the 23 in the LGMD model and the 70 in the LOM extension).

First of all, it is important to note that the extraction model found absolutely no information for the 47 fields, that were in the LOM extensions, and that we considered non-relevant.

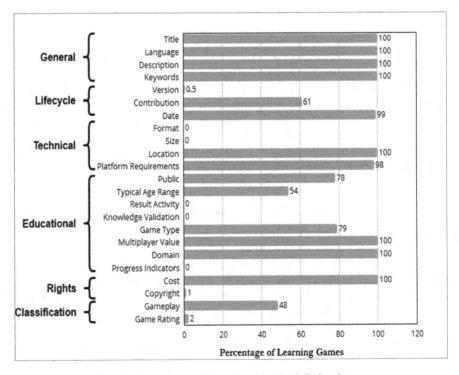

Fig. 2. Percentage of Data Provided by LG developers

As depicted in Fig. 2, out of the 23 fields in LGMD, 10 fields are provided 100% of the time and five fields are provided about 50% of the time. However, it appears to be very hard to find information for the remaining fields. The information for the "copyright" field is only found on 1% of the pages, 2% for the "game rating" and 0.5% for the "version". For the remaining 5 fields of the LGMD (i.e. "format", "size", "result activity", "knowledge validation" and "progress indicators") none of the LG editors of the 736 LGs provide this information (0%). Nonetheless, all fields marked as required or recommended in LGMD are represented at least once. The statistics also show that the completion rate of all the categories in LGMD is at least 50%. For the General, Rights and Classification categories this number goes up to 100% (see Fig. 3).

For the LOM extensions, on the other hand, the completion rate for the categories are much lower. The Meta-Metadata, Relation and Annotation categories have absolutely no fields provided so we did not represent then on the Fig. 3. Only the Rights category has more than 50% of its fields filed out. The data provided for the other categories (e.g. General, Lifecycle, Technical, Educational and Classification) is between 20% and 44%.

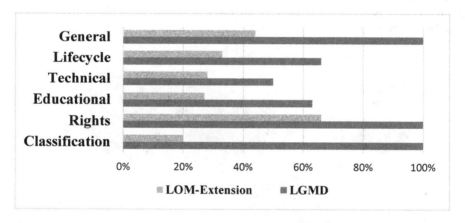

Fig. 3. Percentage of data provided per category in LOM extensions compared to LGMD.

4.3 Discussion

The first interpretation we can make of these results is that the LGMD model covers all the information provided by LG editors, despite the reduced number of its fields. The fact that LG editors do not provide any information for the fields that were not selected for LGMD proves they are not relevant for LGs.

However, the information for some of the fields in LGMD is also very close or equal to 0%. For example, the information regarding the version of the LG is very rarely provided by LG editors. This can be explained by the fact that they probably always provide the latest version of their LGs. However, it is essential that editors provide this information that can guide teachers in their choice of LGs. A new version of a LG may target newer material and teachers may be looking for an earlier game release for older material. Alternatively, a teacher may be looking for a particular version in which emphasis was put on a particular part of a lesson.

Similarly, none of the LG editors provide information for the field "knowledge validation" which could be very useful for teachers. Indeed, the text description written by LG editors only provide information on the educational field without giving a list of the precise target knowledge that one can acquire with the LG. This is probably due to the fact that LG editors are not acquainted with the precise terms used in academia to describe. This can also explain why no information can be found for the field "resulting activity".

Even though very little information can be found on LGs pages for these fields in the current catalogues, we argue that they should be kept in order to encourage LG editors to provide this information that will no doubt help teachers find the appropriate LGs.

Regarding the fields provided at a low percentage such as "game rating", we can observe that for all the LGs where the "typical age range" is provided (e.g. 3 to 6 years old), the "game rating" (e.g. PEGI +3 which means for kids three years and up, ESRB −14 which means for kids younger than 14) is not provided and vice versa (Fig. 4). We explain this phenomenon by the fact that these two fields provide similar types of information on the age of the learners with the "public" field. Perhaps a field that can group the data types of these three fields together would allow for a more concise metadata schema.

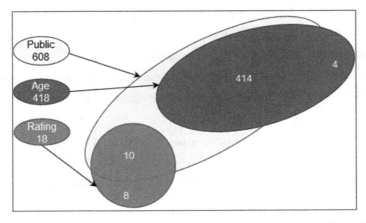

Fig. 4. Distribution of the age and assessment fields in relation to the public field

5 Conclusion

Many Learning Games (LGs) have been created these past years but there is still no centralized platform that allows teachers to search for existing LGs and find those that meet their specific teaching needs. Several researchers have tried to reproduce the success of Learning Object Repositories that are widely used in academia. Several extensions of the Learning Object Metadata (LOM) standard have been proposed. However, these extensions, based on an already heavy model, offer more than 70 fields and use very specific and complex vocabulary. LG editors are not familiar with these standards and are simply not willing to spend so much time providing information for all these fields, including the fact that more than half of the fields are irrelevant for LGs.

In this paper, we propose LGMD (Learning Games Metadata Definition), a lightweight optimal LG metadata model with only 23 fields distributed in 6 categories: general, lifecycle, technical, educational, rights and classification. It contains only the fields of the LOM extensions that are relevant for LGs. Despite its limited number of fields, an analysis of 736 LG web pages, proves that it covers all the data currently provided by LG editors. The information for 2/3 of these fields can be found in more than 50% of the cases. We argue that the remaining eight fields, for with editors rarely provide information, should be kept, in order to encourage them to provide this information, which will help teachers find their ideal LG. In addition, LGMD is retro compatible with the LOM standard. This means that the referencing of an educational resource with the LGMD can be converted into LOM. This compatibility ensures the interoperability with existing learning resource repositories.

The proposed LGMD model is therefore suitable for practical use by editors in the referencing of their LGs. However, further studies are needed to measure how practical LGMD is for the LGs indexing. Moreover, we intent to use this model to reference LGs in a new catalogue. The filtering tools and the vocabulary used will need to be validated with the participation of teachers of all levels and from various disciplines.

References

1. Alvarez, J., Plantec, J.-Y., Vermeulen, M., Kolski, C.: RDU Model dedicated to evaluate needed counsels for Serious Game projects. Comput. Educ. **114**, 38–56 (2017). https://doi.org/10.1016/j.compedu.2017.06.007
2. Fronton, K., Vermeulen, M., Quelennec, K.: LES ECSPER : RETOUR D'EXPERIENCE D'UNE ETUDE DE CAS DE TYPE SERIOUS GAME EN GESTION DE PROJET. Presented at the e-Formation des adultes et des jeunes adultes, 3 June 2015
3. Mitamura, T., Suzuki, Y., Oohori, T.: Serious games for learning programming languages. In: 2012 IEEE International Conference on Systems, Man, and Cybernetics (SMC), pp. 1812–1817 (2012). https://doi.org/10.1109/ICSMC.2012.6378001
4. Gottron, T.: Combining content extraction heuristics: the combine system. In: Proceedings of the 10th International Conference on Information Integration and Web-based Applications & Services, pp. 591–595. ACM, New York (2008). https://doi.org/10.1145/1497308.1497418
5. Serious Game Classification : La classification en ligne du Serious Game. http://serious.gameclassification.com/. Accessed 13 Jan 2020
6. MobyGames: Game Browser. https://www.mobygames.com/browse/games. Accessed 13 Jan 2020
7. La référence Serious Games. https://www.serious-game.fr/. Accessed 13 Jan 2020
8. Neven, F., Duval, E.: Reusable learning objects: a survey of LOM-based repositories. In: Proceedings of the Tenth ACM International Conference on Multimedia, pp. 291–294. ACM, New York (2002). https://doi.org/10.1145/641007.641067
9. Currier, S.: Metadata for Learning Resources: An Update on Standards Activity for 2008. Ariadne (2008)

10. Alvarez, J.: Du jeu vidéo au serious game (2007)
11. Zyda, M.: From visual simulation to virtual reality to games. Computer **38**, 25–32 (2005). https://doi.org/10.1109/MC.2005.297
12. Wirth, C., Fürnkranz, J.: On learning from game annotations. IEEE Trans. Comput. Intell. AI Games **7**, 304–316 (2015). https://doi.org/10.1109/TCIAIG.2014.2332442
13. Massart, D., Shulman, E.: Learning Resource Exchange Metadata Application Profile Version 4.7., vol. 127 (2011)
14. Rajabi, E., Sicilia, M.-A., Sanchez-Alonso, S.: Interlinking educational resources to Web of Data through IEEE LOM. Comput. Sci. Inf. Syst. **12**, 233–255 (2015). https://doi.org/10.2298/CSIS140330088R
15. McClelland, M.: Metadata standards for educational resources. Computer **36**, 107–109 (2003). https://doi.org/10.1109/MC.2003.1244540
16. Pernin, J.-P.: LOM, SCORM et IMS-learning design: ressources, activités et scénarios. In: actes du colloque « L'indexation des ressources pédagogiques numériques » , Lyon (2004)
17. Aouadi, N., Pernelle, P., Marty, J.-C., Carron, T.: A model driven architecture MDA approach to facilitate the serious game integration in an e-learning environment. In: European Conference on Games Based Learning, p. 15. Academic Conferences International Limited (2015)
18. Prensky, M.: Digital game-based learning. Comput. Entertain. **1**, 21 (2003). https://doi.org/10.1145/950566.950596
19. Freire, M., Fernández-Manjón, B.: Metadata for serious games in learning object repositories. IEEE Revista Iberoamericana de Tecnologias del Aprendizaje **11**, 95–100 (2016). https://doi.org/10.1109/RITA.2016.2554019
20. Marfisi-Schottman, I., George, S., Tarpin-Bernard, F.: Un profil d'application de LOM pour les Serious Games. In: Environnements Informatiques pour l'Apprentissage Humain, Conférence EIAH 2011. Editions de l'UMONS, Mons 2011, Belgium, pp. 81–94 (2011)
21. Djaouti, D., Alvarez, J., Jessel, J.-P.: Classifying serious games: the G/P/S model. Handbook of Research on Improving Learning and Motivation through Educational Games: Multidisciplinary Approaches (2011). https://doi.org/10.4018/978-1-60960-495-0.ch006
22. Hendrix, M., Protopsaltis, A., de Freitas, S., Arnab, S., Petridis, P., Rolland, C.: Defining a metadata schema for serious games as learning objects, vol. 6, pp. 14–19 (2012)
23. Dogruel, L., Joeckel, S.: Video game rating systems in the US and Europe: comparing their outcomes. Int. Commun. Gaz. **75**, 672–692 (2013)
24. Elborji, Y., Khaldi, M.: An IEEE LOM application profile to describe serious games « SG-LOM». IJCA **86**, 1–8 (2014). https://doi.org/10.5120/15042-3404
25. Ochoa, X., Klerkx, J., Vandeputte, B., Duval, E.: On the use of learning object metadata: the GLOBE experience. In: Kloos, C.D., Gillet, D., Crespo García, R.M., Wild, F., Wolpers, M. (eds.) Towards Ubiquitous Learning, pp. 271–284. Springer, Heidelberg (2011). https://doi.org/10.1007/978-3-642-23985-4_22
26. Konzack, L.: Pan European game information (PEGI) system. Encycl. Video Games: Cult. Technol. Art Gaming **2**, 474–476 (2012)
27. Bushman, B.J., Cantor, J.: Media ratings for violence and sex: implications for policymakers and parents. Am. Psychol. **58**, 130–141 (2003). https://doi.org/10.1037/0003-066X.58.2.130

Moving Database Cost Models from Darkness to Light

Abdelkader Ouared[✉] and Fatima Zohra Kharroubi[✉]

Ibn Khaldoun University (UIK), Tiaret, Algeria
{abdelkader.ouared,fatima.kharroubi}@univ-tiaret.dz

Abstract. In the database environment, the mathematical cost models plays a crucial role in evaluating non-functional requirements. These requirements comprise query execution performance, energy consumption, resource dimensioning to name a few applications. One of the main characteristics of cost models is that they follow the evolution of database technologies. The main idea behind the survey papers of cost models is to build a framework of a research topic based on the existing literature. Surveying research papers generally means to collect data and results from other research papers. Therefore, cost models become an obscure entity, because they can not be easily exploited by researchers and students for learning, analysis, reproduction purposes, etc. This research address the challenges of cost model categorization, classification, and summary to provide the readers a good overview of the topic. Our research has introduced ideas from the graph database to enable the analysis of changes in database cost models over time, which will fulfill these requirements. Clusterization of an existing database cost model are very interesting to visualize and to show how cost model are related (e.g., authors, papers, committees and topics). In general, all these graphs will allow the resarchers to trace the evolution of database cost models. We believe that, it is very interesting material and it would be in demand by the database community. Our evaluation, demonstrates all the aforementioned capabilities of the technique.

Keywords: Database · Cost model · Graph database · Visual analytics

1 Introduction

Since the Big Data Era arrival, the database community is spending a huge efforts to deal with its characteristics and the impact of their Vs in the traditional solutions that cover their life cycle phases: requirement elicitation and analysis, conceptual modeling, logical modeling, integration, deployment, physical design and exploitation. Newly, it starts dealing with the dark data. Gartner defines dark data as the information assets organizations collect, process and store during regular business activities, but generally fail to use it for other purposes (for example, analytics, business relationships and direct monetizing). IDC

© Springer Nature Switzerland AG 2020
M. Hamlich et al. (Eds.): SADASC 2020, CCIS 1207, pp. 17–32, 2020.
https://doi.org/10.1007/978-3-030-45183-7_2

and EMC estimate that by 2020 the world will have 40 zettabytes of data, and a 2016 Veritas Global Databerg Survey indicates that as much as 85% of this data will be "dark data".

1.1   Problem Statement

Through this paper, we would like to launch a think tank for the database community. It consists in questioning ourselves whether we are doing enough effort to deal with our dark data to bring them to light. An interesting example of these data is the cost models. A cost model is a set of mathematical formulas quantifying metrics of a non-functional requirement such as estimating query execution time, query scheduling, energy consumption, resource pricing, etc. The databse community is continuously developing and updating cost models to satisfy the specificities brought by the different database evolutions in terms of formalisms, modeling, hardware, platforms, storage layouts, new programming paradigms, etc. that touch different phases of their life cycle (e.g. [1,5–8,13,16]). As a consequence, numerous these cost models are available and usually scattered either in scientific papers, usually with fewer details or inside commercial and academic DBMS in codes of their query optimizers. In scientific papers, $\mathcal{CM}$s are represented either by images, formulas, symbol tables (where each symbol represents a parameter of the database dimension), etc. (Fig. 1). In several scientific papers, their authors express the revision and evolution of $\mathcal{CM}$ using natural text notations, for example: "These cost models have been extended by taking into account the different deployment architectures of database applications" [2]. Despite the readability of the text that explains $\mathcal{CM}$s in *scientific papers*, it is difficult for researchers to accurate a big picture of the relationships between CMs entities. This penalizes the researchers and students to benefit from these cost models for learning, analysis and reproduction of the results that becomes a real requirement for some research communities.

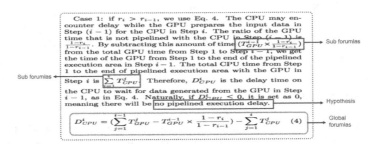

Fig. 1. Example of a cost model described in a scientific paper's discussion.

Recently, a couple of studies proposed systems such as DeepDive dedicated to extract value from dark data [14]. DeepDive helps bring dark data to light by creating structured data (SQL tables) from unstructured information (text documents) and integrating such data with an existing structured database. This extraction is usually performed by machine learning techniques.

1.2   Paper Contributions

In this paper we want to bring cost models from darkness to light, in order to develop cost model, the researcher looks in the literature the previous works to observe cost models evolution and how they are related with each other to extract an interesting knowledge. To face this challenge, we propose a graphical model for sharing and evolving cost models supported by the Graph database. These graphs will allow the community to follow the evolution of the CM and converge towards a unified repository. The Graph-Oriented Database capable of Clusterization an existing cost models. These clusters are very interesting to visualize, and show how CM are related and included in papers citations, and how they relate based on a visual analytic graphs. In general, these graphs will allow researchers to trace the evolution of cost model in database physical design. We believe, it is very interesting material and it would be in demand by the community. For our prototype implementation, we will use Neo4j to store and retrieve the cost models of the databse since it is currently the most popular graph database system[1]. The cost models proposed in litterature will be easily surveilled depends on visual analytics.

1.3   Paper Outline

The rest of the paper is structured as follows. Section 2 presents the background. In Sect. 3 we present our proposed approach. Section 4 highlights the implementation of our proposition and shows its applicability and its benefit. Section 5 is dedicated to discuss the related work. Finally, Sect. 6 summarizes and concludes this paper.

2   Background

This section presents the scientific baseline of this paper. First, we give a brief description of cost models advances. We set out the challenges faced by cost model researchers scientific through a discussion.

2.1   Database Cost Model Description

Database Cost model is a mathematical Function and fundamental part of simulated annealing [8]. The present work builds upon the result of our previous

---

[1] https://dbengines.com/en/ranking/graph+.

paper: In [11] we proposed cost model description language called CostDL [11] to homogenize the way such cost models are expressed. The models describe the different parameters and formulas: which are the layer that are considered, which are the resources of cost (inputs outputs (I/O), CPU, and network costs) that use, which are metrics depending on consumed resources: response time, size and/or energy, etc. We give the formal definition of a $\mathcal{CM}$ [11].

Definition 1 (Cost Model). *A cost model is an entity that can be defined as:* $\mathcal{CM} =< CT_i; cxt_i; func_i; m_i >$ *where:*

- CT_i: *is the cost type which represents the database component considered by the cost model, where* $CT_i \subseteq \{CPU, I/O, Memory, Network\}$.
- cxt_i: *is a context associated to a specific* $\mathcal{CM}_i$
- $func_i$: *is a cost function measuring metrics of a* nfr_i
- m_i: *is a value of the cost model metric* $mi \in \{Response\ time,\ Energy,\ Size\}$.

Definition 2 (Context). *A context is a set of parameters* $cxt = \{p_1, p_2, .., p_n\}$. *Each* $p_i \in P = P_{Database} \cup P_{Hardware} \cup P_{Architecture} \cup P_{Query} = \bigcup cxt_i$, *where every* P_j *is a set of parameters that belong to one of the four categories.*

Definition 3 (Cost function). *The cost function* $func_i$, *of a given cost model* $\mathcal{CM}_i$, *permits to compute the value of the cost model metric* m_i *based on a subset of the context parameters* cxt_i.

The cost function is a tuple $func_i =< Param_i, mf_i >$.

$Param_i \subseteq cxt_i$ *(subset of the cost model context), and* mf_i *is the mathematical formula, where* $mf_i : P^k \rightarrow \mathbb{R}_+$ *and* $k \leq cardinal(Param_i)$.

Researchers and industrials never stop developing cost models to fulfill the requirements of the new databases advances (traditional, Object Oriented, XML, Graph Databases, Semantic Databases, etc.), storage layouts, hardware and platform technology (e.g. [5,7,8,16]).

With advanced database technology, numerous of these cost models are available and usually scattered either in scientific papers with fewer details or inside commercial and academic DBMS in codes of their query optimizers. In scientific papers, $\mathcal{CM}$ are represented by images, formulas, symbol tables (where each symbol represents a parameter of the database dimension), etc. In several scientific papers, the authors do not provide more details about their cost models and use the famous phrase: *for a lack of space the cost models can not be presented.* These cost models are the codes of their implementations, as a consequence, This penalizes the researchers and students to benefit from these cost models for learning, analysis and reproduction of the results that becomes a real requirement for some research communities.

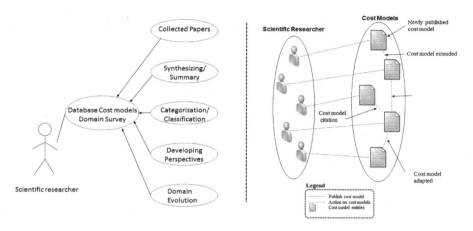

Fig. 2. Survey the database cost models in physical design phase

In Fig. 2 (Left), with use case diagram we show the main phases to survey papers. On the other hand, despite the readability of the text that explain cost models in *scientific papers*, it is difficult for searcher to build an accurate picture of the relationships between CMs entities and survey of their evolution (see Fig. 2) (Right). The CMs that are found in the scientific papers are difficult to understand how their developer respond to their progress and evolving along with the advanced database technology.

2.2 Motivation Example

By reviewing the papers using Google Scholar service and DBLP (Digital Bibliography & Library Project) from the main database conferences (e.g. VLDB, SIGMOD, ICDE) during the period 2000–2019, we found around 2.490.000 papers dealing with cost models which bear out the fact that tracking is a complex task (see Fig. 3). A survey paper is required to collect and classify existing different papers related to the problem, using a well set of classification criteria. However, digital libraries like (e.g., DBLP, Google Scholar or CORE ranking managed by the Australian Research Council) and online bibliographic services offer help on scientific papers, thus providing information (e.g., authors, papers, committees and topics). For instance, one can only consult a cost model for teaching purpose in order to see its shape, its signature and its components, we need to find their respective scientific papers, selection and compare them manually. This process is tedious and time consuming (see Fig. 3). Researchers are instead forced to resort this tedious task of browsing manually different sources (e.g., DBLP, Google Scholar or conference sites) to gather relevant information about a given cost model.

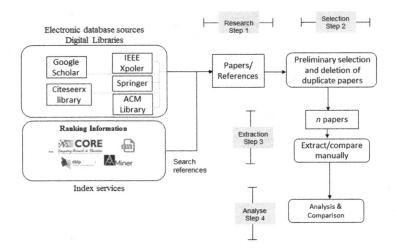

Fig. 3. Paper search and selection process

We need a user-friendly, yet well-formalize query language allowing for the unified processing of databses costs models this solution allows the researchers to select suitable costs models, handle the evolution of costs models domains, as well as exploration technique to analysis them. In this paper we propose a conceptual framework where everyone can interact with via simple queries to get the information that she/he needs. This framework is automatically and incrementally populated with data available online and includes data analysis on cost models graph in order to give the scientific researchers the ability to see how $\mathcal{CM}$s relate.

3   Our Approach

Despite the readability of the text that explains $\mathcal{CM}$s in *scientific papers*, it is difficult for researchers to accurate a big picture of the relationships between $\mathcal{CM}$s entities. Consequently, it would be interesting to explore and analyze $\mathcal{CM}$s to trace how do they evolve. We propose framework dedicated for a comprehensive survey process of database $\mathcal{CM}$s as four-step approach for solving this problem: (1) Categorizing cost model changes, (2) A Graph Model for the $\mathcal{CM}$, (3) Cost models context extraction and (4) Persisting and Exploitation. Figure 4 shows the whole picture of our approach.

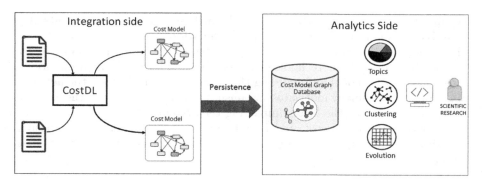

Fig. 4. The whole picture of comprehensive survey process of database $\mathcal{CM}$s

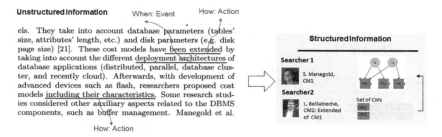

Fig. 5. Example of discussion of $\mathcal{CM}$ extension

3.1   Categorizing Cost Model Changes

We manually compared cost models proposed in the literature and analyzed the relation between them. We have reviewed the scientific papers then state their contributions examining the assumptions of different database cost models to study the changes, we need different versions of a cost model. Developer make different actions on the cost model entity (e.g. calibration, extended, revisited). Each action changes the cost model state is expressed as an operation.

For example, the cost model propose by Bellatreche et al. [2] is an `extension` of the cost model proposed in Manegold et al. [8] (see Fig. 5). In [2], *Bellatreche et al.* shows three changes in context (storage device, model of storage and optimization structures) and considers storage device (HDD, SSD), storage model (ColumnStore, RowStore) and optimization structures (indexes, horizontal partitioning). The author in this paper took the $\mathcal{CM}$ proposed by *S. Manegold et al* and extends it to integrate new SSD requirements and define a $\mathcal{CM}$ that captures the interaction between the two physical structures: indexes and data partitioning in order to estimate I/O cost.

We summarize the categories of changes that pushes the researchers to revisit the cost models defined in the past: In our analysis, we consider the flowing categories of change:

- <u>Calibrate</u> or more <u>expressive</u> cost model which describe the components of a database system in a more or less fine granularity.
- <u>Extended</u> existing cost models by integrating a new dimensions brought by the evolution database Technologies (e.g. extensibility of algorithm pool).
- <u>Revisited</u> a cost model and building them from scratch. Besides, the advance in database technology motivates and pushes researchers to revisit the existing $\mathcal{CM}$s and revisit all the layers impacting the system.
- <u>Cite</u> or <u>Use</u> an existing cost models and invoking it in severals physical design applications like using CM for selecting index with no modifications of it internals.

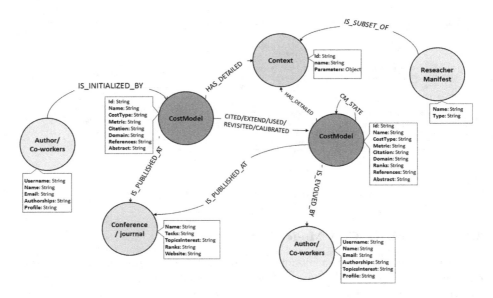

Fig. 6. Graph model for the DB cost model evolution.

3.2 A Graph Model for the $\mathcal{CM}$ Evolution

Based on the requirements discussed above we will now design a graph model for the $\mathcal{CM}$ survey that matches the needs of the scientific researchers.

The $\mathcal{CM}$ survey graph data model consists of five node types: `cost model` nodes, `scientific research manifest` nodes, `context` nodes, `author` nodes and `conference` nodes, Two cost models are linked by six relationship (or edges) types: *cited, extend, used, revisited* and *calibrated*. We look at a $\mathcal{CM}$ survey as a directed graph $G = (V, E)$ where V is a set of nodes and E a set of relationships. In our graph model, cost model $v \in V$ are represented by nodes with label `CostModel`. For each cost model node we store the information parameters and paper references.

Our Graph Model also contains the nodes `Manifest`. The role of this last is to express the needs of the users who look for an appropriate $\mathcal{CM}$. Indeed, manifest node is only composed of context. It is not required to have a well-defined context when users express their manifests, but the more well-defined the manifests context is, the accurate the $\mathcal{CM}$ proposed by the graph database.

For cost models, a <u>Reseacher Manifest</u> is defined as a partial set of the <u>context</u> of cost models to formulate of different Research questions. Let consider a researcher needs to answer several *Research Questions*:

1. What is the cost models are more appropriate for a given context?
2. How did database cost models evolve in physical design phase through time?
3. How can classified a cost models per topic per year and looking how can be related?

One advantage of expressed manifest is bringing into light aspects to be taken into account for what properties needs to be considered that depending of the system under design.

Example 1 (Example of the Researcher Manifest). "A user wants to search $\mathcal{CM}$ that estimate the total <u>energy consumption</u> of queries by considering their <u>I/O</u> and <u>CPU</u> costs. The <u>system under design</u> is described by several parameters related to the database, queries, and the platform. The database parameters are: <u>relational schema</u>, <u>row-oriented storage</u>, no data compression, and a pipeline query processing strategy. The queries parameters considered are: <u>OLAP queries</u> type with no concurrency execution. The platform parameters are: <u>centralized deployments</u> architecture, <u>main memory</u> as a primary storage device, and <u>HDD</u> as a secondary storage device".

Figure 6 depicts the elements of the graph model, which it's `CostModel` node. Every `CostModel` instance is composed of metrics, cost type, has a `Context`. It is also characterized by a name and references which indicated the scientific papers presenting the cost model. Every context of a given cost model is described by a set of database system parameters. Those parameters are related to different categories. To organize them, we propose four categories of parameters: database category, hardware category, architecture category and query category (see our previous work [10]).

3.3   CM Context Extraction

Each database cost model paper has a *context* (cf. Sect. 2) and relation type with other cost models. The context must be extracted automatically as a summary, during this process we will start by the text parsing of the *scientific papers* using deep solutions to identify correctly the $\mathcal{CM}$ context. For the first version, we will define manually a vocabulary of known words (context of cost models) to using a bag-of-words model. The extraction process starts by the input files (e.g. scientific papers) step (1). As it is shown in (Fig. 7(a)) every cost model context in scientific papers explained in a native language. During the second step (Fig. 7(b)) we will use Natural Language Processing (NLP) technique of text modeling known as Bag of Words model [15] to generate the context of database cost models. For instance, the signification of $\sqrt{}$ means that the existence of word is true, while ⊠ symbol means that the world does not appear in the paper. The use of the bag-of-words transforms documents into vectors that will be examined with our CostDL as a final process to identify the dimensions related to database, queries and platform (Fig. 7(c)).

This context must be introduced in our graph database according to our dedicated language called *CostDL* to describe database cost models (for more details, please refer to our previous work of [10]) which is mainly based on the model-driven engineering (MDE). This formalism aims to homogenize the storage of cost models.

Considering the extraction of the relations between cost models entities, these relations can be either identified as an explicite relations which are clear and expressed in a natural language in the research papers or an implicit relations, in this case to facilitate identifying the relation type correctly we compare CMs Contexts. A $\mathcal{CM}_i$ context can be analyzed by a set of tests T to check all the parameters of the CostDL language in order identify the relation type, while $cxt_i \ \mathcal{R}_i \ cxt_j$, with $\mathcal{R}_i \in \{=, \neq \subset\}$.

Here is an example of a test (e.g. t_1: the DB schema is relational $\checkmark$, t_2 the deployment architectures is centralized $\checkmark$, t_3 the storage device is SSD ⊠).

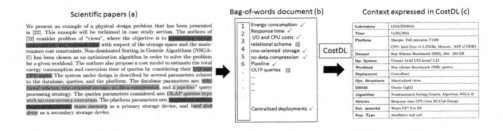

Fig. 7. Context extraction of database cost models

There are possible threats that makes the context incomprehensive because of a limitations of Bag-of-Words. The Meaning discardin the meaning of words in the document (semantics). Context and meaning can offer a lot to the model, that if modeled could tell the difference between the same words differently arranged. In this case, this is a very long and complex task.

4   Implementation Using Neo4j: Persisting and Exploitation

For supporting the exploration of database cost model, we persist the graph model described in Sect. 3.2 into a graph database DB-CM; among many available graph databases, we have chosen Neo4j[2] and we used it query language Cypher to explore the content of our database graph. This noSQL database is considered as appropriate for capturing relations between entities including cost

---

[2] https://neo4j.com/.

models information, detailed context, conference and authors. For the first version of our proposal, we have limited our implementation on analytic side of our proposal (see Fig. 4). We have provided a manual solution to enhance a database by several examples of database cost models with it context and it relation type. Available on Github[3]. The DB-CM Graph connections can be visually explored by the users who understands the entities and the cost models relationships, as well as their connection to a given context, and then navigate on relationships. In our implementation, a scientific researcher manifest is translated into a Cypher query that manipulates the underlying Neo4j graph and reporting the results with Visual Analytics. We next explain four usage scenarios of exploration: **(i)** finding cost models of a given context, **(ii)** visualize how cost model are related and trace there evolution, **(iii)** clustering the existing cost models based on criteria and **(iv)** cost model Recommendation.

4.1   Searching Cost Models

We call "Reseacher Manifest" the characteristics that correspond to a seeker request. We assume that a researcher that looks for cost models which fulfill his/her requirement. Cypher Queries to retrieve results for the formulated research questions. We assume that a *scientific researcher* of database physical design comes up with a manifest and looks for a relevant cost models that fulfills his/her requirements. For instance 1 represents an example of expressing a Manifest presented on Sect. 3.2. Listing 1.1 shows an example of the graph query language.

```
MATCH (cm1:CostModel)
          [HAS_DETAILED] -> (cxt1:Context)
WHERE cm1.costType='InputOutput'
AND cm1.performanceType='performance'
AND cxt1.storageDevice IN ('HDD','SSD')
AND cxt1.processingDevice='CPU'
AND cxt1.type='centralized'
AND cxt1.kind='sharedNothing'
AND cxt1.architecture='centralized'
      RETURN  cm1.Id,
              cm1.Name,
              cm1.References
```

Listing 1.1. Cypher Query Language to a Cost Model of a Given Context

4.2   Tracing Evolution of Database Cost Models

Our graph model will allow us to trace the evolution of database cost models. Users can navigate and explore a cost models via a graph-based visual moreover cost model evolution can be retrieved by using different graph paths (e.g. evolution of $\mathcal{CM}$ in the Era of *distributed database*). Figure 8 shows the group of eight $\mathcal{CM}$ evolution history that contribute to the same research objective. These $\mathcal{CM}$s contain information about versioning and it evolution with six kind of relationship: *cited, extend, used, revisited* and *calibrated.* Then, the exploration

---

[3] https://github.com/OUARED-A/VizCM

connects cost models to their evolution and eventually to their context. Figure 8 shows how multiple nodes (CM, Author and conference) can be retrieved by using different contexts. Once the Items are reached, the user may be interested in understanding content; this is possible by further exploring the Item nodes.

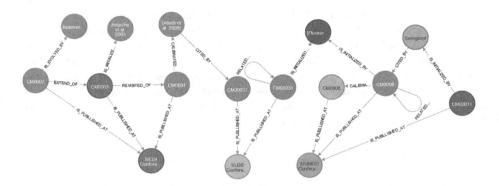

Fig. 8. Excerpt of Visualize the evolution of database cost models

We believe that it would be a helpful tool to better underestand the research trend and its evolutionary characteristics over time. Also topic Evolution help to found an Author's impact in the research community, better research understanding of the database scientific publication network and facilitate data-driven research decisions.

4.3   Clustering an Existing Cost Models

Clusterization of existing database cost models are very interesting to visualize and to how cost models are related (e.g., authors, papers, committees and topics). In other words, the aim is to regroup $\mathcal{CM}$s according to a given *Reseacher Manifest* and classify it using various criteria In other words, the aim is to regroup $\mathcal{CM}$s according to a given manifest and also according to their closeness in terms of categories (see Fig. 9). We propose process for $\mathcal{CM}$s clustering based on Neo4j. We were then able to make node clusters thanks to GraphX, an Apache Spark API[4] for running graph and graph-parallel compute operations on data. The clusters or sub-graphs formed in large graphs are also termed modules (or authors, papers, committees and topics). Finding communities helps in understanding various aspects of a graph, for instance localing the set of nodes that exhibit similar behavior and groups that are strongly connected. Community detection has become an integral part in network science as it helps to exploit large networks to understand them better.

Once the articles are clustered into four groups (see Fig. 9), each cluster will consist of publications from potentially different areas but with similar keywords.

---

[4] https://neo4j.com/docs/graph-algorithms/current/labs-algorithms/triangle-counting-clustering-coefficient/.

For example, result Neo4j Cypher query expressions is shown in Fig. 9, this analysis aims to show to a scientific researcher the similarities and differences between its own cost model and others (already stored in the DB-CM) which rely on the same context of the model under analysis.

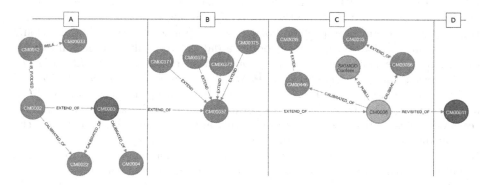

Fig. 9. Excerpt of Clustering an existing cost models based on database source. The cost models are classified according to the database source: (A) Cost models of a relational data source, (B) object data source, (C) semi-structured data source and (D) cloud database.

4.4 Cost Model Recommendation

To properly answer our issue of cost models searching, we believe that recommender systems may assist researchers to make the survey of the databse cost models domain. Using pattern matching with Cypher make graph-based recommendations easier to understand, we want to provide recommendations for Cost Models that a researcher hasn't found (which I am naively assuming that they haven't found the Cost Models yet).

We accomplish this by averaging the Cost Models ratings from that cost models k-nearest neighbors (out of the neighbors who are rated to the relevant Cost Models). We use $k = 3$ for the cost model recommendations; these recommendations should be thought of as estimates of how much the person would search the Cost Models they haven't use or cite and similar to that proposed by the researcher "Ladjel Bellatreche". Listing 1.2 shows an example of Cypher Query using *k-NN Recommendation* Cost Models.

```
MATCH      (A:Author)-[i:IS_INITIALIZED_BY]->(c:CostModel), (b)-[s:SIMILARITY
           ]-(a:Author {name:'Ladjel Bellatreche'})
WHERE      NOT((a)-[:RATED]->(m))
WITH       m, s.similarity AS similarity, r.rating AS rating
ORDER BY   m.name, similarity DESC
WITH       m.name AS CostModel, COLLECT(rating)[0..3] AS ratings
WITH       CostModel, REDUCE(s = 0, i IN ratings | s + i)*1.0/LENGTH(ratings)
           AS year
ORDER BY   year DESC
RETURN     CostModel AS CostModel, references AS Recommendation
```

Listing 1.2. Cypher Query: k-NN Recommendation Cost Model

5   Related Work

From the last decade, the research communities identify the needs to build knowledge based construction. The dark data extraction problem is to populate a relational database with information from unstructured data sources, such as emails, webpages, and PDFs. KBC is a long-standing problem in industry and research that encompasses problems of data extraction, cleaning, and integration. Recently, in [12], Rutuja *and al* introduce a dataset to analyze topics and their evolution in the Database community publication graph e call *Codd's World*. In [4] a work intitle *"'MetaScience: an Holistic Approach for Research Modeling"'* has been accepted at ER2016 [4] proposes a conceptual schema providing a holistic view of conference-related information (e.g., authors, papers, committees and topics). This schema is automatically and incrementally populated with data available online. Similar efforts have been proposed systems such as analyzing the *Panama Papers* with Neo4j [9] and DeepDive dedicated to extract value from dark data [14]. DeepDive helps bring dark data to light by creating structured data (SQL tables) from unstructured information (text documents) and integrating such data with an existing structured database. This extraction is usually performed by machine learning techniques. Other Research Graph project applied in the scholarship domain to establish connections between publications, researchers and research datasets (e.g. [17].

The one of the main characteristics of cost models are that they follow the evolution of database technologies [2,3]. A survey paper of database cost models classify existing different approaches to the problem, using a well set of classification criteria. The main idea behind our paper is to build a framework of a research topic based on existing literature. Surveying research database cost models papers generally mean to collect data and results from research papers. To the best of our knowledge, there is no work address the challenges of cost model categorization, classification, and summary to provide readers a good overview of the topic. Our research have introduced ideas from the graph database to enable the analysis of changes in database cost models over time, which fulfills these requirements. Clusterization of existing database cost model are very interesting to visualize and to show how cost model are related (e.g., authors, papers, committees and topics). In general, all these graphs will allow to trace the evolution of database cost models. We believe, it is very interesting material and it would be in demand by the database community.

6   Conclusion and Future Work

In this paper, we have propose to study the database cost models survey in physical design phases an intuitive graph model of the $\mathcal{CM}$ evolution. We then verified that our proposed graph model has the capability to satisfy the requirement of database cost models survey in physical design phases. In addition, we provided a prototype implementation of our graph data model of cost model for sharing and analyzing. Clusterization of existing databases costs models are very interesting to visualize, to show how cost model are related, include paper citation graph and see how they relate to extract something interesting from this data. In general, all these graphs will permit us to trace the evolution of database cost models. We think it is very interesting material and it would be in demand by the community. For the future, we plan to conduct further experiments to explore the performance and scalability of our approach. Moreover, we will investigate possible design alternatives for our graph model in order to further improve the support provided by the graph database backend for cost models analyzing. We hope to entice the database communities to deal with the identified challenges related to the survey of cost models in database physical design phase.

References

1. Bausch, D., Petrov, I., Buchmann, A.: Making cost-based query optimization asymmetry-aware. In: DaMoN, pp. 24–32. ACM (2012)
2. Bellatreche, L., Cheikh, S., Breß, S., Kerkad, A., Boukhorca, A., Boukhobza, J.: How to exploit the device diversity and database interaction to propose a generic cost model? In: Proceedings of the 17th International Database Engineering & Applications Symposium, pp. 142–147. ACM (2013)
3. Bellatreche, L., et al.: The generalized physical design problem in data warehousing environment: towards a generic cost model. In: 2013 36th International Convention on Information & Communication Technology Electronics & Microelectronics (MIPRO), pp. 1131–1137. IEEE (2013)
4. Cosentino, V., Cánovas Izquierdo, J.L., Cabot, J.: MetaScience: an holistic approach for research modeling. In: Comyn-Wattiau, I., Tanaka, K., Song, I.-Y., Yamamoto, S., Saeki, M. (eds.) ER 2016. LNCS, vol. 9974, pp. 365–380. Springer, Cham (2016). https://doi.org/10.1007/978-3-319-46397-1_28
5. Florescu, D., Kossmann, D.: Rethinking cost and performance of database systems. ACM Sigmod Rec. **38**(1), 43–48 (2009)
6. Gardarin, G., Sha, F., Tang, Z.-H.: Calibrating the query optimizer cost model of IRO-DB, an object-oriented federated database system. VLDB **96**, 3–6 (1996)
7. Leis, V., Gubichev, A., Mirchev, A., Boncz, P.A., Kemper, A., Neumann, T.: How good are query optimizers, really? PVLDB **9**(3), 204–215 (2015)
8. Manegold, S., Boncz, P., Kersten, M.L.: Generic database cost models for hierarchical memory systems. In: VLDB, pp. 191–202 (2002)
9. McGregor, S.E., et al.: When the weakest link is strong: secure collaboration in the case of the panama papers. In: 26th {USENIX} Security Symposium ({USENIX} Security 17), pp. 505–522 (2017)
10. Ouared, A., Ouhammou, Y., Bellatreche, L.: CostDL: a cost models description language for performance metrics in database. In: 2016 21st International Conference on Engineering of Complex Computer Systems (ICECCS), pp. 187–190. IEEE (2016)
11. Ouared, A., Ouhammou, Y., Bellatreche, L.: QoSMOS: QoS metrics management tool suite. Comput. Lang. Syst. Struct. **54**, 236–251 (2018)
12. Pawar, R.S., et al.: Codd's world: topics and their evolution in the database community publication graph. In: Grundlagen von Datenbanken, pp. 74–81 (2019)
13. Selinger, P.G., Astrahan, M.M., et al.: Access path selection in a relational database management system. In: ACM SIGMOD, pp. 23–34. ACM (1979)

14. Shin, J., Wu, S., Wang, F., De Sa, C., Zhang, C., Ré, C.: Incremental knowledge base construction using deepdive. Proc. VLDB Endowment **8**(11), 1310–1321 (2015)
15. Tarnate, K.J.M., Devaraj, M.: Prediction of ISO 9001: 2015 audit reports according to its major clauses using recurrent neural networks (2015)
16. Wu, W., Chi, Y., Zhu, S., et al.: Predicting query execution time: are optimizer cost models really unusable? In: ICDE, pp. 1081–1092. IEEE (2013)
17. Xia, F., Wang, W., Bekele, T.M., Liu, H.: Big scholarly data: a survey. IEEE Trans. Big Data **3**(1), 18–35 (2017)

Building Valid Career Ontologies with B-CPNs

Zakaryae Boudi[1,2(✉)], Abderrahim Ait Wakrime[3], Mohamed Toub[1,2],
and Mohamed Haloua[1]

[1] Ecole Mohammadia d'Ingénieurs, Med V University, Rabat, Morocco
haloua@emi.ac.ma
[2] TrouveTaVoie, Paris, France
{boudi, toub}@trouvetavoie.io
[3] Computer Science Department, Faculty of Sciences,
Mohammed V University, Rabat, Morocco
abderrahim.aitwakrime@um5.ac.ma

Abstract. From straightforward knowledge management to sophisticated AI models, ontologies have proved great potential in capturing expertise while being particularly apposite to today's data abundance and digital transformation. AI and data are reshaping a wide range of sectors, in particular, human resources management and talent development, which tend to involve more automation and growing quantities of data. Because they bring implications on workforce and career planning, jobs transparency and equal opportunities, overseeing what fuels AI and analytical models, their quality standards, integrity and correctness becomes an imperative for HR departments aspiring to such systems. Based on the combination of formal methods, namely, the B-method and CPNs, we present in this paper a preliminary approach to constructing and validating career ontology graphs with what we will define as B-CPNs.

Keywords: B-CPNs · Colored Petri Nets sub-class · B method – HR · Career planning

1 Introduction

Ensuring AI applications in HR are used responsibly is an essential prerequisite for their widespread deployment. Seeking to improve human capital management with unreliable technologies would contradict the core mission and could also spark a backlash, given the potentially critical impact on people involved. For technologies that could affect people's life and well-being, it will be important to have safety mechanisms in place, including compliance with existing specifications and processes. Current HR landscape is characterized by high heterogeneity of models and actors, in an era where careers are constantly reshaped by technological progress. And that is often true even within a same given organization. This highlights the need for systems able to reconcile the heterogeneous HR expertise and processes, all in tracking and making sense of data on employees, candidates, trainings, etc., including records on skills, capabilities, performance, experiences and payroll. Those are typical issues that HR ontology development looks forward to solving. Indeed, ontology-based ICT systems can serve facilitating optimal candidate/job matching, career guidance and staffing

© Springer Nature Switzerland AG 2020
M. Hamlich et al. (Eds.): SADASC 2020, CCIS 1207, pp. 33–46, 2020.
https://doi.org/10.1007/978-3-030-45183-7_3

decisions, bringing a better internal and external view on resources and opportunities, while improving wider coordination and exchange of information between HR departments.

Adjusting career plans to the changing nature of work requires indeed a rethinking of the related processes. HR departments need new ways to help people's careers grow, making them learn and ultimately stay, all regardless of their level, salary or current qualifications. Yet most organizations still rely on pre-set processes and expertise, built on past experience, or based on expert recommendations and advisors' reports. However, the pace of digital transformation, increasing talent competition and high turnover challenges will push managers to rely more on algorithms and AI models to reveal data-driven career evolution alternatives and guide HR decisions, with cost cutting results and efficacy. HR management has its own language: jobs are related to skills, education, qualifications, experience, trainings, responsibilities, compensation, performance, etc., while employees acquire skills, occupy jobs and develop their careers. This language is not only critical to being able to understand organization's career pathways, but it also influences how computer programs identify those things that data systems track and analyse. How things relate to one another makes its way into programs, into data designs, influences AI training, and ultimately dictates whether the data that HR collects is actually of value to the organization. Ontologies can be used here to model career evolution processes, and in the meantime, facilitate the capturing and exchanging of HR data, such as skills, qualifications, hierarchy level and years of experience required to reach a specific occupation. An ontology is generally intended to act as a standard – sort of common language – forming a set of controlled vocabularies and concepts. Overall, these ontologies bring opportunity to HR teams have control on algorithms and data they use, paving the way to create resilient career planning models, increase productivity, and deliver effective guidance to employees and candidates. HR can thus confidently embrace the digital transformation, expanding the boundaries and reshaping traditional patterns.

What is challenging though with AI applications in HR - in building valid ontologies - is to develop at the same time bias-free, fully consistent and performing predictions models. With the available technological potential, how can AI engineers and data scientists decide on the best development strategy, the one that wipes out the unavoidable AI bias and errors, costs less, takes acceptable time to implement, and delivers the objectives? One approach is to use mathematical formal design and verification. With the recent advance in technology, mostly over the past decades, came actually the first use of mathematical tools to produce safe-by-design automation. But in fact, technology is only one of many reasons that brought mathematics in scope. More broadly, the landscape has changed from the regulation perspective, towards a more demanding safety and quality requirements - including need for certification and accreditation – which puts formal analysis in the core of system and software development for many industries. There are also some basics: using mathematical models means that more of software design and control can be automated, leading to reduced costs. One early interesting example of formal methods' application was the development of tools able to generate comprehensive test cases from specifications [1]. Another case, more recent, is theorem proving of systems meeting their specification, which proved cost saving and effective in the verification and validation process [2]. In short, formal methods came to apply software based mathematical modeling on systems in order to help demonstrate they meet their specifications, quality and safety properties. Of course, other cases can involve formal methods in many ways, to build a sound understanding of systems' dynamics and interactions, validate data, generate test cases or reduce the overall development costs [3].

Our present research explores how the combination of Colored Petri Nets and the B-method, particularly for use during the building and validation of a career planning ontology, can contribute to creating automated ontology development frameworks, providing purpose-built solutions to reliably handle algorithms and AI in new HR processes. This paper's contribution is an extension to the introduction of a Petri Nets sub-class, entitled B-sequenced CPNs [4], and can be considered as completing the development of the research exploring the transformation of Petri Nets to Event-B and Classical-B [5, 6], by introducing a broader version we will call B-CPNs, which is also a CPN sub-class. Such a new class of CPNs aims to enhance their features with the B-language annotations and B-method verification tools. It is worth mentioning that several sub-classes of Petri Nets have been introduced in the literature, of which we cite the examples in [7, 8], focused on improving the fineness of system behavior modelling. Still, none of the existing research have covered the combination of other formal annotations to form a Petri net sub-class, whether it is in view of improving the formal specification approaches or for refining models towards correct-by-design code generation.

In considering all these, we discuss in this paper, through a use case addressing the design of a career planning ontology that meets a set of HR rules, how such a sub-class of CPNs integrating Event-B notations, allows the construction and validation of ontology. After recalling the main definitions of graphs, Colored Petri Nets (CPNs) and B-method, the following sections introduce the suggested B-CPNs. On this basis, the case study explains by a concrete application of B-CPNs how this preliminary approach can serve to build and validate career ontology graphs.

2   Combining Formal Methods: Brief Overview

While formal methods are increasingly reaping the rewards of advanced design, cost effective verification and validation, they are still missing out on the benefits they can offer when used in combination, especially in applied industrial setups. The reason we make that statement lies on the fact that the literature on applying combined formal methods is relatively narrow, leading to greatly underutilized potential of modelling and verification techniques. Nonetheless, research interest regarding formal methods' integration is not new, and we can find foundational works from the last century, such as Paige's meta-method for combining formal methods with other formal and semi-formal methods [9], as well as more recent Model Driven Engineering (MDE) approaches to model transformations [10].

In recent contributions within this research line, we introduced several transformation techniques to combine Petri Nets and the B-method or Event-B, in an integrated approach declined as formal transformation rules and definitions from both Place/Transition Petri Nets and CPNs to B abstract machines [4, 5]. Others specific papers explored extensions to these transformations, such as capturing the concept of mathematical sequences and how they can be used as a mean to enhance modelling possibilities and the overall design, verification & validation process [11]. In particular, the tackled transformation was developed in accordance with the mapping approach of Model Driven Engineering [12], using the CPN meta-model presented in [13], which is fully based on Jensen's formal definition. Besides, few other ways to translating Colored Petri Nets have also been investigated by the research community. One is presented by Bon and Collart-Dutilleul in [14], where a set of transformation rules was introduced and applied to a railway signaling scenario. However, after careful consideration, we found that the resulting B machines are outdated and thus, not useable in practice within B tools. Indeed, those B machines used a large amount of looping definitions, and the theoretical aspects of this transformation can be very hard to apply on large CPN models due to the complexity of the rules. A recent research [15] attempted to update and adapt these rules for a pattern of Petri net models, but still needs to demonstrate its scalability to a broader use for bridging Petri Nets to the B-method. Also, authors in [16] presented a mapping from Place/Transition Petri Nets to the B-language, which can be seen as a simplified version of their original transformation form Evaluative Petri Nets to B machines. Although this mapping does not cover colored Petri Nets, the ideas presented are quite close to our approach, and provide principles that can help build a better understanding of the benefits of our transformation as well as the format we used to give its formal definition.

Overall, the work done in developing a transformation approach have raised several limitations, especially with regard to scalability and broad usability in industrial context. As we started thinking of a more fused methodology, a CPN sub-class example "B-sequenced CPNs" was brought in [4], where a concrete application is shown, compared to model transformation, for modeling and validating a safe railway ERTMS Level 3 Movement Authority. B-Sequenced CPNs refer to a particular structure of CPNs which is associated to an Event-B machine and allows the CPN model elements to be annotated with B-language sequence expressions. Such a CPN is intended to support both mathematical modeling and proof of properties through B capabilities and tools.

Formal methods are also used with ontologies, mainly to enrich the way domain knowledge is generated, represented or exploited. For example, in [17], the authors presented a method automatically to generate an OWL ontology from the Petri Net Markup Language and developed the PN2OWL tool that implements the transformation. In [18], the entities of an ontology such as classes, properties, individuals and relations were modeled using the mathematical Pi-Calculus. This formalization was particularly used to describe the operational semantics of how an ontology evolves. Other works focused more on using ontologies as means to consolidate system development. Authors in [19] came for instance with a process based on Event-B, involving a transformation approach – and the development of a Rodin plugin - from ontology context to Event-B, in the purpose of enabling a more comprehensive formal verification on system properties. Another example is [20], where an approach to enrich goal-based models - based on goal-oriented requirements engineering language (SysML/KAOS) - with ontologies is explored, aiming to generate a more complete formal specification in Event-B. In this paper, we look into the control of data-driven ontologies, with the use of a CPN sub-class which leverages Event-B. We provide a formal definition of B-CPNs and show in a practical way how such an approach can help us build and control a HR career ontology.

3 Graphs, Petri Nets and the B Method

Before going further, it is important to have a clear idea on basic definitions when referring, all over this paper, to graphs, Petri Nets, CPNs, B-method or Event-B.

3.1 Graphs and Petri Nets

As with most techniques and technologies, there are few different approaches to represent discrete event systems, including graphs and Petri Nets. Broadly in mathematics' graph theory, a graph is a structure amounting to a set of data, organized as nodes, relationships, and properties - data stored on the nodes or relationships. Nodes are entities holding a number of attributes and properties. Relationships provide directed, named, semantically relevant connections between two node entities. A relationship always has a direction, from an input node to an output node. Like nodes, relationships can also have properties. In most cases, relationships have quantitative properties, such as weights, costs, distances, ratings or time intervals, but can also hold more sophisticated properties like guards. A Petri Net is itself a graph containing two types of nodes. First, the "places", graphically represented by circles, which can contain tokens, and second, the "transitions" represented by bars or boxes. "Places" and "transitions" connect to each other via directed arcs. These arcs can only link a "place" to a "transition" or a "transition to a place". "Transitions" are said to be "enabled" when the input "places" contain a valid token. Also, a Petri net must have an initial state, called initial marking. Detailed explanation is provided in [21]. Petri Nets were initially developed between 1960 and 1962 by Carl Adam Petri, a German mathematician and computer scientist, and became famous in the scope of the MIT Project on Mathematics and Computation (MAC project) in the 1970s. The main benefit from these Petri Nets is the thorough design and analysis they enable for a wide variety of discrete event systems.

While place/transition Petri Nets seem to be suited for small size discrete systems, it is clear they reach many limitations when dealing with big complex systems or models. This led the rise of High-level Petri Nets. Indeed, tokens cannot be distinguished in place/transition Petri Nets. In real life scenarios, the design requires to make the type of tokens changeable by a "transition". High-level Petri Nets cope in fact with token transformation and support first-order languages. One class of High-level Petri Nets known as the "predicate/transition" nets was introduced by Hartmann Genrich [22], followed by Algebraic Petri Nets [23], and then the development of Colored Petri Nets by Kurt Jensen [24]. In brief, Colored Petri Nets (CPNs) are an extension of Petri Nets where a functional language - based on the notion of "typing" - can be used. In other words, each token has a type called "color". Kurt Jensen's formal definition of a Colored Petri net can be found in [11]. To edit and manipulate CPNs, one of the most advanced existing platforms is "CPN-tools", architected by Kurt Jensen, Soren Christensen, Lars M. Kristensen, and Michael Westergaard [25, 26].

3.2   The B-Method and Event-B

The B-method is a formal method initially designed by Jean-Raymond Abrial [27] – it includes theory, modeling language and tools – which enables mathematical specification and rigorous representation and validation of functional properties when designing a given system. The B-method has an end-to-end coverage of the development life cycle, from specification to implementation. Automatic and/or manual mathematical proof is accordingly possible to demonstrate whether invariant properties consistently hold when the system is operated. Many B-method industrial applications have been achieved, mainly found in rail systems such as the automatic train control systems, such as Paris metro line 14 [28] or the automation of Paris line 1 by the RATP. For reference, main B-language notations are found is Jean-Raymond Abrial's B Book [27], where it is explained that properties can be expressed by formulas of first order predicate calculus, constructed with conventional propositional operators such as ($\wedge$), ($\vee$), universally quantification ($\forall$) or existentially ($\exists$) quantified variables. Another major notion of the B-method is "abstract machines". Specifically, abstract machines can be viewed as a form of imperative programing, which sets up operations as a sequence of elementary instructions that will change the program state when executed.

It is important to point out a distinction of "classical" B-method (also called B for software) and Event-B. This distinction lays in the use of the clause "EVENTS" for the latter case rather than "OPERATIONS". The nuance between these two B-method types can be explained by the possibility to generate and implement code from classical B "OPERATIONS", in the context of software development. Such a possibility is not allowed for "EVENTS", which are intended for system specification and can only be refined. The success of the B-method in the industry is highly driven its comprehensive tools for development and automatic proof/model checking. Most known tools are ProB[1], animator and model checker of abstract machines, and Atelier-B[2], IDE and theorem prover.

4   Definition of B-CPNs

B-CPNs refer to a particular structure of CPNs which is associated to an Event-B machine and allows the CPN model elements to be annotated with B-language expressions. Such a CPN is intended to support both mathematical modeling and proof of properties through B capabilities and tools.

Definition. We formally define a B-CPN as a tuple $B\_CPN = (\Sigma, P, T, A, N, C, G, E, I)$, which is derived from Jensen's CPNs formal definition and associated to an Event-B machine such as:

---

[1] http://www.stups.uni-duesseldorf.de/ProB/index.php5/Download.

[2] http://www.atelierb.eu/telecharger-latelier-b/.

(i) Σ is a finite set of colors Σi, defined as the sets *Color_Σi* under the clause DEFINITIONS, using sets declared in the clause SETS of the Event-B machine.

```
MACHINE B_CPN
SETS
S1,....Si
DEFINITIONS
color_Σi == formula
```

(ii) **P** is a finite set of places of type Σi; and for each $p \in P$, we have:

```
VARIABLES
State_p
INVARIANT
State_p : color_Σi
```

(iii) **T** is a finite set of transitions, such that for each $t \in T$, there is a B event corresponding to the firing of t:

```
EVENTS
t
```

(iv) **A** is a finite set of arcs such that: $P \cap T = P \cap A = T \cap A = \emptyset$.

(v) **N** is a node function. It is defined from A into $P \times T \cup T \times P$.

(vi) **C** is a color function. It is defined as $C(P) = Seq\_\Sigma$.

(vii) **G** is a guard function. It is defined from T into expressions such that: $\forall t \in T : [Type(G(t)) = Bool \wedge Type(Var(G(t))) \subseteq Seq\_\Sigma]$.

(viii) **E** is an arc expression function. It is defined from A into expressions such that: $\forall a \in A : [Type(E(a)) = C(p(a))_{MS} \wedge Type(Var(E(a))) \subseteq \Sigma]$
and $\forall t \in T, \forall a'' \in A$ provided that a'' is an output arc of t:

```
EVENTS
t = [SELECT, ANY...WHERE]
        G(t) & State_p'(a)
        THEN State_p"(a) := E(a")
        END
```

Where $p(a)$ is the place of $N(a)$, $p'(a)$ is the place of $N(a) \cap P \times T$, and $p''(a)$ is the place of $N(a) \cap T \times P$.

(ix) **I** is an initialization function. It is defined from P into closed expressions such that: $\forall p \in P : [Type(I(p)) = C(p)_{MS}]$.

5   Case Study: Career Planning Ontology

5.1   Description

Let's consider an analytical model for HR departments, built by the French start-up TrouveTaVoie[3], which, for every given candidate, predicts the best fit target jobs and existing skill gaps to be considered, all based on the company's or the sector's job and skill galaxies. Galaxies are graphs constructed by processing a data sample comprised by thousands of employee resumés, all by using an artificial intelligence model that normalizes job titles to international standardized classifications - ESCO or ROME [29, 30], and custom ontologies built to link jobs and skills. To make it simple, each galaxy (job galaxy and skill galaxy) is a directed graph where nodes represent a normalized job or skill, and each two nodes are bound by an arche if they correspond to two successive jobs or subsequent skills (Fig. 1).

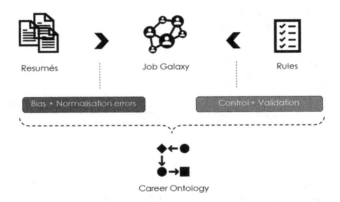

Fig. 1. Process of building a career ontology

What's actually at stake for if these galaxies don't get right? The problem to solve is in fact how to control the bias resulting from the quality of input data, which is free natural text from employee resumés. Bias of this kind may come about through problematic historical data, including unrepresentative or inaccurate sample sizes. Also, even if a model achieves a desired level of accuracy on test data, new or unanticipated error cases often appear in real-life scenarios. In other words, how can we make sure that the successive normalized jobs in our galaxy do always respect inherent specificities, such as succession of seniority levels or adapted qualification. This problem sends us back to how we build a company job galaxy. The initial data is a set of employee resumes, let's say 1000 resumés. The first step of the process is to derive an employee job graph that retraces all his professional experiences and education. Second, the job titles of employee occupations in that graph are normalized using an AI model, normal jobs being those listed in the ESCO classification. Finally, a super graph is derived from all individual employee job graphs, creating edges according to the

---

[3] www.trouvetavoie.io.

statistical probability that two normalized jobs (nodes) have a directed link between them, and weighting them with metrices and information such as average years of experience required, minimum performance scores or most relevant diplomas. For practical reasons, we will take as example and for reasoning purposes a small size and simplified job galaxy.

First, let's consider a hypothetical IT company where employee résumés show some occupations as presented below, with their associated normalization – performed using a specialized AI, including a few errors highlighted in red: a "Progammer" for example was normalized to "Programme manager" instead of "software programmer", or a "Test analyst" was normalized to "Control tester" instead of "Software tester".

Occupation	Normalization	ESCO Job Family
Programmer	Programme manager	Policy and planning managers
Web app developer	Web developer	Web and multimedia developers
Manager of web projects	Web project manager	Information technology service managers
Backend developer	Web developer	Web and multimedia developers
Test analyst	Control tester	Product graders and testers
App analyst	Software analyst	Software developers

This kind of errors typically leads to a job galaxy (Fig. 2) that encompasses a number of doubtful links between some jobs – here arche weights represent the number of years of experience required to move from an occupation to another.

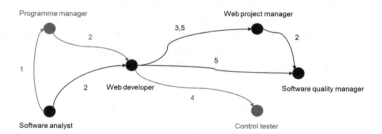

Fig. 2. Example job galaxy

The control solution we develop as part of this example is a B-CPN model that proves the job galaxy used for career planning verifies all company career development rules, which are specifying the requirements to move into a given role. In this case, one rule will relate to the number of years of experience required to step in the target roles, with respect to their ESCO Job Family, which we will all express in B-language as predicates. First, we formalize the job galaxy (graph) into a B-CPN model, then implement the HR rules into the model's Event-B abstract machine, at the INVAR-IANT clause, and finally, run automated proof and model checking to determine which nodes or archers from the galaxy cause invariants to be violated. Let's consider the two following HR career development rules:

1- Occupations of "Policy and planning managers" can be accessed from other families only if the employee has 7 years of experience AND at least two separate experiences.

2- Occupations of "Product graders and testers" cannot exist within the company.

5.2   The B-CPN Model

How will a B-CPN model compound the task of controlling such a critical job galaxy and help build a valid career ontology? Referring the earlier definition presented in this paper, we design a B-CPN model that is representative of the job galaxy – future work will detail this modelling process, especially how we look forward to automating B-CPN models from graphs. We will then demonstrate how we detect the anomalies using Event-B, and ultimately, verify whether the galaxy meets HR career planning rules. Note that the example in this case involves relatively small numbers of nodes for understandability purposes. But when we add them up at the scale of a large company or an industry, that's a big number, where a formal verification of this kind becomes absolutely relevant.

B-CPN models are well suited to carry both a graphical representation of the galaxy dynamics, and a mathematical description intended to run formal verification with Event-B. In effect, the example model in Fig. 3 contains one "place" representing the Employee state, which can correspond to the job galaxy nodes – possible states. As an output, the B-CPN transitions represent the links between those nodes – career transitions - and are associated to the "EVENTS" clause of the Event-B machine, translating the information between each two nodes of the job galaxy into an action with conditions. We notice that, in accordance of the definition of B-CPNs, all places have a type "Employee", noted *Color_Employee == Occupations * (Job_Families * NATURAL * NATURAL)* in the Event-B machine. The type reflects the information considered to describe an employee, namely, his/her occupation, job family, years of experiences and the number of experiences (Fig. 4).

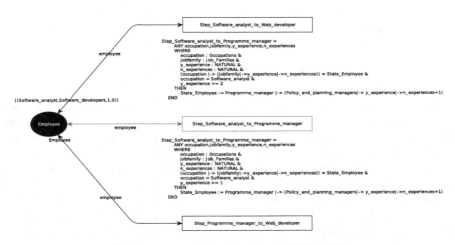

Fig. 3. Excerpt of the job galaxy B-CPN model

```
MACHINE HR_Planning_Case

SETS
Job_Families = {Poli-
cy_and_planning_managers,Web_and_multimedia_developers,Information_and_communic
ations_technology_service_managers,Product_graders_and_testers,Software_develop
ers} ;
Occupations = {Pro-
gramme_manager,Web_developer,Web_project_manager,Control_tester,Software_analys
t}

DEFINITIONS
Color_Employee == Occupations * (Job_Families * NATURAL * NATURAL)

VARIABLES
State_Employee

INVARIANT
State_Employee : Color_Employee &

//property: Occupations of type "Policy and planning managers" can be accessed
from other families only if the employee has 7 years of experience AND at least
two separate experiences.

!(vv,xx,yy,zz).(vv:Occupations & xx:Job_Families & yy : NATURAL & zz : NATURAL
& vv|->(xx|->yy|->zz) = State_Employee & xx=Policy_and_planning_managers =>
yy>=7 & zz>=2)

INITIALISATION
State_Employee := Software_analyst |-> (Software_developers|->1|->0)

EVENTS

Step_Software_analyst_to_Programme_manager =
ANY occupation,jobfamily,y_experience,n_experiences
WHERE
occupation : Occupations & jobfamily : Job_Families & y_experience : NATURAL &
n_experiences : NATURAL &
(occupation |-> (jobfamily|->y_experience|->n_experiences)) = State_Employee &
occupation = Software_analyst &
y_experience >= 1
THEN State_Employee := Programme_manager |-> (Policy_and_planning_managers|->
y_experience|->n_experiences+1)
END;
...
END
```

Fig. 4. Excerpt of B-CPN mode: Event-B machine

5.3 Formal Control Using Event-B

The first step is formalizing the HR career development rules as mathematical predicates, with a clear view on the variables to be used, here *State_Employee*. For example, the HR property stating that *occupations of "Policy and planning managers" can only be accessed from other families if the employee has 7 years of experience AND at least two separate experiences*, sits in a formal predicate as follows (Fig. 5):

```
!(vv,xx,yy,zz).(
          vv : Occupations &
          xx : Job_Families &
          yy : NATURAL &
          zz : NATURAL &
          vv|->(xx|->yy|->zz) = State_Employee &
          xx=Policy_and_planning_managers
          => yy>=7 & zz>=2
          )
```

Fig. 5. HR rule invariant

The EVENTS' incumbent triggering conditions correspond to the actual galaxy information. In this example, EVENT outputs keep the years of experience constant, and increment the number of experiences. To make sure all possible cases are covered with regards to years of experience, we iterate the verification process from different initial states, where the number of years of experience will vary for example, from 0 to 30. This process can be automated using specific scripts.

When we've run ProB and Atelier B, setting each time the initial state repetitively to cover all possible positions from where the career planning may start, we could determine where the job galaxy errors and inconsistencies come from. One way to showcase that was the use of ProB state space projection, highlighting the wrong states, and thus, the transition we should eliminate from the galaxy - In this case, ProB model checker revealed that the transition from a "Software analyst" role to a "Programme manager" with only one year of experience is not possible. When we do that analysis, we can imagine several ways to implement the formal verification in driving the career planning process. For example, a solution could be to run the formal verification at the career prediction level, meaning that we will break down the job galaxy for each employee and then filter out the states and transitions not fitting HR rules. Another way is simply to use the formal verification to exclude the conflicted nodes directly from the job galaxy, sustaining only the valid part for the career prediction. A more careful study of pros and cons will be conducted with regards to the best way to go.

6   Conclusion and Perspectives

When we dig deeper in AI models, we realize that ontologies have great potential in capturing and integrating the key HR expertise that is necessary to control what AI algorithms may predict. Based on the combination of formal methods, namely, the B-method and CPNs, we introduced in this paper B-CPNs as a CPN sub-class and presented a preliminary approach to constructing and validating career ontology graphs with a B-CPN model. Compounding formal methods and ontologies is not a totally new practice, but still, so little or quasi no development is seen with regards to controlling AI systems using such a fused approach with CPNs and Event-B, which is giving rise to a new window of applied research that could advance the way HR AI models are developed and controlled. In this paper, we particularly focused on the introduction of the formal definition of B-CPNs, and how Event-B machines can be exploited for modeling and control of career graphs. What's more, the development of this CPN sub-class has been driven by a practical career planning case, based on an AI and its related ontology, all developed by the French startup TrouiveTaVoie.

Further, deploying and sustaining AI models will require a by-design control with regards to some aspects, in a way that can maintain or improve the models and extract meaningful outputs from them. For this reason, we look forward to exploring in future work, a reinforcement deep learning approach, based on the formal validation of ontology derived invariants, using the opportunities offered by interfacing Colored Petri Nets and the B-method. This research aims to consolidate our AI to fit company specifications, making sure there isn't any bias built in and increasing people's confidence in AI driven HR management. This is also one perspective to effectively apply formal methods in the artificial intelligence space. From what comes next, we can recall the development of a methodology to automatically generate B-CPN models from graphs, the configuration of HR rules and properties as a pre-ontology able to infer formal invariants, and ultimately, building a reinforcement learning approach that could interface with existing B-method tools such as ProB and Atelier B.

References

1. Toth, K.C., Donat, M.R., Joyce, J.J.: Generating test cases from formal specifications. In: 6th Annual Symposium of the International Council on Systems Engineering (1996)
2. Richard, D., Chandramouli, K.R., Butler, R.W.: Cost effective use of formal methods in verification and validation (2003)
3. Ait Wakrime, A., Limet, S., Robert, S.: Place-liveness of ComSA applications. In: Lanese, I., Madelaine, E. (eds.) FACS 2014. LNCS, vol. 8997, pp. 346–363. Springer, Cham (2015). https://doi.org/10.1007/978-3-319-15317-9_21
4. Boudi, Z., Ait Wakrime, A., Collart-Dutilleul, S., Haloua, M.: Introducing B-Sequenced Petri Nets as a CPN sub-class for safe train control. In: Proceedings of the 14th International Conference on Evaluation of Novel Approaches to Software Engineering, pp. 350–358. SCITEPRESS-Science and Technology Publications, Lda, May 2019
5. Boudi, Z., Ben-Ayed, R., El Koursi, E.M., et al.: A CPN/B method transformation framework for railway safety rules formal validation. Eur. Transp. Res. Rev. 9(2), 13 (2017). https://doi.org/10.1007/s12544-017-0228-x
6. Boudi, Z., El Koursi, E.M., Collart-Dutilleul, S.: Colored Petri Nets formal transformation to B machines for safety critical software development. In: International Conference on Industrial Engineering and Systems Management (IESM), Proceedings, pp. 12–18. IEEE (2015)
7. Chiola, G., Franceschinis, G.: Colored GSPN models and automatic symmetry detection. In: Petri Nets and Performance Models, The Proceedings of the Third International Workshop, PNPM 1989, pp. 50–60. IEEE Computer Society (1989)
8. Ait Wakrime, A.: Une approche par composants pour l'analyse visuelle interactive de résultats issus de simulations numériques. A component based approach for interactive and visual analysis of numerical simulations results. Ph.D. thesis (2015)
9. Paige, R.F.: A meta-method for formal method integration. In: Fitzgerald, J., Jones, C.B., Lucas, P. (eds.) FME 1997. LNCS, vol. 1313, pp. 473–494. Springer, Heidelberg (1997). https://doi.org/10.1007/3-540-63533-5_25
10. De Putter, S., Wijs, A.: A formal verification technique for behavioural model-to-model transformations. Formal Aspects Comput. 30(1), 3–43 (2018)

11. Boudi, Z., Ait Wakrime, A., Collart-Dutilleul, S., Haloua, M.: Petri Nets to Event-B: handling mathematical sequences through an ERTMS L3 case. In: Abdelwahed, E.H., et al. (eds.) MEDI 2018. CCIS, vol. 929, pp. 50–62. Springer, Cham (2018). https://doi.org/10.1007/978-3-030-02852-7_5

12. Combemale, B., Crégut, X., Garoche, P.L., Thirioux, X.: Essay on semantic definitions in MDE - an instrumented approach for model verification. JSW **4**(9), 943–958 (2009)

13. Istoan, P.: Methodology for the derivation of product behavior in a Software Product Line. Ph.D. thesis, University of Rennes 1, University of Luxembourg, February 2013

14. Bon, P., Collart-Dutilleul, S.: From a solution model to a B Model for verification of safety properties. J. UCS **19**(1), 2–24 (2013)

15. Sun, P., Bon, P., Collart-Dutilleul, S.: A joint development of coloured Petri Nets and the B method in critical systems. J. Univ. Comput. Sci. **21**(12), 1654–1683 (2015)

16. Korečko, S., Sobota, B.: Petri Nets to B-language transformation in software development. Acta Plotechnica Hungarica. **11**(6), 187–206 (2014)

17. Ma, Z., Cheng, H., Yan, L.: Automatic construction of OWL ontologies from Petri Nets. Int. J. Semant. Web Inf. Syst. (IJSWIS) **15**(1), 21–51 (2019)

18. Zhang, R., Guo, D., Gao, W., Liu, L.: Modeling ontology evolution via Pi-Calculus. Inf. Sci. **346**, 286–301 (2016)

19. Mohand-Oussaid, L., Ait-Sadoune, I.: Formal modelling of domain constraints in Event-B. In: Ouhammou, Y., Ivanovic, M., Abelló, A., Bellatreche, L. (eds.) MEDI 2017. LNCS, vol. 10563, pp. 153–166. Springer, Cham (2017). https://doi.org/10.1007/978-3-319-66854-3_12

20. Mammar, A., Laleau, R.: On the use of domain and system knowledge modeling in goal-based Event-B specifications. In: Margaria, T., Steffen, B. (eds.) ISoLA 2016. LNCS, vol. 9952, pp. 325–339. Springer, Cham (2016). https://doi.org/10.1007/978-3-319-47166-2_23

21. Murata, T.: Petri Nets: properties, analysis and applications an invited survery paper. Proc. IEEE **77**(4), 541–580 (1989)

22. HJ, G.: Predicate/transition nets. In: Jensen, K., Rozenberg, G. (eds.) High-Level Petri Nets. Theory and Application, pp. 3–43. Springer, Heidelberg (1991). https://doi.org/10.1007/978-3-642-84524-6_1

23. Reisig, W.: Petri Nets and algebraic specifications. Theor. Comput. Sci. **80**(1), 1–3 (1991)

24. Jensen, K.: Coloured Petri Nets - Basic Concepts, Analysis Methods and Practical Use-Vol. 1. EATCS Monographs on Theoretical Computer Science, pp. 1–X, 1–236. Springer, Berlin (1992)

25. Jensen, K., Kristensen, L.M., Wells, L.: Coloured Petri Nets and CPN tools for modelling and validation of concurrent systems. Int. J. Softw. Tools Technol. Transf. (STTT) **9**(3–4), 213–254 (2007)

26. Ratzer, A.V., Wells, L., Lassen, H.M., et al.: CPN tools for editing, simulating, and analysing coloured Petri Nets. In: van der Aalst, W.M.P., Best, E. (eds.) ICATPN 2003. LNCS, vol. 2679, pp. 450–462. Springer, Heidelberg (2003). https://doi.org/10.1007/3-540-44919-1_28

27. Abrial, J.-R.: The B-Book: Assigning Programs to Meanings. Cambridge University Press, Cambridge (1996)

28. Behm, P., Benoit, P., Faivre, A., Meynadier, J.-M.: Météor: a successful application of B in a large project. In: Wing, J.M., Woodcock, J., Davies, J. (eds.) FM 1999. LNCS, vol. 1708, pp. 369–387. Springer, Heidelberg (1999). https://doi.org/10.1007/3-540-48119-2_22

29. Pôle Emploi: Répertoire Opérationnel des Métiers et Emplois. http://www.pole-emploi.org/opendata/repertoire-operationnel-des-meti.html?type=article. Accessed 27 Aug 2019

30. le Vrang, M., Papantoniou, A., Pauwels, E., Fannes, P., Vandensteen, D., De Smedt, J.: ESCO: boosting job matching in Europe with semantic interoperability. Computer **47**(10), 57–64 (2014)

Modeling Input Data of Control System of a Mining Production Unit Based on ISA-95 Approach

Atae Semmar[1,2,3(✉)], Nadia Machkour[3,4], Reda Boutaleb[3,4],
Hajar Bnouachir[1,2,3], Hicham Medromi[1,2], Meriyem Chergui[2],
Laurent Deshayes[3], Mohamed Elouazguiti[3], Fouad Moutaouakkil[2],
and Mourad Zegrari[3,4]

[1] Research Foundation for Development and Innovation in Science
and Engineering, Casablanca, Morocco
atae.semmar.as@gmail.com, bnouachirhajar@gmail.com,
hmedromi@yahoo.fr
[2] Engineering Research Laboratory (LRI), System Architecture Team (EAS),
National and High School of Electricity and Mechanic (ENSEM),
Hassan II University, Casablanca 8118, Morocco
fmoutaouakkil@hotmail.com
[3] Innovation Lab for Operations, Mohammed VI Polytechnic University,
Benguerir, Morocco
nadia.machkour@gmail.com, zegrari.ensam@gmail.com,
{reda.boutaleb, laurent.deshayes,
mohamed.elouazguiti}@um6p.ma
[4] Structural Engineering, Intelligent Systems and Electrical Energy Laboratory,
Ecole Nationale Supérieure des Arts et Métiers, University Hassan II,
Casablanca, Morocco

Abstract. Digital transformation is an important part of the performance improvement strategies and the modernization of the information system of several companies, including the Moroccan leader in the mining sector, the Cherifien Office of Phosphates – OCP - Group. The quality of the information will make the performance analyses of its industrial units more reliable and allow more relevant corrective action plans to be put in place. Indeed, providing the right information to the right people at the right time optimizes the management and monitoring of the performance of fixed installations on mining sites. This article presents generalities about industrial piloting and presents a case study on the classification of fixed installation input data of the OCP group based on ISA 95 standard.

Keywords: Industrial control · ISA-95 approach · Purdue Enterprise Reference Architecture Modeling · Data classification

1 Introduction

In order to remain competitive and conquer new markets, manufacturers must improve the way they manage production at the strategic and operational level. At the strategic level, it is necessary to modify and adapt their means of production to reduce their

© Springer Nature Switzerland AG 2020
M. Hamlich et al. (Eds.): SADASC 2020, CCIS 1207, pp. 47–55, 2020.
https://doi.org/10.1007/978-3-030-45183-7_4

manufacturing times. And at the operational level, it is necessary to be able to react in the very short term to unexpected events such as a modification or cancellation of an order, an arrival of an urgent order or random disruptions of the production system [1]. In this case, reactive piloting and corrective piloting will be used. Reactive Piloting takes place during the execution of production, once the launch has been completed. Its purpose is to correct the values of the decision variables when an unforeseen event occurs. This control reacts in real time. Unpredictable events can occur, without being able to anticipate them by predictive or proactive piloting. Reactive control becomes necessary to analyze the consequences of this unforeseen event in relation to the production objective and, if necessary, to determine the control parameters to be corrected to minimize the impact of this disturbance. In the event that we cannot control a drift and bring a parameter back to the expected values, then we need an approach that modifies the production objective. In fact, this level is carried out following a limit value, which signifies the actual appearance of a hazard such as a machine failure. Reaching this limit declares the initiation of a corrective approach, for example by carrying out corrective maintenance. In any case, it is necessary to memorize the facts in a database for later use. Therefore, it is very important to react at the right time. The piloting of industrial installations is a solution to this problem. Piloting concerns the organization of the relations between the physical subsystem and the decision-making subsystem and the organization related to decision-making [2]. Thus, its purpose is to ensure the consistency of decisions between orders resulting from short-term management planning and actions carried out at the level of the production system.

According to the American production and inventory control society (APICS) [3], piloting is the function that consists of guiding and distributing the work to be done in production units as well as piloting suppliers. Workshop piloting covers the principles, methods and techniques necessary to schedule, manage, measure and evaluate the efficiency of production operations. Management and piloting use data from the field to update and communicate the status of production orders and load centers, as well as to control material movements in the plant [4].

The control system is supported by the Manufacturing Execution System (MES) software, which allows the structure and management of the flow data exchange between the physical production system and the management system [5]. It bridges the gap in-between planning system and controlling systems and uses the manufacturing information (such as equipment, resources and orders) to support manufacturing processes [6]. Based on the ISA-95 Standard, MES provides several functions such as [4]: Scheduling Resource, Allocation Quality Management, Process Management, Dispatching Maintenance, Management Document, Control Product Historian, Data Acquisition Operations, Analysis Labor Management, these functions operate to "translate" the real-time data occurring on the factory floor into information which can be used to analyze the performance and make a good decision. Successful MES functions require good technical data collections and reliable reporting of information.

Morocco, with its large share of the world's phosphate reserves, is the leading exporter of phosphate and its derivatives. Phosphate deposits in Morocco occur in three areas - the Khouribga area (Oulad Abdoun Plateau), the Gantour area (Youssoufia area) and Layoune-BouCraa. They are managed by the OCP group. The demand and the phosphate quality requirements on the world market have prompted the OCP group to modernize its management of the mining sites production.

It is in this context that the GUENTOUR-BENGURIR OCP has set up an MES information system based on the recommendations of the Manufacturing Enterprise Solution Association (MESA) and on the ISA 95 standard. It ensures the automatic real-time feedback of field data and uses it to refine the piloting of its fixed installations on mining sites and optimize performance. This will subsequently allow the optimization of decision-making. However, this system has experienced limitations since its implementation: data not accessible, or manually entered, and a lack of performance indicators for production management.

The objective of our studies is the development of the existing information system to a system whose objectives are to collect data in real time. These collected data are subsequently used to carry out a number of analysis activities and to ensure better management of production facilities. The main trigger for this study is the group's awareness of the importance of reliable information given to the right people at the right time in managing and managing performance. Indeed, this project aims to manage operational performance in an efficient manner by providing the manager with adequate interfaces, based on appropriate, reliable and timely indices.

The objective of this article is to present a conceptual model of input data classification for the control system of the BENGUERIR fixed installation unit. To do this we have adopted the ISA-95 approach. This approach focuses on information architecture more than on business process. The ISA-95 model divides production systems into 5 levels, based on the Purdue Enterprise Reference Architecture (PERA) model.

This paper is organized as follows: Sect. 2 presents definitions and general information about, ISA95 standard and PERA modeling. Section 3 presents a case study on the classification of fixed installation input data on the basis of ISA 95. Section 4 ends with conclusion.

2 ISA-95 Standard and PERA Modeling

2.1 ISA-95 Standards

The ISA (International Society of Automation) [7] is an American association of 39,000 members of the industry. Originally turned towards instrumentation, it extended the scope of its work to automation, and is at the origin of many independent standards.

The efficient coupling of production in the supply chain is critical for industrial dynamics. The ISA-95 deals with the different operational domains that support the production (inventory, quality, maintenance) to ensure the continuity of the processes through the concerned applications: ERP (Enterprise resource planning), control systems (SCADA, API/PLC, SNCC/DCS ...), MES (Manufacturing Execution Systems), but also LIMS (Laboratory Information Management Systems), WES (Warehouse Execution Systems), LES (Logistics Execution Systems), CMMS (Computerized Maintenance Management System). ISA-95 takes into account the interactions of the development of the company with the operational domain (PLM - Product lifecycle management).

The objectives of ISA-95 are multiple. A first objective was to share with industrialists a common terminology for the notions handled by the MES. Indeed, manufacturers are used to using the terms specific to their job to designate them, which thwarts a generic approach to problems. One of the objectives of the ISA-95 was therefore to clarify the field by providing this common terminology.

With the considerable increase of ERP in companies, the dialogue of the MES with this software has clearly emerged as a necessary passage for the MES. The second objective of the ISA95 was therefore to provide a set of exchange models between the MES and the ERP.

The work of ISA-95 subsequently developed to the point of providing an operational model for the MES that can serve as a basis for the structuring of market software.

Parts 1, 2, 4 and 5 of the standard define consistent, flexible and extensible data models for describing and implementing communication flows between these applications and for master data management.

Part 3 describes the area of production facility management commonly referred to as Manufacturing Operations Management (MOM) through an informal functional model that facilitates the mapping and definition of functional requirements in so-called "MES" projects.

The development of the ISA-95 standard, which continues to cover the communication needs between the IT systems of the plant. Parts 6 to 8 under development successively deal with communication services, reference alignment, and the grouping of dependent transactions associated with events.

The ISA-95 is a meta-model that offers an ontological basis for the representation of the production systems to support the development of the company. Indeed, it presents a framework of reflection for our work in the measure of defining the models of data exchange and the level of automation required for this case study.

This standard was chosen because the industry has widely adopted the ISA-95 to facilitate the interoperability of computer applications and the complexity of integrating related to the production system. The main purpose of ISA 95 is to understand the problem of production control more simply. In other words, the standard seeks to facilitate the strategic choices to be put in place through the creation of a master plan or a preliminary study while specifying the nature and scope of the different systems. Additionally, a neutral institution has conducted a survey [8] in various MES products provided by global vendors on the market using questionnaires, in which the ISA-95 standard was considered as one of important criterion for product evaluation.

The article [9] shows the guidelines for defining the specifications of the needs of users of MES based on the ISA-95 standard.

2.2   PERA Modeling

Research at the Purdue Laboratory for Applied Industrial Control led to the development of the Purdue Enterprise Reference Architecture (PERA) [10] to address the complexities of industrial enterprises, emphasizing the human involvement within the enterprise system [11, 12]. The objective of PERA is to make the process of implementing enterprise systems more understandable and predictable. This can be accomplished by applying several basic principles that relate to any enterprise [13] (Fig. 1).

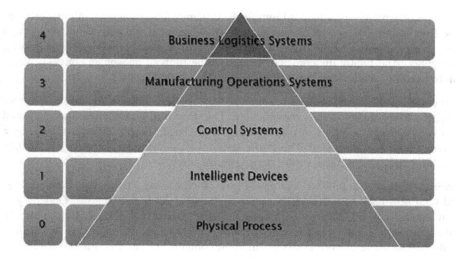

Fig. 1. The Purdue Enterprise Reference Architecture.

ANSI/ISA-95 establishes the basic standard of how to manage a production environment based on the 5 levels of PERA. Level 0 is associated to the physical process of manufacturing; level 1 to the intelligent devices that measure and manipulate the physical process; level 2 represents the control and supervision of the underlying activities; level 3 involves the management of the operations. Finally, level 4 is associated to the business activities of the entire firm. This architecture represents, in a synthetic way, the different activities and functions of a production system. Besides, it establishes the way in which the different levels are communicated; in particular that in traditional productions settings, each level interacts only with its adjacent levels. On the other hand, PERA defines a hierarchy in the decision making process and the global control of the system. Level 4, the top one, establishes the goals and guidelines for the underlying levels, down to level 0, which is in charge of carrying out the plan [14].

3 Case Study: Classification of Inputs Data of Fixed Installation According to ISA-95

The case study focuses on the part relating to the production management of fixed installations (FIs) at the OCP Group's mining site, which consists of three phases: de-stoning, screening and train loading.

De-stoning This phase is composed of four elements; the feed hopper, stone removal, crushing and conveyor. The facility has two hoppers that receive the phosphate transported by the trucks. Then, the stone removal is done by two-stage screens, the rejection of screens larger than 90 mm feeds a channel that discharges into the crusher. The latter reduces the screen rejection into a small fragment and reduces the blocks to a size ranging from 0 to 300 mm, so that they can be transported by the slag heap conveyors. And finally the conveyor, which in the form of phosphate conveyor belts, binds fixed installations and tank farms.

Screening. The screening station contains five hoppers that are fed by a conveyor using a variable opening distribution chute. The de-stoned phosphate is then screened by five screens at the outlet of the hopper. The screened phosphate is transported by a conveyor to the loading yard. The sterile material is conducted by a conveyor for final screening before being sent to the sterile storage area.

Train Loading. The product is removed from storage using a two-wheel bucket wheel and then sent back to a 300 m^3 capacity hopper that feeds the wagons. Generally, a train consists of 60 wagons with an average capacity of 61 tons. Before this, a homogenization of the phosphate is necessary to achieve a mixture of the desired quality, since there are ore layers of different contents. To do this, the de-stoned and screened phosphate is stored in alternate passes.

For the purpose of managing and controlling fixed installations, the input data of each phase is identified and then classified based on the ISA-95 standard using the PERA modeling. Indeed, this identification subsequently made it possible to make a conceptual model of the inputs of the global management system for fixed installations and to model the information streams between production operations management, quality operations management, maintenance operations, operations management and inventory operations management. The objective of this classification is to decompose and make reliable the input data in order to allow a perfect automation of the fixed installations. This classification will approve the intelligent modernization of the control system and a complete integration of the digitalization of production into the OCP group.

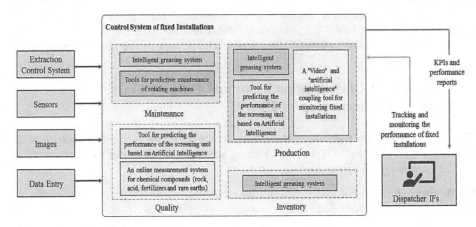

Fig. 2. Conceptual model of a fixed installation control system.

Figure 2 presents the global model of the fixed installation control system that integrates the different projects affiliated to it, namely: Intelligent greasing system,

Tools for predictive maintenance of rotating machines, Tool for predicting the performance of the screening unit based on Artificial Intelligence, A "Video" and "artificial intelligence" coupling tool for monitoring fixed installations and An online measurement system for chemical compounds (rock, acid, fertilizers and rare earths). The various projects are classified according to ISA-95. The System's input data may contain all of the following: images data, sensors data and phosphate extraction control system, or part of it. The system receives real-time feedback on the operation of the installations through the dispatcher. The model also illustrates the inputs of the global system that are linked to the outputs that present in our case the Key Performance Indicators (KPIs) and performance reports. The monitoring and monitoring of the performance of fixed installations is done through a dispatcher who is communications personnel responsible for receiving and transmitting pure and reliable messages, tracking vehicles and equipment, and recording other important information.

Figure 3 shows the detailed inputs that can be classified into measures data and seizure/Parameters data. These data are classified according to the four pillars of the ISA95 standard, namely maintenance (M), Production (P), Quality (Q), Inventory (In). The collection of these data can be visualized in the Manufacturing control and supervisory control section. The processing of this data and decision-making is done in the management part through the calculation of the various KPIs. A few KPIs were proposed for each project. These KPIs were determined according to the needs and

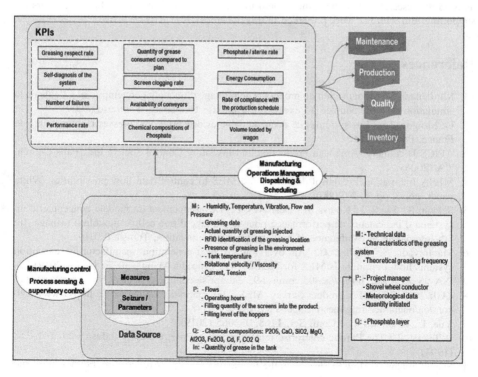

Fig. 3. Data modeling of the fixed installation control system.

requirements expressed by the OCP group by doing multiple brainstorming sessions with managers and operational staff. Once the KPIs are calculated, they are displayed in a dashboard accessible by all the stakeholders concerned.

The paper focuses on a specific system. Specific insights to this system can also be generalized and used for other systems. Indeed, that can be generalized for all the manufacturing systems and the different operational domains that support the production (inventory, quality, maintenance).

4 Conclusion

This work presents a general context of industrial piloting systems. Also, it provides an overview of ISA-95 approach and PERA modeling. A case study has been proposed that models the classification, based on ISA-95, of the input data of the control system for the three phases of the fixed installations at the OCP Group's mine site, namely: Destoning phase, Screening phase and Train loading phase. The next step is to define the different parameters influencing the KPIs in order to generate calculation formulas and help decision-making.

Acknowledgments. This research was supported by The OCP Group. We thank our colleagues from Mohammed VI Polytechnic University who provided insight and expertise that greatly assisted the research. Also, the author would like to express his gratitude to his supervisors for supporting him with the work presented in this document.

References

1. Mirdamadi, S.: Modélisation du processus de pilotage d'un atelier en temps réel à l'aide de la simulation en ligne couplée à l'exécution. Toulouse University, Toulouse (2009)
2. Le Moigne, J.L.: Les systèmes de décision dans les organisations. Presses Universitaires de France, Paris (1974)
3. APICS Dictionary: American Production and Inventory Control Society Inc., Falls Church, VA (2004)
4. MESA International: Control definition and MES to control data flow possibilities. White paper, no. 3, pp. 1–7 (2000)
5. Sekkat, S., Saadi, J., Kouiss, K., Deshayes, L.: Développement du modèle conceptuel d'un système d'indicateurs de performance pour le pilotage d'une cellule flexible d'usinage. In: 8th Internationale Conference of modélisation and simulation, Tunisia (2010)
6. Mantravadi, S., Møller, C.: An overview of next-generation manufacturing execution systems how important is MES for Industry 4.0. Procedia Manuf. **30**, 588–595 (2019)
7. ISA-95 approach. https://isa-95.com/isa-95-enterprise-control-systems/
8. CGI: 2018 CGI MES Product Survey. MESA International, USA (2018). https://www.cgi.com/en/manufacturing/mes-product-survey
9. Yue, L., et al.: J. Phys: Conf. Ser. **1168**, 032065 (2019)
10. Williams, T.: The Purdue enterprise reference architecture. Comput. Industry **24**, 141–158 (1994)
11. Schekkerman, J.: How to Survive in the Jungle of Enterprise Architecture, Frameworks, 2nd edn. Trafford Publishing, Victoria (2004)

12. PERA: PERA Enterprise Integration. http://pera.net
13. Williams, T., Rathwell, G., Li, H.: A Handbook on Master Planning and Implementations for Enterprise Integration Programs - Based on the Purdue Enterprise Reference Architecture and the Purdue Methodology (2001)
14. Rossit, D., Tohmé, F.: Scheduling research contributions to smart manufacturing. Manuf. Lett. **15**, 111–114 (2018)

Cyber Physical Systems and Block-Chains

Towards a Security Reinforcement Mechanism for Social Cyber-Physical Systems

Samir Ouchani$^{(\boxtimes)}$

LINEACT Laboratory, École d'Ingénieur CESI, Aix-en-Provence, France
souchani@cesi.fr

Abstract. Cyber-physical systems (CPS) are heterogeneous inter-operating parts of different aspects that can be physical, technical, networking, and even social like agent operators in smart grids. The main concerns of CPS are ensuring security and well-functioning against attacks that can either be technical or socio-technical based threats. To detail how well security policies are expressed, integrated, and reinforced within a CPS, we rely on formal methods to develop a sound approach that models CPS entities, especially their demeanor and interactions. Further, the approach proposes to specify formally security requirements and policies in CPS. For security analysis, we propose an algorithm that reinforces the specified security policies and also quantifies the validity of requirements for CPS. Finally, we validate the approach on a real case scenario of CPS in the presence of social and technical treats.

Keywords: Cyber-physical systems · Socio-technical systems · Security policies · Access control · Security requirements · Probabilistic model checking

1 Introduction

Safeguarding information is an important but complex goal for such systems. Information can be protected by putting controls on how data are managed and accessed. In the physical infrastructure, offices have doors and rooms have drawers: they can guard documents and can be locked. In the digital infrastructure, files are the carriers of informational assets: they can be encrypted and their access is protected by access control mechanisms. There are other ways to control risks. A system can also adopt security policies for best practices. For example in an organization, they may educate employees to encrypt files and communications (*like* demanding that confidential documents are not left on top of desks, nor forgot at the printer.). In adopting such rules an organization hopes to reduce the risk that an intruder could steal data which is sensitive for the organization's business.

The protection of **CPS! (CPS!)** assets is usually done through cryptography, or by their equivalent in the physical world, a safe or a locked drawer. However,

© Springer Nature Switzerland AG 2020
M. Hamlich et al. (Eds.): SADASC 2020, CCIS 1207, pp. 59–73, 2020.
https://doi.org/10.1007/978-3-030-45183-7_5

from the level of abstraction, protecting pieces of information also means to protect the physical devices that carry them. Information, in fact, is stored in USB keys, in hard disks or it is written on papers and notebooks which can be locked in drawers, kept in folders, even carried in one's pockets. Information can also find place in people's minds.

To model **CPS!** with physical and digital objects, we must look on constraints of physical and digital worlds. We also define the capabilities of an adversary acting in the same environment as the **CPS!**'s employees do. A physical space, like an organization's building, where people move and interact with objects. The physical space is organized in rooms and rooms are connected by doors. Rooms contain objects, some of which can be containers, such as drawers, boxes and closets that are able to host other objects [1]. Doors and containers can be locked: their inside is accessible only to whom has the opening keys. An actor's fetching, carrying, and exchanging objects and his movements inside the physical space occur with a certain probability or are guided by non-deterministic choices. Such interactions define patterns of behaviours.

Another challenge rather than modeling CPS is how to enforce their security. We were concerned with modelling such patterns to analyse the security of a CPS. In particular, we looked into whether objects of value are sufficiently protected against an adversary who can move and act like other agents, but with additional adversarial capabilities including picking locks, stealing objects, and deceiving honest agents, for instance by stealthily using them to carry objects out. Of course, these capabilities are restricted by the laws of physics about space and time, preventing the adversary to walk through walls, teleport himself, be ubiquitously present or move objects by telekinesis. The adversary's resources are also limited in the sense that we can assign a cost measure to his actions, allowing us, for instance, to express that picking a door's lock costs more time than opening the door with a key. We used the PRISM [2] model checker, to estimate the probability of a system to be secure and the adversary's cost when executing an attack, given a set of adversary capabilities and a specific amount of resources. Security requirements were expressed as PCTL properties over CPS entities.

In this paper we extend that model in several ways. We enrich the model to be able to represent *informational assets*, such as files or pieces of stored information. Similarly to physical objects, informational objects can be hidden (*i.e.*, encrypted) and carried along by agents; differently from objects, informational assets can be cloned. Agents and the adversary's abilities are updated accordingly as to cope with informational objects. For example, they can copy, create, and destroy information. Further, we define *policies*. Policies model different constraints that we assume enforced on the system (*e.g.*, that an agent does not enter unaccompanied into other offices other than his own). Besides, we define how a CPS evolves when constrained by its policies, and we develop a methodology to analyse a system's security with and without the constraints imposed by the policies. We are interested in checking under which policies a system matches its security requirements. The goal is to find a set of policies that, when enforced, imply security. With the help of this framework we can, for instance, check whether a system S is secure (*i.e.*, satisfies a specific requirement) assuming policies π are enforced. If enforcing π on the real system is considered possible, we have evidences to sustain that the real system will match its security requirements.

The next sections overview the overall reinforcement framework and clarify how to model physical and digital objects and formally define the notion of a policy and what it means to enforce a policy (Sect. 4). We clarify the relation between policies and requirements, and show how to efficiently generate the model that represents the system constrained by the polices. Finally, we propose an algorithm to model check efficiently whether the system meets its security requirements in the constrained model.

2   Security Analysis of CPS

We use a security expression ϕ to specify a policy as well as a requirement to be verified against a system S. Also, we denote by $\gamma(S, \phi) \models \phi'$ the satisfiability of a property ϕ' in a system S enforced with the policy ϕ. Our analysis approach is depicted in Fig. 1 and sketched as follows. For the evaluation of $\gamma(S, \phi) \models \phi'$,

The CPS model resulting from $\gamma(S, \phi)$ is mapped to a PRISM program. This step maps each element of the CPS model into a PRISM module by encoding the actors and the transition rules that have an effect, the objects and the transition rules that have an effect on objects. Also, it encodes the physical space, locations and doors, and the transition rules affecting them. Besides, it encodes the intruder and the transition rules of the intruder's actions. The global PRISM program is the composition, by synchronization, of the encoded PRISM modules. Finally, PRISM checks the satisfiability of the property (ϕ') in the considered model (the PRISM code of $\gamma(S, \phi)$), and produces the verification result.

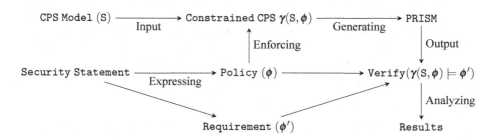

Fig. 1. Schema of the verification of the constrained CPS model.

3   CPS Formal Model

3.1   Syntax

A CPS is a tuple $\langle Phy, Obj, Act, Struc \rangle$, where Phy is the physical space made of rooms and locked/unlocked doors; Obj are the objects found in the space including containers holding physical as well as information content; Act are the actors (*i.e.*, the people, malicious agent) and their interactions with and within the physical space; $Struc$ defines the structure of the physical space by telling what rooms are adjacent and which are connected by doors. Formally, we describe the CPS tuple as follows:

A) *Phy* is a tuple $\langle L, D, key_D \rangle$, where
  – L is a finite set of locations (with elements l, l', etc.).
  – D is a finite set of doors (with elements d, d', etc.).
  – $key_D \colon D \mapsto O$ is a partial function that returns the object (*i.e.*, the key) that can lock/unlock a door. $Dom(key_D)$ is the set of doors that can be locked.
B) *Obj* is a tuple $\langle O, type_O, attr_O, key_O \rangle$, where
  – O is a finite set of objects (with elements o, o', etc.).
  – $type_O \colon O \to \{p, d\}$ returns the type of object, physical (p) or digital (d).
  – $attr_O \colon O \to 2^{\{c,m,d,n\}}$ returns a set of attributes of an object, that is, container (c), movable (m), destroyable (d), and clonable (n).
  – $key_O \colon O \mapsto O$ is a partial function that returns the object (*i.e.*, the key) that can lock/unlock a physical object (resp. encrypt/decrypt a digital object). $Dom(key_O)$ are digital objects and containers that can be locked. Note that a password can lock a safe, and a physical key used to encrypt (lock) a file.
C) *Act* is a tuple $\langle A, I, \Sigma \rangle$, where
  – A is a finite set of actors (with elements a, a', etc.).
  – $I \notin A$ is the intruder. We use A_I as a shorthand for the set $A \cup \{I\}$.
  – Σ is the set of basic actions that any agent can perform: moving from one location to another through a door, locking/encrypting, unlocking/decrypting, drop or pick objects from rooms or containers, destroy, clone information, exchange objects and information with other peers, or do nothing. Assuming that $l, l' \in L$, $d \in D$, $o, o' \in O$, $a \in A$, and $x \in L \cup O$, and $v \in D \cup O$, we have

$$\Sigma = \{MoveTo(d, l, l'), Lock(v, o), UnLock(v, o), Put(o, x), Get(o, x),$$
$$Destroy(o), Clone(o, o'), Give(o, a), Rec(o, a), Stop\}.$$

Informally, the following actions as their names mean are related to a given actor where $MoveTo(d, l, l')$ leads to move from location l to l' through door d, $Lock(v, o)$ to lock v with o, $UnLock(v, o)$ to unlock v with o, $Put(o, x)$ to put o in x, $Get(o, x)$ to get o from x, $Destroy(o)$ to destroy o, $Clone(o, o')$ to clone o in o', $Give(o, a)$ to give o to a, $Rec(o, a)$ to receive o from a, and $Stop$ means ending the actors' behavior.

– $bv_A \colon A \to \mathscr{L}$ returns the expression that describes the behaviour of an actor. $\mathscr{L}$ is a language described by $B ::= \alpha \cdot (B+B)$ where $\alpha \in \Sigma$, '·' and '+' are the sequential and the non-determinism operators respectively. We assume a structural equivalence $=$ on expressions, defined as the smallest relation that satisfies the following equalities:
  - $B + B = B$,
  - $(B_1 + B_2) + B_3 = B_1 + (B_2 + B_3) = B_1 + B_2 + B_3$, and
  - $Stop.B = Stop$.

D) *Struc* is a multi-graph $\langle V, E, C \rangle$, representing how the entities are connected, where
  – $V = \{b\} \cup L \cup A_I \cup O$, *i.e.*, the vertices, is the set of all the entities plus b the root, which may be considered the name of physical space.
  – $E \subseteq (\{b\} \times L) \cup (L \times (A_I \cup O)) \cup (A_I \times O) \cup (O \times O)$
  – $\langle V, E \rangle$ is a tree rooted in b.
  – $C \subseteq L \times D \times L$ is a set of edges labelled by doors representing the rooms' connection.

3.2 Semantics

We represent the execution of actions in a CPS by a labeled state transition system $\langle \mathbf{S}, S_0, \Rightarrow \rangle$, where: $\mathbf{S}$ is the set of all possible CPS states, $S_0 \in \mathbf{S}$ is the initial state, and $\Rightarrow \ \subseteq (\mathbf{S} \times \Gamma \times \mathbf{S})$ is the transition relation between states for a set of labels Γ. It is the smallest relation that satisfies the transition rules.

We express each transition by $s \overset{\ell}{\Rightarrow} s'$ (See Fig. 2), where the states are represented by the relevant part of the multi-graph. The edge labels and the nodes in the graph express elements of the state that relate to them. We display only those elements that express a condition for the occurrence of the transition or that change due to the transition. For example, the semantic rule depicted in Fig. 2 shows the execution of $Clone(o'', o)$ that clones the object o'' from o' to o, where o' and o are container objects, and o'' is a movable and clonable object. Further since there is no methodology that calculates probabilities and provides cost of actions in CPS, we omit these two features from the CPS model formalism presented in [3].

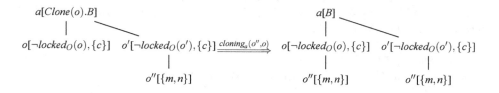

Fig. 2. Semantic rule for clone action.

Further, we define two auxiliary functions. They keep a history of whether doors and containers have been locked/encrypted and by whom.

- $Hist_D : \mathbf{S} \times D \rightarrow 2^{\mathbb{B} \times A}$ returns a list of pairs, each pair saying whether the door has been locked (**true**) or unlocked (**false**) and the actors performing that action;
- $Hist_O : \mathbf{S} \times O \mapsto 2^{\mathbb{B} \times A}$ returns a list of pairs, each pair saying whether the object has been locked (**true**) or unlocked (**false**) and the actors performing that action.

4　Security Policies and Security Requirements

We intend to incorporate our CPS model in a framework to deal with *security policies* and *security requirements*.

A security policy constraints the system traces by restricting the actors' behaviour [4]. When a policy is enforced, it limits what can happen. In our model we assume policies to be enforced by mechanisms acting upon the **CPS!**. For instance, what agents can do on objects and files is determined by access control systems; how people behave is determined by accepted moral or social rules, or by regulations that people follow in fear of punishment. In modeling policies, we abstract the real reason of the enforcement and focus on the effect that policies have on the semantics of our model.

A security requirement is a property that we would like to hold on the constrained CPS. The requirement must hold despite specific threats, coming from an adversary or from people acting dishonestly, that is, breaking the rules and the regulations assumed on the CPS. We discuss a framework that checks whether a constrained CPS model satisfying a requirement or not by considering a requirement as a set of states or a sequence of states. Further, we define a set of templates expressing the requirements.

4.1　Security Policies vs. Security Requirements

We express policies and requirements using the language of *security statements* given in Definition 1 based on the next operator and bounded until of **LTL!** (**LTL!**).

Definition 1 (Security Statement). *A security statement denoted by ϕ is an expression of the language generated by the following grammar, whose rules are written in Backus-Naur form:*

$$\phi ::= \psi_{SP} \mid \psi_{PL} \mid \psi_{TL}$$
$$\psi_{SP} ::= d \in conn(l, l') \mid o \in key_D(d) \mid (x, a) \in Hist_D(d) \mid$$
$$\quad y \in attr_O(o) \mid z \in type_O(o) \mid loc_O(o) = l \mid o \in key_O(o') \mid o \in cont_O(o') \mid$$
$$\quad (x, a) \in Hist_O(o) \mid loc_A(a) = l \mid o \in cont_A(a)$$
$$\psi_{PL} ::= \top \mid \neg\phi \mid \phi \wedge \phi$$
$$\psi_{TL} ::= \bigcirc\phi \mid \phi \mathrm{U}^{\leq k} \mid \phi \mathrm{U}\phi \mid \diamond\phi \mid \Box\phi$$

The boolean operators $\wedge$ and $\neg$ give the full power of propositional logic; operators $\bigcirc$ and $U^{\leq k}$ are sufficient to derive the other linear temporal operators.

$$\varphi_1 U \varphi_2 \overset{def}{=} \varphi_1\ U^{\leq \infty}\ \varphi_2 \qquad \Diamond \varphi \overset{def}{=} \mathbf{true} U \varphi \qquad \Box \varphi \overset{def}{=} \neg \Diamond \neg \varphi$$

From the non-terminal symbol φ_{SP} we derive the *state propositions*, which are propositions over a CPS's state. Their informal meaning can be evinced from the name of the statement. So, for instance, $o \in key_D(d)$, where o ranges over the objects O, evaluates true if and only if o is the key that opens door d. The formal semantics is given in Table 1. It defines $[\![\cdot]\!]_S$ the function that returns a φ's truth value given a particular CPS's state $S \in \mathbf{S}$. All the items (set of nodes, labels, edges) in Table 1 must be intended as those defined in S.

Table 1. Interpretation of the state formulas give an CPS's state S. Here E^+ is the transitive closure of E.

$$[\![d \in conn(l, l')]\!]_S \text{ iff } (l, d, l') \in C$$
$$[\![(x, a) \in Hist_D(o)]\!]_S \text{ iff } (x, a) \in Hist_D(o)$$
$$[\![(x, a) \in Hist_O(o)]\!]_S \text{ iff } (x, a) \in Hist_O(o)$$
$$[\![y \in attr_O(o)]\!]_S \text{ iff } y \in attr_O(o)$$
$$[\![z \in type_O(o)]\!]_S \text{ iff } z \in type_O(o)$$

$$[\![loc_O(o) = l]\!]_S \text{ iff } (l, o) \in (E)^+$$
$$[\![loc_A(a) = l]\!]_S \text{ iff } (l, a) \in E$$
$$[\![o \in key_D(d)]\!]_S \text{ iff } o = key_D(d)$$
$$[\![o \in key_O(o')]\!]_S \text{ iff } o = key_O(o')$$
$$[\![o \in cont_O(o')]\!]_S \text{ iff } (o', o) \in (E)^+$$
$$[\![o \in cont_A(a)]\!]_S \text{ iff } (a, o) \in (E)^+$$

The semantics of φ is the standard semantics of **LTL!** formula (*e.g.*, see [ ]). It is the set $Words(\varphi) = \{\rho \in 2^{\varphi_{SP}} : \rho \models \varphi\}$ of all ω-words (*i.e.*, infinite words) that satisfy φ, where the satisfaction relation $\models \subseteq 2^{\varphi_{SP}} \times \mathbf{LTL!}_\varphi$ is the smallest relation satisfying the following properties (here, if $\rho = s_1 \cdots s_2 \ldots$, $\rho[i] = s_i \cdots s_{i+1} \ldots$):

- $\rho \models \top$
- $\rho \models \varphi_{SP}$ iff $[\![\varphi_{SP}]\!]_{\rho[0]}$
- $\rho \models \neg \varphi$ iff $\rho \not\models \varphi$
- $\rho \models \varphi_1 \wedge \varphi_2$ iff $\rho \models \varphi_1$ and $\rho \models \varphi_2$

- $\rho \models \bigcirc \varphi$ iff $\rho[1 \ldots] =, 1 \ldots \models \varphi$
- $\rho \models \varphi_1 U \varphi_2$ iff $\exists\, j \geq 0, \forall 0 \leq i < j$: $\rho[j \cdots] \models \varphi_2$ and $\rho[i \cdots] \models \varphi_1$

We model a policy that can bound the CPS behaviour (*e.g.*, agent a should never enter in location l) which explicitly affects the CPS's semantics (*e.g.*, there will be no state where a is in location l). This raises the question about whether the real policy, that we are modeling, is actually capable to cause on the system (*e.g.*, is it really true that imposing that a cannot enter in l, implies that there will be no state where a is in l?). This may depend on the policy, but we will chose to model policies in such a way that the answer of this question is positive (*e.g.*, yes it is true that imposing an actor a to not enter in l implies that there will be no state where a is in l). In contrast, the requirement describes functional and non-functional guidelines to ensure the behavioral correctness of the CPS model within the policy. Further, a requirement needs to be satisfied in order to ensure security and the correct behavior of an CPS model.

In our CPS context we consider a security policy as a safety property or the negation of a liveness property. We assert that a security requirement any security statement that the CPS model must satisfy. We denote by π a security policy and by p a security requirement.

Definition 2 (Security Policy). *A security policy is security statement that express either a safety property of the form $\Box\neg\varphi_{SP}$ or a negation of a liveness property written as $\neg\Box(\varphi_{SP} \to \Diamond\varphi_{SP}))$.*

Definition 3 (Security Requirement). *A security requirement is security statement.*

5   Reinforced CPS Semantics

Definition 4 (Requirements/Policies Affectedness). *Let p be a requirement and π be a policy and S a model of execution of a CPS!. Let $\texttt{traces}(S, p)$ be the set of traces in S that satisfy p, and $\texttt{traces}(S, \neg\pi)$ the set of traces where π is not satisfied. We say that p is affected by π in S, and we write $p \hookleftarrow \pi$ when $\texttt{traces}(S, p) \cap \texttt{traces}(S, \neg\pi) = \emptyset$.*

Definition 5 illustrates an CPS model constrained with a policy.

Definition 5 (Constrained CPS). *Let $S = \langle \mathbf{S}, S_0, \Rightarrow \rangle$ to be an CPS, π a security statement represents a policy for S, and p a security statement represents a requirement for S, then, S constrained with a policy π, written (S, π) is a new CPS, $S' = \langle \mathbf{S}', S_0, \Rightarrow' \rangle$ such that:*

1. *If $S \not\models \pi$ then $(S, \pi) \models \pi$;*
2. *For all π such that $p \not\hookleftarrow \pi$ then if $S \models p$ then $(S, \pi) \models p$;*

Definition 6 (Constraining CPS). *For a given $S = \langle \mathbf{S}, S_0, \Rightarrow \rangle$ and a policy π, constraining S with π produces S' by executing three actions defined as follows.*

1. CLEANS $\triangleq$ *If $\exists s \in \mathbf{S}$ where $s \models \phi$:*
   - $\mathbf{S}' = \mathbf{S}\backslash\{s\}$, *and*
   - *If $\exists(s', s) \in\Rightarrow$: $\Rightarrow'= (\Rightarrow \backslash\{(s', s)\}) \cup \{(s', s')\}$, and*
   - *If $\exists(s, s') \in\Rightarrow$: $\Rightarrow'= (\Rightarrow \backslash\{(s', s)\})$.*
2. CLEANT $\triangleq$ *If $\exists\rho = [s_i, \ldots, s_{j-1}, s_j]$ where $\rho \models \pi$:*
   - $\Rightarrow'= (\Rightarrow \backslash\{(s_{j-1}, s_j)\}) \cup \{(s_{j-1}, s_{j-1})\}$.
3. CLEANR $\triangleq$ *If $\exists s' \in \mathbf{S}'$, $\not\exists(s'', s') \in\Rightarrow': \mathbf{S}' = \mathbf{S}'\backslash\{s'\}$.*

To produce the semantics of an CPS S constrained with a policy ϕ, we parse, with a depth-first search, the CPS transition system. Algorithm 1 does this search and constructs a policy constrained semantics of an CPS S.

The algorithm first checks if a policy ϕ is of type ψ_{SP}, ψ_{PL} (line 4), or ψ_{TL} (line 10). In the case of a state statement, the procedure γ looks for states satisfying the policy ϕ (line 6) to exclude them from the original CPS by calling the function CLEANS (line 7). For the case of path statements, the procedure finds the path that satisfies ϕ (line 12) and calls the function CLEANT (line 13). Finally, the function CLEANR (line 17) cleans the unreachable state.

The function CLEANS (lines 19–30) replaces the incoming edges of a state with loops (line 22 and 23), and ignores its outgoing edges (line 26). Finally, it excludes the state from the set of states in S (line 29). The function CLEANT (lines 31–34) replaces the last transition of the path formula with a loop, and the function CLEANR (lines 35–56) finds the predecessors of states (lines 38–42), and it excludes them (line 49) as well as its successors (line 46) from the state space, and the set of transitions, respectively. CLEANR terminates when all states are reachable.

Example 1. Now we enforce the model of the presented example with the policy $\Box(\neg(loc_A(I) \neq l_0))$ that claims an intruder should never access the infrastructure. Figure 3 shows only the retained steps on the CPS model presented after enforcing this policy. Further, we enforce again the model with a policy that claims if the object o_2 has been possessed by a_1, then, it will never be possessed by a_2. It is expressed as $\Box(\neg(\{o_2\} \subseteq cont_A(a_2) \rightarrow \Diamond(\{o_2\} \subseteq cont_A(a_1)))$. As a result, Fig. 4 shows the added transition loop in green and the deleted one in red from the initial CPS formal model.

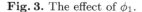
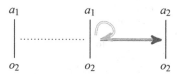

Fig. 3. The effect of ϕ_1.   **Fig. 4.** The effect of ϕ_2.

Algorithm 1. Policy Constrained Algorithm.

```
1:  procedure γ(S,φ)
2:      Input:
        1. S = ⟨S, S₀, ⇒⟩;                                    ▷ A tuple modeling an CPS.
        2. φ;                                                  ▷ A security statement.
3:      Output:
        1. S = ⟨S′, S₀′, ⇒′⟩;                                ▷ A policy-based constrained CPS.
4:      if φ.type() ∈ {SP, PL} then                          ▷ The case of state formula.
5:          for each s ∈ S do
6:              if s ⊨ φ then
7:                  CLEANS(S,s);                              ▷ Clean the states that satisfy φ.
8:              end if
9:          end for
10:     else if φ.type() ∈ {TL} then                         ▷ The case of path formula.
11:         for each ρ ∈ 2⇒ do
12:             if ρ[sᵢ,…,s_{j−1},s_j] ⊨ φ then
13:                 CLEANT(S,s_{j−1} ⇒ s_j);                  ▷ Clean the last transition of the path ρ.
14:             end if
15:         end for
16:     end if
17:     CLEANR(S);                                            ▷ Clean the unreachable states.
18: end procedure
19: function CLEANS(S,s)
20:     for each s′ ∈ S do
21:         if s′ ⇒ s ∈⇒ then
22:             ⇒ ← (⇒ \{s′ ⇒ s});                           ▷ Exclude the predecessors of the state s.
23:             ⇒ ← ⇒′ ∪{s′ ⇒ s′};                           ▷ Adding a loop on the state s.
24:         end if
25:         if s ⇒ s′ ∈⇒ then
26:             ⇒ ← ⇒ \{s ⇒ s′};                             ▷ Exclude the successors of the state s.
27:         end if
28:     end for
29:     S = S\{s};                                            ▷ Exclude the state s.
30: end function
31: function CLEANT(S,s_{j−1} ⇒ s_j)
32:     ⇒ ← ⇒ \{s_{j−1} ⇒ s_j};                              ▷ Exclude the transition s_{j−1} ⇒ s_j.
33:     ⇒ ← ⇒ ∪{s_{j−1} ⇒ s_{j−1}};                          ▷ Adding a loop on the state s_{j−1}.
34: end function
35: function CLEANR(S)
36:     Inₛ = ∅;                                              ▷ List of transitions.
37:     for each sᵢ ∈ S do
38:         for each s_j ∈ S do                               ▷ Find the predecessors of a state s_j.
39:             if s_j ⇒ sᵢ ∈⇒ then
40:                 Inₛ ← {s_j ⇒ sᵢ};
41:             end if
42:         end for
43:         if Inₛ = ∅ then                                   ▷ The case of unreachable state s_j.
44:             for each s_k ∈ S do
45:                 if s_j ⇒ s_k ∈⇒ then
46:                     ⇒=⇒ \{s_j ⇒ s_k};                     ▷ Exclude the successors of the state s_j.
47:                 end if
48:             end for
49:             S = S\{s_j};                                  ▷ Exclude the state s_j.
50:             Inₛ = ∅;
51:             CLEANR(S);
52:         else
53:             return S;                                     ▷ The constrained CPS.
54:         end if
55:     end for
56: end function
```

---

6   Proof of Concept

We show the effectiveness of the approach presented in Fig. 1 by enforcing the security policies expressed as security statements on the model depicted in Fig. 5.

First, we express two security policies. One is about forbidding the access to a location and the other is about restricting the possession of objects. Both policies are described and expressed as follows.

1. The object o_1 is a fixed printer and it should never be possessed: $\forall a_i \in A : \Box\neg(\{o_1\} \subset cont_A(a_i))$.
2. If the object o_2 has been possessed by a_2 then it should never be possessed by a_1: $\Box\neg((\{o_2\} \subset cont_A(a_2)) \rightarrow (\{o_2\} \subset cont_A(a_1)))$.

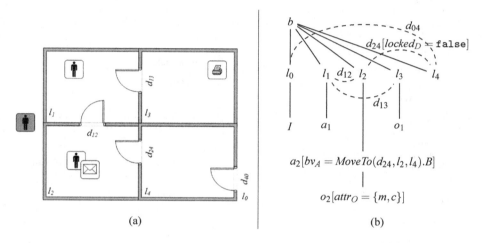

(a)   (b)

Fig. 5. (a) An CPS's floor plan; (b) The formal representation of the CPS.

To check the validity of the policies on the CPS model, we encode the model depicted in Fig. 5 as a PRISM program. The program includes five modules representing the behaviors of the actors a_1 and a_2, the intruder, and the objects o_1 and o_2. Table 2 shows parts of the code fragment that represents these entities as five modules: Actor_{a_1}, Actor_{a_1}, intruder, Object_{o_2} and Object_{o_2}. Each module is composed from a sequence of commands where each represents a transition in the CPS transition system. For example, line 15 in the module $\text{Actor}a_1$ shows the command representing the moving transition of a_1 from l_1 to l_2. The action of this transition is denoted by $M_{l,2}$ between brackets ([]), the current transition of a_1 is represented by the guard of this command which is $(l_{a_1} = 1)$ and the next state of this presentation is represented by the update of the command $(l_{a_1} = 2)$ (in the right side). The command T_{o_2} in line 20 describes taking o_2 if it is not possessed by another actor and if location of a_1 is the same as o_2. The

Table 2. PRISM code fragment of the CPS model.

```
1   mdp
2   module Actor_{a_1}
3   l_{a_1}: [0..4] init 1;
4   a_{o_1}: bool init ⊥;
5   a_{o_2}: bool init ⊥;
6   //Moving actions
7   [M_{0,0}] (l_{a_1}=0)⇒(l_{a_1}'=0);
8   [M_{0,4}] (l_{a_1}=0)⇒(l_{a_1}'=4);
9   [M_{4,0}] (l_{a_1}=4) ⇒ (l'_{a_1}=0);
10  [M_{4,2}] (l_{a_1}=4) ⇒ (l'_{a_1}=2);
11  [M_{4,4}] (l_{a_1}=4) ⇒ (l'_{a_1}=4);
12  [M_{2,2}] (l_{a_1}=2) ⇒ (l'_{a_1}=2);
13  [M_{2,4}] (l_{a_1}=2) ⇒ (l'_{a_1}=4);
14  [M_{1,1}] (l_{a_1}=1) ⇒ (l'_{a_1}=1);
15  [M_{1,2}] (l_{a_1}=1) ⇒ (l'_{a_1}=2);
16  [M_{1,3}] (l_{a_1}=1) ⇒ (l'_{a_1}=3);
17  [M_{3,1}] (l_{a_1}=3) ⇒ (l'_{a_1}=1);
18  [M_{3,3}] (l_{a_1}=3) ⇒ (l'_{a_1}=3);
19  //The actor a_1 takes o_2
20  [T_{o_2}] (l_{a_1}=l_{o_2}&¬(a_2)_{o_2}&¬I_{o_2})⇒(a_1)'_{o_2}=⊤;
21  //The actor a_1 receives o_2 from a_2
22  [X_{o_2,a_1}](l_{a_1}=l_{o_2})&((a_2)_{o_2})⇒(a_1)'_{o_2}=⊤);
23  [X_{o_2,a_1}](l_{a_1}=l_{o_2})&((a_2)_{o_2})⇒(a_1)'_{o_2}=⊥);
24  ...
25  endmodule
26  module Actor_{a_2}
27  l_{a_2}: [0..4] init 2;
28  a_{o_1}: bool init ⊥;
29  a_{o_2}: bool init ⊤;
30  //Moving actions
31  [M_{0,0}] (l_{a_2}=0)⇒(l_{a_2}'=0);
32  [M_{0,4}] (l_{a_2}=0)⇒(l_{a_2}'=4);
33  [M_{4,0}] (l_{a_2}=4) ⇒ (l'_{a_2}=0);
34  [M_{4,2}] (l_{a_2}=4) ⇒ (l'_{a_2}=2);
35  [M_{4,4}] (l_{a_2}=4) ⇒ (l'_{a_2}=4);
36  ...
37  //The actions of a_2 with o_1
38  //The actor a_1 takes o_2
39  [T_{o_2}](l_{a_1}=l_{o_1}&¬(a_1)_{o_1}&¬(a_2)_{o_1}&¬I_{o_1})⇒(a_1)'_{o_1}=⊤;
40  [T_{o_2}](l_{a_1}=l_{o_1}&¬(a_1)_{o_1}&¬(a_2)_{o_1}&¬I_{o_1})⇒(a_1)'_{o_1}=⊥;
41  //The actions of a_2 in l_2
42  [M_{2,l_i}] (l_{a_1}=l_2&¬(a_2)_{o_2}&¬I_{o_2})⇒(a_1)'_{o_2}=⊤;
43  [T_{o_2,l_i}] (l_{a_1}=l_2&¬(a_2)_{o_2}&¬I_{o_2})⇒(a_1)'_{o_2}=⊤;
44  //The actor a_2 puts o_2 in l_i
45  [P_{o_2,l_i}] (l_{a_2}=l_{o_2})&(l_{a_2}=l_i)&((a_2)_{o_2})⇒((a_2)'_{o_2}=⊥);
46  //The actor a_2 gives o_2 to a_1
47  [X_{o_2,a_1}](l_{a_1}=l_{o_2})&((a_2)_{o_2}))⇒((a_2)'_{o_2}=⊥);
48  [X_{o_2,a_1}](l_{a_1}=l_{o_2})&((a_2)_{o_2}))⇒((a_2)'_{o_2}=⊤);
49  ...
50  endmodule

1   module Intruder
2   l_I: [0..4] init 0;//Locations
3   I_{o_1}: bool init ⊥;
4   I_{o_2}: bool init ⊥;
5   //Moving actions
6   [M_{00}] (l_I=0)⇒(l_I'=0);
7   [M_{04}] (l_I=0)⇒(l_I'=4);
8   [M_{40}] (l_I=4) ⇒ (l'_I=0);
9   [M_{42}] (l_I=4) ⇒ (l'_I=2);
10  [M_{44}] (l_I=4) ⇒ (l'_I=4);
11  //Stealing o_2
12  [S_{o_2}] (l_I=l_{o_2}) ⇒ (I'_{o_2}=⊤);
13  //Slipping o_2
14  [L_{o_2,a_1}] (l_I=l_{a_1}) & (I_{o_2}) ⇒ (I'_{o_2}=⊥);
15  [L_{o_2,a_2}] (l_I=l_{a_2}) & (I_{o_2}) ⇒ (I'_{o_2}=⊥);
16  //Putting o_2 !in! location l_i
17  [P_{o_2,l_i}] (l_I=l_i) & (I_{o_2}) ⇒ (I'_{o_2}=⊥);
18  //Destroyinging o_2
19  [D_{I,o_2}] (I_{o_2})⇒ (I'_{o_2}=⊥);
20  ...
21  endmodule
22
23  module object_{o_1}
24  l_{o_2}:[0..4] init 3;
25  exist_{o_1}:bool init ⊤;
26  //Moving o_2 with the possessor
27  [M_{a_1,o_1}] (exist_{o_2})⇒ (l'_{o_2}=l_{a_1});
28  [M_{a_1,o_1}] (exist_{o_2})⇒ (l'_{o_2}=l_{a_2});
29  [M_{I,o_2}] (exist_{o_2})⇒ (l'_{o_2}=l_I);
30  //Destroyinging o_2 by the intruder
31  [D_{I,o_2}] (exist_{o_2}∧I_{o_2})⇒ (exist'_{o_2}=⊥);
32  ...
33  endmodule
34
35  module object_{o_2}
36  l_{o_2}:[0..4] init 2;
37  exist_{o_2}:bool init ⊤;
38  //Moving o_2 with the possessor
39  [M_{a_1,o_2}] (exist_{o_2}) ⇒ (l'_{o_2}=l_{a_1});
40  [M_{a_1,o_2}] (exist_{o_2}) ⇒ (l'_{o_2}=l_{a_2});
41  [M_{I,o_2}] (exist_{o_2})⇒ (l'_{o_1}=l_I);
42  //Destroyinging o_2 by the intruder
43  [D_{I,o_2}] (exist_{o_2}∧I_{o_2})⇒ (exist'_{o_2}=⊥);
44  ...
45  endmodule
```

command X_{o_2,a_1} in line 22 synchronizes with the command of 47 for the module $Actor_{a_2}$ that describes exchanging o_2.

The verification of the CPS Model under test shows that both policies are violated. For the first policy, initially, o_1 is in l_3 (module $Object_{o_1}$, line 24). We enforce the model with the first policy by excluding the command T_{o_1} from each module in the PRISM code and we add a loop transition. For example the transition T_{o_1} of Module Actor$_{o_1}$ in line 39 with red color is excluded and we added a loop transition expressed by the command of line 40 with blue color. For the second policy, the command $X(o_2, a_1)$ that represents exchanging o_2 between a_1 and a_2 has been excluded (line 22 and 47 in red) and the loop command is added (line 23 and 48 in blue).

After model checking the new enforced CPS model, the verification results show that both policies hold.

7   Related Work

We compare the presented work with the existing formalisms and techniques used to express and enforce security principally in CPS.

Ouchani [1] proposes IoT-SEC framework that covers the probability and costs of actions, formalizes IoT, analyzes the correctness and measures their security level by relying on the probabilistic model checking PRISM. The proposed model covers five entities: object and users devices, computing services, and social actors. To ensure the functional correctness of an IoT-based system, IoT-SEC develops five steps: defines the IoT components, formalizes the architecture in a process algebra expression. Then, it expresses the IoT requirements in PCTL and transforms the IoT model into the PRISM input language. Finally, PRISM checks how much a requirement is ensured on the IoT model. The results can be qualitative or quantitative. IoT-SEC has been applied on a use case presenting a smart healthcare emergency room. The analysis is automatic and covering the components that might exist in an environment. However, the proposed framework involves a large amount of data and messages which make the probabilistic model checking expensive in terms of time and memory.

Hartel et al. [4] consider a policy as a process concurring with the system. Both polcies and the system are modeled as transition systems and implemented in SPIN. They present four use case protocols—the Unix command **ping**, payment with a smart card, peer-to-peer music sharing, and accessing a database for testing versus for using it—together with four specific policies with the goal to check whether the system composed with the policies, complies with a security principle. This work is limited to four use cases and does not show how it can be applied to different cases. Further, the composition makes the system more complex for verification compared to our approach.

Jaume classifies the security policies into three categories [5]: (i) property-based policies where a security target is satisfied in a state of a transition system, (ii) access control policies which are defined through subjects, objects, and access modes (iii) flow policies that control flows between subjects and objects by specifying a set of authorized flows between them. Jaume shows the equivalence between the different classes of security policies. Our approach combines these three categories in a well-formed easy-to-express class. However, Jaume does not show how to constrain a policy.

Ranise et al. [6] extend the action language STRIPS to specify policies in smart spaces. The security requirements in the new language called ALPS are expressed as first-order logic assertions and the model is described as a timed transition system. The Groove model checker has been used to verify security requirements that are defined as a reachability properties. In this work, the security policies are considered as requirements and are not enforced within the model.

Tschantz *et al.* [7] introduce two concepts: purpose and planning. The planning is used to determine the executed actions to achieve a purpose. It is modeled as a non-redundant MDP where the redundant actions are replaced by stop ones, and the purpose is considered as a state logic formula. The actions are defined by using an MDP strategy that optimizes the reward functions of the MDP. Compared to our approach, this one focuses more on state formulae, and it does not show how the planning has been determined after execution.

Bertolissi and Fernandez [8] extend the access control model RBAC to cover location and time features. The resulting access model called LTRBAC uses the term rewriting systems to specify discrete time and location access control policies. The LTRBAC model has been implemented in Maude and OCAML. Fong [9] models the access control policies in ReBAC as a set of predicates expressing the owners, the accessors, and the relation between identifiers in a social network graph. The modal logic is proposed to express the policies for ReBAC. Compared to our work, the policies expressed in LTRBAC and ReBAC do not cover the relation between the models' entities and do not express a sequence of actions. Further, LTRBAC focuses only on constraining a specific location at a time.

Ouchani et al. [10,11] propose an algorithm that converts the attack models into pCTL to express security requirements. They propose to use PRISM for security assessment by generating attacks related to systems that are designed by using SysML activity diagrams. The generation of attacks is based on attack surfaces detection and instantiating from a predefined library of attacks the possible potential attacks proper to the detected attack surface. This approach deals only with the generation of security requirements instead of enforcing security policies.

8   Conclusion

The presented research sets the foundations for ensuring security of CPS. One way to achieve this is to enforce security of an CPS with security policies. We presented a formal language to express security policies and a methodology to enforce and to verify security in CPS models. Besides that, the proposed language has been used to express the security requirements for verification. We validated the presented approach on a real scenario. The results affirms the effectiveness and the efficiency of our approach. The presented work will be extended in the following directions. First, we want to reduce the complexity of the proposed algorithm and optimize the generated CPS models. Further, we would like to provide a catalogue of templates expressing security policies and security requirements. Also, we intend to apply our framework on different real cases, especially those related to product chains and cyber-physical systems.

References

1. Ouchani, S.: Ensuring the functional correctness of IoT through formal modeling and verification. In: Abdelwahed, E.H., Bellatreche, L., Golfarelli, M., Méry, D., Ordonez, C. (eds.) MEDI 2018. LNCS, vol. 11163, pp. 401–417. Springer, Cham (2018). https://doi.org/10.1007/978-3-030-00856-7_27

2. Ouchani, S., Ait Mohamed, O., Debbabi, M.: Efficient probabilistic abstraction for SysML activity diagrams. In: Eleftherakis, G., Hinchey, M., Holcombe, M. (eds.) SEFM 2012. LNCS, vol. 7504, pp. 263–277. Springer, Heidelberg (2012). https://doi.org/10.1007/978-3-642-33826-7_18

3. Lenzini, G., Mauw, S., Ouchani, S.: Security analysis of socio-technical physical systems. Comput. Electr. Eng. **47**(C), 258–274 (2015)

4. Hartel, P., van Eck, P., Etalle, S., Wieringa, R.: Modelling mobility aspects of security policies. In: Barthe, G., Burdy, L., Huisman, M., Lanet, J.-L., Muntean, T. (eds.) CASSIS 2004. LNCS, vol. 3362, pp. 172–191. Springer, Heidelberg (2005). https://doi.org/10.1007/978-3-540-30569-9_9

5. Jaume, M.: Semantic comparison of security policies: from access control policies to flow properties. In: 2012 IEEE Symposium on Security and Privacy Workshops (SPW), pp. 60–67, May 2012

6. Ranise, S., Traverso, R.: ALPS: an action language for policy specification and automated safety analysis. In: Mauw, S., Jensen, C.D. (eds.) STM 2014. LNCS, vol. 8743, pp. 146–161. Springer, Cham (2014). https://doi.org/10.1007/978-3-319-11851-2_10

7. Tschantz, M.C., Datta, A., Wing, J.M.: Formalizing and enforcing purpose restrictions in privacy policies. In: 2012 IEEE Symposium on Security and Privacy (SP), pp. 176–190, May 2012

8. Bertolissi, C., Fernandez, M.: Time and location based services with access control. In: New Technologies, Mobility and Security, NTMS 2008, pp. 1–6, November 2008

9. Fong, P.W.L.: Relationship-based access control: protection model and policy language. In: Proceedings of the First ACM Conference on Data and Application Security and Privacy, CODASPY 2011, pp. 191–202 (2011)

10. Ouchani, S., Mohamed, O.A., Debbabi, M.: A security risk assessment framework for SysML activity diagrams. In: 2013 IEEE 7th International Conference on Software Security and Reliability (SERE), pp. 227–236 (2013)

11. Ouchani, S., Mohamed, O.A., Debbabi, M.: Attacks generation by detecting attack surfaces. Procedia Comput. Sci. **32**, 529–536 (2014). The 5th International Conference on Ambient Systems, Networks and Technologies (ANT-2014), the 4th International Conference on Sustainable Energy Information Technology (SEIT-2014)

Smart Cyber-Physical System for Pattern Recognition of Illegal 3D Designs in 3D Printing

Anton Vedeshin[1]([✉]), John Mehmet Ulgar Dogru[1], Innar Liiv[2],
Sadok Ben Yahia[2], and Dirk Draheim[3]

[1] 3DPrinterOS, 3D Control Systems, Inc., San Francisco, CA, USA
{anton,john}@3dprinteros.com
[2] Department of Software Science, Tallinn University of Technology, Tallinn, Estonia
{innar,sadok.ben}@taltech.ee
[3] Information Systems Group, Tallinn University of Technology, Tallinn, Estonia
dirk.draheim@taltech.ee
https://3DPrinterOS.com

Abstract. The method to protect intellectual property (IP) in automated manufacturing (AM) and 3D printing industry particularly, presented in this paper, is based on a smart cyber-physical system and the radical improvement of preventive and detective controls to find potential cases of automated manufacturing copyrights infringement. The focus of this paper is not the ecosystem of managing a large network of physical 3D printers, but a smart application and data analysis of data flow within the ecosystem to solve a problem of IP protection and illegal physical objects manufacturing. In this paper, we focus on the first step in this direction – pattern recognition of illegal physical designs in 3D printing, and detection of firearms parts particularly. The proposed method relies on several important steps: normalization of 3D designs, metadata calculation, defining typical illegal designs, pattern matrix creation, new 3D designs challenging, and pattern matrix update. We classify 3D designs into loose groups without strict differentiation, forming a pattern matrix. We use conformity and seriation to calculate the pattern matrix. Then, we perform the analysis of the matrix to find illegal 3D designs. Our method ensures simultaneous pattern discovery at several information levels - from local patterns to global. We performed experiments with 5831 3D designs, extracting 3728 features. It took 12 min to perform pattern matrix calculation based on the test data. Each new 3D design file pattern recognition took 0.32 s on four core, 8 GB ram, 32 GB SSD Azure VM instance.

Keywords: Pattern recognition · Intelligent manufacturing systems · Technology social factors · Distributed computing

1 Introduction

The method to protect intellectual property (IP) in automated manufacturing (AM) and 3D printing industry particularly, presented in this paper, is based

© Springer Nature Switzerland AG 2020
M. Hamlich et al. (Eds.): SADASC 2020, CCIS 1207, pp. 74–85, 2020.
https://doi.org/10.1007/978-3-030-45183-7_6

on the radical improvement of preventive and detective controls on software, firmware, and hardware levels of AM machines. These controls would help to find potential cases of copyright infringement, illegal objects, and firearms manufacturing with the use of AM machines. In this paper, we focus on the first step in this direction – pattern recognition of illegal physical objects in 3D printing, and detection of 3D designs with firearm parts.

Recently, we have witnessed the advent of cloud manufacturing, where F500 enterprises, small and medium businesses, and home users use devices such as 3D printers, CNC mills, laser jets, and robotics to manufacture products locally at the point and time of need. The impressively fast adoption of these technologies strongly indicates that this novel approach to manufacturing can become a crucial enabler for the real-time economy of the future, i.e., a possible paradigm shift in manufacturing towards cloud manufacturing. Now it is possible to manufacture a real working part or a usable product from a CAD design in just hours using cloud manufacturing. Companies and people would not buy a ready-made product at the shop, but obtain raw material and produce products locally, utilizing their own or nearby accessible automated manufacturing machinery. With all the benefits of the new way to manufacture things, there is a growing threat to society. Firstly, there is a need to protect intellectual property (IP) in the form of 3D designs and manufacturing files. Secondly, there is an increased risk and real cases [5, 17, 33] of people producing firearms at home using desktop 3D printers.

With the growing popularity of automated manufacturing (AM), robotic process automation (RPA), the need to protect the intellectual property (IP) at every stage of the AM process became more important: from idea, CAD design to machine instructions and manufacturing files. Companies and people should be able to protect their IP by claiming their technical, mechanical, and chemical solutions through a decentralized platform that protects their IP. Moreover, there should be a measure established which would protect the society from a potential leakage of firearm designs and manufacturing of illegal objects.

In this paper, we are going to address this problem and present one of the possible solutions using a smart cyber-physical system. Our proposed digital ecosystem for personal manufacturing enables one to link the physical world (3D printers) with virtual cloud-based operating system [29]. The focus of this paper is not the ecosystem of managing a large network of physical 3D printers, but a smart application and data analysis of data flow within the ecosystem to solve a problem of IP protection and illegal physical objects manufacturing. In the following, we glance at the main contributions of this paper:

1. We discuss the motivation for the creation of the cloud-based manufacturing operating system to address an evolving critical problem of IP protection and illegal physical objects manufacturing;
2. We introduce a novel cloud-based manufacturing operating system architecture to protect IP and detect illegal physical objects using pattern recognition;

The remainder of the paper is organized as follows: In Sect. 2, we discuss the related work and our motivation to do this task. In Sect. 3, we describe the logic behind patter recognition for illegal 3D objects detection. In Sect. 4, we discuss the experiments and performance of our solution. In Sect. 5, we conclude the paper and give directions for future work.

2   Related Work

In this section, we present related work and the overview of existing ways to protect IP copyright for automated manufacturing (AM).

In their work [13], Hou et al. cover traditional ways to secure 3D files. The authors describe solutions from digital rights management (DRM) to an embedding visual shapes into 3D printed models' internal structure. Later, the scanning of internal structures allows one to figure out it is an original part or a copy. Their work does not cover the whole AM workflow and focuses on protection methods, which can help after manufacturing already happened, for example, watermarking and tagging an object with RFID chips. Although it helps to detect whether the part was original, it does not protect from copying the part or preventing from manufacturing an illegal part. Moreover, by scanning a 3D printed part, it is hard to reverse engineer it due to internal structures, and the exact way it is manufactured. To reproduce the physical part, it is not enough to only obtain the shape of the object, 3D printer toolhead movements, speed, temperature used at that exact path - everything is important and affects the final physical properties of the object. IP protection is essential, mostly before manufacturing.

Nein-Hsien et al., in their research [23], describe a method to encode 3D models into a Jpeg stream, to transfer 3D designs. It is not a comprehensive solution and has definite limitations. Their paper does not handle AM end-to-end workflow, nor prevents an illegal 3D design manufacturing.

In our prior research [25] we only theoretically touched the protection of IP rights for 3D printing. We have described a paradigm applied to secure 3D content delivery called the *live matrix*. This prior work is purely theoretical, lacking technical details. The current paper is the first paper to explain IP copyright protection and illegal 3D part detection technically. This paper's contribution is to extend the initial idea with the implementation details, bring it to the next level, technically broaden it to the illegal 3D parts detection before the part is manufactured.

In our previous works [14,15,30], we have emphasized in detail the necessity to enforce the 3D files' copyrights through secured content delivery - 3D files streaming. Our previous work targets a very niche case to secure 3D designs data at rest and to be transferred from the server to a 3D printer. Previous solution [14,15] is technically dense, has multiple drawbacks. Moreover, it lacks the protection of IP at any other stage of IP handling, nor illegal 3D part detection and manufacturing prevention of illegal parts [30]. In this paper, we contribute a reliable and fast way to detect IP copyrights infringement and extend it to the illegal physical objects detection and prevention from manufacturing.

In their work [24], Mattingly et al. describe a method for three-dimensional printing with blockchain controls. Their work does not precisely describe how the copyright is given and what happens with the file. The idea of just closing the block with the list of transactions is a nature of blockchain; however, this is not clear, how it helps to grant access to the IP. The solution they propose is, basically, a log file that contains the records of what has happened in the past, regardless of whether the IP owner authorized the transaction or not. Smart contracts are not mentioned; thus, it is not clear how exactly the access is granted. The work lacks the details of implementation.

In their work [12], Holland et al. propose copyrights protection for additive manufacturing with a blockchain approach. They utilize the property of blockchain to eliminate the 3rd party so that the blockchain poses a trusted 3rd party or notary, which governs the exchange of transaction data. In their work, 3D design files are not stored in the blockchain, and the blockchain is used only for granting the license and number of prints. Their method lacks the process for the 3D printer to report to the blockchain. 3D printer should send a transaction to update how many times the file was printed and decrease the license quantity.

In the work [16], the authors present a method, which adds a distinctive nanomaterial chemical signature to the parts and registers it in the blockchain. Their method helps to check after the file was manufactured, whether it is an original file or a counterfeit. Their solution does not defend the file nor detects and prevents an illegal 3D file from being manufactured. In their work, the blockchain is a shared resource between the manufacturer of a 3D part and a part receiving party so that both have access to the blockchain instance, and then the counter-party can see the transactions made by the manufacturer. From their work, it is not clear what would stop the user from updating blockchain data without receiving the part? The confirmation of receiving the part or not confirming is not giving much to the security. Their solution is solving mostly audit and integrity problems, and the method works best for a genuine check after the manufacturing or during usage of the part.

Many other works [6,7,11] describe how the user uploads a file to the cloud and how the design is protected using digital rights management (DRM); however, they do not present a viable solution to protect the copyright of 3D files in the long term. These works do not describe how to protect files from being exposed to 3rd parties nor the possibility to detect and prevent illegal parts manufacturing. Our solution proposes a real solution to enforce copyright protection, illegal parts detection, and prevention of manufacturing.

While it is essential to allow users and manufacturers to determine if any restrictions exist on reproducing a 3D object, ideally there must also be a mechanism in place to prevent the unauthorized reproduction of the 3D object, primarily when the 3D design represents an illegal or dangerous part, like a firearm. As the 3D file itself representing the 3D object according to this scenario does not necessarily have any means attached preventing unauthorized use of the 3D file, the known methods cannot be used. The authorization means must be integrated with the manufacturing device itself, e.g., before the start of each manufacturing job, the manufacturing device needs an authorization from the rights holder or confirmation that no restrictions exist. However, with the use

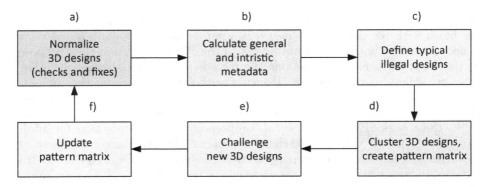

Fig. 1. The proposed method concept

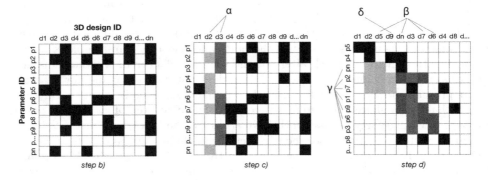

Fig. 2. *step b)* - Calculate general and intrinsic metadata, and store into binary matrix, *step c)* - Define typical illegal objects, *step d)* - Cluster 3D designs and produce pattern matrix, α - illegal 3D designs that were initially marked, β - adjacent illegal designs similar to the ones initially marked, γ - parameters that unify the illegal designs, δ - the design in-between two groups, not strictly differentiated to any of the major groups.

of our cloud manufacturing operating system and ecosystem [29], the detection and protection from illegal parts manufacturing can be performed in the cloud. In the case of our proposed method, there is no need for significant modifications on the AM machine side to support a safe and legal method to produce parts.

3   Proposed Method

To achieve the detection of 3D designs IP copyright infringement and illegal physical objects in 3D printing, we use pattern recognition based on the seriated matrix of 3D designs and their important parameters. The proposed concept relies on several important steps depicted in Fig. 1:

a) *Normalize 3D designs*, this steps includes 87 different checks and fixes. We check the CAD file consistency on three different levels: file format level, 3D design mathematical consistency level, and physical consistency level, e.g., watertight, wall thickness within a certain threshold, and many more. We mathematically reassemble the model [19,28] and fix non-manifold edges, remove duplicate faces, remove hidden malicious geometry, and more.

b) *Calculate general and intrinsic metadata* to find important parameters to be used in clustering and pattern recognition. Create initial matrix of objects and parameters, presented on Fig. 2, step b). We extract more than 150 different *general parameters* from the CAD design, e.g., scale factor to find the original measurement units, number of triangles, bounding box enclosing the object, maximum outer dimensions, volume, shadow volume, voxelized shape, center of mass, skeleton, corpus indicator, detail indicator, deviation of angles, bounding corners density, average deviation of points, and many more.

   Additionally, we extract parameters intrinsic to IP, which should be protected, and illegal objects to detect, e.g., firearms. For example, to find *intrinsic parameters* for firearms, we perform analysis of adjacent faces of a 3D design, so that faces lie on the open cylinder surface of the same cylinder with a certain threshold. We can extract the number of cylindrical shapes, the diameter of cylindrical shapes, the height of cylindrical shapes, the number of triangles participating in cylindrical shapes, the ratio of missing triangles in a cylindrical shape, and many more. For the pattern matrix and the step d) below, we would need a binary representation of parameters. Thus, from 150 parameters, we get more than 3750 by discretizing non-binary parameters into categories.

c) *Define typical illegal designs* as a part of a supervised machine learning process. Later, in the process, these parts will become indicators or contrasting bodies, to detect groups and classes we are looking for, depicted in Fig. 2, step c). For our experiments, we mark objects, which we already know are firearms or contain firearm parts or firearm inverted parts, e.g., a section of an injection mold for firearm production.

d) *Cluster 3D designs* into loose groups without strict differentiation, forming a pattern matrix. We are using conformity and seriation [21,22,32] to calculate our pattern matrix. Then, we perform the analysis of the matrix in automated mode to find classes with a certain threshold. However, the pattern matrix would provide an interesting insight to analyze the data visually. Our method ensures simultaneous pattern discovery at several information levels - from local patterns to global [21,22]. Initial matrix example is shown on Fig. 2, step b), seriated and transformed matrix example is shown on Fig. 2, step d).

e) *Challenge new 3D designs* against the pattern matrix. Firstly, a newcomer 3D design is normalized in step a), then based on the metadata calculated in step b), we perform a fast classification by matching with other 3D designs, which already positioned in the pattern matrix and have close parameters. Finally, we can understand which class of objects it belongs to. Copyright holders can run different types of searches and investigations for the copyright infringements. For example, it is easy to perform a quick check of whether the object fits into one of the classes of illegal objects. Challenging a new 3D design does not require a recalculation of the pattern matrix.

f) *Update pattern matrix* with the new designs. When there is a considerable amount of new 3D designs within a certain threshold, then the pattern matrix will be recalculated to accommodate new designs. Adjacent designs within a certain threshold could automatically or with operator supervision be marked as common illegal objects. Then, the process repeats over and over again. Over time, the system can adjust for new types of IP to be protected or new types of illegal objects, e.g., new shapes of firearms.

Similarly, the solution could be implemented inside the firmware of the AM machine, like a 3D printer. As an option, an exported pattern matrix can be stored on a hardware chip to help AM machines to challenge 3D designs sent to a job queue. The possibility for a fast classification, whether it is an illegal object to manufacture, would not allow the AM machines to produce illegal or dangerous parts.

4   Evaluation

A software architecture used to perform the evaluation of the proposed method is depicted in Fig. 3:

a) *Commander module* is used to launch the workflow described in the proposed method concept Fig. 1. The module consists of Python scripts that send commands and files to *Normalizer module* and *Clustering module.*

b) *Normalizer module* is used to normalize 3D designs, calculate general and intrinsic metadata, and challenge new 3D designs against the pattern matrix. It stores 3D designs to Hadoop Distributed File System (HDFS) [26].

c) *Extracted features database* keeps the general and intrinsic metadata on all 3D designs. We use Apache Cassandra [18] as it is a highly available, scalable, and fault-tolerant column-oriented key-value storage with the ability to store over two billion values per row. It is easy to store pattern matrix and perform CQL [9] queries to match new 3D design parameters against pattern matrix. We are also able to keep several versions of pattern matrices in the Cassandra database.

d) *3D design storage* is an HDFS file storage used by the Normalizer module to initially store processed files and then revisit the files if new parameters are added.

e) *Clustering module* is implemented as the Hadoop Map/Reduce Job. It is important to use parallel Map/Reduce implementation of conformity calculation and seriation. Conformity calculation and seriation sequential algorithms implementation require an exponential increase in computational time for binary matrices larger than 10×10. Our Hadoop Map-Reduce parallel implementation of conformity calculation significantly outperforms sequential algorithms.

This module is responsible for updating the pattern matrix in case of the number of new designs reaches a threshold preset in the settings file.

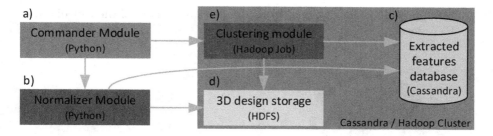

Fig. 3. Architecture of the proposed method

Experiments were performed on a test database with 5831 design files in STL [27] format. 3D design files were selected from Thingiverse [8] and other sources [1,3,4]. Test database included 3D designs from different areas of life: animals, architecture, kitchen appliances, toys, movie characters, vehicles, interior objects, firearms, and many others.

Normalization stage with checks and fixes was implemented on Python language with the usage of CGAL [10] library. As a next step, all files were run through a batch job to find general and intrinsic metadata parameters. We were able to obtain 3728 parameters for the test dataset.

We performed *normalization* stage on a 4 core, 8 GB ram, 32 GB SSD Azure VM instance, compute optimize type (Standard_F4s_v2). On average, it took 2.31 s for 1 MB, 10.46 s for 5 MB, 48.14 s for 20 MB, 283.58 s for 100 MB, 35 min 36 s for 500 MB, and 1 h 48 min 12 s for 1 Gb respectively. Total, all file size was 6.19 GB, and the total time for 5831 files was 6 h 37 min 34 s.

For the experiment, we selected 28 different indicative objects containing firearm shaped parts and marked those 28 designs as common illegal objects for our algorithm.

Then we run the algorithm to classify 3D objects based on the indicators and parameters which should help to detect firearms. We have implemented Conformity calculation [20,32] and matrix seriation [21,22] using Hadoop Map-Reduce framework [31]. We run Map-Reduce jobs on a cluster of 4 machines in Microsoft Azure cloud [2], each machine having 4 cores, 8 GB RAM, 30 GB SSD. It took 12 min to perform pattern matrix calculation based on the test data.

Each new 3D design file pattern recognition (search by the parameters in the pattern matrix) took 0.32 s on 4 core, 8 GB ram, 32 GB SSD Azure VM instance.

For new incoming illegal 3D designs tested against the pattern matrix, we were able to obtain a very close class of objects similar to initially selected firearm 3D designs. Example visualization of correctly detected Liberator barrel is shown in Fig. 4. 3D design in-between two groups, not strictly differentiated as a firearm, the test visualization is shown in Fig. 5. Something which was not detected as a firearm example is shown in Fig. 6.

Further tests showed that the solution would find not only a direct shape of the firearm but also an inverse shape, like an injection mold, or a tool to create a firearm.

This approach, similarity, could be extended to any type of multimedia, not just 3D objects.

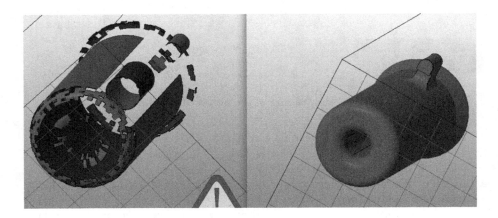

Fig. 4. The Liberator barrel detected as a part of a firearm

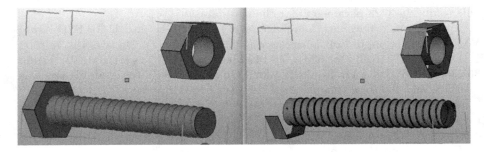

Fig. 5. 3D design in-between two groups, not strictly differentiated as a firearm

Fig. 6. 3D design that was not detected as a firearm

5   Conclusion

We believe that in order to detect and withstand the global threat of IP copyrights violation efficiently, firearms spreading, illegal 3D objects manufacturing, especially firearms manufactured with the help of AM and 3D printing particularly, we need preventive and detective controls on software, firmware, and hardware levels. The method to protect intellectual property (IP) in automated manufacturing (AM) presented in this paper is based on the radical improvement of preventive and detective controls on software, firmware, and hardware levels. These controls would help to find potential cases of copyrights infringement, illegal objects, and firearms manufacturing with the use of automated manufacturing (AM) machinery. The manufacturing of illegal physical objects on a software level could be prevented through the cloud manufacturing operating system controls, which would not allow sending a manufacturing file to an AM machine. On the machine level, the prevention of manufacturing of illegal parts cloud be implemented through encoding the proposed method into the AM machine firmware, or into a chip integrated into the hardware.

In future research, interesting enough will be to perform experiments on a bigger dataset of 2.14M files and extend the presented approach to a fast 3D design search.

References

1. Defense distributed. https://defcad.com. Accessed 29 Sept 2019
2. Microsoft azure. http://azure.microsoft.com. Accessed 25 Sept 2019
3. Thingiverse. https://www.thingiverse.com. Accessed 29 Sept 2019
4. Youmagine. https://www.youmagine.com. Accessed 28 Sept 2019
5. All3DP: 2019 3D printed gun digest: all you need to know. all3dp.com, July 2019. https://all3dp.com/1/3d-printed-gun-firearm-weapon-parts/
6. Astovasadourian, A., Naro, O., Cabanel, V.: 3-D printing protected by digital rights management. US Patent App. 14/950,431, 20 April 2017
7. Badhani, H., Chopra, A., Goel, N.P., Panda, A.S.: Method and apparatus for controlling printability of a 3-dimensional model. US Patent 9,457,518, 4 October 2016
8. Buehler, E., et al.: Sharing is caring: assistive technology designs on Thingiverse. In: Proceedings of the 33rd Annual ACM Conference on Human Factors in Computing Systems, pp. 525–534. ACM (2015)
9. Chebotko, A., Kashlev, A., Lu, S.: A big data modeling methodology for apache Cassandra. In: 2015 IEEE International Congress on Big Data, pp. 238–245. IEEE (2015)
10. Fabri, A., Teillaud, M.: CGAL-the computational geometry algorithms library. In: 10e colloque national en calcul des structures, p. 6 (2011)
11. Glasgow, D., MacLaurin, M.B., Sherman, C.E., Ramadge, D.: Digital rights and integrity management in three-dimensional (3D) printing. US Patent 9,595,037, 14 March 2017
12. Holland, M., Nigischer, C., Stjepandić, J., Chen, C.: Copyright protection in additive manufacturing with blockchain approach. Transdiscipl. Eng.: Paradigm Shift 5, 914–921 (2017)

13. Hou, J.U., Kim, D., Ahn, W.H., Lee, H.K.: Copyright protections of digital content in the age of 3D printer: emerging issues and survey. IEEE Access **6**, 44082–44093 (2018)
14. Isbjornssund, K., Vedeshin, A.: Method and system for enforcing 3D restricted rights in a rapid manufacturing and prototyping environment. US Patent App. 13/973,816, 27 February 2014
15. Isbjörnssund, K., Vedeshin, A.: Secure streaming method in a numerically controlled manufacturing system, and a secure numerically controlled manufacturing system. US Patent App. 14/761,588, 3 December 2015
16. Kennedy, Z.C., et al.: Enhanced anti-counterfeiting measures for additive manufacturing: coupling lanthanide nanomaterial chemical signatures with blockchain technology. J. Mater. Chem. C **5**(37), 9570–9578 (2017)
17. Kietzmann, J., Pitt, L., Berthon, P.: Disruptions, decisions, and destinations: enter the age of 3-D printing and additive manufacturing. Bus. Horiz. **58**(2), 209–215 (2015)
18. Lakshman, A., Malik, P.: Cassandra: a decentralized structured storage system. ACM SIGOPS Oper. Syst. Rev. **44**(2), 35–40 (2010)
19. Leong, K., Chua, C., Ng, Y.: A study of stereolithography file errors and repair. Part 1. Generic solution. Int. J. Adv. Manuf. Technol. **12**(6), 407–414 (1996)
20. Liiv, I.: Visualization and data mining method for inventory classification. In: 2007 IEEE International Conference on Service Operations and Logistics, and Informatics, pp. 1–6. IEEE (2007)
21. Liiv, I.: Pattern Discovery Using Seriation and Matrix Reordering: A Unified View, Extensions and an Application to Inventory Management. TUT Press, Tallinn (2008)
22. Liiv, I.: Seriation and matrix reordering methods: an historical overview. Stat. Anal. Data Min.: ASA Data Sci. J. **3**(2), 70–91 (2010)
23. Lin, N.H., Huang, T.H., Chen, B.Y.: 3D model streaming based on JPEG 2000. IEEE Trans. Consum. Electron. **53**(1), 182–190 (2007)
24. Mattingly, T.D., Tovey, D.G., O'brien, J.J.: System and methods for three dimensional printing with blockchain controls. US Patent App. 15/913,382, 13 September 2018
25. Sepp, P.-M., Vedeshin, A., Dutt, P.: Intellectual property protection of 3D printing using secured streaming. In: Kerikmäe, T., Rull, A. (eds.) The Future of Law and eTechnologies, pp. 81–109. Springer, Cham (2016). https://doi.org/10.1007/978-3-319-26896-5_5
26. Shvachko, K., Kuang, H., Radia, S., Chansler, R.: The hadoop distributed file system. In: 2010 IEEE 26th Symposium on Mass Storage Systems and Technologies (MSST), pp. 1–10. IEEE (2010)
27. Stroud, I., Xirouchakis, P.: STL and extensions. Adv. Eng. Softw. **31**(2), 83–95 (2000)
28. Szilvśi-Nagy, M., Matyasi, G.: Analysis of STL files. Math. Comput. Model. **38**(7–9), 945–960 (2003)
29. Vedeshin, A., Dogru, J.M.U., Liiv, I., Draheim, D., Ben Yahia, S.: A digital ecosystem for personal manufacturing: an architecture for cloud-based distributed manufacturing operating systems. In: Proceedings of the 11th International Conference on Management of Digital EcoSystems, MEDES 2019, pp. 224–228. Association for Computing Machinery, New York (2019). https://doi.org/10.1145/3297662.3365792

30. Vedeshin, A., Dogru, J.M.U., Liiv, I., Yahia, S.B., Draheim, D.: A secure data infrastructure for personal manufacturing based on a novel key-less, byte-less encryption method. IEEE Access **8**, 40039–40056 (2019)
31. Verma, J.P., Patel, B., Patel, A.: Big data analysis: recommendation system with hadoop framework. In: 2015 IEEE International Conference on Computational Intelligence & Communication Technology, pp. 92–97. IEEE (2015)
32. Võhandu, L.: Fast methods in exploratory data analysis. Trans. TTU **705**, 3–13 (1989)
33. Walther, G.: Printing insecurity? The security implications of 3D-printing of weapons. Sci. Eng. Ethics **21**(6), 1435–1445 (2015)

Crowdsourcing and Blockchain-Based E-Government Applications: Corruption Mapping

Hasna El Alaoui El Abdallaoui$^{(\boxtimes)}$, Abdelaziz El Fazziki,
and Mohamed Sadgal

Computing Systems Engineering Laboratory (LISI), Faculty of Sciences
Semlalia, Cadi Ayyad University, Marrakech, Morocco
h.elalaoui@edu.uca.ac.ma

Abstract. Corruption represents a fundamental threat to the stability and prosperity of Morocco. Fighting it requires approaches based on both appropriate principles and practices. Information and Communication Technologies (ICT) allow initiatives such as the Smarter Crowdsourcing project innovated by GovLab to open new perspectives for the prevention, the detection and the criminalization of corrupt acts. In the same context, we propose a digital framework based on the principle of crowdsourcing, blockchain technology and the principle of smart contracts for the implementation of a tool for mapping corrupt acts. The framework is inspired by the concept of blockchain and would allow citizens to publish photos and videos with their reports on suspicious transactions. The developed application collects, aggregates, displays and stores the reported information in a secure manner on a limited access ledger based on a blockchain. Reporters will then be able to track and monitor the government's response to actions taken via the application. Once confirmed, reports on suspicious transactions are reported to a public document-oriented database.

Keywords: Blockchain · Crowdsourcing · Corruption · Mapping · Smart contracts

1 Introduction

Corruption is a universal phenomenon that affects us all and is a major threat to countries around the world. It threatens the economy by allowing unfair competition and discouraging investment and trade [1]. Caused by the result of several shortcomings that are ethical, economic, intellectual, and organizational in addition to the lack of sanctions, it is felt more by the most disadvantaged population [1]. The negative effects of widespread corruption constitute conditions that are not conducive to sustainable development and poverty reduction. Corruption, which is perpetrated by individuals who are anxious to protect their personal interests, creates favorable conditions for the presence of factors contributing to a reduction in economic growth, thus leading to slippage in the management of public affairs [1].

Corruption takes the form of an agreement (the "corrupt pact") between the corrupt and the corrupter [2]. The existence of this agreement constitutes an offense without any

© Springer Nature Switzerland AG 2020
M. Hamlich et al. (Eds.): SADASC 2020, CCIS 1207, pp. 86–99, 2020.
https://doi.org/10.1007/978-3-030-45183-7_7

need to consider its effects. This consideration can take different forms in practice and can benefit both the corrupt and his relatives: free housing, interest-free loan, reduction of a purchase price, the benefit of a job without financial compensation, etc. [3].

In Morocco, complex bureaucratic procedures requiring a multitude of steps and approvals generally pave the way for corruption. Opportunities to demand or offer bribes tend to increase when transactions between citizens and officials are conducted in person, as is still often the case in our country [4]. Recognizing this problem, the government is aggressively reducing red tape by simplifying and digitizing administrative processes. By automating services and putting them online, the government is leaving less chance for the corrupt to make arbitrary decisions.

The design and the implementation of an integrated anti-corruption framework is an effective step to protect society against fraudulent transactions. However, this may seem a complex and daunting task. It is difficult to know where to start: what should the different components be and how do they fit together? Which ones should we focus on first? How can we get the most out of the investments made in this area? Users can report the nature, number, configuration, types, location, frequency and values of actual corruption.

The design of an anti-corruption platform based on the principle of crowdsourcing [5] is an undeniable means of detecting and preventing corruption as they are oriented from and towards the citizen [6]. However, most current systems are based on a centralized architecture, which consists of a central entity subject to reliability risks. This central entity remains highly susceptible to manipulation. This leads to several security problems, such as the disclosure of private data and the dissemination of inaccurate information [7]. Therefore, the use of more independent technology such as blockchain can increase transparency and prevent fraud, thus improving control and accountability [8]. Over the last two or three years, anti-corruption activists and policy makers have increasingly turned to this technology and the concept of the smart contracts [8] as a support for highly sensitive activities.

From these findings and mechanisms based on blockchain technology, we have therefore focused in this research work on designing and developing an anti-corruption complaints framework aiming at considerable citizen engagement. The major objective was to develop a mapping tool to provide visibility on corruption risks.

The Paper Organization. The first section is dedicated to present the main concepts used in this research paper in addition to a brief literature review of the most known anti-corruption platforms. Then, the proposed framework, its components and structure are described in the following section. The results of some experiments are presented before a conclusion section.

2   Background

2.1   Crowdsourcing

Initiated in 2006 by Jeff Howe and Mark Robinson, both editors of Wired Magazine, the term "crowdsourcing" [5, 9] is a combination of two words: "crowd" and "outsourcing". The term refers to a public solicitation (with or without certain qualifications) for help with tasks, new ideas or content generation [10]. Crowd-sourcing is a production model and a distributed problem-solving system that has gained strength over the last decade. In addition to examples of purely for-profit use, crowdsourcing has gained importance as a tool for participation in governance [11].

At this stage, crowdsourcing is a concept used for a wide range of governance activities to help government and citizens become more engaged in collective activities: many frameworks have been implemented for decision making [12], awareness raising and crisis situations [13] or as a means to make cities smarter [14]. If well implemented, these government platforms can be very powerful and effective, especially in cases of anti-corruption.

2.2 Blockchain

The blockchain is widely known as the technology behind Bitcoin [15], a digital currency. But it is also used to record real estate transactions and to combat dubious transactions in general.

The Blockchain is a technology that promises increased transactional security by storing information in a digital ledger as "blocks" where each block contains data about a transaction [16]. Blockchain copies are stored on a large number of servers in a decentralized peer-to-peer network structure. By this design, the copies represent a verifiable record that cannot be changed without modifying subsequent blocks, thus limiting the possibility of undetected malicious acts [17]. This can be particularly useful in environments with low levels of trust, often also characterized by high levels of corruption.

Smart contracts are another much-discussed concept of this technology: they are a mechanism that is automatically triggered when predetermined conditions agreed by both parties are met [18]. Although the use of the blockchain technology in the fight against corruption is still relevant, potential uses include increased security in public procurement or land registries and the securing of financial transactions against fraud [17].

2.3 Existing Anticorruption Platforms

Several approaches based on the principle of crowdsourcing for the denunciation of corrupt acts have emerged [3, 19, 20]. Platforms provide citizens with adequate information and mechanisms to report abuses of power and suspicious transactions, enabling them to fight against such behavior [21]. As an example, the Mexican government's trials on a project called "Smarter Crowdsourcing", based on a methodology developed by the GovLab at New York University [21].

In India, the IPaidABribe[1] (IPAB) platform is considered a success as it involved a large number of people. According to their own statistics, IPAB receives between 25 and 50 denunciations per day and has claimed responsibility for more than 112,500 estimated reports of corruption since its launch in 2010 through 2015 [20]. However, the site is not intended as an anti-corruption tool, but only as an awareness-raising tool,

---

[1] http://www.ipaidabribe.com/.

according to several studies conducted to measure the effectiveness of initiatives such as IPAB. For example, Ryvkin, Serra and Tremewan [20] found that the demand for bribes did not decrease after the launch of IPAB. According to the same authors, the reason is that the platform does not provide the possibility to fully report information or make it publicly available.

Several crowdsourcing-based anti-corruption initiatives have been launched in Morocco such as the complaints portal 'Chikaya'[2]. Its objectives are multiple, including receiving, monitoring and responding to citizens' complaints. Whether it is the website, the mobile application or the call center, this initiative has facilitated the procedure for filing complaints and has enabled the various public administrations to have a mechanism for managing and taking into account the complaints.

All these projects may have contributed to a greater or lesser extent to motivate citizens to fight corruption and to take actions against the problems that contaminate the public administration services. However, these projects suffer from shortcomings and some of them have not been active or functional for years.

3   A Blockchain and Crowdsourcing Based Approach

We present a framework based on crowdsourcing and inspired by blockchain technology for reporting corrupt acts. In this context, the following objectives have been set:

1. **To ensure full transparency:** the integrity of the participants holds a copy of the submitted and validated complaints. However, an information can only be added, removed or altered with the consent of the entire network. It is impossible to modify or destroy the published facts.
2. **To facilitate data sharing and protection:** thanks to the decentralized aspect, data are secured and there is no central point of failure.
3. **To guarantee traceability:** the blockchain will ensure that acts of corruption can be traced and dealt with this technology.
4. **Provide every citizen with a digital identity:** a whistle-blower's private information will be encrypted and can only be decrypted using a key that only the whistle-blower has.
5. **Mapping corruption:** thanks to a dashboard, confirmed acts of corruption will be mapped, giving decision-makers an idea of the corruption risks.

We start with a general overview of the proposed solution before the architecture, the actors and their interactions are defined. The proposed claims process is described in the second part of this section.

3.1   The Corruption Mapping

A collaborative online tool would allow Moroccan citizens to identify, understand and follow the evolution of the acts and the sanctions related to corruption on Moroccan

---

[2] https://www.chikaya.ma/.

territory. The mapping could mainly be enriched thanks to the Crowdsourcing, which feeds it with information provided by the citizens and the investigators. The public data register provides information both on convictions in the public or private sector, corrupted persons, corrupters, intermediaries, recorded convictions, classified acts, etc. The data is also used to identify the most serious cases of corruption in Morocco.

The tool is easy to use and allows every citizen to report information on corrupt acts and to monitor the fairness of judgements in the fight against corruption. Just by clicking on an area of the map, we can get all the information on the convictions handed down in the city/region, to find out about court decisions and the type of punishment, or to see the time elapsed between the date of the acts and the date of conviction. The map also makes it possible to identify the most frequently repeated offenses on Moroccan territory and their geographical distribution. It is possible to carry out an advanced search according to the place, the type of the offense and the organization. A real panorama of corruption cases in the country. The dashboard developed will make it possible to retrieve qualitative and quantitative information on the corruption situation in the country by aiming at a set of objectives illustrated in the Fig. 1.

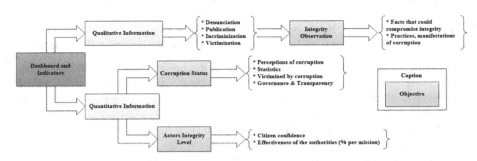

Fig. 1. Objectives of the development of the Corruption Mapping Tool

3.2   A General Overview

A citizen will be able to use the platform in order to report information on a suspicion of corruption. The report is considered a suspicious transaction if the user supports his submission with supporting documents. Smart contracts, used in parallel with the Blockchain technology, are integrated into the proposed framework in order to check the validity of a transaction and the solvency of a whistle-blower. These contracts are directly linked to an oracle that is a component that automatically checks and executes the terms and the conditions of the contract by reading the rules and the codes stored in a database.

A validated transaction is then passed to a shared ledger in a secure manner that allows transparent processing of transactions to determine the corrupt acts and prosecute those responsible. These transactions are also recorded in a public database accessible to all citizens and are mapped in a dashboard. The Fig. 2 outlines the general idea of the proposed system.

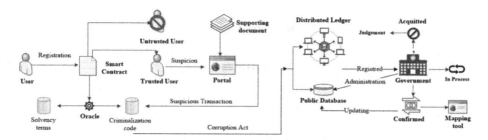

Fig. 2. The general overview of the proposed solution

3.3   The System Components

Using computers and mobile devices, citizens can access the system for different purposes; either to file a whistle-blowing report or to view a list of corrupt services/persons. The data is stored in a document-oriented public database.

Also, any suspicious transactions submitted are distributed in a secure registry through a blockchain network. In order to verify the solvency of the whistle-blower and to validate the corrupt act, the Smarts Contracts are developed. In case of validation, governmental or non-governmental organizations are notified in order to process the transaction; the public database and the blockchain registry are synchronized. This structure is illustrated in the Fig. 3 below:

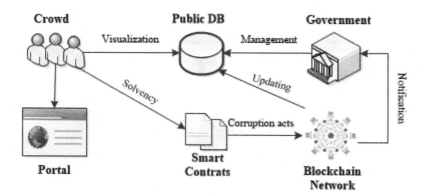

Fig. 3. The system components

3.4   The General Architecture

This section presents a multi-layered model characterizing the architecture of the proposed system and briefly describes its underlying techniques. As shown in the Fig. 4, the structure of the system consists of five superimposed layers, as described below.

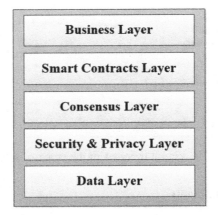

Fig. 4. The general architecture

Data Layer. This layer provides the structure of the data blocks as well as their sequence (the structure of the whole blockchain). Each block contains all the data related to a participant and the declared transaction. It is divided into 2 parts: the header part specifies the meta-information and the body part encapsulates all the verified data. All blocks are chained in chronological order from the initial block (Genesis block) to the most recently inserted block (Fig. 5).

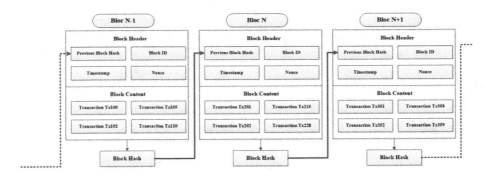

Fig. 5. The blockchain structure

Security and Privacy Layer. This layer specifies the encryption and the hash algorithms used to secure the system. In the proposed system, we use PKI (Public Key Framework), an encryption/decryption mechanism that ensures the authenticity and confidentiality of shared messages. The PKI signature algorithm used is ECDSA (Elliptic Curve Digital Signature Algorithm). Upon registration, a participant has a cryptographic private key S_k that he uses to sign a claim. The signature is attached to the transaction and the public key P_k, corresponding to the private key, is used by the network nodes to prove the authenticity of a transaction.

Consensus Layer. By synthesizing the most common consensus protocols [22], the PoW (Proof-of-Work), PoS (Proof-of-Stake), PoC (Proof-of-Capacity), PoA (Proof-of-Activity), DPoS (Delegated Proof-of-Stake) and PoET (Proof of Elapsed Time) algorithms were tested simultaneously.

Contract Layer. The system includes 2 smart contracts. Firstly, the 'Objectivity Analysis' contract contains various functions (Roles Distinction Function (RDF), Trust Management Function (TMF) and Access Control Function (ACF)) that define the entities and their roles, allow the management of denunciations and control the access of the users to the system. Secondly, the 'Criminalization Code' contract determines whether a suspicious transaction is a corrupt act according to the Criminalization Code defining the laws and the legislations.

Business Layer. The Fig. 6 illustrates the main functions allowed by the proposed system and that are described as follows:

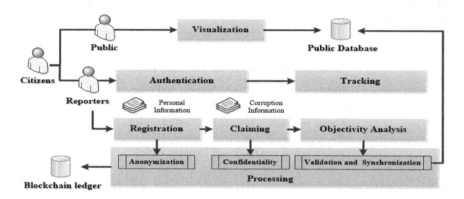

Fig. 6. The proposed system process

- Registration: The proposed system anonyms the personal data of the participants once they register via the platform.
- Claiming: Victims/witnesses of the corrupt act capture all details of the suspicion and can attach supporting documents.
- Processing: Once submitted, claims are subject to specific processing based on the blockchain concept as described above. Before a transaction is validated, an objectivity analysis is required to check the solvency of the whistle-blower through the Contract Layer. If it is objective, the anonymization processes, information protection and claim validation follow. The Contract Layer also allows the transaction to be validated as a corrupt act.

- Tracking: a citizen who has already lodged a suspicion will be able to follow its progress and the phases of its processing thanks to the proposed system.
- Visualization: every citizen has the right to information. To this end, the proposed system contains a database accessible to the public.

4   Implementation and Experimentations

4.1   Description

We implement the proposed system using the Python language (Version 3.7) and test its performance in a Windows 10 64-bit environment (with 3.20 GHz Intel® Core™ i5-5200U CPU and 8G RAM) and an Android 9.0 environment (with 2.20 GHz Octa-Core CPU and 3G RAM). For the experiment, we used the Flask framework, a Python-based web development framework, to create a REST API to interact with the nodes of the blockchain network (the miners) and its clients (whistle-blowers and institutions) as described in Table 1 below:

Table 1. Description of the simulated nodes

Nodes	Number and type
Miners	20 Desktop nodes
Whistle-blowers	10 Desktop nodes 3 Mobile nodes
Governmental institutions	5 Desktop nodes

We created the smart contracts using Python and the SmartPy development tool, an Integrated Development Environment (IDE) to analyze, test and formally prove the properties of smart contracts.

4.2   User Interfaces

Crowd Interfaces. The interfaces for registration and claiming are HMIs suitable for web and mobile devices. The Fig. 7 includes a form for entering data about the corrupt act. This includes information on the date, the time and the amount of the act, the service/administration concerned and the person bribed. The whistle-blower may attach a document supporting his or her complaint.

Fig. 7. The interface for reporting the transaction information

The different corrupt acts and the services involved are then structured to be stored in a document-oriented database such as MongoDB [23]. The stored data is publicly available online for visualization by citizens (Fig. 8). It is important to mention that due to the unavailability of real data, we only present the results of experiments carried out with simulated fictitious data.

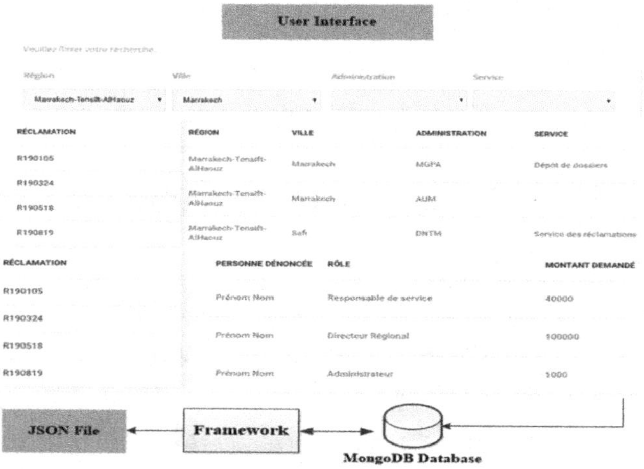

Fig. 8. Filtered acts of corruption by region, city, administration and department

Mapping Interfaces. The proposed system is also a simple and interactive mapping tool. It allows, through a dashboard, to visualize, by region or by city, all condemned or not condemned corrupt acts by the administration and by service (Fig. 9) and according to their types and natures (Fig. 10) and also deals with the victimization aspect (Fig. 11). This is a very practical way for policy makers to measure corruption risks.

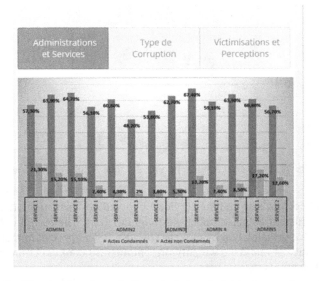

Fig. 9. Mapping interface: dashboard of the administrations and services

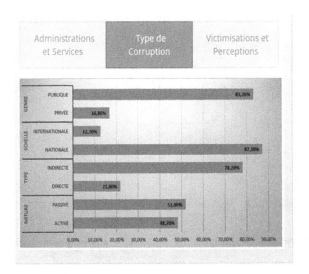

Fig. 10. Mapping interface: dashboard of corrupt acts by type

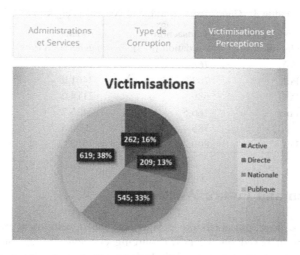

Fig. 11. Mapping interface: dashboard of the corruption victimizations and perceptions

4.3 System Evaluation

In this section, we test the performance of the system considering the mining and the block generation operations. The experiments established using the PoS (Proof-of-Stake) algorithm are presented. We first varied the claims throughput; that is, the number of claims received per minute; and observed how these variations affect the validation time of a transaction and therefore the block generation time. The Table 2 summarizes the results obtained. Then, we perform an evaluation of our system by testing different consensus algorithms (Table 3).

Table 2. Timeframes for validating a claim and generating a block in relation to the flow of transactions

Claims number/min	Claim validation delay(s)	Block generation delay (s)
2	795	1867
5	744	1804
10	675	1724
15	442	1552
20	350	1400
30	855	2210
50	907	2544

Table 3. Comparison of different consensus algorithms

Consensus algorithm	Transaction validation (in s)	Block generation (in s)
PoW	760.5	2223.8
PoS	787.9	2461.2
PoC	689	2114.2
PoA	766.5	2425.2
DPoS	785.4	2200.5
PoET	800.2	2558

5 Conclusion and Future Work

In this paper, we have presented the design and the development of a system for reporting corruption based on the crowdsourcing concept and the blockchain technology. The aim is to fight corruption with the help of citizens, the first victims and first witnesses of the scourge of corruption. The system also integrates a mapping tool that can help decision-makers evaluate the corruption risks.

Thanks to its independent, secure and anonymous nature, the system encourages denunciation to the competent authorities by offering the possibility that investigations be carried out, justice be seized, the culprits unmasked and the embezzled public funds be confiscated and returned to the State.

The various experiments carried out on the proposed system prove its efficiency and high performance. Even if this performance weakens at a certain threshold (30 claims/min), the system is still quite reliable due to its smart contracts and low consumption of material resources.

The mining and the block insertion processes were performed by Desktop nodes. Given the performance of the system, we thought about integrating mobile nodes as miners in improved versions of the system. Furthermore, a comparison of the different consensus mechanisms revealed that, while some are quite powerful such as PoW or PoC, they remain expensive in terms of the physical resources required for processing. This leads us to the idea of a future direction, consisting in developing a combination between several algorithms or developing a new algorithm appropriate to the proposed system.

References

1. Aladwani, A.M.: International journal of information management corruption as a source of e-government projects failure in developing countries: a theoretical exposition. Int. J. Inf. Manag. **36**(1), 105–112 (2016)
2. Elbahnasawy, N.G.: E-government, Internet adoption, and corruption: an empirical investigation. World Dev. **57**, 114–126 (2014)
3. Jeppesen, K.K.: The role of auditing in the fight against corruption. Br. Acc. Rev. **51**, 100978 (2019)

4. Denoeux, G.P.: Corruption in Morocco: old forces, new dynamics and a way forward. Middle East Policy **14**, 134 (2007)
5. Howe, B.J.: The rise of crowdsourcing. Wired Mag. **14**(6), 1–4 (2006)
6. Martinez, R., Kukutschka, B.: Technology against corruption: the potential of online corruption- reporting apps and other platforms, no. 20, pp. 1–10 (2016)
7. Fazekas, M.: Are emerging technologies helping win the fight against corruption in developing countries? Curbing corruption in development aid-funded procurement view project skills beyond school: country studies of postsecondary professional training View project, April 2018
8. De Souza, R.C., Luciano, E.M., Wiedenhöft, G.C.: The uses of the blockchain smart contracts reduce the levels of corruption: some preliminary thoughts. In: ACM International Conference Proceedings Series, pp. 5–6 (20180
9. Howe, J.: Bringing essential knowledge & book summaries to high Achievers C ROWDSOURCING why the power of the crowd is driving the future of business
10. Law, E., Von Ahn, L.: Human computation. Synth. Lect. Artif. Intell. Mach. Learn. **5**(3), 1–121 (2011)
11. Clark, B.Y., Zingale, N., Logan, J., Brudney, J.: A framework for using crowdsourcing in government. Int. J. Public Adm. Digit. Age **3**(4), 57–75 (2016)
12. Chiu, C.M., Liang, T.P., Turban, E.: What can crowdsourcing do for decision support? Decis. Support Syst. **65**(C), 40–49 (2014)
13. Ren, J., Zhang, Y., Zhang, K., Shen, X.: SACRM: social aware crowdsourcing with Reputation Management in mobile sensing. Comput. Commun. **65**, 55–65 (2015)
14. Benouaret, K., Valliyur-ramalingam, R., Benouaret, K., Valliyur-ramalingam, R., Benouaret, K., Valliyur-ramalingam, R.: CrowdSC: building smart cities with large scale citizen participation. Internet Comput. IEEE **17**(6), 57–63 (2013)
15. Nakamoto, S.: Bitcoin: a peer-to-peer electronic cash system. J. Gen. Philos. Sci. **39**(1), 53–67 (2008)
16. Zheng, Z., Xie, S., Dai, H., Chen, X., Wang, H.: An overview of blockchain technology: architecture, consensus, and future trends. In: Proceedings - 2017 IEEE 6th International Congress Big Data, BigData Congress June 2017, pp. 557–564 (2017)
17. Sharmila, K., Kamalakkannan, S., Devi, M.R., Shanthi, M.C.: A comprehensive study on blockchain with its components, taxonomy and consensus, May 2019
18. Luu, L., Chu, D.H., Olickel, H., Saxena, P., Hobor, A.: Making smart contracts smarter. In: Proceedings of ACM Conference on Computer and Commununication Security, 24–28 October, pp. 254–269 (2016)
19. Mittal, M., Wu, W., Rubin, S., Madden, S., Hartmann, B.: Bribecaster, p. 171, (2012)
20. Ryvkin, D., Serra, D., Tremewan, J.: I paid a bribe: an experiment on information sharing and extortionary corruption. Eur. Econ. Rev. **94**, 1–22 (2017)
21. Noveck, B.S., Koga, K., Aceves, R., Deleanu, G.H., Cantú-Pedraza, D.: Smarter crowdsourcing for anti-corruption, April 2018
22. Bach, L., Mihaljevic, B., Zagar, M.: Comparative analysis of blockchain consensus algorithms. In: MIPRO Opatija Croatia, pp. 1545–1550 (2018)
23. Bhojwani, N., Shah, A.P.V.: A survey on Hadoop HBase system. Int. J. Adv. Eng. Res. Dev. Sci. J. Impact Factor (SJIF) **3**(1), 82–87 (2016)

Recommender Systems

A Multimodal Route Recommendation Framework Based on Urban Congestion Management

Sara Berrouk[(✉)] and Mohamed Sadgal

Computing Systems Engineering Laboratory (LISI), Cadi Ayyad University,
Marrakesh, Morocco
berrouk.sara@gmail.com, sadgal@uca.ma

Abstract. This paper represents a novel solution to the traffic and bus transit congestion issue by proposing a multimodal route recommendation framework. The framework relies on simulating the traffic and transit data, modeling the multimodal road network, computing a congestion index for each road segment and finally providing route plans for the framework's users. As a result, road congestion can be diminished and the use of public transport can be encouraged. The multimodal network is represented using a weighted multi-layered graph, where the weights changes depending on the computed congestion indexes. A novel method is suggested to calculate the congestion indexes, it takes into consideration multiple aspects of congestion by combining three commonly used congestion measures. For the multimodal least congested pathfinding, a solution is proposed to provide relevant recommendations; it takes into account all viable constraints for an optimal route suggestion.

Keywords: Traffic congestion · Multimodal route recommendation · Congestion measures

1 Introduction

Traffic congestion is a complex problem that most big cities have to deal with. Many approaches tried to lessen traffic congestion by creating new transport infrastructure. However, this can worsen the traffic situation leading to more congested roads, not forgetting that these solutions are expensive arrangements. A more efficient way to reduce traffic congestion is to manage the cities 'intelligent transportation system. This can be done by improving route guidance systems, traffic signals, public transport, and accident management. Such solutions require a better understanding of the congestion phenomena and its different aspects and dimensions. Assessing the level of congestion is also mandatory for better optimization of the traffic flow.

The congestion phenomena have no unified definition, however, it can be judged as "a situation in which the capacity of the transportation infrastructure is under the demand of people, leading to low speed, traffic delays and waste of time, money and energy" [1]. Since the congestion can be seen from several aspects, its evaluation and measuring also can be done differently. The traffic flow, the average speed, the delay

© Springer Nature Switzerland AG 2020
M. Hamlich et al. (Eds.): SADASC 2020, CCIS 1207, pp. 103–116, 2020.
https://doi.org/10.1007/978-3-030-45183-7_8

and the travel time can contribute, separately or in combinations, in the calculation of the level of congestion. Considering that the private vehicles cause higher fuel consumption and pollution emission compared to public transportation transfers per traveler. This has led to the high promotion of using public transportation in the last decades. In this sense, multiple web/mobile applications exist these days for determining and envisioning routes over public transportation systems. However, these applications commonly determine the shortest path in term of distance or the shortest time paths and do not take into account alternative objectives, for example, the least congested path with minimal congestion indicators and measures such as volume-to-capacity ratio, the alternation between private and public transport modes within a minimal number of changes, the option of minimal use of a specific transport mode such as walking or the resident users preferences.

The objective of this study is generating multimodal route recommendations as a solution to traffic congestion increasingly growing in Marrakesh-city. The suggested framework is capable of modeling the multimodal transportation network, of computing the proposed congestion index for the three most used transport modes in cities which are: walking, riding a bus and driving a car and applying the proposed optimal multimodal path-finding algorithm. The computed congestion indexes reflect the traffic conditions; they allow providing pertinent data to travelers and suggestions about the best ways to take to make a journey. To test our proposed approach, traffic and transit records simulation are used since there is yet no Intelligent Transportation System placed in Marrakesh-City and even with the multiple traffic and transit data collections means placed in some of the city's areas, unfortunately, the access to these data was not granted. The constraints of the constantly changing traffic and transit data and the prevention of candidate congestion in the route recommendations should be taken into account.

This paper is organized as follows: Sect. 2 presents the state of the art, Sect. 3 overviews the multimodal route recommendation process. Subsection 3.1 illustrates the multimodal network modeling. Subsection 3.2 describes the proposed method for computing the congestion index. Subsection 3.3 presents the proposed algorithm for optimal pathfinding in the multimodal transportation network. Section 4 illustrates the experimentation results followed by the discussion and conclusion in Sect. 5.

2 State of the Art

2.1 Traffic Congestion Measures

In the literature, many congestion measures have been defined and proclaimed to be the best in assessing traffic conditions. These measures are also categorized differently; for example time associated measures, cost associated measures, etc. However, the congestion measure can be categorized under two relevant categories which are mobility measures and reliability measures [2]. The frequently used mobility measures are: the Total Delay which is introduced as the sum of time wasted because of congestion in a roadway segment [3], the Volume-To-Capacity ratio that reflects the count of vehicles passing through a roadway segment divided by the capacity of that roadway segment

[4], the Travel Time which can be represented by the division of the length of a roadway segment on the speed recorded on that same roadway segment [5] and the Travel Time Index that compares between the peak and free-flow travel conditions while taking into account both recurrent and non-recurrent congestion. For the reliability congestion measures, transportation agencies [6–8] mainly use the Buffer Index that reflects the extra time needed to guaranty an acceptable arrival time for the majority of trips and the Planning Time Index which is presented as the extra time that road users consider when planning a trip at peak hours, it can also be obtained as 95% of the Travel Time Index.

However, the use of single congestion indicators to estimate traffic congestion on urban roadways can be misleading because of the complex nature of the phenomenon. For this reason, recent studies are focusing on using multiple congestion indicators to correctly asses the traffic state. In [5], the Travel Time and speed measures are both used to evaluate the traffic conditions on freeways. Similarly, [9] adopted the transit Automatic Vehicle Location in the traffic data collecting phase and used the same congestion measures to evaluate the traffic state on freeways.

2.2 Multimodal Optimal Pathfinding

Retrieving multimodal route recommendations for road users relies on solving the shortest path algorithm. Classical ways to find the shortest path using static graphs are either label-setting or label-correcting algorithms [10]. The more adapted to route planning in transport networks, which is a one-to-one shortest path problem, is the label-setting since it can stop when reaching the destination node previously named. The static shortest path problem can be solved in polynomial time. When having a dynamic shortest path issue; where edges 'costs change over time, the label-setting algorithm can be flexible to solve it. When the time is determined as a discrete variable, this latter can elaborate on an explicit time-space expansion of the graph [11]. Unfortunately, this strategy can procure in increasing the size of the graph and running time.

When dealing with multimodal transportation, more constraints are added to the shortest path problem to provide a feasible solution while considering the available transport modes. A route recommendation that takes into account multimodality must be constituted from a sequence of mono-modal sub-paths, the beginning and end of these latter take place in a suitable and possible location. These rules are defined as viability constraints [12]. The viability constraints are represented in formal language using a finite automaton by [13], labeling algorithms can be used on the resulting product of the first introduced graph that illustrates the multimodal network while the finite automaton providing the constraints in the formal language. Table 1 illustrates a bunch of existing multimodal pathfinding solutions in the literature.

Table 1. Existing multimodal pathfinding solutions.

Literature document	Description	Transport mode	Weight function
[14]	A multicriteria routing algorithm to solve an itinerary planning problem	Railway, bus, tram, and pedestrian	Travel time, number of transfers and the total walking time
[15]	The use of an automaton and label-correcting algorithm to answer the point-to-point multimodal shortest path issue	Private vehicle mode, metro mode and, other modes'	Cost, number of mode changes
[16]	An algorithm to deal with the multimodal shortest path problem with more reduced time complexity	Walking, driving and transit mode	Delays at mode and arc switching points
[17]	The adaptation of a label-setting shortest path algorithm for one-way and two-way routing in multimodal route planning	Walking, cycling, driving, public transport	Travel time

According to the literature review, existing works on finding the optimal path in a multimodal network do not take into account congestion measures and the state of traffic and most of these works do not consider the extension of their proposed algorithm to the two-way multimodal shortest path.

3   The Proposed Multimodal Route Recommendation

The proposed solution in this work aims to deal with the traffic congestion problem by generating multimodal route recommendations to road users. The process of the proposed approach, illustrated in Fig. 1, starts with the traffic and transit data simulation along with the multimodal network data gathering that includes the road network of three transportation modes which are car driving, bus riding and walking. The next step of the process consists of generating the multi-layered graph. The traffic and transit data simulated are used in the congestion indexes calculation for both car and bus modes. The following step performs the multilayer graph weights computation. Since the objective of this work is to avoid the most congested road segments while preventing the generation of additional traffic congestion, the last step of the process includes the application of the optimal multimodal path algorithm to deliver to the system's users the best route to make their journeys.

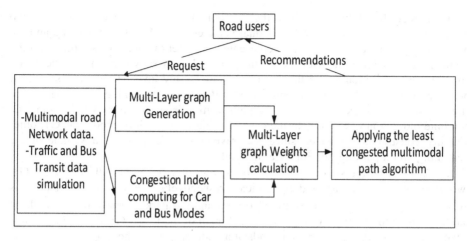

Fig. 1. The multimodal route recommendation process

3.1 The Multimodal Network Modeling

A lot of systems tried to simulate transport by modeling only one mode of transport. In this study, the use of a multimodal transportation network is considered. The multimodal trips are based on private vehicles (i.e. cars) and public transport (i.e. busses) modes and are composed of several components such as driving, walking, parking the car (on-street or in a car park), waiting at a bus stop and using the bus to make a journey. To represent all these components, the network structure will consist of three mono-modal layers interconnected together to form a multilayer graph (see Fig. 2). Each layer represents a different transport mode (car, walking or bus). Each node in the graph is a road intersection, a bus station or a bus stop. Edges represent either a segment between two bus stops in the bus layer or a segment between two intersections having similar properties (capacity, maximum speed permitted, number of lanes…) in the car and walking modes.

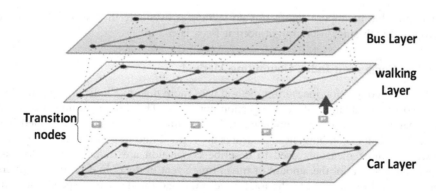

Fig. 2. The multimodal graph structure

In respect of viability constraint, the transport modes can be categorized into two groups: G1 represents the use of individual vehicles and G2 units the walking and the public transport modes. The path is represented via a set of segments starting with the origin node and finishing with the destination node. As shown in Fig. 2, the graph contains also transition nodes that do not belong to any layer. These nodes make it possible to alternate from or to a mode of G1. They represent parking spaces, either on-street areas or car parks. Therefore, the path from a departure to an arrival point can combine more than one mode. In the case of using a sub-path of mode $x \in$ G1, other viability constraints are added since the traveler must dispose of a vehicle at the beginning and a parking possibility at the end.

Let TN $\subseteq$ N be the set of transition nodes. For all $y \in$ TN and all modes $x \in$ G1, two Boolean attributes a_{yi}^x and b_{yi}^x indicate respectively if a vehicle of mode x is available in y at the beginning of the algorithm and if a parking space for a vehicle of mode x can be found in y. A mono-modal sub-path of mode $x \in$ G1 always begins at a node $y_0 \in$ TN, where $a_{y_0}^x =$ true and ends at a node $y_f \in$ TN, where $b_{y_f}^x =$ true. For all edges (i, j), a transport mode $tm_{ij} \in \{car, walking, bus\}$, and a weight w_{ij} are associated. The weights for the walking mode are time-independent considering that it is not affected by the congestion level. For the car and bus modes, the weights are time-dependent and computed for each segment based on multiple parameters that change periodically. The proposed weight function computation method is detailed in Subsect. 3.2.

Once the multimodal graph is generated and the weight functions and mode attributes are assigned to each segment, a label-setting algorithm will be applied. This later provides a multimodal route for a one-way trip between D and A but can be easily extended in future works to deal with the two-way trip problem. The algorithm should respect the following specific features:

- The solution path respects viability constraints;
- The weight functions are time-independent or time-dependent, different for each transport mode and calculated from traffic data simulated and delivered to the system;
- Individual vehicles located at any transition node in the network can be used in the routing process;
- It is possible to impose that a private vehicle is available in A at the end of the proposed path since users might need it for a later trip.

3.2   The Congestion Index Computing Method

The proposed congestion measuring method uses more than one indicator to provide a better and true evaluation of the congestion condition. The three measures are calculated separately based on the simulated traffic and transit data and are combined into one measure. Details on how these measures are formed into a single measure are cited bellow. The three measures used to describe congestion are traffic volume to road segment capacity ratio, the amount of travel time spent in delay in each road segment (beneath 5 km/h) compared to the total travel time and the decreased speed rate. The combination of these three measures gives a preview of the congestion state while taking into consideration changes in speed while traveling, the passengers' sense of annoyance and displeasure by considering the V/C Ratio (volume to capacity ratio) as well as making use of vehicle's speed variation.

The V/C Ratio. Equation (1) reflects the ratio between the counts of vehicles passing through a road segment i and the maximum number of vehicles that can support that road segment.

$$V/C\,Ratio(i) = \frac{volume\ of\ vehicles(i)}{capacity\ of\ road\ segment(i)} \tag{1}$$

This value ranges from 0 to values sometimes greater than 1. A value near "0" represents the best traffic state (free flow) as for a value near or greater than 1, it represents the worst traffic state (severely congested).

Low-Speed Rate. Equation (2) represents the ratio between the travel time spent at very low speed and the total travel time both associated to the same road segment i.

$$Low\ speed\ rate(i) = \frac{travel\ time\ spent\ in\ delay(i)}{tota\ travel\ time(i)} \tag{2}$$

This value ranges from 0 to 1, 0 represents the best condition (free flow/no delay), and 1 represents the worst condition (very congested/delay). The delay here is determined as the amount of travel time spent at a speed of less than 5 km/h.

Decreased Speed Rate. Equation (3) denotes the rate of reduced speed of the vehicle passing through a road segment i due to congested situation. This measure represents the traffic condition for non-peak and peak periods.

$$Decreased\ speed\ rate(i) = \frac{NonPeakAvgSpeed(i) - PeakAvgSpeed(i)}{NonPeakAvgSpeed(i)} \tag{3}$$

This value ranges from 0 to 1, 0 being the best condition when the Peak average speed is bigger than or equal to the Non-Peak average speed, and 1 being the worst condition when Peak's average speed is near to 0.

Coupling the Low-Speed Rate, the Volume-To-Capacity Ratio and the Decreased speed rate measures, the segment congestion index is represented by CongIndex(i) used by the proposed system (Eq. (4)).

$$CongIndex(i) = \frac{\begin{pmatrix} Low\ speed\ rate(i) \times Cf1 + \\ V/C\,Ratio(i) \times Cf2 + \\ Decreased\ speed\ rate(i) \times Cf3 \end{pmatrix}}{(Cf1 + Cf2 + Cf3)} \tag{4}$$

Cf1, Cf2, and Cf3 denote coefficients related to the costs of the Low-Speed Rate value, the volume to capacity ratio value, and the decreased speed rate value respectively. When new measurements of traffic and transit data are provided to the system, the congestion indexes are recalculated and therefore the weights of both car and bus networks are directly updated. Otherwise, the proposed system computes the weights using the available measurements.

3.3   Optimal Multimodal Path-Finding Algorithm

Finding optimal paths in a weighted multi-layer graph is in another-way finding the shortest feasible paths between a departure D and an arrival point A. The path is composed of a set of road segments to travel between two nodes. The weight calculation of each road segment depends on the transport mode to which it belongs. It is a combination of the different nature of the cost of using that particular road segment. For the car driving mode, the weights are computed based on the congestion indexes, the segment lengths and the delays in the two intersections in the extremities of the segment. As for the bus mode, the weights combine the congestion indexes with the segment lengths, the delay and the average waiting time in the two bus stops existing in the start and the end of the road segment. And finally, for the walking mode, the weights are time-independent and are calculated based on travel time required to cross a particular segment.

The following formula is adopted to compute the weights of the car network segments (Eq. (5)).

$$W_{i,j}(car) = \frac{CongIndex_i \times C_1 + Length_i \times C_2 + \left(\frac{Delayintersection_1}{a} + \frac{Delayintersection_2}{b}\right) \times C_3}{(C_1 + C_2 + C_3)} \tag{5}$$

Where $CongIndex_i$ is the computed congestion index of the segment i from the previous subsection, $Delayintersection_1$ and $Delayintersection_2$ are respectively the delays spent in the nodes forming the edge i, a and b are respectively the number of edges joined in the nodes forming the edge i and finally C_1, C_2, and C_3 are three coefficients controlled by decision-makers to optimize the function of the weight segment computing.

Similarly, the following formula is adopted to compute the weights of the bus network segments (Eq. (6)).

$$W_{ij}(bus) = \frac{CongIndex_i \times Coef_1 + Length_i \times Coef_2 + \left(\frac{DelayBStop_1}{a} + \frac{DelayBStop_2}{b}\right) \times Coef_3 + \left(\frac{AvgWtimeBStop_1}{a} + \frac{AvgWtimeBStop_2}{b}\right) \times Coef_4}{(Coef_1 + Coef_2 + Coef_3 + Coef_4)} \tag{6}$$

Where $CongIndex_i$ is the obtained congestion index of the segment i from the previous subsection, $Length_i$ is the length of the segment i, $DelayBStop_1$ and $DelayBStop_2$ are the delays spent in the two bus stops forming the edge i, $AvgWtimeBStop_1$ and $AvgWtimeBStop_2$ are respectively the average of time spent waiting for the bus to arrive in both bus stops forming the segment, a and b are respectively the number of edges joined in the nodes forming the edge i and finally $Coef_1$, $Coef_2$, $Coef_3$ and $Coef_4$ are four coefficients managed by decision-makers to optimize the calculation function of the weight segment.

The proposed labeling algorithm in this study focuses on finding the one-way multimodal shortest way to travel between a start to an endpoint. A feasible multimodal path can be distinguished by several conditions that differ according to the final node. The conditions can range from Car Accessible (CA), Driving Car (DC) and Inaccessible Car (IC). Figure 3 illustrates the automaton that defines the possible mode combinations. Transitions from a condition to another are either traveling transitions or update transitions. It can be represented respectively by a continuous labeled line or a dashed labeled line. Labels lb in the traveling transitions refer to the transport mode tm_{ij} used to go through edge (i, j). The update transition corresponds to a change in the ongoing condition. It occurs along the path when coming across a transition node where a car is accessible or a parking space is found.

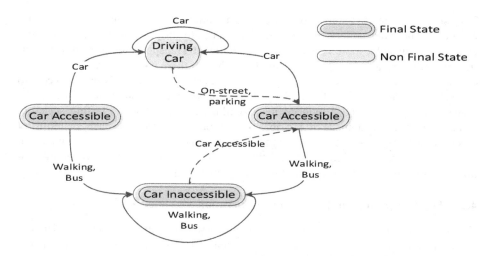

Fig. 3. A finite-state automaton for the viable mode combinations definition

A trajectory from D to $i \in N$ can be presented by the pair (i, c_0) where c_0 is the condition associated with the trajectory. The label-setting procedure consists in scanning all the possible (i, c_0) pairs. Let $\delta^+(i)$ be the set of successor nodes for i. When (i, c_0) pair is scanned, the nodes $j \in \delta^+(i)$ are examined and the concatenation of (i, c_0) with each edge (i, j) is tried. This concatenation corresponds to a traveling transition from condition c_0 and with label tm_{ij} in the automaton. If the transition is not possible, j is considered as unreachable from (i, c_0). Otherwise, the condition c_f associated to the new path from D to j can be determined by the automaton. If j corresponds to a transition node and if a parking space or a car is available at this node, condition c_f can be modified with an update transition. For example, arriving with condition $c_f = DC$ at a transition node where a parking space is available implies an update to the condition $c_f = CA$. Finally, the path (j, c_f) is labeled with three values:

- The potential $\pi^j_{c_f} \leftarrow \min\left(\pi^j_{c_f}, \pi^i_{c_0} + w_{ij}\left(\pi^i_{c_0}\right)\right)$ calculated as usual in labeling algorithms,
- $\text{pred}^j_{c_f} \leftarrow i$ which gives the predecessor of the node j in the path,
- $\text{predCondition}^j_{c_f} \leftarrow c_0$ which gives the condition associated with the sub-path going from D to $\text{pred}^j_{c_f}$.

A path ending in A cannot be labeled with the condition DC, as each car used has to be parked before arriving. If the user requests a private car available in A, a modification of the automaton can be made to accept only CA as the final condition.

4   Experimentation and Results

4.1   Description

This study was at first intended to deal with traffic congestion in Marrakesh-City, Morocco. The latter suffers from congestion especially in peak hours and in specific areas. Unfortunately, there is yet no urban Intelligent Transportation System (ITS) infrastructure to measure traffic in the city. Even though there are some traffic and transit data collection means placed all over the city and even inside the city's buses, access to these data was not possible. To validate our system, we ought to simulate the traffic and transit data and we used a reduced map of Marrakech-city for the testing scenario. Generating these data made it possible to test our proposed approach in terms of modeling the multimodal network, computing the proposed congestion index and use it as weights in the generated graph and finally deliver multimodal route recommendations by applying the proposed multimodal optimal pathfinding.

4.2   The Congestion Indexes Values Generation

The proposed congestion model is applied to a real-world multimodal network. Table 2 shows an example of the congestion indexes generation for some segments of the car network. The simulated traffic data for the car mode i.e. distance between consecutive intersections, the capacity of the segment, travel time, delay time, traffic counts are required for computing the independent congestion measures which are the v/c ratio, the Low-speed rate, and the decreased speed rate. The measures are computed for each link using the Eq. 1, Eq. 2, and Eq. 3. The resulting congestion indexes are obtained in the last column using the Eq. 4. These congestion indexes show the congestion status of each link while taking into consideration multiple aspects of congestion.

Table 2. A portion of the input data and the resulting Congestion Index

Car road segment From	To	Length (km)	Capacity (vehicles)	Traffic volume (vehicles)	Travel time (sec)	Time spent in delay (sec)	Non-peak average speed	Peak average speed	V/C	Low-speed rate	Decreased speed rate	The resulting congestion index
1	2	0.4	70	58	39.8	22.1	36.5	24.25	0.82	0.55	0.33	0.67
2	3	0.25	50	22	25	7.7	37.2	16.7	0.46	0.308	0.55	0.39
3	4	0.4	70	39	46.6	11.6	31.04	13.5	0.59	0.248	0.56	0.45
2	4	0.3	65	18	25,7	4.2	27.2	15.4	0.27	0.16	0.44	0.24

4.3   The Optimal Multimodal Path-Finding

In the multimodal route planning implementation, the generated multimodal graph should represent a particular area that answers the road user's need. An example of such a request is illustrated in Fig. 4; a test request is supposed to make the journey from point O to point D using both car and bus modes. Once the request is launched, the framework generates the graph that represents the surrounding area and calculates or updates the congestion indexes that represent the costs of the graph segments.

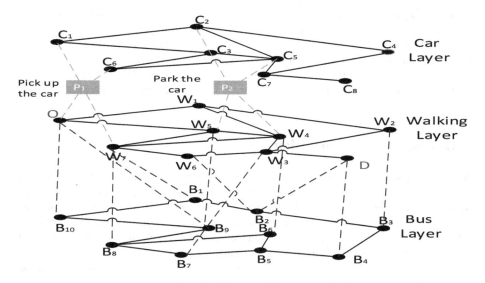

Fig. 4. The generated multimodal graph

For each segment of the generated multimodal graph, the weight Wi is computed differently depending on the mode of transport it belongs to. The congestion indexes are computed using the Eq. 4. The proposed algorithm for optimal pathfinding in the multimodal transportation network detailed in Subsect. 3.3 is then applied, to generate an optimal trajectory recommendation while considering the transport modes selected by the user. An example of the resulting shortest path is presented in Table 3.

Table 3. The least congested path found beside the Level of congestion for each segment.

The least congested path from O to D	
Directions	Congestion index value/the level of congestion
1. Walk from start point O to parking space P1 and Pick up the car	O→ P1 = 0.12/Low
2. Drive from the parking space P1 to node C1, take the segment relying on C1 to C1, after that the segment mapping between C1 and C5 and finally drive to parking space P2 and park the car in it	P1→ C1 = 0.1/Low C1→ C3 = 0.34/Moderate C3→ C5 = 0.24/Low C5→ P2 = 0.4/Moderate
3. Walk from the parking space P2 to node W4 and then to node B6 of the bus layer	P2→W4 = 0.12/Low W4→B6 = 0.14/Low
4. Take bus number 13 that will travel from bus stop B6 to B4 while passing through B5	B6→ B4 = 0.26/Moderate B4→ B5 = 0.5/Moderate
5. Walk from bus stop B4 to Destination D	B4→D = 0.18/Low

5 Discussion and Conclusion

This research study aims to propose a convenient solution to the worldwide issue of road congestion in urban areas. The proposed congestion management framework relies on simulating a testing scenario with traffic and transit data. It was implemented using the Java programming language and was tested using a cut map of Marrakesh multimodal road network. The generated multimodal graph is weighted with the simulated traffic and transit data stored in a database.

To manage the urban traffic congestion, the condition of the road network should be first evaluated. As presented in the research survey (Sect. 2), many congestion measures have been introduced by several studies throughout the years to assess the road conditions such as volume-to-capacity ratio, Travel Time Index, etc. None of these independent measures reflects the reality of the complex nature of the traffic state. To overcome this limitation, a lot of studies considered the combination of more than one measure to form a single congestion index that evaluates the traffic conditions from different aspects [18, 19]. Inspired by the cited works, a part of the contribution of this work emerges in the proposition of a novel method that computes and asses the road states, detailed in Subsect. 3.2. With this method, A congestion index is calculated, it represents a combination of three independent congestion measures. To our knowledge, no previous works have measured the congestion in the same manner, especially for the bus mode which its congestion is mainly evaluated using travel time.

The framework also provides a route recommendation service that takes into consideration car, bus and walking modes and lies on the computed congestion indexes. When a system user asks for the best alternatives to travel from a start to an endpoint, he can choose the transport modes by which he desires to make his journey. The framework generates the corresponding weighted graph with the congestion indexes and other parameters, applies the proposed algorithm detailed in Subsect. 3.3 and recommends the least congested path back to the system user. Figure 4 and

Table 3 illustrate an example of a resulting least congested path of a test request that selected the option of using both car and bus modes to travel from point O to point D. The proposed multimodal shortest path algorithm provides a one-way path while taking into account all viability constraints for efficient recommendations but it can be easily adapted to provide two-way path solutions.

The experimentation results reflect the efficiency of the shortest pathfinding algorithm applied to the simulated data. However, the major limitation of this study is the lack of real-world data. In our future works, we will consider other parameters besides the computed congestion indexes to give more pertinent recommendations. Besides, the proposed one-way multimodal shortest path algorithm will be adapted to answer the two-way multimodal route recommendations.

References

1. Weisbrod, G., Vary, D., Treyz, G.: Economic Implications of Congestion. National Academy Press, Washington D.C. (2001)
2. K. transportation Cabinet, "Congestion Measures."
3. Lomax, W., Schrank, T.J., Eisele, D.L.: The keys to estimating mobility in urban areas, applying definitions and measures that everyone understands. Texas Transport Institute, Texas A&M University System College Station Texas, May 2005
4. Lindley, J.A.: Urban freeway congestion: quantification of the problem and effectiveness of potential solutions. ITE **57**(1), 27–32 (1987)
5. Bertini, M.L., Robert, L., Lovell, D.J.: Generating performance measures from Portland's archived advanced traffic, Washington DC (2001)
6. Federal Highway Administration (FHWA). https://ops.fhwa.dot.gov/publications/tt_reliability/ttr_report.htm. Accessed 28 Feb 2019
7. Minnesota Department of Transportation (Mn/DOT). http://www.dot.state.mn.us/. Accessed 01 Mar 2019
8. The Washington State Department of Transportation (WSDOT). http://www.wsdot.wa.gov/. Accessed 01 Mar 2019
9. Coifman, B., Kim, S.: Measuring freeway traffic conditions with transit vehicles. Transp. Res. Rec. J. Transp. Res. Board **2121**(1), 90–101 (2009)
10. Kirchler, D., Kirchler, D.: Efficient routing on multimodal transportation networks (2013)
11. Pallottino, S., Scutellà, M.G.: Shortest path algorithms in transportation models: classical and innovative aspects. In: Marcotte, P., Nguyen, S. (eds.) Equilibrium and Advanced Transportation Modelling. CRT, pp. 245–281. Springer, Boston (1998). https://doi.org/10.1007/978-1-4615-5757-9_11
12. Battista, M.G., Lucertini, M., Simeone, B.: Path composition and multiple choice in a bimodal transportation network. In: The 7th WCTR (1995)
13. Barrett, C., Bisset, K., Jacob, R., Konjevod, G., Marathe, M.: Classical and contemporary shortest path problems in road networks: implementation and experimental analysis of the TRANSIMS router. In: Möhring, R., Raman, R. (eds.) ESA 2002. LNCS, vol. 2461, pp. 126–138. Springer, Heidelberg (2002). https://doi.org/10.1007/3-540-45749-6_15
14. Dib, O., et al.: A multimodal transport network model and efficient algorithms for building advanced traveler information systems To cite this version: HAL Id: hal-01586874 ScienceDirect a multimodal transport network model and efficient algorithms for building advanced traveler information systems (2017)

15. Lozano, A., Storchi, G.: Shortest viable path algorithm in multimodal networks. Transp. Res. Part A **35**, 225–241 (2001)
16. Ziliaskopoulos, A., Wardell, W.: An intermodal optimum path algorithm for multimodal networks with dynamic arc travel times and switching delays. Eur. J. Oper. Res. **125**(3), 486–502 (2000)
17. Aur, B., Sophie, C., Noureddin, E.F.: On the adaptation of a label-setting shortest path algorithm for one-way and two-way routing in multimodal urban transport networks introduction and state of the art, pp. 1–8 (2009)
18. Hamad, S., Kikuchi, K.: Developing a measure of traffic time congestion: fuzzy inference approach. Transp. Res. Rec. J. Transp. Res. Board **1802**, 77–85 (2002)
19. Patel, N., Mukherjee, A.: Categorization of urban traffic congestion based on the fuzzification of congestion index value and influencing parameters. Theor. Empir. Res. Urban Manag. **9**(4), 36–51 (2014)

Hybrid Recommendation of Articles in Scientific Social Networks Using Optimization and Multiview Clustering

Lamia Berkani[1,2]($\boxtimes$) (ID), Rima Hanifi[2], and Hiba Dahmani[1,2]

[1] Laboratory for Research in Artificial Intelligence (LRIA),
Department of Computer Science, USTHB University,
16111 Bab Ezzouar, Algiers, Algeria
lberkani@usthb.dz, l_berkani@hotmail.com
[2] Department of Computer Science, Faculty of Computer and Electrical
Engineering, USTHB University, 16111 Bab Ezzouar, Algiers, Algeria

Abstract. Several published articles are shared every day through scientific social network, which make it very difficult for researchers to find highly valuable and appropriate articles. To solve this issue, we propose in this paper a novel hybrid recommendation of articles combining an improved version of the content based filtering (CBF) and the collaborative filtering (CF) algorithms. First, the profiles of researchers and articles are built integrating the social tag information into the CBF algorithm. Then, the social friend information was integrated into the CF algorithm. Due to the problem sparsity of the CF, we have considered the singular matrix factorization (SVD) and unified probabilistic matrix factorization (PMF) algorithms. Finally, in order to further improve the performance of the CF, an optimized clustering has been applied using the Kmedoids algorithm and the BAT meta-heuristic. Different hybridization have been proposed: (1) a weighted hybrid algorithm which combines the two improved versions of the CBF and CF algorithms; and (2) the multiview clustering based hybrid algorithm. Experimental results conducted on the CiteULike dataset demonstrate that the proposed approach has significantly improved the recommendation accuracy and outperforms the baselines and exiting methods.

Keywords: Article recommendation · Hybrid recommendation · Content-based filtering · Collaborative filtering · Clustering · Multiview clustering · Optimization

1 Introduction

The rapid development of information technologies and Web 2.0 has encouraged the proliferation of online communities and social media including a variety of platforms that enable collaborative content sharing, creation and modification among users. Among them, the social network, a typical application of Web 2.0, has become one of the most exploited and the fastest growing online information interaction communities in recent years. A simple search on the web reveals the variety of areas and domains

© Springer Nature Switzerland AG 2020
M. Hamlich et al. (Eds.): SADASC 2020, CCIS 1207, pp. 117–132, 2020.
https://doi.org/10.1007/978-3-030-45183-7_9

related to these platforms where we can find, in addition to the mainstream social networks (e.g. Facebook, Tweeter), other more specialized networks such as the professional social networks (e.g. LinkedIn) or those grouping communities of researchers (i.e. scientific social networks like ResearchGate and CiteULike). Scientific social networks allow researchers different ways for collaboration and sharing of their articles, offering them new opportunities and activities that are of great importance as they can keep up-to-date the current trends in their research fields. However, as other similar platforms, the increasing rate of new published articles has led to the information overload problem, making it difficult for researchers to find the most appropriate scientific articles according to their profiles (their research field and interests). Accordingly, the article recommendation has attracted many researchers and many approaches have been developed to automatically suggest articles for a given researcher [1]. According to Wang et al. [2], these approaches can be classified into three categories: CBF approaches [3, 4], CF approaches [5, 6], and hybrid approaches [7, 8]. In order to improve the performance of article recommendation, Wang et al. [2] proposed a novel hybrid approach integrating social information in scientific social network (HAR-SI). The results obtained in this work outperformed the exiting approaches. However, by considering a very large number of data the performance of this algorithm could be reduced due to the scalability problem.

We focus in this article by this issue and we propose an extension of the HAR-SI approach, which combines the improved CBF and the improved CF algorithms. The improved CF is enriched using an optimized clustering algorithm (the Kmedoids partitioning algorithm and the BAT meta-heuristic algorithm have been employed). The, a novel hybrid recommendation of articles using a multiview clustering has been proposed. The users are iteratively clustered from the views of both rating patterns (the improved CF) and content information (the improved CBF). Finally, based on the multiview clustering, recommendations are generated. In order to evaluate our approach, experiments have been conducted using the collected CiteULike dataset and where different baselines and related work have been considered.

The remainder of this article is organized as follows: Sect. 2 provides some related work on article recommendation. Section 3 presents the details of the proposed article recommendation. The experiments results and analysis are given in Sect. 4. Finally, the conclusion and future perspectives are discussed in Sect. 5.

2 Related Work

According to Adomavicius and Tuzhilin [9] the CBF approach attempts to retrieve useful information (usually textual data) from articles that the researchers have appreciated in the past in order to construct article feature profiles and researcher preference profiles. The state of the art shows that different techniques have been employed. For instance, in Nallapati et al. [10], the text and citation relationship were jointly modeled under the framework of topic model. Hong et al. [11] proposed a personalized research paper recommendation system using keyword extraction based on user profile. Researcher profiles could be constructed through explicit declaration [12] (such as in CiteSeer) or observation of researchers' implicit interaction (their historical browsing behaviors by analyzing their previously read documents) [13]. Then semantic-expansion approach was adopted in [14], where the researcher profile is represented as a keyword vector in the form of a hierarchical category structure.

With the popularity of social networking websites, the CF approach has attracted more attentions for article recommendation. This algorithm recommends articles for researcher based on the relationships between other like-minded individuals or articles that have similar preferences or features as the target researcher [5]. However, as occurring in the other domain, such as E-commerce, the application of CF in article recommendation also encounters the data sparsity and cold start problems. To overcome the data sparsity problem, Vellino proposed a hybrid multi-dimensional approach where usage-based and citation-based methods for recommending research articles were combined [6]. Besides collective relations involved in user-item pairs, some attempts have been made to incorporate social relations into CF methods, considering for example a group trust [15] or a personal trust model [16].

To minimize these limitations and leverage the advantages made by either CBF or CF at the same time, hybrid recommendation approaches have been proposed. For instance, the recommendation for online book communities [8], using ontology network analysis for research document recommendation to infer the preference of researchers [17], and applying the social information to extract negative instance, then used to conduct a unified probability matrix factorization with the negative instance added data [18].

The study of these works shows the importance of combining the CBF and CF algorithms including social information, as proposed in [2]. However, to our best knowledge, none of the existing work in this context has addressed the problem of data volume, which is growing exponentially. Previous work using CF with social information based on optimized clustering has performed the recommendation accuracy [19]. We therefore propose a recommendation approach combining the CBF and CF algorithms with social information on the one hand and by applying clustering and optimization techniques on the other hand.

3   Adapted Hybrid Approach for Article Recommendation

This section describes our approach based on multiview clustering and optimization techniques, using the improved CBF and CF algorithms proposed in [2]. Figure 1 gives an overview of our approach by highlighting the proposed algorithms in bold.

3.1   Enrichments of the Improved CBF Model

The main tasks of the improved CBF approach proposed in [2] include: article feature profiling, user preference profiling, similarity computing and prediction. First, the

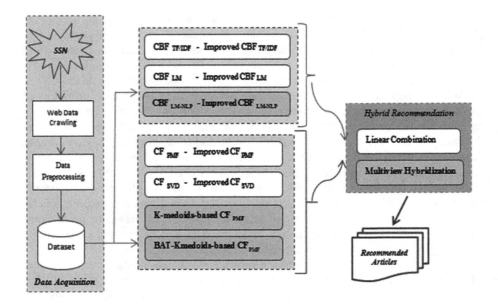

Fig. 1. Overview of the proposed article recommendation approach

article profiles are built based on the title and all tags labeled by researchers. It contains a set of features that describe and characterize a particular article. The Language model (LM) method is used to compute the profiles similarity between the target researcher and articles unread by the researcher. In order to solve the sparsity problem, LM approach uses a data smoothing method. The objective is to adjust the probability of maximum likelihood estimation to reduce the probability of having zero and non-zero values (for improving the overall accuracy of the model).

In our model, we have made a modification of the CBF approach by applying automatic natural language processing techniques (NLP) for data pretreatments. We first considered the titles of the articles, and then we considered a combination of these titles with the tags. Several preprocessing operations were carried out on each article in order to improve the quality of this data. We have implemented an algorithm which performs the preprocessing below in order to extract a list of keywords as follows:

- *Segmentation of the title.*
- *Delete stop words.*
- *Stemming:* this operation allows us to represent the words of an article by their roots. This will allow several variants of a term to be grouped together in a single representative form, thereby reducing the number of distinct terms that are needed to represent an article.

- *N-grams:* the N-grams allow us to construct a subsequence of *n* consecutive words. They allow us to contextualize the order of appearance of a set of words. We have considered a set of words up to 3-grams.

After these pretreatments, the computation of the weights and similarity is done according to the same steps used in [2], as described above.

3.2   The Optimized Clustering-Based Improved CF Model

The CF based on an optimized clustering is applied according to the following steps:

1. Use of the evaluations given by the researchers on the articles (a value ranging from 1 to 5) and construction of the usage matrix by one of the SVD or PMF matrix factorization methods.
2. Partitioning of users using the Kmedoids clustering algorithm. This classification will allow us to group the researchers into different groups so that individuals that belong to the same group are considered as neighbors (without noisy individuals, such as false profiles, that affect the results of clustering).
3. Optimization of the partitioning using the BAT algorithm.
4. Prediction of evaluations based on the optimized partitioning.

k-Medoids-Based CF. Described as an improvement on K-means, K-medoids remains similar to its predecessor but less sensitive to outliers. Cluster centers represent real users unlike k-means where cluster centers can sometimes represent points that don't belong to the dataset. K-medoids is considered the most robust partitioning algorithm, trying to minimize the distance between users that belong to a cluster. A user designated as the center of this cluster is called medoid. It can be defined as the object of a cluster whose average dissimilarity compared to all the objects in the cluster is minimal, i.e. it is the most centralized point of the cluster.

The distance function adopted in this work is as follows:

$$d\,(A,\,B) = 1 - sim\,(A,\,B) \tag{1}$$

where: *sim(A, B)* is the cosine similarity measure as described by this formula:

$$sim\left(u_i, v_j\right) = \frac{\sum_t u_i(t) v_j(t)}{\sqrt{\sum_t u_i(t)^2 \sum_t v_{ij}(t)^2}} \tag{2}$$

where:

u_i: denotes the vector model of a researcher *u*.

v_j: represents one of the vectors of articles which have not yet been read by this researcher u_i.

The k-medoids algorithm using the PAM version has been implemented. The complexity of the k-medoids-PAM algorithm is equal for each iteration to $O\ (k\ (n - k)\ 2)$, where n represents the size of the dataset and k the number of clusters.

BAT-Kmedoids-Based CF. The application of BAT metaheuristic will allow a rapid convergence to the initial stages of the k-medoids algorithm from exploration to exploitation. The BAT algorithm is based on the simulation of the echolocation behavior, i.e. biological sonar allowing them to detect the distance separating them from obstacles/prey [20].

Representation of a Solution for the k-*Medoids Algorithm.* Since a solution represents a set of starting medoids for the k-medoids algorithm, then the latter will be represented by vectors of k elements, where each element represents a point in the data set.

The position x_i, of each virtual bat defines a set of cluster medoids $(C_1, C_2 \ldots C_k)$ where k represents the number of clusters (i.e. the number of medoids). Thus, to find the best set of k medoids having a minimum cost, each bat adjusts its speed as well as its position and frequency to reach an optimum.

In order to simulate the displacement of a given bat, it would be necessary to define the rules for updating their positions x_i^t and their speeds v_i^t in a two-dimensional space at each iteration t. The following formulas are used:

$$f_i = f_{min} + (f_{max} - f_{min})\beta \tag{3}$$

$$v_i^t = v_i^{t-1} + (x_i^t - x_*)f_i \tag{4}$$

$$x_i^t = x_i^{t-1} + v_i^t \tag{5}$$

where:

x_*: designates the best current global solution which is updated by comparing the solutions of all the bats;

$\beta \in [0, 1]$ is a random vector from a uniform distribution; and

f_i: designates the pulse frequency initialized randomly for the bat x_i located between $[f_{min}, f_{max}]$.

The BAT-based k-medoids clustering algorithm is described as follows:

```
Algorithm 1: BAT-based Clustering
Input:
(a) Number of clusters k;
(b) Maximum number of iterations maxIter;
(c) Data set D;
(d) Population size p;
Output:
(a) medoids
(b) Output clusters.
Begin
- Generate a random position xᵢ= (xᵢ₁,xᵢ₂ ...xᵢₖ) for each batᵢ;
- Define the pulse frequency fᵢ of each position xᵢ;
- Initialize the pulsation rate rᵢ and the volume Aᵢ;
While t < maxIter Do
   For i == 1 To p Do
      Generate a new solution by adjusting the frequency and
      updating the speed and position with formulas 3, 4, 5;
      If xᵢ ∉ D then Search-for-neighbors (xᵢ);
      EndIf
   Call k-medoids with the solution xᵢ;
   Evaluate xᵢ;
   If rand > rᵢ then
      - Select a solution from the best solutions;
      - Generate a local solution around the best generated
        solution x* using a transformation integrating a
        random factor;
   EndIf
   If rand < Aᵢ and fitness (xᵢ) < f(x*) then
      -  Accept the new solution;
      -  Increase Aᵢ and decrease rᵢ ; // increase the pulse
         emission rate and decrease the sound amplitude
   EndIf
   Done
Revise the global best solution x* according to the fit-
   ness;
Done
End.
```

Search for Neighbors. The search for neighbors is represented by a heuristic which allows the different points to really belong to our dataset. In each iteration, the positions of the bats are changed using formula 5. However, this can sometimes lead to a position that does not belong to our initial data set. Therefore, we used a heuristic which, for each modified point (medoid), ensures that this point belong to our dataset. Otherwise, the closest point (i.e. according to the shortest distance) of this point will be selected.

Update of the Bats Movement Equations. As mentioned in the algorithm above, the movement of bats is calculated by the three formulas 3, 4 and 5. Each artificial bat uses the formula 3 to select a frequency f_i in the frequency range $[f_{min}, f_{max}]$, where f_{min} and f_{max} are two integers in the range $[1, n]$ such that n represents the size of our data set. Then they use the formula 4 to update their speed. Thus, the resulting value is applied in the third equation (Formula 5) in order to calculate the next position.

Complexity Calculation. The optimization of the k-medoids algorithm by the BAT algorithm contains two internal loops when passing through the population p and when searching for neighbors n and an external loop for the iteration t. Moreover, for each solution, the k-medoids clustering algorithm is called to test the performance of this solution generated by a given bat. Accordingly, the worst-case complexity is equal to O (np (k (n − k) 2 i) t) ≈ O (ptkn 3), where, O (k (n − k) 2 i) represents the complexity of k-medoids algorithm.

3.3 Multiview Clustering for HAR (MVC-HAR)

In this section we propose a new form of hybridization between the improved CBF and the improved CF algorithms using a new method based on a multiview clustering.

Clustering-based recommender systems suffer from relatively low accuracy and coverage. To address these issues, Guo et al. [21] developed a multiview clustering method through which users are iteratively clustered from the views of both rating patterns and social trust relationships. We were inspired by this proposal (multiview clustering for recommendation in a social context) which we adapted to our research by considering the two views: content (the improved CBF) and evaluations (the improved CF). A multiview hybridization would group the users according to the similarity on the one hand and on the other hand according to the content of their histories.

First, users are grouped using similarity between users. Then, separately, the users are grouped using the information on the content of their articles in order to be able to calculate the distance separating them from the others. We have adapted the cosine measure as follows:

$$sim(t_i, t_j) = \frac{\sum_{k \in K} t_i(k) t_j(k)}{\sqrt{\sum_k t_i(k)^2} \sqrt{\sum_k t_j(k)^2}} \tag{6}$$

where:

$K = t_i \cap t_j$: is the set of terms common to both profiles.

t_i and t_j: represent the profiles of users i and j containing their histories, where the values represent the frequency of appearance of a term in the history of a given user.

```
Algorithm 2: Multiviews k-medoids
Input:
  D_c : Content-based distance matrix;
  D_s: Similarity-based distance matrix;
  k: number of clusters;
  maxIter : maximum number of iterations;
Output:
  C: output clusters.
Begin
- p←0;
- Randomly select k medoids m_c  from D_c ;
- Make a clustering from D_c  with the medoids m_c ;
While medoids changed and t <maxIter do
// In the view of similarity
- p←p + 1;
- m_s  ← m_c  ;
- Swap (m_s  , u), u ∈ content-based clusters of the step
(p-1);
- Calculate cost_s (u), u ∈ content-based clusters;
- Calculate cost_s (m_c ), u ∈ content-based clusters;
If cost_s (u) < cost_s (m_c ) then ms ←u;
EndIf
- Make a clustering from D_s  with the medoids m_s ;
// In the view of content
- p ← p + 1;
- m_c  ← m_s  ;
- Swap(m_c , u), u ∈ similarity-based clusters of the step
(p-1) ;
- Calculate cost_c  (u), u ∈ similarity-based clusters;
- Calculate cost_c (m_s ), u ∈ similarity-based clusters;
If cost_c (u) < cost_c (m_s ) then m_c  ←u;
EndIf
- Make a clustering from D_c  with the medoids m_c  ;
End
Return Integration(Ccontent , Csimilarity )
End.
```

In this algorithm, the similarity-based distance matrix based on the evaluations D_s and the content-based distance matrix D_c are taken as inputs to the multiview clustering algorithm that generates user clusters. We start by randomly selecting k users as initial medoids, and form a set of content-based medoids in the step p = 0. Then, we form clusters with these medoids where the users of the dataset will be assigned to the nearest cluster (taking into account the closest distance). The multiview clustering method will iterate the users of two different views and combine the two views as final results. In particular, in the first view (i.e. the similarity view), we initialize the similarity medoids with the content medoids which are determined in the previous step. Then, they are updated by exchanging each medoid with other users u within the Cc clusters (i.e. the content clusters) which reach the minimum cost of pairwise distances. Finally, user clusters in the similarity view are generated.

Similarly, in the content view where the similarity medoids generated previously will be assigned as initial content medoids in step p. Content medoids are updated based on content distances and produce a new set of user clusters. This iterative process will continue until no medoid is changed, or the maximum number of iterations is reached. Finally, user groups from different views are combined by the Cluster Integration and Pruning algorithm (in this algorithm, content and similarity clusters are taken as input).

Integration and Pruning. In order to obtain user clusters as output, integration will be triggered when the number of individuals belonging to the same cluster is less than the value of a given threshold θ, i.e. for each cluster C_c^i in the clusters C_c, if this criterion is satisfied then the integration continues. First, it would be necessary to find another cluster C_c^j which reaches the minimum average distance between each user $u \in C_c^i$ and the medoid m_c^j of the cluster C_c^j. If such a cluster is found, all users of the C_c^i cluster will be merged into the C_c^j cluster. The cluster C_i will be pruned in both cases, whether it is merged or not. After processing the content clusters C_c, the same procedure is repeated, replacing C_c with similarity clusters C_s. We note that a user will be able to belong to two different clusters after having completed the integration and pruning process.

Prediction. Once the multiview clustering as well as the integration and pruning phases have been completed, it would be possible to make article predictions for a given user. As mentioned above, the integration phase sometimes allows users to belong to two different clusters. While the pruning phase, allows users to belong to no cluster. The following three cases are distinguished:

- *First case:* If a user belongs to only one cluster, in this case, we have adapted the weighted sum equation which considers the closest neighbors of a given user, as follows:

$$Pred(u, i) = \frac{\sum_{v \in U} sim_s(u, v).sim_c(u, v).(r_{v,i} - r(\vec{v}))}{\sum_v sim_s(u, v) + sim_c(u, v)} \tag{7}$$

where
$Pred(u, i)$: denotes the prediction of user u on item i.

$sim_s(u, v)$ and $sim_c(u, v)$: denote the similarity between user u and v considering the ratings and the content respectively. We adopted the cosine similarity measure and the modified cosine similarity measure for the similarity calculation.

- *Second case:* If a user does not belong to any cluster (i.e. in the case of pruning), in order to predict a vote for a given item, we have in this case taken into account the average of its votes.
- *Third case:* In the case a user belongs to two different clusters, to predict a vote of a user u on an article i, we calculated the average of the two predictions of each cluster namely $pred_1$ and $pred_2$ as follows:

$$Pred(u, i) = \frac{pred_1(u, i) + pred_2(u, i)}{2} \tag{8}$$

where:

$pred_1(u, i)$: represents the prediction of user u on item i in the first cluster.
$pred_2(u, i)$: represents the prediction of user u on item i in the second cluster.

4   Evaluation

To evaluate our approach we have developed all the modules described in Fig. 1 including those proposed by Wang et al. [2]. Our system was implemented using the Python language, using several libraries (Numpy, NLTK, Pandas, Scikit-learn …).

Empirical experiments have been conducted to study two main research questions: (1) whether integrating multiple views of user correlations can improve the recommendation accuracy; and (2) demonstrate the added value of the optimization in the clustering.

4.1   Experimental Dataset and Metrics

In order to demonstrate the effectiveness of the proposed recommendation approach, a real-life dataset from CiteULike was used. The dataset was crawled, where all article content and social information, including article title, tag, friend relation, and browsing history, were extracted. We have selected all users with a number of articles between 50 and 500 in their libraries. The details of the final dataset are described in Table 1.

Table 1. Statistics of filtered CiteULike dataset

Description	Value
Number of researchers	621
Number of articles	45 720
Number of tags	21 149
Number of groups	500

To evaluate the different algorithms of the proposed approach, we used the precision and recall metrics specifying the top M predictions, according to these formulas:

$$Precision@M = \frac{Number\ of\ correctly\ recommended\ articles\ in\ top\ M}{Number\ of\ recommended\ articles} \qquad (9)$$

$$Recall@M = \frac{Number\ of\ correctly\ recommended\ articles\ in\ top\ M}{Number\ of\ collected\ articles} \qquad (10)$$

4.2 Evaluation Results

Evaluation of the Improved CBF Algorithm. We have evaluated the improved CBF_{LM} algorithm using the NLP module (CBF_{LM-NLP}). The results obtained show that the NLP module has considerably improved the evaluation metrics compared to the LM (based on title) and Improved LM (based on title and tag) approaches. The following tables represent the results obtained in terms of precision and recall (Tables 2 and 3).

Table 2. Precision results for the CBF algorithm

Precision@	LM	Improved LM	LM-NLP	Improved LM-NLP
10	0.0436	0.048	0.052	0.0548
15	0.0495	0.0554	0.0604	0.06049
20	0.0593	0.07102	0.0746	0.0806
25	0.0836	0.0989	0.0929	0.1089

Table 3. Recall results for the CBF algorithm

Recall@	LM	Improved LM	LM-NLP	Improved LM-NLP
10	0.07592	0.14085	0.08542	0.16458
15	0.06931	0.10513	0.0798	0.116933
20	0.05656	0.08374	0.07482	0.097186
25	0.04269	0.07499	0.0628	0.07631

Contribution of Clustering on the CF Algorithm. We started by evaluating CF algorithms based or not on social information (friendships) by considering the two variants of PMF and SVD. The results obtained confirm those obtained in [2] which show the contribution of social information on the CF and that the methods of PMF can reach higher performances compared to the methods of SVD. We therefore considered in the following evaluations the Improved CF algorithm based on PMF which gave the best performances in terms of precision and recall.

In order to test the contribution of clustering on the CF, we varied the number of clusters in order to be able to fix them for the next evaluations. We notice that a large number of clusters do not improve our performance, which remains relatively stable. This may be due to the sparsity problem.

Finally, we evaluated the CF algorithm based on an optimized clustering, given that we considered the best value of clusters obtained in the previous evaluation (K = 55). The following figures summarize the results obtained, where we can see a clear improvement with clustering and a slight improvement with optimization.

We note that the quality of clustering is not always proportional to the quality of the prediction. The good clustering does not necessarily imply good prediction, especially when the number of individuals remains relatively small (as is the case in our data sample) because BAT aimed to improve the clustering (Fig. 2).

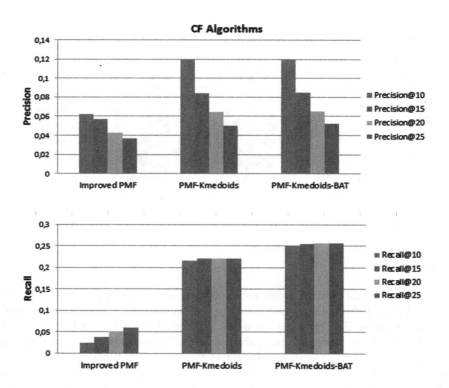

Fig. 2. Precision and recall for the CF algorithms

Comparison Between Hybrid Filtering Algorithms. The results of the evaluations show that the algorithm based on a multiview clustering gave better performances compared to the linear hybridization proposed in HAR-SI [2]. This demonstrates that this technique has surpassed the results of the state of the art with a considerable improvement as illustrated in Fig. 3. In addition, we can also see that the NLP module has also slightly improved this performance.

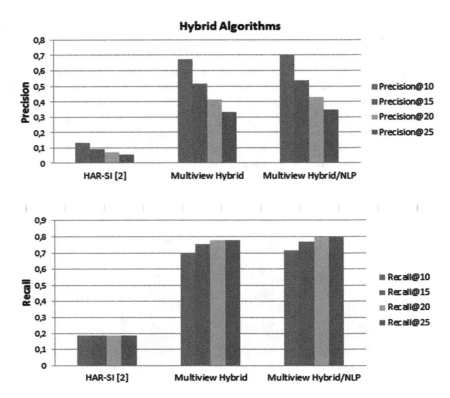

Fig. 3. Evaluation of the hybrid filtering based on multiview clustering.

5   Conclusion

We focus in this article on the article recommendation in scientific social network. We propose a novel hybrid recommendation of articles combining an improved version of the content based filtering (CBF) and the collaborative filtering (CF) algorithms. The CBF has been improved using the social tag information and employing the Language model and a Natural Language Processing module. While the CF has been improved with the social friend information and using an optimized clustering method (BAT-Kmedoids algorithm). Furthermore, the novelty of our approach is the proposition of the multiview hybrid algorithm where the users are iteratively clustered from the views of both rating patterns (the improved CF) and content information (the improved CBF). The experimental results conducted on the CiteULike dataset demonstrate the effectiveness of our approach which has significantly improved the recommendation accuracy and outperforms the baselines and exiting methods.

In our future work, we envisage to further improve these results by incorporating other information such the expertise of researchers and the quality of their articles, considering other social networks with a more larger database and optimizing our multiview clustering based hybrid algorithm.

References

1. Wang, C., Blei, D.M.: Collaborative topic modeling for recommending scientific articles. In: Proceedings of the 17th ACM SIGKDD International Conference on Knowledge Discovery and Data Mining. ACM (2011)
2. Wang, G., XiRan, H., Ishuga, C.I.: HAR-SI: a novel hybrid article recommendation approach integrating with social information in scientific social network. Knowl.-Based Syst. **148**, 85–99 (2018)
3. Vivacqua, A.S., Oliveira, J., De Souza, J.M.: i-ProSE: inferring user profiles in a scientific context. Comput. J. **52**(7), 789–798 (2009)
4. Chandrasekaran, K., Gauch, S., Lakkaraju, P., Luong, H.P.: Concept-based document recommendations for CiteSeer authors. In: Nejdl, W., Kay, J., Pu, P., Herder, E. (eds.) AH 2008. LNCS, vol. 5149, pp. 83–92. Springer, Heidelberg (2008). https://doi.org/10.1007/978-3-540-70987-9_11
5. Bogers, T. Antal, V.D.B.: Recommending scientific articles using CiteULike. In: ACM Conference on Recommender Systems, Recsys, Lausanne, Switzerland, October 2008
6. Vellino, A.: A comparison between usage-based and citation-based methods for recommending scholarly research articles. Proc. Am. Soc. Inf. Sci. Technol. **47**, 1–2 (2010)
7. Sun, J., Ma, J., Liu, Z., Miao, Y.: Leveraging content and connections for scientific article recommendation in social computing contexts. Comput. J. **57**(9), 1331–1342 (2014)
8. Kim, H.K., Oh, H.Y., Gu, J.C., Kim, J.K.: Commenders: a recommendation procedure for online book communities. Electron. Commerce Res. Appl. **10**(5), 501–509 (2011)
9. Adomavicius, G., Tuzhilin, A.: Toward the next generation of recommender systems: a survey of the state-of-the-art and possible extensions. IEEE Trans. Knowl. Data Eng. **17**(6), 734–749 (2005)
10. Nallapati, R.M., Ahmed, A., Xing, E.P., Cohen, W.W.: Joint latent topic models for text and citations. In: Proceedings of the 14th ACM SIGKDD International Conference on Knowledge Discovery and Data Mining. ACM (2008)
11. Hong, K., Jeon, H., Jeon, C.: Personalized research paper recommendation system using keyword extraction based on user-profile. J. Converg. Inf. Technol. **8**(16), 106 (2013)
12. Bollacker, K.D., Lawrence, S., Giles, C.L.: Discovering relevant scientific literature on the web. IEEE Intell. Syst. Appl. **15**(2), 42–47 (2000)
13. Liang, T.-P., Yang, Y.-F., Chen, D.-N., Ku, Y.-C.: A semantic-expansion approach to personalized knowledge recommendation. Decis. Support Syst. **45**(3), 401–412 (2008)
14. Chen, C.C., Chen, M.C., Sun, Y.: PVA: a self-adaptive personal view agent. J. Intell. Inf. Syst. **18**(2–3), 173–194 (2002)
15. Lee, D.H., Brusilovsky, P.: Using self-defined group activities for improving recommendations in collaborative tagging systems. In: 4th ACM Conference on Recommender Systems (2010)
16. Lai, C.H., Liu, D.R., Lin, C.S.: Novel personal and group-based trust models in collaborative filtering for document recommendation. Inf. Sci. **239**(4), 31–49 (2013)
17. Weng, S.-S., Chang, H.-L.: Using ontology network analysis for research document recommendation. Expert Syst. Appl. **34**(3), 1857–1869 (2008)
18. Wang, G., He, X., Ishuga, C.I.: Social and content aware one-class recommendation of papers in scientific social networks. PLoS One **12**(8), 1–30 (2017)
19. Berkani, L.: Social-based collaborative recommendation: bees swarm optimization based clustering approach. In: Schewe, K.-D., Singh, N.K. (eds.) MEDI 2019. LNCS, vol. 11815, pp. 156–171. Springer, Cham (2019). https://doi.org/10.1007/978-3-030-32065-2_11

20. Yang, X.S.: A new metaheuristic bat-inspired algorithm. In: González, J.R., Pelta, D.A., Cruz, C., Terrazas, G., Krasnogor, N. (eds.) NICSO 2010. SCI, vol. 284, pp. 65–74. Springer, Berlin (2010). https://doi.org/10.1007/978-3-642-12538-6_6
21. Guo, G., Zhang, J., Yorke-Smith, N.: Leveraging multiviews of trust and similarity to enhance clustering-based recommender systems. KBS J. **74**, 14–27 (2015)

Toward a Recommendation System: Proposition of a New Model to Measure Competences Using Dimensionality Reduction

Safia Baali[1]([⊠]), Hicham Moutachaouik[1], and Abdelaziz Marzak[2]

[1] Structural Engineering, Intelligent Systems and Electrical Energy, ENSAM,
Hassan II University, Casablanca, Morocco
safia.baali@gmail.com
[2] Information Technology and Modelling Laboratory,
Faculty of Sciences Benmsik, Casablanca, Morocco

Abstract. To assure the delivery 's performance in IT Digital services company, we must assign the best collaborator's profile in the adequate project. The objective of our study is to develop a Recommendation system for Human Resources Data with based-content and collaborative filtering, that allows recommending potential collaborators for a new job offer, using multicriteria analysis (AHP) and the matching between job offer of new project and collaborators profiles. We propose in the first step a model of criteria to measure competences for the Information Technology team, we validate it by a survey carried out in the IT service company based in Morocco. The data collected is analyzed using dimensionality reduction (PCA) method (Principal Component Analysis). The results indicate that six factors can measure the collaborator's competences in the team (collective competence): Technical competence, Integrity, Proactivity, Communication, Cooperation, and Benevolence/ Interpersonal Relationship. These criteria will be used in the AHP function to allow a recommendation of potential collaborators for the adequate project.

Keywords: Collective competence · Recommendation system · Trust model · Dimensionality reduction · PCA · AHP method

1 Introduction

One of the most challenging problems in the Human Resources (HR) domain in the Digital services company is to affect the best profiles to the adequate project and predict the success of collaborator, then the success of delivery and customers' satisfaction. in this paper, we propose a recommendation system with based-content and collaborative filtering. The objectives of our contribution are:

- To propose a new model of criteria to measure collaborator's competences which be used in an AHP method to give a score for each collaborator
- To propose a recommendation system for ranking/matching collaborators profiles, with content-based and collaborative filtering to assign the potentials profiles to the adequate project (profiles who have an estimated end date of actual project assignment).

© Springer Nature Switzerland AG 2020
M. Hamlich et al. (Eds.): SADASC 2020, CCIS 1207, pp. 133–145, 2020.
https://doi.org/10.1007/978-3-030-45183-7_10

- Predict the success of the collaborator in the job offer of the new project.

There are many studies that take into account the measure of collective competence. On one hand the study of Janaina Macke and Kelly Menezes Crespi [1], that elaborates an instrument for measure collectives competences in IT work team and identify four factors (Proactivity, Cooperation, Communication and Interpersonal- Relationship) on the other hand, we note the works of Lucile Callebert [2], who develops a multi-agent system, that generates the behaviors of agents on the team in a virtual environment, he approves the importance of each criteria of trust for the team's performance, these criteria are (Integrity, Benevolence, technical competence) they are related to the Model of Trust MDS (Mayer, David, Shoorman), the measure of collective competence must also take into account the Trust model, in this reason we propose a Hybrid model that associates these two models. We examine this proposition by a study based on a survey carried out in an IT Digital services company. We aim to define the criteria of measuring collective competences from the analysis of the collected data (opinions about the attitudes and collaborative behaviors in the IT team) using PCA method. These criteria will be used in the AHP function to allow the recommendation of potential collaborators for the adequate project. The structure of this article is as follows: First, we present the literature review, then we present our contribution, we discuss the results, conclude in the final section and indicate the gains and perspective of our study.

2   Literature Review

Despite the simplicity of Competences Management's concept, its application is relatively complicated [3] According to Bonotto [4], this concept is devised in tow approaches: individual and organizational. Otherwise, many authors take a great importance for the coordination of these competences and present it as a principal factor of success and performance [5]. There are many studies in relation to collective competences and are based on the articulation between competences and organization by project. As a result, in the project management's context, there are autonomous or semi-autonomous teams and groups that emerge around a professional objective [6].

2.1   Instrument for Measure of Collective Competence

Many studies have focused on the measure of competences within a team, Janaina Macke and Kelly Menezes Crespi [1], have developed an instrument to measure the collective competences of IT teams. that four factors can measure the collaborator's competences (Proactivity, Cooperation, Communication, Interpersonal Relationship).

According to Janaina Macke and Kelly Menezes Crespi [1], we present the definition of each criterion below:

- **Proactivity:** According to Zarifian [7] Proactivity present an important attitude for developing competences, that present the strong relation between competence and capacity to take responsibilities toward complicated situation in the work.
- **Cooperation:** According to Zarifian [7], Cooperation is the mutualization of the ways to solve problems.

- **Communication:** According to (Le Boterf, [8]) communicate cannot eliminate tension and conflict, but allows the team to manage it and consider it as normal.
- **Inter-personal Relationship:** Colleagues need to know each other's strengths and weaknesses so that they can diagnose each other's needs and plan adequate actions.

2.2 Model of Trust

Trust presents a basic element for success and the group's performance. According to Lucile Callebert [2], and related to the trust model proposed by MDS (Mayer, David, Shoorman) [9, 10] trustor's intention to trust relies on the assessment of the following characteristics of the trustee:

- **Technical competence:** The evaluation of the trustee's competence by the trustor is related to a specific field and area of expertise.
- **Integrity:** The trustor's perception of trustee integrity is described by Mayer as the trustor's sentiment (where he or she believes that the trustee adheres to the values that he or she deems acceptable). Integrity is also linked to the regularity of the trustee's behavior and to the coherence between his words and his actions.
- **Benevolence:** The trustor will perceive the trustee as benevolent if he has the impression that the trustee wants his property.

According to these studies, we note that the instrument proposed by Janina Macke is relatively limited. Many factors can influence the collective competence, especially the factors related to the trust model. Therefore, we propose a model that assemble these criteria to have a better definition of how to me measure a collective competence.

3 Contribution

3.1 Proposition of a Hybrid Model of Competence's Measure

According to Janaina Macke and Kelly Menezes Crespi [1] study, and following validation with the studies of several authors, this instrument is based on the four main factors: proactivity, communication, cooperation, and interpersonal relationship. This study did not focus on the addition of the trust model that is important in the group's performance (technical competence, integrity, benevolence). We propose a Hybrid model that assembles these two models as follows: We will proceed in the next paragraph by evaluating the reliability of this model by a case study in an IT service company (Fig. 1).

In order to test the validity of the model of measure collective competence, we processed by a survey established in an IT service company, the data are analyzed by the PCA method in order to determine factors of measure collective competences.

The different steps of this study are as follows:

3.1.1 Conception of the Hypotheses of the Survey and Data Collect

In this phase, we proceed with the same methodology adopted by Janaina Macke study [1], the formulation of the hypotheses is based on the following studies [11–13].

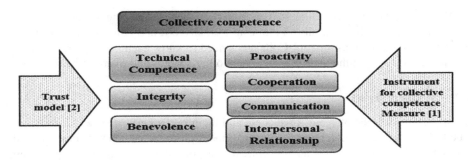

Fig. 1. The proposed model for measuring collective competence

To test the criteria related to the trust model, we make a hypothesis related to each of these criteria: technical competence, integrity, benevolence, according to the definition adopted by the different authors. The hypotheses of the survey include the description of the attitudes and collaborative behaviors of the IT team, we have 43 hypotheses. The opinions on the hypotheses of the survey are the five Likert-type scale levels, 1 to 5, (1 for strongly disagree and 5 for strongly agree).

3.1.2 Data Analysis

In this paragraph, we explain the method used to analyze the data collected from the survey, according to many studies of PCA method.

1. Dimensionality reduction: is a method used to project data from a large space into a smaller space. This operation is crucial in machine learning to fight against what is called the scourge of large dimensions (the fact that large dimension alters the efficiency of methods).
2. PCA method: The principal Component Analysis [14] is a powerful tool for information compression and synthesis, very useful when there is a large quantitative data to be processed and interpreted, this method is a factorial analysis, it produces factors that present a linear combination of the initial, hierarchical and independent variables. It is mostly used as for exploratory data analysis to make predictive models.

In our study, the survey includes 43 hypotheses, it represents the variables that explain the basis of collective competences, we have 200 collaborators that give a response for each variable, to explain the content of this data, we have to reduce the dimensionality of these variables using PCA method. The analysis is carried with Varimax rotation, a Kaiser-Meyer-Olkin (KMO) adequacy index of 0.912 and a Bartlett sphericity test of 0.000, indicating Data factorability. The first cycle of the analysis identified eight factors, with variables with a low factor load, and other variables that significantly saturate on more than one factor, this signifies that these variables should be removed since they did not have one position on a one factor. These variables are excluded from the second analysis. In the second cycle of our analysis, six determinants of collective competence are found with an explained variance about 90%, the presentation of the variables are significant only on five factors, and after a Varimax rotation of the factorial planes, normalization of Kaiser with convergence, we obtain a presentation on six factors as presented in the next paragraph (Table 1).

Table 1. Presentation of variables and factors

Variable	Hypotheses	Factor 1	Factor 2	Factor 3	Factor 4	Factor 5	Factor 6
V1	Our team often finds creative ways to solve problems.	,777	-,036	,037	,007	,096	-,018
V2	On our team, there is a balanced distribution of tasks among members	,700	-,036	,037	,007	,096	-,018
V3	In our team, people are interested in learning more about their colleagues.	,650	-,036	,037	,007	,096	-,018
V4	When a problem hinders our progress, team members show motivation to solve it.	,644	-,036	,037	,007	,096	-,018
V5	In our team colleagues usually share their knowledge.	,640	-,036	,037	,007	,096	-,018
V6	My colleagues often cooperate so that the team can achieve their goals.	,630	-,036	,037	,007	,096	-,018
V7	When I have problems, my teammates usually help me.	,600	-,036	,037	,007	,096	-,018
V8	My colleagues encourage me to meet or exceed my personal and professional goals	-,078	,750	,069	,073	,216	,211
V9	We often adopt the goals of other team members in an altruistic manner	-,078	,750	,079	,073	,216	,211
V10	We always trust that each teammate helps us to achieve the collective goal	-,068	,700	,069	,073	,216	,211
V11	My colleagues understand my strengths and weaknesses.	-,078	,650	,089	,073	,216	,211
V12	When I have a complaint, I feel free to talk to a colleague(s) about it.	-,068	,644	,069	,073	,216	,211
V13	The team members have proved their kindness many times. Their help was indispensable in the various problems encountered.	-,066	,600	,069	,073	,216	,211
V14	Delivery times are always respected	,039	,037	,800	,127	,061	,086
V15	We always make the privilege of collective goals on personal goals in order to succeed together	,039	,027	,750	,127	,061	,076
V16	We are honest about our words; we think what we say and we say what we think	,071	,129	,700	-,116	,076	,042
V17	We are always honest and committed to our collective goal	,071	,159	,650	-,116	,066	,042
V18	In our team the members privilege the realization of the tasks for which they are competent	-,148	,040	-,105	,915	,100	,134
V19	The competence of the team members is crucial for the success of the project	-,148	,24	-,105	,900	,100	,134

(*continued*)

Table 1. (*continued*)

V20	We often trust the teammate's skill to do a common task	,211	,174	,143	,831	-,130	-,221
V21	We measure the levels of competence with the resultant levels or the execution time of tasks requiring this skill	,211	,174	,143	,831	-,130	-,221
V22	We pay attention to the moods in our team.	,267	,496	,109	-,008	,820	,020
V23	Relationships in our team are based on cooperation.	,267	,496	,109	-,008	,790	,020
V24	My colleagues have ways to show they care about each other.	,267	,496	,109	-,008	,700	,020
V25	In our team we recognize the efforts of colleagues	,267	,496	,109	-,008	,650	,020
V26	In our team we tell colleagues if they are doing something considered unacceptable	-,024	,385	,090	-,033	,017	,750
V27	We often discuss how to manage our difficulties.	-,024	,385	,090	-,033	,017	,730
V28	We recognize a tense situation and talk about it with team members.	-,024	,385	,090	-,033	,017	,700

3.1.3   Results and Discussions

According to the results described above, we find that the variables are distributed on the following six factors:

- **Factor 1 [Proactivity]:** V1 to V7 (table above). According to the study of Janaina Macke and Kelly Menezes Crespi [1], proactivity is crucial in the evaluation of collective competence. According to Zarifian, [5] one of the most important attitudes to skills development is proactivity, which means that competence is related to one's ability to take responsibility for working situations as well as act proactively in the face of unforeseen events. According to Le Boterf [15] be competent means being able to act and take initiatives, evaluation can no longer be reduced to controlling the compliance with a standard.
- **Factor 2 [Benevolence/Interpersonal relationship]:** V8 à V13, we note that this factor reassembles benevolence and interpersonal relationships. Benevolence can refer to a specific relationship between the Trustor and Trustee, and therefore, it is more important when the Trustor and the trustee strongly know each other [2].
- **Factor 3 [Integrity]:** V14 à V17, these four variables are the most important determinants of integrity. We note that the integrity is essential in the determination of the collective competence. To achieve the common goal every team member must be honest and dedicated toward his or her engagements as well as respect the planning and task completion.
- **Factor 4 [Technical competence]:** V18 à V21, these variables are mainly associated with technical competence. This factor is a determinant of trust and group

performance, and according to Sabrina Loufrani-Fedida [6], individual competence is a key element in achieving collective competence.

- **Factor 5 [Cooperation]:** V22 à V25, these variables are mainly associated with cooperation. According to the work [1], cooperation is a way to converge the actions and processes between the team's groups. This factor is essential in the group's performance.
- **Factor 6 [Communication]:** V26 à V28, these variables are most closely associated with the communication. Communication is a very important element in teamwork, according to le Boterf [7]. Being able to communicate does not eliminate the problems and crises, but promotes the ability to manage and consider them as normal.

3.2   Proposition of Recommendation System to Assign Collaborator to a Job Offer of the New Project

3.2.1   Recommendation System in Human Resources

Recommendation systems provide users with suggestions to meet their needs and preferences. The different approaches related are based-content filtering which makes recommendations by comparing the content of resources with the user's preferences [16], collaborative filtering which makes recommendations by analyzing, the users' opinions and those of other users about the resources they have consulted [17]. In Human Resource, for the internal assignment in the company [18] the author proposes a prototype of a recommendation engine based on a Big Human Resources Data platform, allowing to retrieve the best candidates for a specific mission, using the matching of CV/Mission and different types of scoring. In the E-recruitment, we note the work [19], the author proposes a recommendation system using content-based filtering, he uses the matching of the job offer and candidate profile by the indexation and full text search using the engine LUCENE, he progresses the accuracy of the system using the automatic detection of the activity area with supervised machine learning. To match the candidates profiles the specific job offer, there is many approaches, in the work [20] the author proposes a system that directed to adopt a clustering algorithm to match the profile of the job seekers against the requirements of the job posted by the prospect employers.

3.2.2   Proposed Model for the Recommendation of Potentials Profiles

In our approach we need to develop a recommendation system that allows recommending potential collaborator, using content-based (target relevant candidate profiles using the information provided by the recruiter) and collaborative filtering (score given by the other project managers), the principal's parts are:

1 The automatic matching of the subject and required competences of the job offer in the new project with the technical competences of the collaborator.
2 Ranking each collaborator by the score given by the last project manager using the AHP method (Fig. 2).

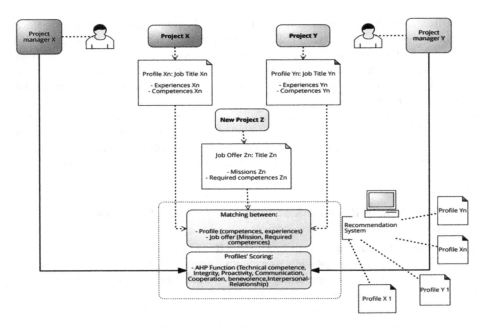

Fig. 2. Proposed model of recommendation system

3.2.3   The Matching Between Competences, Experience of Profile and Job Offer

According to the works related to the matching between Job offer and candidate profile [19, 21], the matching is applied through the extraction of useful information from the job offer, and profiles search:

1. Extraction of useful information from job: Job Title, Competences, years of experience.
2. Profiles search: Realized by the indexation and full-text search for profiles using the Lucene engine (https://lucene.apache.org/) [22, 23]

– Search for the job title in the positions held by profiles using a Lucene field **expfunc**, and search for the competences extracted from the job offer among the competences entered in a profile using a Lucene field **skillname**.
 Example of query: **expfunc** = "lead developer" **AND skillname**: (JAVA development, Unit Testing)

3.2.4   Proposition of Function to Give a Score for Collaborator

In our approach, we propose a function that assembles the different criteria of the new proposed model to evaluate collaborator,according to the studies on the methods of multicriteria analysis [24, 25] we opted for the method AHP (Hierarchical Analysis Process), that is characterized by its way of determining the weights of criteria by binary combinations of each level of hierarchy with respect to the elements of the highest level. According to the principles of the AHP method, the proposed function is:

$$f(x) = \sum \alpha i X i (i = 1 \rightarrow n)(0 < \alpha i < 1; \sum \alpha i = 1)$$

Function 1: AHP Function to give a score to the collaborator
Xi = Criteria related to the validation of collective competence; αi = Weight of each criteria

- The criteria are: **X1** = Technical competence, **X2** = Integrity, **X3** = Proactivity, **X4** = Cooperation, **X5** = Benevolence/Interpersonal relationship, **X6** = Communication
- The weights related to the criteria will be defined by the judgment of the experts
- We consulted the project managers to give us the weighting for each criterion as presented in the table below (Table 2).

Table 2. Criteria matrix for determining the binary importance

	Technical competence	Benevolence/relationship	Integrity	Proactivity	Cooperation	Communication
Technical competence	1	4	4	4	4	4
Benevolence/relationship	1/4	1	1/2	1/3	1/2	1/3
Integrity	1/4	2	1	2	2	2
Proactivity	1/4	3	1/2	1	2	2
Cooperation	1/4	2	1/2	1/2	1	2
Communication	1/4	3	1/2	1/2	1/2	1

We compare the importance of criteria in line with the importance in column: 1 = equal importance, 2 = moderate importance, 3 = strong importance, 4 = very strong importance, 5 = extreme importance. The next step is to calculate the weight of each criterion (Table 3):

Table 3. Calculation of criteria's weight

	Technical competence	Benevolence /Relationship	Integrity	Proactivity	Cooperation	Communication	Criteria Average
Technical competence	0.44	0.266	0.57	0.48	0.4	0.35	0.417
Benevolence / Relationship	0.11	0.066	0.07	0.04	0.05	0.029	0.06
Integrity	0.11	0.13	0.14	0.24	0.2	0.176	0.166
Proactivity	0.11	0.2	0.07	0.12	0.2	0.176	0.146
Cooperation	0.11	0.13	0.07	0.06	0.1	0.176	0.107
Communication	0.11	0.2	0.07	0.06	0.05	0.088	0.096

The Function will be as follow:

$$F(x) = 0.417\ X1 + 0.166\ X2 + 0.146\ X3 + 0.107\ X4 + 0.096\ X5 + 0.06\ X6$$

X1 = Technical competence, X2 = Integrity, X3 = Proactivity, X4 = Cooperation, X5 = Communication, X6 = Benevolence/Interpersonal relationship

3.2.5 Evaluation of the Recommendation System

To evaluate the accuracy of our recommendation system, we have taken a manual evaluation for 60 collaborators who change the project to a new assignment.

Strategy: A new project with the Job offers: (the project was started 6 months ago), we present in the table below the collaborators assigned to the new project (Table 4).

Table 4. List of collaborators assigned to the new project

Job offer	Required technical competence
15 Business analyst	Functional conception, Quotation, Strategic planning, Functional testing, Reporting…
15 JAVA consultants	Technical design, Develop and execute unit tests, Correct anomalies of the different test cycles, Struts 1, JSF 2, Swing/Awt…
20 .NET consultants	Technical design, Develop and execute unit tests, Correct anomalies of the different test cycles, Web development-ASP. NET AJAX…

The collaborators in the table above have a specific technical competence that is required for the new project. and have also another aspect of collective competences that are related to the behavior in the last team project (proactivity, cooperation, integrity, benevolence/interpersonal relationship, communication). We assign these collaborators from different other projects, to the new project in where they spend six months.

1 We ask the project manager of the last project to give us a score evaluation for each collaborator based on AHP function.
2 For the collaborator who have required competences for the new job, we recommend it, based on the score given by the last project manager.
3 Have the opinion of the new project manager about the collaborator 'performance.

After analysis of the recommendation proposed by our approach, and the satisfaction of the new project manager we present an example of results (Table 5):

Table 5. Example of some recommendation's evaluation

Collaborator	Rating in the last project assignment (with AHP function)	Recommendation	Performance in the current project	Recommendation result
Business analyst	2	Recommended	OK	Successful
Business analyst	2	Recommended	KO	Unsuccessful
JAVA consultant	1	Recommended	OK	Successful
JAVA consultant	4	Not Recommended	KO	Successful
.NET consultant	1	Recommended	OK	Successful
.NET consultant	2	Recommended	OK	Successful

After analysis of the evaluation's result (almost 60 collaborators), the accuracy obtained is about 80%, this first result is encouraging, we must continue with other cases to conclude the improvements that we can replicate to the recommendation system.

4   Conclusion and Perspectives

In this paper, we have proposed a new criteria to evaluate the collaborator in the project, the six criteria are (Technical competence, Integrity, Proactivity, Communication, Cooperation, and Benevolence/Interpersonal Relationship). These criteria are used as the main criteria in a function defined by the AHP method, in order to give an evaluation' score for each collaborator. we proposed a recommendation system based on collaborative and content-based filtering, that allows recommending potential collaborators (who have an end date of actual assignment) to the adequate job offer of the new project, by the matching of the subject and required competences of the offer, with the technical competences of the collaborator ranked by the evaluation's score given to each collaborator. This new model helps us to predict the collaborator's success in the adequate project, and then the delivery's performance and customer's satisfaction. The limit of the proposed recommendation system is the cold start problem, the perspective of this limit is to consider the data of the collaborator's profile from a social network (LinkedIn, Viadeo). We must also take into account the progression of the competence ontology for matching job offer and profiles and propose a new approach to the recommendation of a new CV candidates for E-Recruitment.

References

1. Macke, J., Crespi, K.M.: "One swallow does not make a summer": the development of an instrument for measuring collective competences in information technology teams. SAGE Open 6(2), 2158244016642497 (2016)
2. Callebert, L.: Activités collaboratives et génération de comportements d'agents: moteur décisionnel s'appuyant sur un modèle de confiance (2017). (https://tel.archives-ouvertes.fr/tel-01522687)
3. Ruas, R.L.: Gestão por competências: uma contribuição estratégia das organizações. aprendizagem organizacional e competências, pp. 34–35. Porto Alegre, Brazil (2005)
4. Bonotto, F.: The elements of the collective competences in workplace groups—The experience of Copesul, Doctoral thesis (2005)
5. Zarifian, P.: Objective Competence: A new Logic. Atlas, São Paulo (2001)
6. Loufrani-Fedida, S.: Thesis Management des compétences et organisation par projets (2012). https://tel.archives-ouvertes.fr/)
7. Dutra, J.S.: Competences: Concepts and Tools Human Resource Management in the Modern Business. Atlas, São Paulo (2007)
8. Le Boterf, G.: Developing the Competence of Professional. Porto Alegre (2003)
9. Shoorman, F.D., Roger, C.M., James, H.D.: An integrative model of organizational trust: past, present and future. Acad. Manag. Rev. 32(2), 344–354 (2007)
10. Bowen, Q., Elbahtimy, H., Hobbs, C., Moran, M.: The human side of verification: trust and confidence. In: Trust in Nuclear Disarmament Verification (2018)
11. Closs, L.Q.: Cross-cultural study of group emotional competence: validation of a US research tool for use in the Brazilian context. Master's thesis. Federal University of Rio Grande do Sul. School of Management, Porto Alegre (2004)
12. Pereira, M.A.C.: Competences for teaching and research: a survey of chemical engineering faculty. Doctoral dissertation. University of São Paulo, São Paulo (2007)
13. Rosa, J.S.: The dynamics of collective competences in a context of cooperation networks. Master's thesis. University Vale do Rio dos Sinos, São Leopoldo (2007)
14. Liu, W., Zhang, H., Tao, D., Wang, Y., Lu, K.: Large-scale paralleled sparse principal component analysis. Multimed. Tools Appl. 75, 1481–1493 (2016). https://doi.org/10.1007/s11042-014-2004-4
15. Le Boterf, G.: Une innovation pédagogique pour la professionnalisation des étudiants en kinésithérapie. KINE, 826 p. (2018)
16. Yu, L., Han, F., Huang, Y., Luo, Y.: A content-based goods image recommendation system. Multimed. Tools Appl. 77, 4155–4169 (2018). 10.1007/s11042-017-4542-z
17. Mao, Y., Zhang, F., Xu, L., Zhang, D., Yang, H.: A bidirectional collaborative filtering recommender system based on EM algorithm. In: International Conference on Smart Vehicular Technology, Transportation, Communication and Applications. Springer (2017)
18. Darmon, P., Mazouzi, R., Manad, O.: Team Builder: D'un moteur de recommandation de CV notés et ordonnés à l'analyse sémantique du patrimoine informationnel d'une société. hal.archives-ouvertes.fr (2018)
19. Casagrande, A., Gotti, F., Lapalme, G.: Cerebra, un système de recommandation de candidats pour l'e-recrutement. hal.archives-ouvertes.fr (2017)
20. Rodriguez, L.G., Chavez, E.P.: Feature selection for job matching application using profile matching model. In: IEEE 4th International Conference 2019. (2019). ieeexplore.ieee.org
21. Dieng, M.A.: Développement d'un système d'appariement pour l'e-recrutement. papyrus. bib.umontreal.ca (2016)

22. Azzopardi, L., Moshfeghi, Y.: Lucene4IR: Developing information retrieval evaluation resources using Lucene. ACM SIGIR Forum(2017)
23. Białecki, A., Muir, R.: Apache Lucene 4 information retrieval. academia.edu (2012)
24. Domański, C., Kondrasiuk, J.: AHP as support for strategy decision making in banking. In: Jajuga, K., Sokołowski, A., Bock, H.H. (eds.) Classification, Clustering, and Data Analysis. Studies in Classification, Data Analysis, and Knowledge Organization, pp. 447–453. Springer, Heidelberg (2002). https://doi.org/10.1007/978-3-642-56181-8_49
25. Gaikwad, S.M., Joshi, R.R., Kulkarni, A.J.: Cohort intelligence and genetic algorithm along with AHP to recommend an ice cream to a diabetic patient. In: Panigrahi, B.K., Suganthan, P.N., Das, S., Satapathy, S.C. (eds.) SEMCCO 2015. LNCS, vol. 9873, pp. 40–49. Springer, Cham (2016). https://doi.org/10.1007/978-3-319-48959-9_4

Unsupervised Deep Collaborative Filtering Recommender System for E-Learning Platforms

Jamal Mawane$^{(\boxtimes)}$ ⓘ, Abdelwahab Naji, and Mohamed Ramdani

IT Department FST Mohammedia, Hassan II University, Casablanca, Morocco
ja.mawane@gmail.com

Abstract. With the rapid development of the online learning resources, trying to respect the differences between learners in terms of cognitive ability and knowledge structure. Traditional collaborative filtering recommendation algorithms cannot identify useful learning resources which will be interesting and simple to understand. Furthermore, the redundant recommended content and the high-dimensional and nonlinear data on online learning users cannot be effectively handled, leading to inefficient resource recommendations. To enhance learning resource recommendations efficiency, this paper presents a two steps efficient resource recommendation model based on, Kohonen card unsupervised deep learning to identify the instrumental approximation of learning styles, and deep auto-encoder, whose interest is not the prediction of resource in as such, but the transformation learned by the self-encoder, which serves as an alternative representation of the input and estimate the success rate of the proposed resource to the learner. This model need deeply mines learner features course content attribute features assessment attribute features and incorporates learner platform interactions features to build Learner features vector as input for the first step and Learner-Content ratings vector to choose the more efficient learning resource to recommend.

Keywords: E-Learning · Clustering · Unsupervised learning · Deep learning · Recommendation systems · Collaborative filtering

1 Introduction

The recommendation systems are a tools that limit the excessive choice of users. Given the explosive growth of resources, users are often greeted with too many resources, films or restaurants as examples on e-commerce platforms, or showered with Learning resources with the same content objective by e-Learning platforms. As such, the recommendation is a strategy of which the goal is to simplify user experience. These systems play an indispensable role in various access to information systems to stimulate business and facilitate the decision-making process. They constitute the new trend of web and e-commerce techniques and/or media websites [2]. Recommendation items lists are generated

© Springer Nature Switzerland AG 2020
M. Hamlich et al. (Eds.): SADASC 2020, CCIS 1207, pp. 146–161, 2020.
https://doi.org/10.1007/978-3-030-45183-7_11

based on user preferences, item characteristics, past user-item interactions, and additional information such as users segmentation or the items trends. The recommendation techniques are mainly classified into three categories: collaborative filtering recommendation systems, content-based recommendation systems and hybrid recommendation systems. The last decades have seen a strong return of machine learning, based on neuron networks and the new machines exponential evolution of computation averages and storage as well as the rate of success of the applications of the deep learning in many application areas, such as computer vision and speech recognition. The scientific and industrial world are in perpetual race to find new deep learning applications fields, armed by the reason of its capacity to understand many tasks, and the density of the datasets of available examples. Deep learning may be a radically reformed proposal design and increased opportunities to improve the recommendation applications. Deep learning can be a point of setback and reform in the design of recommendation systems, the advanced uses led by deep learning gives a very encouraging look to overcome the limitations of standard models and to propose High quality systems of recommendations. Deep learning makes it possible, to understand the inherent contextual links between users or between users and the elements proposed by the recommendation system. In the recommendation systems of e-learning platforms, the use of deep learning aims to increase the relevance and assimilation rate as well as the item' adaptability proposed by the recommendation systems to learners. To verify our model's effectiveness, an offline experimental analysis, using a Real word dataset was conducted to show that the Unsupervised Deep Collaborative Filtring recommendation system has greater accuracy than previous recommendation methods. In the field of recommendation systems research, numerous methods have been used to select the relevant items for platforms users. This can be done through classic data-mining techniques that compute a similarity score to each user or item, and utilize the top-scoring ones in similarity or comparison elements of selection to recommend it.

1.1 Recommendation Systems

In general, recommendations can be generated based on users preferences, item features, user-item transactions, and other environmental factors such as time, season, location [1]. In the recommendation literature these are categorized into three primary categories: collaborative filtering (using only the user-item interaction information for recommendation), content based filtering (using users preferences, item preferences or both) and hybrid recommendation models (using both interaction information as well as user and item metadata) [21]. Models under each of these categories have their own limitations such as data sparsity, cold start for users and items. Figure 1 gives an overview of the three strategies used in the recommendation systems and the scientific research themes published over the last years. Recommendation Systems are used for:

– **Improve retention:** Constantly satisfying users makes them more loyal to the service.

- **Increase sales:** Quick sales of new products through their links or similarities to old ones.
- **Form Habits:** Develop habits by influencing customer experiences.
- **Accelerate Work:** Suggestions for new relevant content necessarily reduce work time.
  The Fig. 1 gives a recommendation techniques overview as well as the most strategies cited in the literature

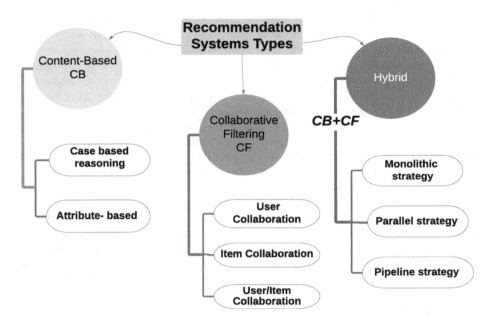

Fig. 1. Recommendation systems techniques' overview .

1.2   Unsupervised Deep Learning

As extended field of artificial neural network, deep learning is also a subset of machine learning which is featured by multiple non-linear processing layers and tries to mine hidden data' aspect [7,22]. For the time being,this research topic is growing very fast and generating various deep learning architectures in which new models are being developed constantly. The community is quite open and there are a number of deep learning tutorials and books of good-quality [12,17,19] (Fig. 2).

Self-Organized Map (Kohonen Maps). A Self-Organized Map (SOM): [9] is an unsupervised and a high data dimensional reducer. It is capable of projecting input data onto a low-dimensional (usually two dimensions are sufficient) map

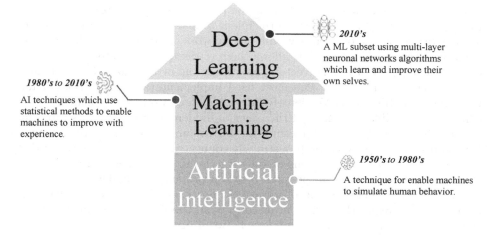

Fig. 2. Theorical position of deep learning.

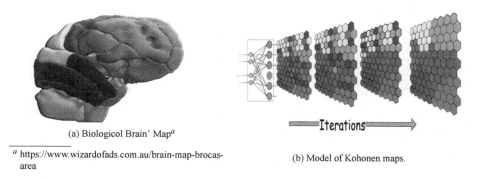

(a) Biologicol Brain' Map[a]

[a] https://www.wizardofads.com.au/brain-map-brocas-area

(b) Model of Kohonen maps.

Fig. 3. Kohonen maps concept and procedure

[10,14]. Like the human Brain, various neural functions are mapped onto identifiable regions of the brain Fig. 3a. Thus, a SOM is a nonlinear projection of data that tries to preserve the topology of the input attributes from the multidimensional space. Self-organized maps have been utilised in several recommendation application systems [4,5]. The unsupervised nature of this approach provides an alternative tool to conventional algorithms, compared in our previously published work, thus opening the possibility of developing a dynamic classifier that does not depend on the number of clusters, as is the case with classical algorithms, as well as the ability to focus the work on internal links within each cluster. Another important feature of a SOM is the ability to produce a structured order of new output data that is similar to the training sample and that will be mapped to neighboring neural nodes of the trained features map, subsequently offering to match new learners of the platform to its homogeneity cluster Fig. 3b.

Boltzmann Machines. [20] A Boltzmann machine is a complete graph (hence the symmetry) of which operating principle is to make stochastic decisions as to the activation or not of a path within the network. Boltzmann machines have a simple learning algorithm that allows them to discover interesting features in datasets composed of binary vectors, as well as the evolutionary trend thanks to its stochastic dynamics. The most used implementation of the Boltzmann machine is the Restricted Version (RBM), which has two layers of neurons, one composed of visible neurons and the other of hidden neurons. As illustrated in Fig. 4a. In this restricted architecture, the Boltzmann machines' graph is transformed from a complete graph to a strongly connected graph, by eliminating the connections between the neurons of the same layer [8,16]. The visible layer of the model is associated with the input observations and the hidden layer shapes the dependencies between the observations. For example, in the handwritten recognizing problem, the visible layer collects all the pixels of an image, while the hidden layer represents dependences between pixels [6,15].

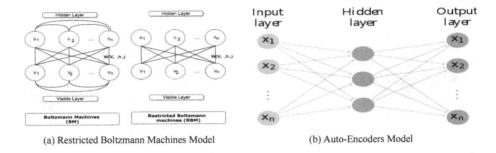

(a) Restricted Boltzmann Machines Model   (b) Auto-Encoders Model

Fig. 4. Restricted Boltzmann machines & Auto-Encoders model

Autoencoder (AE). An autoencoder (AE) is an unsupervised artificial neural network, also known as an auto-associator network, which uses feedforward approach to encode the input into some representation, and reconstitute the output from it (Hinton and Salakhutdinov 2006). As illustrated in Fig. 4b, An autoencoder has three essential parts: an encoder, a code and a decoder. This means that the input is compressed in the first part of the autoencoder network, and then sent to be decompressed as output in the second part, which is often similar to the original input. An autoencoder provides compression functionality in the field of machine learning [18].

1.3   E-Learning Recommendation System

E-Learning has become a leveraging domain in big data, due to the exponentially growing number of e-learning platforms. Thus, machine learning and data analysis have also become essential to exploit the growing amount of collected data generated in this area. The recommendation system is a field of machine

learning and data analysis that is proposed as a solution to deal with the growth
of collected data. These algorithms are tools that can use data, behavior, and
finding interesting models on it. E-learning recommendation systems offer a set
of elements to learners, in order to draw the most effective paths specific to their
learning styles through an abundance of learning resources. The relevance of
recommendations is the purpose of e-learning recommendation systems, as preferences and abilities related to learners' learning styles are constantly evolving.
All recommendations must be relevant to increase the effectiveness of learning
and ensure an attachment to the learning system in the long term. Some research
has been done to study learners' learning activities and to provide corresponding adaptive recommendations. Learners' learning profiles are updated through
certain facets of interactivity with the e-Learning platform. The Fig. 5 presents
a summary of the most prominent papers associated with the recommendation
techniques as well as the most important themes in literature. In recommendation systems, the correspondence score between Learners and Items is num-
ber $\in [|1, 5|]$. This score in E-learning platforms represents either the learner's
personalised items recommended satisfaction or the score obtained in an item
assessment. Formally, an E-learning platform items' recommendation is a func-
tion (R) from $\mathbb{L}$ to $\mathbb{I}$, where $\mathbb{L}$ is the Learners set and I refers to the Learning
items resource set which is assumed to be very large. For each user $L_i \in \mathbb{L}$, The
function (R) must select the learning items $I_{[|0,k|]} \in \mathbb{I}$ to satisfy the Learner's
needs. for this, the function can have the following mathematical expression:

$$R: \begin{cases} \mathbb{L} \longrightarrow \mathbb{I} \\ L_i \longmapsto \underbrace{max_1(I_R) + \cdots + max_k(I_R)}_{k_{items}} \end{cases} \tag{1}$$

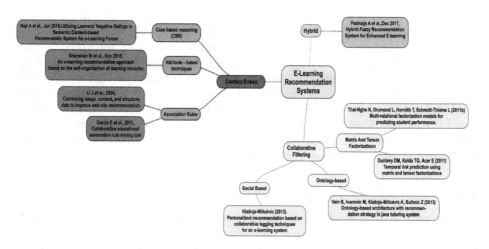

Fig. 5. Literature E-Learning recommendation systems

2   Unsupervised Deep E-Learning Recommender System

Deep learning neural networks have strong capabilities for detecting and extracting the intrinsic characteristics of input data. The purpose of this paper is to propose a two-block collaborative recommendation model based on two unsupervised deep learning networks, the framework of which is presented in Fig. 7. The first block' s objective is to establish the connection between the learners, in order to form groups of the same profile, and select relevant items related to each cluster to recommend. The set of selected input characteristics serve a single personality aspect of the learners (Personal Aspect, Results obtained, and the volume of interactivity with the system), the graphical representation Fig. 6 shows that no learner' s characteristic is strongly correlated with another; in this configuration, no group seems natural, in this context, the attraction forces' Kohonen map will determine both the learners of each group as well as the number of closer groups. The second Block based on a Deep AutoEncoder predicts the learner' s score among the list of items best achieved among all learners, Finally, the last step compares the two blocks results ,in order to chose relevant items to recommend. In summary, this collaborative recommendation model supported by a pre-grouping of learners based on all the learners' palpable aspects (personal information, interaction with the platform, learning style, results obtained,......), the elements proposed by all learners and supported by the results of its congeners will have a better accuracy of success, in addition to the cold start congeners can ensure a reassuring recommendation at the beginning... In the remainder of this section, we present this approach step by step.

2.1   Architecture

A system of recommendation by its nature offers a considerable number of elements to the learner. Nevertheless, anything that can be offered can not be helpful. The purpose of this paper is to present a vision of the collaborative filtering recommendation based on the unsupervised approach of deep learning, in order to recommend elements with a very high accuracy of success, through the selection of elements achieved by learners with the same learning profile, the prediction of the most relevant elements and finally the validation and evaluation of relevance. Profile matching is based on three facets of learners: personal information, previous results, and interactivity and attachment to the system. In the rest of this section, we present this approach step-by-step.

2.2   Data Collections and Processing

The purpose is to analyze the learner' s interest latent characteristics with unsupervised deep learning machines, and discover the best learner' s interresting items. In general, the model needs to be independent on any e-learning data collection, directly related to learners' aspects. For this reason, data pre-processing, often neglected, is a one major step, which can even distort the training and results of machine learning. Data collection methods are often poorly controlled,

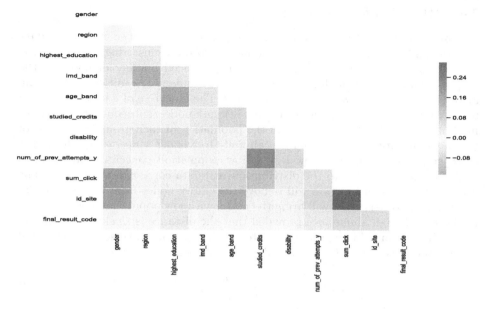

Fig. 6. Features correlations

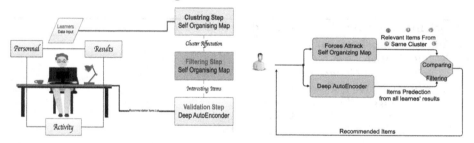

Fig. 7. System architecture

and sometimes fail to detect impossible combinations of data (for example, Age: 10, Level: High School) giving false or misleading results. Thus, the pretreatment of the quality of the data is an essential phase above all data analysis. The training phase is unable to discover knowledge if a redundant or irrelevant or noisy or unreliable information is present in the data collection. Data preprocessing includes:

- Data Cleaning,
- Data Integration,
- Data Transformation,
- Data Reduction.

Thus the machine training database is ready after all these steps, despite the time taken by the preprocessing of the data, to the discovery of latent knowledge in the data source.

2.3   Attraction Forces' Kohonen Map

The main purpose of the kohonen map algorithm is to reduce the size of data vectors, and this may present an alternative to data clustering, based on the intrinsic distance of input vectors, and for a reduced number of nodes in the map network, this algorithm may give results similar to traditional clustering algorithms such as K-Means and K-Medians. The objective of adding attraction forces to the nodes is to merge the closest network nodes, subsequently determining both the number of clusters and the population of each group, regardless of the initial network configuration. In all Self-Organizing Maps, especially larger ones, get sheets (i.e. empty nodes) or low population concentration nodes is probable, generally due to the distribution real data correspondances' law. The attraction-repulsion function will remove the empty nodes from the network, in the first step, otherwise it will bring the nodes with low population density closer to those with high abundance provided that the distance is as close as possible. So, the attraction will be proportional to the distance and inversely proportional to the abundance of nodes +1(in order to avoid being divided by 0).

$$Actract(N_i, N_j) = \frac{dist(N_i, N_j)}{Pop(N_i) * Pop(N_j) + 1} \tag{2}$$

Algorithm 1. Attract method to reduce nodes'clusters

---

   function REDUCE(*Som*)
      Initialization : $k = NL * NC$
      Initialization $Change \leftarrow True$
      while $Change \neq False$ **do**
         $Change \leftarrow False$
         for $i \leftarrow 1, NL$ & $j \leftarrow 1, NC$ **do**
            if $Atract(i, j) < limit_{distance}$ **then**
               $Change \leftarrow True$
               if $pop(i) > pop(j)$ **then**
                  $j \leftarrow i$
               else
                  $i \leftarrow j$
         $k \leftarrow k - 1$
      return k

2.4   Prediction

Our model is based on Autoencoders, which are unsupervised neural networks with feedback effects that aims to construct a prediction on the initial input. The objective of our model is, first of all, to predict the score of the recommended items within its clusters provided by attract Map, and to discover probable items not identified by the cluster.

2.5   Filtering and Validation

The last stage of our recommendation method, developed to improve the learners' experience on an online learning platform, aims to filter among the items that should be recommended to a learner those that have a strong certainty of success. This block has a decision-making nature, it cross-references the two deep networks' results, in order to select three different items. The first items to be filtered are those which the first Attraction forces' Kohonen map does not select, and the deep Autoenconder gives low score' predicts. The second items strongly recommended are those that are opposed to the first ones. The last items proposed as discovery items not proposed by the first block, but had a very high predictive score.

3   Results

To evaluate the present effectiveness of our recommendation system at this stage, we will use both comparisons on our initial test basis to evaluate the results of our system compared to conventional recommendation systems. Different measurement methods are used to evaluate the performance of our system. This study uses a python implementation program, with pytorch library, to create both an adapted self Organizing Maps and the deep Autoencoder network. In ordre to evaluate our mode's accuracy, tested on off-line realistic DataSet (OULAD) Fig. 8 [11]. Based on the learner' s prediction score of items not seen before, we used the metrics Root Mean Squared Error (RMSE) to calculate the difference between the predicted score and the actual score to reflect the accuracy of the recommendation related to a number of training iterations.

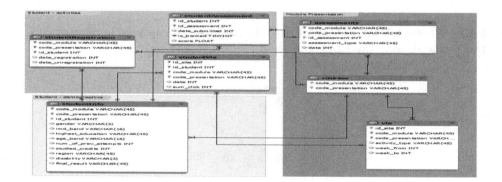

Fig. 8. Data set structure

3.1 Kohonen Map Evaluation

To evaluate the proposed bloc, we study the Kohonen map convergence on a Map example, then, we evaluate the results similarity between Kohonen Map and classical clustering method (Optimum k finding with ElBlow method is used). The evaluation results are as follows:

Clusters' Number Evaluation. On a Kohonen 5X5 two-dimensional Map' size, map nodes' population changes in relation to the number of iterations of the individual dispatching process.

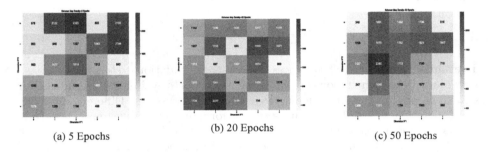

(a) 5 Epochs   (b) 20 Epochs   (c) 50 Epochs

Fig. 9. Kohonen map nodes' population density related to epochs

The Figs. 9 above show that from 20 iterations onwards, the map stabilizes and approximates the areas of proximity in terms of density.

Force Attract VS K-Means,Fuzzy K-Means. The optimal number of clusters deduced using the ELBow method is equal to 4 (Fig. 10).

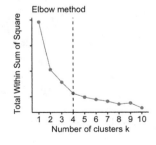

Fig. 10. The optimal clusters number find it with ELBow method

Algorithm 2. Find Optimal K with Elbow Method

procedure ELBOW(*dataSet*)
    Initialization : $k = 1$
    while $cost_k \neq 0$ **do**
        $k \leftarrow k + 1$
    End

The table below shows the rate of the true likelihood between the 4 clusters of the methods and the 4 nodes of our kohonen map reduced to 2X2.

Table 1. Clustering algorithm cross similarity rate

		Kohonen VS KMeans		Kohonen VS Fuzzy-KMeans	
		1X4	2X2	1X4	2X2
		Similarity' average rate			
Epoch	40	46%	13%	36%	4%
	80	57%	0%	43%	0%
	150	0%	88%	12%	0%
	200	0%	88%	12%	0%

From the previous Table 1, we can see that there is an identical similarity between cluster $N°1$ and the KMeans algorithm, knowing that generalize the similarity ratio between the methods is estimated at 53% between Kohonen and Kmeans, 25% between Kohonen and Fuzzy KMeans, while the similarity is 26% between KMeans and Fuzzy KMeans, so the similarity between the other algorithms is higher than the one between them.

3.2 Deep AutoEncoders

Independent tests performed on the two parameterized auto-encoder network, namely the depth of the network to the activation functions, in order to create the most efficient network possible To determine the optimal value of the first parameter of our network, the test used just the Sigmoid activation function, and we vary the depth of our network. While for the second parameter, studies have been concluded on our network:

– The first study tested the influence of certain linear functions, "rectified linear units" (RELU), reticence rectified linear units (LRELU), associated with Sigmoid at the output layer [3].
– The second study compares the performance of a single function, for example "linear exponential scale units" (SELU) or hyperbolic tangent (TANH) along all networks [13] .

Losses' Deep Evaluation. The Fig. 11 below, shows the evolution of losses in AutoEncoder relating to its depth.

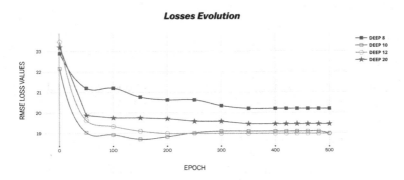

Fig. 11. Losses evolution related to AE' deep

For only 500 computation' Epochs, with 4 symetric autoencoder' deep configurations models, we notice that the network converges to a smallvalue of losses, about $0.2 = 20/100$ (100 is final mark), in this context, the Deep 12' network provides an efficient result comparing to the others.

Losses' Activation Functions Evaluation. The Fig. 12, show the evolution of losses in AutoEncoder related to used layers' activation function.

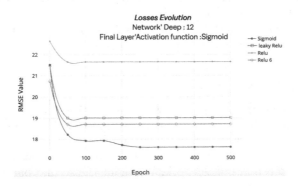

Fig. 12. Losses evolution related to AE' deep activation function

For our autoencoder network, Relu and its variants (LRelu and Relu 6) do not converge, unless the Sigmoid activation function is used in the output layer, despite this combination, sigmoid used in all layers is more efficient. The Fig. 13 gives a comparison between Sigmoid and other activation functions.

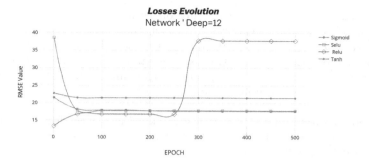

Fig. 13. Losses evolution related to AE' deep with same activation function

We can deduce that Sigmoid and Selu are the two most suitable functions for our autoencoder network.

4   Deep AutoEncoders VS Recommendation Algorithm

We compared the recommendation quality obtained by our method with other collaborative filtering approaches based on the closest neighbours, User-Item-Based CF and RBM. Table 2 shows the efficiency result of each method tested on Oulad DataSet.

Table 2. Unsupervised deep E-Learning RS compared to relevant methods

Evaluation	
RS methods	Root-mean-square error value
RBM	22.55
User-item-based CF	22.55
Unsupervised deep CF	17

From the results obtained on Oulad dataSet, it can be seen that our model is more efficent than both RBM and User-Item-Based Collaboratif Filtering.

5   Conclusions

This paper sets off a hybrid collaborative recommendation system' model, dedicated to E-Learning platforms, and based on learners' profiling' aspects to avoid the problem of cold start learning(collaborative systems shortcome), and a parallel items prediction, of which the cross-results validate the recommended items within a profile group and the discovery of new items proposed by the platform. With E-Learning platforms' efficiency in terms of use, exchanges and learning, data' volume is increasing exponentially on these platforms. Our model uses two deep artificial learning networks to extract, generalize, and discover possible intrinsic relationships from data. In this context, deep learning can lead to practical solutions for E-Learning platforms. Deep architectures are able to perform complex operations compared to traditional algorithms, exhibiting classification' skills and rapid convergence predictions.

Acknowledgements. All the experiment work part was conducted on OULAD Dataset. For this, our thanks to The Open University members, for giving us the opportunity to verify our model.

References

1. Adomavicius, G., Tuzhilin, A.: Toward the next generation of recommender systems: a survey of the state-of-the-art and possible extensions. IEEE Trans. Knowl. Data Eng. **6**, 734–749 (2005)
2. Aggarwal, C.C.: An introduction to recommender systems. Recommender Systems, pp. 1–28. Springer, Cham (2016). https://doi.org/10.1007/978-3-319-29659-3_1
3. Banerjee, C., Mukherjee, T., Pasiliao, Jr., E.: An empirical study on generalizations of the ReLU activation function. In: Proceedings of the 2019 ACM Southeast Conference, ACM SE 2019, pp. 164–167. ACM, New York (2019). https://doi.org/10.1145/3299815.3314450
4. Cottrell, M., Fort, J.C., Pagès, G.: Theoretical aspects of the som algorithm. Neurocomputing **21**(1–3), 119–138 (1998)
5. Cottrell, M., Olteanu, M., Rossi, F., Villa-Vialaneix, N.: Theoretical and applied aspects of the self-organizing maps. In: Merényi, E., Mendenhall, M.J., O'Driscoll, P. (eds.) Advances in Self-Organizing Maps and Learning Vector Quantization. AISC, vol. 428, pp. 3–26. Springer, Cham (2016). https://doi.org/10.1007/978-3-319-28518-4_1
6. Dargan, S., Kumar, M., Ayyagari, M.R., Kumar, G.: A survey of deep learning and its applications: a new paradigm to machine learning. Arch. Comput. Methods Eng. (2019). https://doi.org/10.1007/s11831-019-09344-w
7. Du, X., Cai, Y., Wang, S., Zhang, L.: Overview of deep learning. In: 2016 31st Youth Academic Annual Conference of Chinese Association of Automation (YAC), pp. 159–164, November 2016. https://doi.org/10.1109/YAC.2016.7804882
8. Hinton, G.E.: A practical guide to training restricted boltzmann machines. In: Montavon, G., Orr, G.B., Müller, K.-R. (eds.) Neural Networks: Tricks of the Trade. LNCS, vol. 7700, pp. 599–619. Springer, Heidelberg (2012). https://doi.org/10.1007/978-3-642-35289-8_32
9. Kohonen, T.: The self-organizing map. Proc. IEEE **78**(9), 1464–1480 (1990). https://doi.org/10.1109/5.58325
10. Kohonen, T.: Self-organized formation of topologically correct feature maps. Biol. Cybern. **43**(1), 59–69 (1982)
11. Kuzilek, J., Hlosta, M., Zdrahal, Z.: Open university learning analytics dataset 4, 170171. https://doi.org/10.1038/sdata.2017.171
12. Lin, L., Zhang, D., Luo, P., Zuo, W.: The foundation and advances of deep learning. Human Centric Visual Analysis with Deep Learning, pp. 3–13. Springer, Singapore (2020). https://doi.org/10.1007/978-981-13-2387-4_1
13. Ramachandran, P., Zoph, B., Le, Q.V.: Searching for activation functions (2017)

14. Ritter, H., Schulten, K.: Kohonen's self-organizing maps: exploring their computational capabilities. In: IEEE 1988 International Conference on Neural Networks, pp. 109–116, July 1988. https://doi.org/10.1109/ICNN.1988.23838

15. Salakhutdinov, R., Hinton, G.: Deep Boltzmann machines. In: Artificial intelligence and statistics, pp. 448–455 (2009)

16. Salakhutdinov, R., Mnih, A., Hinton, G.: Restricted Boltzmann machines for collaborative filtering. In: Proceedings of the 24th International Conference on Machine Learning, ICML 2007, pp. 791–798. ACM, New York (2007). https://doi.org/10.1145/1273496.1273596

17. Schreiber, A., Bock, M.: Visualization and exploration of deep learning networks in 3D and virtual reality. In: Stephanidis, C. (ed.) HCII 2019. CCIS, vol. 1033, pp. 206–211. Springer, Cham (2019). https://doi.org/10.1007/978-3-030-23528-4_29

18. Strub, F., Gaudel, R., Mary, J.: Hybrid recommender system based on autoencoders. In: Proceedings of the 1st Workshop on Deep Learning for Recommender Systems, DLRS 2016, pp. 11–16. ACM, New York (2016). https://doi.org/10.1145/2988450.2988456

19. Thiagarajan, J.J., Kim, I., Anirudh, R., Bremer, P.: Understanding deep neural networks through input uncertainties. In: ICASSP 2019–2019 IEEE International Conference on Acoustics, Speech and Signal Processing (ICASSP), pp. 2812–2816, May 2019. https://doi.org/10.1109/ICASSP.2019.8682930

20. Upadhya, V., Sastry, P.S.: An overview of restricted Boltzmann machines. J. Indian Inst. Sci. 99(2), 225–236 (2019). https://doi.org/10.1007/s41745-019-0102-z

21. Wan, S., Niu, Z.: A hybrid e-learning recommendation approach based on learners' influence propagation. IEEE Trans. Knowl. Data Eng. 1 (2019). https://doi.org/10.1109/TKDE.2019.2895033

22. Zhang, S., Yao, L., Sun, A., Tay, Y.: Deep learning based recommender system: a survey and new perspectives. ACM Computing Surveys (CSUR) 52(1), 5 (2019)

Machine Learning Based Applications

Decision Tree Model Based Gene Selection and Classification for Breast Cancer Risk Prediction

Mohammed Hamim[1]([⊠])(iD), Ismail El Moudden[2](iD), Hicham Moutachaouik[1], and Mustapha Hain[1]

[1] I2SI2E Laboratory, ENSAM-Casablanca, University Hassan II, Casablanca, Morocco
mohamed.hamim@gmail.com, gotohicham@gmail.com, infohain@gmail.com
[2] EVMS-Sentara Healthcare Analytics and Delivery Science Institute, Eastern Virginia Medical School, Norfolk, VA, USA
elmouddenismail@gmail.com

Abstract. Breast cancer is considered the most frequently diagnosed cancer in worldwide women and ranked second after lung cancer. Early diagnosis of this cancer may increase the chance to get an early treatment, which can increase the chance of survival for women suffering from this disease. Recently, Microarray data technology has brought a great opportunity to make diagnose cancer faster and easy. However, the most common challenge of gene expression data is high dimensionality, i.e., thousands of genes, and a few tens of patients, which makes any prediction approach difficult to apply. To take this challenge, a C5.0 based feature selection approach is being proposed. The strongest point of our approach resides in the combination of two feature selection techniques: the fisher-score based filter method and the inner feature selection ability of C5.0. The classification algorithms used to assess our approach in terms of prediction accuracy are Artificial neural Networks, C5.0 Decision Tree, Logistic Regression, and Support Vector Machine. Compared to the state-of-the-art models, our approach can predict breast cancer with the highest accuracy based on a strict minimum of genes.

Keywords: Breast cancer · Gene selection · Cancer risk prediction · Microarray technology

1 Introduction

Recently, with increased life expectancy and increased unhealthy lifestyles, a significant breast cancer increase has observed in several countries and specifically in developed ones. Although it represents 25.1% of all types of cancers, breast cancer is considered as the first cancer type among women [2]. However, the detection at an early stage may reduce the risk and side effects of this disease. Hence, a breast cancer prediction system with high accuracy became a necessity

© Springer Nature Switzerland AG 2020
M. Hamlich et al. (Eds.): SADASC 2020, CCIS 1207, pp. 165–177, 2020.
https://doi.org/10.1007/978-3-030-45183-7_12

to fight this fatal disease. With the development of gene expression technology and machine learning methods, the idea of developing a breast cancer prediction model became more realistic than before. However, the presence of a huge number of genes in microarray datasets versus a small number of samples may affect the outcome of any cancer prediction model, which makes the concretization of this idea more difficult. Hence, reducing the original research space by selecting only the most relevant genes seems a great solution for improving the accuracy of any future cancer prediction system. Generally, feature selection is the process that aims at building a subset of the original features by keeping only features that contribute most in learning models [1]. There are too many gene selection methods. In terms of contribution in the context of breast cancer prediction, our study presents a new C5.0 based gene selection approach. The new approach combines the fisher-score based filter method and the inner feature selection ability of C5.0. The whole approach was combined with the classification process to improve breast cancer modeling.

The remainder of the present paper is structured as follows: In the next section, we briefly review previous work. Materials and methods are outlined in the third section. The experiment results are discussed in Sect. 4. In the final section, we draw a conclusion.

2   Related Works

S. Turgut et al. in their work, first, eight classifiers -Adaboost, Gradient Boosting Machines, k-Nearest Neighbors (KNN), Multilayer Perceptron (MLP), Support Vector Machine (SVM), Logistic Regression (LR), Decision Trees and Random Forest- are applied on breast cancer microarray data without any dimension reduction techniques. Then the same classifiers were applied after two genes selection techniques, Recursive Feature Elimination (RFE) and Randomized Logistic Regression (RLR). Without genes selection, the best classification accuracy of 67.42% was achieved by Random Forest, while after genes selection the highest accuracy of 88.82% with 50 selected genes was obtained by SVM [4].

Based on ensemble classifier Deep Neural Network (DNN) and SVM, Al-Quraishi et al. developed a breast cancer risk prediction model. First, the ensemble classifier was applied to data without any gene selection methods. Secondly, the Decision Tree algorithm (DT-FWD), Correlation-based filter method (FCBF), Symmetrical Uncertainty Criteria (SUC) and Regularized Random Forest algorithm (RRF) were used to select genes that are more representative before using the ensemble classifier. Experimental results show that the ensemble classifier DNN+SVM combined with FCBF achieved the highest accuracy of 96.11% with 112 genes [5].

Aldryan et al. have presented a new classification system using Modified Back-propagation with Conjugate Gradient Polak-Ribiere and Ant Colony Optimization (ACO) as a gene selector. All of the experiments and tests were conducted on 5 public microarray datasets (Breast cancer, Colon Tumor, Leukemia, Ovarian Cancer, and Lung Cancer). For Breast cancer, the experiment achieved an accuracy of 64.12% when involving only 10% of genes (2448 genes) [6].

Evaluated on 11 public cancer microarray datasets, Jain et al. have proposed two phases, hybrid model for gene selection and cancer classification. In the pre-filtering phase, the Correlation-based Feature Selection (CFS) method was used to eliminate redundant, irrelevant or noisy genes. Then, in gene optimization and cancer classification phase, improved-Binary Particle Swarm Optimization (iBPSO) uses genes retained by the previous phase to select the optimal subset of genes with the help of Naive-Bayes classifier. The study achieved 94% accuracy for Breast cancer dataset using an average of 32 genes as predictors [7].

Li et al. proposed a new version of SVM-RFE (SVM on Recursive Feature Elimination) method that overcomes the time consumption of old versions of the same approach (SVM-RFE) without degrading the feature selection quality. The proposed method was evaluated on six public gene expression datasets, and results show a comparable improvement in terms of time consumption and classification accuracy [8].

3   Materials and Methods

3.1   Description

A new model is proposed for improving breast cancer prediction performance (Fig. 1). The suggested model is based on feature selection using the Fisher score and C5.0 algorithm, and classification using ANN, C5.0, logistic regression and SVM algorithms.

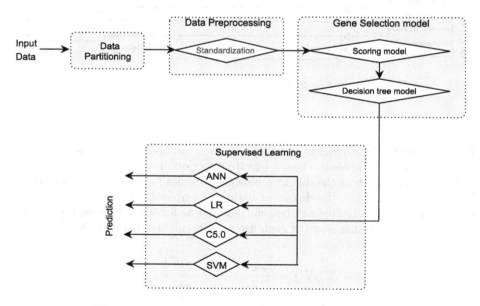

Fig. 1. Learned model for identifying predictive genes

3.2　Genes Selection Methods

Feature Selection is considered a powerful tool to reduced the data dimensionality in many research fields, especially when it comes to working with a huge number of variables (dimensions). In the context of genes expression data analysis, the presence of a small number of samples versus a huge number of genes may increase the time and space complexity when processing microarray data, which makes classification technics difficult. A more common technic to overcome this problem of curse of dimensionality is feature selection [3,9]. The main idea behind this technic is to reduce the dimensionality of input space by discarding any irrelevant or noisy genes from the original data. Feature selection problem can be reformulated as follows: from the input features $X = (X_1, X_2, .., X_k)$, find a subset $X_{sub} = (X_1, X_3, .., X_{p<k})$ while retaining only most relevant features (Fig. 2).

In the proposed approach, we implement two feature selection techniques, the fisher-score based filter method and the connate feature selection ability of the C5.0 algorithm.

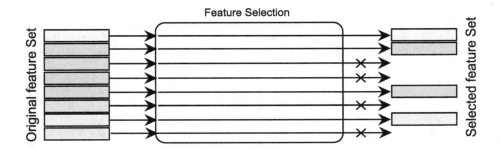

Fig. 2. Feature selection process

Fisher Score: Considered as a supervised filter method used in binary classification problems, fisher-score based feature selection aims at finding a subset of features (genes) such as the distance between samples for different classes are as large as possible, while the distances between samples in the same class are as small as possible [10]. This can be reformulated as follows: given an input data matrix, then the Fisher score of each feature j is calculated using Eq. (1).

$$F\left(X^j\right) = \frac{\sum_{k=1}^c \eta_k \left(\mu_k^j - \mu^j\right)^2}{\sum_{k=1}^c \eta_k \left(\sigma_k^j\right)^2} \tag{1}$$

With μ_k^j, σ_k^j the mean and standard deviation of k-th class, corresponding to the j-th feature. μ^j denotes the mean of the whole j-th feature in the X.

As the Fisher score of each feature(gene) is computed independently, from original genes, only 10% of the highest-ranked genes were selected to achieve the classification process.

C5.0 Decision Tree: The decision tree is a popular machine-learning algorithm used in classification for its high speed, high classification performance, and its efficiency when it comes to working on datasets with a large scale. Besides its ability in classification, decision tree is considered as an efficient feature selection algorithm [11–14]. As an improved version of C4.5, C5.0 Decision Tree algorithm is favored for its powerful boosting technique, can deal with missing data, its easy to understand, and manages efficiently memory use which makes it faster than the other machine learning algorithms in terms of time consumption [15]. In the present work, we take both advantages of C5.0, its ability as a powerful feature selection tool combined with the Fisher score, and as a classifier to achieve the classification phase in our framework.

In the context of gene selection using C5.0 Decision Tree, all genes were initially compared by using the following process: first of all, we set the pruning degree (Pruning is a technique that consists in reducing the size of decision trees by eliminating branches of the tree that provide little information which can reduce the complexity of classifier, thus improving classification performance) to 75% as default value to prevent overfitting. Then, the information gain ratios of each gene is calculated using the formula as follows [17]:

$$GainRatio(G) = \frac{Info(S) - Info(S/G)}{Split(G)}$$
$$= \frac{Equation\,(3) - Equation\,(4)}{Equation\,(5)} \qquad (2)$$

Where :

-$Info(S)$ is the Information Entropy which calculated as follows:

$$Info(S) = -\sum_{i=1}^{m} p_i log_2(p_i) \qquad (3)$$

$With$:

m	: Number of classes in the training set (in our case m $= 2$)
S	: denotes a given set of n samples ($|S| = n$)
$p_i = \frac{n_i}{|S|}$	(with n_i be the number of class C_i samples)

-$Info(S/G)$ denotes the Conditional Information Entropy which is defined as follows:

$$Info(S/G) = -\sum_{j=1}^{\nu} \frac{|S_j|}{|S|} \sum_{i=1}^{m} \frac{n_{ij}}{|S_j|} log_2(\frac{n_{ij}}{|S_j|}) \qquad (4)$$

Assuming that G divide the set S into ν subsets $(S_1, S_2, ..., S_\nu)$, then n_{ij} denotes the number of classes C_i samples in the subset S_j with $|S_j| = \sum_{i=1}^{m} n_{ij}$ and $|S| = n$.

And $Split(G)$ is defined as:

$$Split(G) = -\sum_{j=1}^{\nu} \frac{|S_j|}{|S|} log_2 (\frac{|S_j|}{|S|}) \tag{5}$$

The feature with the highest information gain ratio is voted to be the root node of the tree. Remained features are divided into branches by computing and assigning the highest information gain ratio to each branch node. The process continues until a predefined criterion is accomplished. As the tree was pruned, the optimal feature subset is determined [15, 17]

3.3   Classification Algorithms

In our study, we constructed our ensemble of classifiers by employing four machine learning algorithms namely the Regression Logistic (LR), C5.0 Decision Tree, Support Vector Machine (SVM) and Artificial Neural Network (ANN). We opted for the choice of these algorithms for their ability to improve the prediction performance in cancer microarray data classification analysis [3, 4, 8]. First, these machine learning algorithms were applied to the data without any feature selection techniques. Then the feature selection approach was applied. All results of the classifications are compared with each other and with the results obtained before and after using our new feature selection approach.

3.4   Artificial Neural Network

ANN is an artificial representation that attempts to simulate the biological neural systems of the human brain. Generally, an ANN is an interconnected group of a large number of processing nodes called artificial neuron [18]. As a family of pattern recognition algorithms, the ANN is characterized by its ability to learn by lots of examples, which make it suitable for cancer predicting using gene expression. Different architectures of ANN exist, the most commonly used, the multilayer perceptron (MLP). In the MLP architecture, the neurons (nodes) are arranged in at least three layers: an input layer, a hidden one, and an output one (Fig. 3). Except for the neurons in the input layer, each neuron uses a nonlinear activation function (usually logistic).

3.5   Logistic Regression

Logistic Regression (LR) is a probabilistic statistical machine learning technique that was used across different disciplines such as pattern recognition, biological research field, and social sciences [16]. Using the Eq. (6), the Logistic Regression

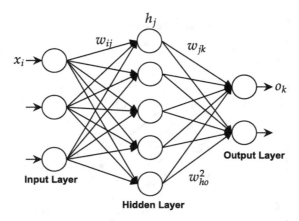

Fig. 3. Architecture of multi-layer perceptron (MLP) neural network

is a powerful extension of Linear one, which is used when it comes to dealing with a dichotomous dependent variable.

$$L(x) = \frac{1}{1 + e^{-y}} \quad with \ y = a_0 + a_1 x_1 + a_2 x_2 + \dots + a_n x_n \tag{6}$$

3.6 Support Vector Machine

Support Vector Machine (SVM) is a learning algorithm, allowing to learn a separator, it is a discriminating model which tries to minimize learning errors while maximizing the margin separating data from classes (Fig. 4). Maximizing the margin is a regularization method that reduces the complexity of the classifier. The SVM belongs to the category of linear classifiers (which use a linear separation of the data), and which has its own method to find the border between the categories. However, in a real classification context like ours, the research space is usually linearly non-separable. In the present paper a Gaussian kernel (Eq. (7)) was used to deal with the problem of non-linearity.

$$k(x_i, x_j) = \exp(-\gamma \parallel x_i - x_j \parallel^2) \qquad \gamma > 0 \tag{7}$$

Where :

d denotes the degree of the kernel, $\parallel x_i - x_j \parallel^2$ is the squared Euclidean distance, and γ represents parameter that sets the spread of the kernel.

3.7 C5.0 Decision Tree

C5.0 decision tree has become recently a powerful machine learning tool used in many research fields as it provides high classification accuracy [21–23]. As an extension developed from C4.5, the C5.0 draw its power by keeping all characteristics of C4.5 and introducing new technologies such as the purring technology, boosting, and cost-sensitive tree.

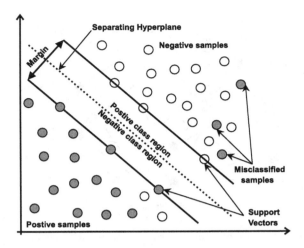

Fig. 4. Support Vector Machine (SVM) classifier

3.8 Performance Evaluation

Evaluating the performance of any learning algorithms is a crucial step in any prediction system. The most common metrics to evaluate the quality of the classification process is the confusion matrix (Fig. 5) which reports the results of prediction in terms of incorrectly and incorrectly classified samples for each class. However, all information reported in the confusion matrix about the outcome of the classifier is difficult to compare and discuss. To make reading confusion matrix easy, some common parameters calculated from it are used such as the accuracy (Eq. (8)).

		Predicted classes	
		Positives	**Negatives**
Observed classes	**Positives**	**TP** True Positive	**TN** True Negative
	Negatives	**FP** False Positive	**FN** False Negative

Fig. 5. Confusion matrix for binary classification

$$Accuracy = \frac{TP + TN}{TP + TN + FP + FN} \tag{8}$$

In the context of breast cancer prediction, the meaning of each values reported in the confusing matrix is as follow:

- **TP:** Represents the number of patients that have been diagnosed with cancer, and the model also predicted that they have cancer.
- **FP:** Represents the number of patients that the model predicted them with cancer, but in reality, they are not.
- **TN:** Represents the number of patients that are not diagnosed with cancer and also the model predicted them as healthy.
- **FN:** Represents the number of patients that are diagnosed with cancer but the model predicted them as healthy.

In the present work, the average accuracy of training and testing set (Eq. (9)) was used to evaluate the quality of our generated cancer prediction models.

$$Accuracy_{Mean} = \frac{Accuracy_{Train} + Accuracy_{Test}}{2} \tag{9}$$

4   Experimental Results and Discussion

4.1   Dataset Description

All experiments were conducted on publicly available microarray breast cancer gene expression data [19]. The dataset contains 24,481 gene expressions with 97 patients (samples). The 97 samples are divided into the training set and testing set. The training data contains 78 samples, 44 of which are healthy (labeled as non-relapse) and the rest are diagnosed with cancer (labeled as relapse). Consequently, there are 7 samples labeled non-relapse and 12 samples labeled as relapse in the testing set. Table 1 summarize data description.

Table 1. Microarray datasets characteristics

Dataset	Genes	Patterns	Classes	Missing values	Ref.
Breast cancer	24481	97	2	Yes	[19]

4.2   K-Fold Cross Validation

To ensure the credibility of our approach in terms of results, we adopted the K-Fold Cross Validation technique to split the data. This technique aims at limiting problems of overfitting and underfitting by splitting the entire data into k folds. Then the $k - 1$ folds are used to fit the model and the remaining K_{th} fold is used to validate the model. In this study, all the experiments were conducted using stratified 10-fold cross-validation. We have opted for 10 folds because it is a common choice in this research area and the stratified strategy to ensure that the proportions of instances in terms of classes are equal in both, the training set and testing set.

4.3 Data Preprocessing

In order to optimize classification results in terms of time cost and accuracy, a standardization phase was applied before any process step in our framework (Fig. 1). The standardization technique used in this paper aims at transforming normal variants to standard score form [20]. Given a set of features X, the standardization formula is defined as (Eq. (10)):

$$z_{ij} = \frac{x_{ij} - \mu^j}{\sigma^j} \tag{10}$$

With μ^j, σ^j denote the sample mean and standard deviation of the j-th feature. z_{ij}, x_{ij} denote the data point and z-score of j-th feature.

4.4 System Configuration

In order to test the performance of our proposed framework, we have implemented it in Python 3.7 programming language in Ubuntu 18.04.3 64bits running on a PC with system configuration Intel E5-2637 v2 3.5 GHz with 64 GB of RAM.

4.5 Results and Discussion

This section aims at evaluating the performance of new approach by examining the experimental results (Generated models) on the basis of three criteria: classification accuracy, the number of selected genes and consumption time.

To show to the power of our new model, first, we applied our proposed machine learning algorithms without applying any feature selection process, then we applied the feature selection approach and compared the experimental results. Table 2 shows the prediction accuracy without the proposed model (using full breast cancer gene expression dataset). As we can notice, the ANN exhibited a higher accuracy rate of 86.99%, while C5.0 shows the lowest accuracy rate of 79.01%.

Table 3, shows the proposed framework performance in terms of accuracy matched with the number of selected genes. As we can notice, the dimensionality of our research space (the number of genes) was reduced in two steps. First, the number of genes passed from p = 24481 genes to k = 2448 using the Fisher score based filter method - the new k represents 10% of the original number of genes (p) that have the highest score-. In the second step, the previously k selected genes was reduced for a second time using the inner feature selection ability of C5.0, and the k passed from 2448 genes to five genes (k' = 5). Thereafter, the new space of five predictors (genes) was used to construct four classifiers (SVM, LR, ANN, and C5.0). As result of our proposed approach, all generated shrinkage models produced high classification accuracy that exceeds 80%, which considered as higher than human experts. In addition to the high degree of dimensional reduction achieved by gene selection models, our proposed framework improved significantly the prediction accuracy when using SVM or C5.0 (Fig. 6).

As our aim is to find a prediction model that involves the strict minimum of predictors and classifies with high accuracy new observations, and regarding the results obtained by Table 3, the FC.0-C5.0 model can provides the highest accuracy of 93.28% by using only five genes, which can make our proposed model a more strong and accurate competitor than all what was reported in the related works.

Table 2. Prediction accuracy without using the feature selection approaches

Input data	Original genes number	Gene selection	Classification model	Time (s)	Accuracy (%)
Breast cancer	24481	Pristine	SVM	1	80.05
			LR	13	83.91
			ANN	42	86.99
			C5.0	25	79.01

Table 3. Performance measurement using Gene Selection models

Input data	Original genes number	Gene selection models		Selected genes	Classification model	Time (s)	Accuracy (%)
		Fisher score (F)	C5.0				
Breast cancer	$p =$ 24481	$k = 2448$	$k' = 5$	NM_3438, AL137615, NM_3477, Contig26768_, Contig55662_	FC5-SVM	31	85.4
					FC5-LR	31	81.78
					FC5-ANN	31	86.21
					FC5-C5.0	**31**	**93.28**

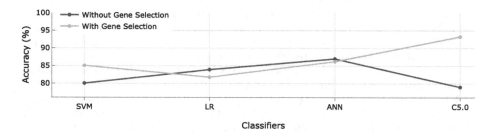

Fig. 6. Prediction accuracy using gene selection and using full genes

5 Conclusion and Future Work

To improve the prediction of breast cancer risk, the present paper proposed a two-phase model for gene selection and classification using gene expression data

The model combines two feature selection methods to improve classification performance, the Fisher score based filter method to reduce the dimension of our search space by eliminating irrelevant and noisy genes from the dataset, and C5.0 classifier to select an optimal subset of important genes. Four classifiers (C5.0, ANN, SVM, and LR) are combined with the gene selection process to classify each sample into binary classes (1, 0). Compared to the state-of-the-art, experimental results show that the proposed approach significantly reduced the dimensionality of research space (only five dimensions are retained instead of 24481), which can achieve a higher prediction accuracy that attains 93.28%. In our future work, we will attempt to test the ability of the proposed approach on new microarray datasets with different properties in terms of the number of genes, the number of samples, and the number of classes.

References

1. Antoniadis, A., Lambert-Lacroix, S., Leblanc, F.: Effective dimension reduction methods for tumor classification using gene expression data. Bioinformatics **19**(5), 563–570 (2003). https://doi.org/10.1093/bioinformatics/btg062
2. Ghoncheh, M., Pournamdar, Z., Salehiniya, H.: Incidence and mortality and epidemiology of breast cancer in the world. Asian Pac. J. Cancer Prev. **17**(sup3), 43–46 (2016). https://doi.org/10.7314/APJCP.2016.17.S3.43
3. Moutachaouik, H., El Moudden, I.: Mining prostate cancer behavior using parsimonious factors and shrinkage methods. SSRN J. (2018). https://doi.org/10.2139/ssrn.3180967
4. Turgut, S., Dagtekin, M., Ensari, T.: Microarray breast cancer data classification using machine learning methods. In: 2018 Electric Electronics, Computer Science, Biomedical Engineerings' Meeting (EBBT), Istanbul, pp. 1–3 (2018). https://doi.org/10.1109/EBBT.2018.8391468
5. Al-Quraishi, T., Abawajy, J.H., Al-Quraishi, N., Abdalrada, A., Al-Omairi, L.: Predicting breast cancer risk using subset of genes. In: 2019 6th International Conference on Control, Decision and Information Technologies (CoDIT), Paris, France, pp. 1379–1384 (2019). https://doi.org/10.1109/CoDIT.2019.8820378
6. Aldryan, D.P., Adiwijaya, Annisa, A.: Cancer detection based on microarray data classification with ant colony optimization and modified backpropagation conjugate gradient Polak-Ribiére. In: 2018 International Conference on Computer, Control, Informatics and its Applications (IC3INA), Tangerang, Indonesia, pp. 13–16 (2018). https://doi.org/10.1109/IC3INA.2018.8629506
7. Jain, I., Jain, V.K., Jain, R.: Correlation feature selection based improved-Binary Particle Swarm Optimization for gene selection and cancer classification. Appl. Soft Comput. **62**, 203–215 (2018). https://doi.org/10.1016/j.asoc.2017.09.038
8. Li, Z., Xie, W., Liu, T.: Efficient feature selection and classification for microarray data. PLoS ONE **13**(8), e0202167 (2018). https://doi.org/10.1371/journal.pone.0202167
9. El Moudden, I., Ouzir, M., ElBernoussi, S.: Feature selection and extraction for class prediction in dysphonia measures analysis: a case study on Parkinson's disease speech rehabilitation. THC **25**, 693–708 (2017)
10. Gu, Q., Li, Z., Han, J.: Generalized fisher score for feature selection. arXiv:1202.3725 (February 2012)

11. Wang, Y.Y., Li, J.: Feature-selection ability of the decision-tree algorithm and the impact of feature-selection/extraction on decision-tree results based on hyperspectral data. Int. J. Remote Sens. **29**(10), 2993–3010 (2008). https://doi.org/10.1080/01431160701442070

12. McIver, D.K., Friedl, M.A.: Using prior probabilities in decision-tree classification of remotely sensed data. Remote Sens. Environ. **81**(2–3), 253–261 (2002). https://doi.org/10.1016/S0034-4257(02)00003-2

13. Qi, Z., Yeh, A.G.-O., Li, X., Lin, Z.: A novel algorithm for land use and land cover classification using RADARSAT-2 polarimetric SAR data. Remote Sens. Environ. **118**, 21–39 (2012). https://doi.org/10.1016/j.rse.2011.11.001

14. Deng, L., Yan, Y., Wang, C.: Improved POLSAR image classification by the use of multi-feature combination. Remote Sens. **7**(4), 4157–4177 (2015). https://doi.org/10.3390/rs70404157

15. Revathy, R., Lawrance, R.: Comparative analysis of C4.5 and C5.0 algorithms on crop pest data. Int. J. Innov. Res. Comput. Commun. Eng. **5**, 2017 (2019)

16. Chen, M.-Y.: Predicting corporate financial distress based on integration of decision tree classification and logistic regression. Expert Syst. Appl. **38**, 11261–11272 (2011)

17. Pang, S., Gong, J.: C5.0 classification algorithm and application on individual credit evaluation of banks. Syst. Eng. - Theory Pract. **29**(12), 94–104 (2009). https://doi.org/10.1016/S1874-8651(10)60092-0

18. Rajasekaran, S., Pai, G.A.V.: Neural Network. Fuzzy Logic and Genetic Algorithms - Synthesis and Applications. Prentice-Hall, Upper Saddle River (2005)

19. van 't Veer, L.J., et al.: Gene expression profiling predicts clinical outcome of breast cancer. Nature **415**(6871), 530–536 (2002). https://doi.org/10.1038/415530a

20. Mohamad, I., Usman, D.: Standardization and its effects on k-means clustering algorithm (2013). https://doi.org/10.19026/rjaset.6.3638

21. Puspita Siknun, G., Sitanggang, I.: Web-based classification application for forest fire data using the shiny framework and the C5.0 algorithm. Procedia Environ. Sci. **33**, 332–339 (2016)

22. Bujlow, T., Riaz, T., Myrup Pedersen, J.: A method for classification of network traffic based on C5.0 machine learning algorithm (2012)

23. Ranjbar, S., Aghamohammadi, M., Haghjoo, F.: Determining wide area damping control signal (WADCS)based on C5.0 classifier (2016)

Dynamic Partitioning of Transportation Network Using Evolutionary Spectral Clustering

Pamela Al Alam[1,2]($\boxtimes$), Denis Hamad[1], Joseph Constantin[3], Ibtissam Constantin[3], and Youssef Zaatar[2]

[1] LISIC-ULCO, 50 rue Ferdinand Buisson, BP 699, 62228 Calais Cedex, France
pamela.al.alam@gmail.com
[2] Applied Physics Laboratory (LPA), Lebanese University, Campus Fanar, BP 90656, Jdeidet, Lebanon
[3] Research Laboratory in Networks, Computer Science and Security (LaRRIS), Lebanese University, Campus Fanar, BP 90656, Jdeidet, Lebanon

Abstract. Traffic congestion appears with different shapes and patterns that may evolve quickly over time. Static spectral clustering techniques are unable to manage these traffic variations. This paper proposes an evolutionary spectral clustering algorithm that partitions the time-varying heterogeneous network into connected homogeneous regions. The complexity of the algorithm is simplified by computing similarities in a way to obtain a sparse matrix. Next, the evolutionary spectral clustering algorithm is applied on roads speeds in order to obtain clusters results that fit the current traffic state while simultaneously not deviate from previous histories. Experimental results on real city traffic network architecture demonstrate the superiority of the proposed evolutionary spectral clustering algorithm in robustness and effectiveness when compared with the static clustering method.

Keywords: Dynamic transportation network · Evolutionary spectral clustering · Snakes similarities · Road-traffic congestion

1 Introduction

Road congestion problems have increased recently due to population growth and changes in population density. The traffic system is complex because traffic changes are uncertain [2]. Many approaches are taken into consideration such as the partitioning of roads according to traffic congestion in order to conceive strategies for resolving it. Partitioning a heterogeneous network into homogeneous zones can be extremely useful for traffic control considering the fact that

This work was funded in part by the University of the Littoral Opal Coast in France and the Agence Universitaire de la Francophonie with the National Council for Scientific Research in Lebanon through a doctoral fellowship grant under ARCUS E2D2 project. We would like to thank Clélia Lopez for her valuable help with the data sets.

M. Hamlich et al. (Eds.): SADASC 2020, CCIS 1207, pp. 178–186, 2020.
https://doi.org/10.1007/978-3-030-45183-7_13

the congestion is spatially correlated in adjacent roads and it is propagated with different speeds [8]. Spectral clustering algorithms have been successfully applied on the partitioning of transportation network based on the spatial features of congestion on specific times [11]. However, spectral clustering which is based on the use of an eigen-system resolution is not suited for large amount of data that change over time [13]. Incremental spectral clustering algorithms have been applied in dynamic environments to handle similarity changes among objects that evolve over time. However, the objective of these researches is to improve computation efficiency at the cost of lower cluster quality [6].

In this paper, we focus on how to obtain clusters that evolve smoothly over time, for partitioning an urban transportation network. In order to improve the network performance, the similarity matrix is computed in a way to put more weights on neighboring road segments in order to facilitate the connectivity of the clusters [7]. The similarity in this case will be a sparse matrix as some road segments have zero similarity which can simplify the complexity of the clustering algorithm. Next, an evolutionary spectral clustering algorithm is applied in the context of time varying road traffic. The preserving cluster quality and cluster membership concepts of the evolutionary spectral clustering algorithm are used in order to partition the road network smoothly and to fit the current traffic well while simultaneously not deviate too dramatically from previous history. Experimental results on a real transportation network of Amsterdam city [3] demonstrate the superiority of the proposed evolutionary spectral clustering algorithm in effectiveness and robustness compared with the static spectral clustering method in case of dynamic environment where the traffic data evolve over time. The paper is structured as follows: in Sect. 2, we introduce the spectral clustering algorithm and then describe how to design the snake similarity matrix to partition the transportation network, we also present the proposed evolutionary spectral clustering algorithm. Section 3 shows the experimental results and finally the paper is summarized with a conclusion in Sect. 4.

2   Methodology

Traffic data changes quickly, hence static spectral clustering algorithms are unable to deal with data where the characteristics of the roads speeds to be clustered change over time. We are interested to develop an algorithm to partition dynamically the traffic network into connected and homogeneous clusters. First, we present the static spectral clustering algorithm, then we derive the evolutionary spectral clustering frameworks through normalized cut.

2.1   Spectral Clustering

In order to apply spectral clustering, we need to convert the road network structure into a graph. A graph $G(V, E)$ is built in which $V = \{v_1, \ldots, v_N\} \in \mathbb{R}^N$ is the set of nodes, with N the number of nodes in the network, and E is the set of edges. The idea of spectral clustering is to partition the graph by minimizing the objective function which can be of type K-way normalized cut [9,10]. For a set of clustering results $C = \{C_1, \ldots, C_K\}$ such that $C = \cup_{k=1}^{K} C_k$, the K-way normalized cut (NC) is defined as follows:

$$NC = \sum_{k=1}^{K} \frac{cut(C_k, \overline{C_k})}{cut(C_k, V)} \tag{1}$$

where K is the number of clusters, $\overline{C_k} \subset V$ is defined as the complementary set of C_k. The cut-weight between 2 subsets C_k and $\overline{C_k}$ is defined as:

$$cut(C_k, \overline{C_k}) = \sum_{v_i \in C_k} \sum_{v_j \in \overline{C_k}} W(i, j) \tag{2}$$

where W is the similarity matrix. A partition can be expressed as an n-by-K cluster indicator matrix Z, with $Z(i, j) = 1$ if and only if the node i belongs to cluster j. We normalize Z by dividing the k-th column of Z by $\sqrt{|C_k|}$, where $|C_k|$ is the size of C_k. Finding the optimal partition Z for the normalized cut is NP-hard [10]. So a relaxed version of the optimization problem is solved by computing the eigenvectors of the Laplacian matrix based on the similarity matrix W, projecting the data points to $span(X)$ and applying the K-means algorithm to the projected data in order to obtain the clustering results. In this paper $span(X)$ is defined as the subspace spanned by the columns of X, and X is the matrix containing the top K-eigenvectors of the Laplacian matrix [12].

There are many proposed ways in the literature to construct the similarity matrix W, such as, the inner product of feature vectors, the Gaussian similarity and cosine similarity [10]. In our case study, we adopt the idea of snake similarity. In the context of road traffic, the design of the graph requires a special attention based on the idea of snake. A snake is represented by a node of the network and is defined as a sequence of roads segments where the vehicles have approximately the same speeds. The idea is therefore to calculate the similarity between pairs of nodes-snakes by considering the homogeneous neighboring segments in terms of speeds [3,7]. This similarity choice utilizes the fact that traffic jam has strong spatial correlation in transportation networks. Each sequence of road segments is called snake $S_i[L] = \{s_{i1}, \ldots s_{iL}\}$, where $s_{il} = \{identifier, speed\}$, with $1 \leq l \leq L$, and $L \leq N$ is the size of snake. A snake is built starting by a single road segment and grows by adding at each step the adjacent road segment which gives the closest variance value to the average value of previously added road segments in that sequence. Each snake only contains connected roads segments in the network which have a high degree of homogeneity. The neighborhood of a given snake is defined as the road segments spatially connected to it. The variance value of the snake at each step l can be computed by:

$$\sigma_l^2 = ((l - 1)\sigma_{l-1}^2 + (x_l - \overline{x}_l)(x_l - \overline{x}_{l-1}))/l \tag{3}$$

where $\bar{x}_l = ((l-1)\bar{x}_{l-1} + x_l)/l$ denotes the mean of the snake with size l and x_l is the speed of the road segment added in l-th step. After obtaining all snakes of the network, the snake similarity is defined as follows:

$$W(i,j) = \sum_{l=1}^{L} \phi^l \times card(S_i[l] \cap S_j[l]), \qquad i,j = 1,\ldots,N \qquad (4)$$

where $S_i[l]$ and $S_j[l]$ are l size snakes corresponding to road segments i and j and $card(S_i[l] \cap S_j[l])$ is the number of common road segments identifiers between the two snakes. The weight coefficient ϕ is assigned by the user, with $0 < \phi \leq 1$. As the size of the snake grows, the measure of similarity gives less weight on the road segments that are collected. In this case, we obtain a sparse similarity matrix.

2.2 Evolutionary Spectral Clustering

Spectral clustering approaches are usually static algorithms, and hence they need to be adapted in case of clustering traffic data that change over time. In order to solve this problem and obtain clusters that evolve smoothly over time, the current clusters should depend on both the current traffic features at time t and the previous traffic features at time $(t-1)$ [1].

In this section, we apply the two frameworks of evolutionary spectral clustering for the partitioning of dynamic transportation networks: the preserving cluster quality (PCQ) and the preserving cluster membership (PCM). Both frameworks propose to optimize a total cost function which is defined as a linear combination of a snapshot cost (SC) and a temporal cost (TC). In both frameworks, the snapshot cost (SC) refers to minimizing the K-way normalized cut (NC) at time t, however, they differ by how the temporal cost (TC) is defined.

Preserving Cluster Quality (PCQ): In this framework, the temporal cost refers to how well the current partition clusters data at time $(t-1)$. Consider that two partitions, Z_t and Z_t', cluster the data at time t equally well. However, to cluster historic data at time $(t-1)$, the clustering performance using partition Z_t is better than using Z_t'. In this case, partition Z_t is preferred over Z_t' because Z_t is more consistent with historic data. The total cost is defined by:

$$Cost = \alpha SC + (1-\alpha)TC = \alpha NC_t|_{Z_t} + (1-\alpha)NC_{(t-1)}|_{Z_t} \qquad (5)$$

where $|_{Z_t}$ means evaluated by the partition Z_t, $NC_t|_{Z_t}$ is the normalized cut value at time t under the partition Z_t which is called the snapshot cost, where a higher snapshot cost implies worse snapshot quality. $NC_{t-1}|_{Z_t}$ is the temporal cost, where a higher temporal cost implies worse temporal smoothness. The smoothness parameter $0 \leq \alpha \leq 1$ is assigned by the user, it reflects the user's emphasis on the current snapshot and the previous data matrix.

The PCQ clustering method consists to find the optimal solution that minimizes the total cost. This problem can be converted to a trace maximization, where the solution is the matrix X_t, such that $X_t^T X_t = I_k$, whose columns are the top K-eigenvectors associated with top K-eigenvalues of the evolutionary Laplacian matrix defined by the combination of both Laplacian matrices at time t and $(t-1)$ [1]:

$$L_{PCQ} = \alpha(D_t^{-1/2} W_t D_t^{-1/2}) + (1-\alpha)(D_{t-1}^{-1/2} W_{t-1} D_{t-1}^{-1/2}) \tag{6}$$

where D is a diagonal matrix with $D(i,j) = \sum_{j=1}^{n} W(i,j)$.

Preserving Cluster Membership (PCM): In this framework, the temporal cost (TC) is expressed as the difference between the clustering result at time t and the clustering result at time $(t-1)$. Consider that two partitions, Z_t and Z_t', cluster the data at time t equally well. However, when compared with the historic partition $Z_{(t-1)}$, Z_t is preferred because it's more similar to $Z_{(t-1)}$ than Z_t', so we can say it is more consistent with historic partition. The total cost is defined by:

$$Cost = \alpha SC + (1-\alpha)TC = \alpha NC_t|_{Z_t} + (1-\alpha)P_{(t-1)} \tag{7}$$

where, $NC_t|_{Z_t}$ is the snapshot cost and $P_{(t-1)} = \frac{1}{2} \left\| X_t X_t^T - X_{t-1} X_{t-1}^T \right\|^2$ is the temporal cost.

The PCM clustering method consists to find the optimal solution that minimizes the total cost. This problem can be converted to a trace maximization, where the solution is the matrix X_t whose columns are the top K-eigenvectors associated with top K-eigenvalues of the evolutionary Laplacian matrix defined by [1]:

$$L_{PCM} = \alpha(D_t^{-1/2} W_t D_t^{-1/2}) + (1-\alpha)(X_{t-1} X_{t-1}^T) \tag{8}$$

In both frameworks, the final clusters can be attained by projecting data into $span(X_t)$ and then apply the k-means algorithm to obtain the final clusters.

3   Experimental Results

In order to perform network partitioning, both the network topology and the road segment speeds for all time periods are needed. However, real data are often incomplete, especially data collected by classic urban measurements. Therefore, data preparation is needed to create a validated data set for partitioning. Real data gathered from the Amsterdam urban area were used [3]. The Amsterdam network has been simplified and reduced to about 208 road segments. The speeds of roads segments were estimated from the individual travel times [4]. The mean speed information is available every period of 10 min between 7 A.M and 3 P.M for all 208 road segments during 35 days. In this case, for every day, we have a 48 time periods [3]. This study focuses on only 1 day of data, and it is considered to be a weekday. We fix the number of clusters to $K = 2$ in order to differ between crowded and not crowded road segments. In our experiments, we compare both frameworks of evolutionary spectral clustering algorithms with the normalized spectral clustering algorithm [5], which we named IND, it independently partitions the speeds of road segments only at current time step t and ignores all historic information before t. For a fair comparison, we use the NC cost defined for the spectral clustering problem as the measure of performance, where a smaller value means a better result.

In the first experiment, we show that the evolutionary frameworks are able to control the swap between the snapshot quality and the temporal smoothness. Figures (1a–1b) present the average snapshot cost and the temporal cost for the 48 time periods under different values of the parameter α. We change the value of α from 0 to 1 with a step of 0.1. As expected, when the value of α increases, we get a better snapshot quality at the price of worse temporal smoothness. In the upcoming experiments, we chose a value of $\alpha = 0.7$ in order to emphasize more on the snapshot cost but still consider at same time the temporal cost. In the second experiment, we consider the time periods from 1 through 48 and we evaluate all costs for all three methods. For all costs, a lower value means better result. In Figs. 2a–2b, we report the SC and TC. As can be seen, the IND method gives a low snapshot cost with higher temporal cost. In comparison, both PCQ and PCM frameworks give a low temporal cost and an increase in snapshot cost over IND. Figure 2c shows that the PCQ framework assures the best performance in minimizing the total cost and the PCM framework improves over the IND method. In order to show the performance and the smoothness of the evolution-

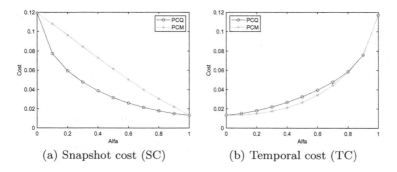

(a) Snapshot cost (SC)   (b) Temporal cost (TC)

Fig. 1. The performance of (a) snapshot cost and (b) temporal cost

ary spectral clustering algorithm in separating homogeneous connected clusters that fit the current data while simultaneously not deviate from previous history, we plot in the third experiment the partitioning results for all three methods. Figure 3 illustrates the partitioning results of 4 consecutive time periods from $t = 7$ through $t = 10$ which correspond to day hours from 8:00–8:30 A.M. one of the peak times of a weekday. Figures (3a–3d), (3e–3h) and (3i–3l) illustrate the clustering results of IND, PCM and PCQ frameworks, respectively. In these figures, a bold color for any road segment indicates its deviation from one cluster to another. We obtain the same clustering results for all the three methods

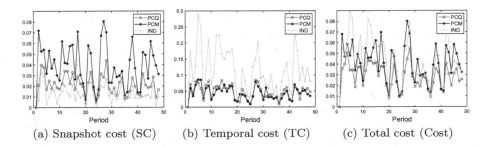

(a) Snapshot cost (SC)   (b) Temporal cost (TC)   (c) Total cost (Cost)

Fig. 2. The performance on Amsterdam traffic data

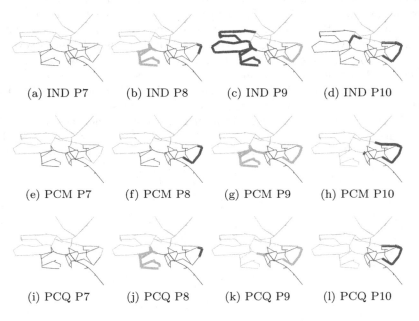

(a) IND P7   (b) IND P8   (c) IND P9   (d) IND P10

(e) PCM P7   (f) PCM P8   (g) PCM P9   (h) PCM P10

(i) PCQ P7   (j) PCQ P8   (k) PCQ P9   (l) PCQ P10

Fig. 3. Clustering results for periods 7 to 10 with K = 2 for IND, PCM and PCQ frameworks

during the first period. We can see that from periods $t = 8$ through $t = 10$ for IND method, the number of road segments in a cluster is changing rapidly and inconsistently. On the other hand, the number of road segments in PCM and PCQ frameworks is more stable when compared with historic data. The results depicted in Table 1 gives an example of the corresponding average speed value for each partition and the normalized total variance (TV_n) for period $t = 10$ for the three methods. The TV_n evaluation metric is used to evaluate the performance of the algorithm and the homogeneity of the clusters [8]. It is defined as:

$$TV_n = \frac{\sum_{k=1}^{K} N_k \times var(C_k)}{N \times var(C)} \tag{9}$$

where N_k is the number of road segments in cluster C_k. It is based on the assumption that a given cluster is composed of road segments with similar speeds. A small TV_n value implies an improvement gained by partitioning. It is obvious that the average speed between the partitions is dissimilar for all three methods with a little improvement for the PCQ framework over PCM. The PCQ and PCM frameworks have lower values for (TV_n), which means that the intra-cluster similarity is better than the IND method.

In addition, we tested the average run-time in seconds over 48 periods for both of the evolutionary spectral clustering frameworks and the normalized spectral clustering (IND). These algorithms are implemented in Matlab and experiments were conducted on Intel Core i7 PC with 2 Intel CPUs at 2.80 GHZ and 16 GB of RAM. The average run-time is equal to 0.020 for the IND method and 0.013 for both PCM and PCQ frameworks. We find that the PCM and the PCQ frameworks assure a better performance in time complexity than IND method. It is shown that the required run-time for the two evolutionary spectral clustering frameworks is small, so they can be used to make online decisions. These experiments also demonstrate that compared with the static clustering method (IND), our algorithms provide clustering results that are more stable, consistent and robust because it takes historic information into account.

Table 1. Average speed values of road segments and the TV_n for the period t = 10.

Method	Blue cluster	Red cluster	TV_n
IND	10.3	7.8	0.9
PCM	9.8	7.2	0.8
PCQ	10.0	7.2	0.8

4 Conclusion

The goal of our study was to partition a transportation network when road segments speeds evolve over time using the evolutionary spectral clustering. Two frameworks of evolutionary spectral clustering are presented to partition the network. In the first framework, the temporal cost is expressed as how well the current partition clusters historic variation of road segments speed. In the second framework, the temporal cost is expressed as the difference between the current partition and the historic one. In both frameworks, a cost function is defined in order to regularize the temporal smoothness. Experimental studies demonstrate that these two frameworks provide results that are stable and consistent in case of clustering dynamic transportation network where traffic can change over time. Future work will investigate a way to optimize the run-time of the two frameworks of evolutionary spectral clustering. In this case, a real proof based on run-time can be performed between the evolutionary spectral clustering frameworks and other static clustering methods.

References

1. Chi, Y., Song, X., Zhou, D., Hino, K., Tseng, B.L.: Evolutionary spectral clustering by incorporating temporal smoothness. In: Proceedings of the 13th ACM SIGKDD International Conference on Knowledge Discovery and Data Mining, pp. 153–162. ACM (2007)
2. Li, R., et al.: Crowded urban traffic: co-evolution among land development, population, roads and vehicle ownership. Nonlinear Dyn. **95**(4), 2783–2795 (2019). https://doi.org/10.1007/s11071-018-4722-z
3. Lopez, C., Krishnakumari, P., Leclercq, L., Chiabaut, N., Van Lint, H.: Spatiotemporal partitioning of transportation network using travel time data. Transp. Res. Rec. **2623**(1), 98–107 (2017)
4. Lopez, C., Leclercq, L., Krishnakumari, P., Chiabaut, N., Van Lint, H.: Revealing the day-to-day regularity of urban congestion patterns with 3D speed maps. Sci. Rep. **7**(1), 1–11 (2017)
5. Ng, A.Y., Jordan, M.I., Weiss, Y.: On spectral clustering: analysis and an algorithm. In: Advances in Neural Information Processing Systems, pp. 849–856 (2002)
6. Ning, H., Xu, W., Chi, Y., Gong, Y., Huang, T.: Incremental spectral clustering with application to monitoring of evolving blog communities. In: Proceedings of the 2007 SIAM International Conference on Data Mining, pp. 261–272. SIAM (2007)
7. Saeedmanesh, M., Geroliminis, N.: Clustering of heterogeneous networks with directional flows based on "snake" similarities. Transp. Res. Part B: Methodol. **91**, 250–269 (2016)
8. Saeedmanesh, M., Geroliminis, N.: Dynamic clustering and propagation of congestion in heterogeneously congested urban traffic networks. Transp. Res. Procedia **23**, 962–979 (2017)
9. Shi, J., Malik, J.: Normalized cuts and image segmentation. IEEE Trans. Pattern Anal. Mach. Intell. **22**(8), 888–905 (2000)
10. Von Luxburg, U.: A tutorial on spectral clustering. Stat. Comput. **17**(4), 395–416 (2007)
11. Yang, S., Wu, J., Qi, G., Tian, K.: Analysis of traffic state variation patterns for urban road network based on spectral clustering. Adv. Mech. Eng. **9**(9) (2017). https://doi.org/10.1177/1687814017723790
12. Zaki, M.J., Meira Jr., W., Meira, W.: Data Mining and Analysis: Fundamental Concepts and Algorithms. Cambridge University Press, Cambridge (2014)
13. Zhao, Y., Yuan, Y., Nie, F., Wang, Q.: Spectral clustering based on iterative optimization for large-scale and high-dimensional data. Neurocomputing **318**, 227–235 (2018)

Towards a Feature Selection
for Multi-label Text Classification
in Big Data

Houda Amazal$^{(\boxtimes)}$, Mohammed Ramdani, and Mohamed Kissi

Laboratoire Informatique de Mohammedia, Faculty of Sciences and Technologies,
Hassan II University of Casablanca, BP 146, 20650 Mohammedia, Morocco
houda.kamouss@gmail.com, ramdani@fstm.ac.ma, mohamed.kissi@univh2c.ma

Abstract. Feature selection is an important task in machine learning.
It can improve classification accuracy and effectively reduce the dataset
dimensionality by removing no discriminative features. Though a large
body of researches were focused on feature selection for text classification, few works addressed the problem for multi-label data in big data
context. Therefore, this paper proposes a distributed feature selection
approach for multi-label textual big data based on the weighted chi-
square method. First, a standard multi-label approach to transform the
multi-label data into single-label data is applied. Then, the algorithm
assigns different weights to the features based on the category term frequency and then calculates the chi-square based on the weight of each
feature. The proposed method is implemented on Hadoop framework
using MapReduce programming model. At last, a set of experiments
were conducted on three benchmarking text datasets to evaluate the
effectiveness of the proposed approach. A comparative analysis of the
results with the state-of-the-art techniques proves that our method is
efficient, robust and scalable.

Keywords: Chi-square · Feature selection · Hadoop · MapReduce ·
Multi-label · Text classification

1 Introduction

Text classification is an essential process in machine learning which aims to
assign a text document to one or multiple predefined categories, according to
its content. This process includes single-label text classification and multi-label
text classification. In single-label text classification a text is associated with one
predefined topic and assigned to only one category [17,24], while in multi-label
text classification, a text document is associated with multiple predefined topics
and assigned to multiple categories [7]. For example, a news document can be
classified under various labels like "movie", "music", and others. Also, an article
about computers may be assigned to the topics of "computers" and "software

© Springer Nature Switzerland AG 2020
M. Hamlich et al. (Eds.): SADASC 2020, CCIS 1207, pp. 187–199, 2020.
https://doi.org/10.1007/978-3-030-45183-7_14

engineering". In the real world, it is very common for a text to be associated with multiple topics, so it is more adequate to study multi-label text classification.

Feature selection is a fundamental step in multi-label text classification which reduces the feature space dimensionality and improves performance of the classifiers. It removes irrelevant features and only keeps the features with robust category discrimination ability to construct the feature subset [16]. Filter methods are a type of feature selection techniques. Because of their simplicity, lower computational complexity and promising score [12], filter methods are usually suitable. Besides, they require a statistical analysis on a feature set without applying any learning algorithm.

The Term Frequency (TF) [1] and chi-square (CHI) [23] are two commonly used filter methods. However, the selected features using TF do not automatically have strong category discrimination ability. For instance, assume that the feature "science" appears often in the whole training set, so using the TF method, "science" is considered as a relevant feature. However, such feature may have the same TF score in each category of the training set, so it does not have category discrimination ability indeed. On the other hand, assume that for a specific category, the feature "science" appears frequently in some documents and disappears in others, this feature could be discarded by the CHI method since it only considers whether the feature occurs or not and does not take into account the feature distribution. Thus, to select the most discriminative features, the importance of features should be evaluated taking into consideration two aspects; namely the frequency of features as well their correlation with categories.

Therefore, in this paper we propose a weighted CHI feature selection approach which is called distributed category term frequency based on chi-square (CTF-CHI). The contributions of features to category discrimination are calculated from the aforementioned two aspects, and the relevance of the features is achieved with the combination of them. In addition, since distributed platforms such as Hadoop implement only a few feature selection techniques and still lack improved ones, especially for multi-label data, we have implemented the proposed method manually using MapReduce.

In this paper, we propose a parallel filter feature selection method for multi-label text. Firstly, multi-label documents are transformed into single-label documents using the Label Powerset method. Next, the importance of each feature is calculated using the proposed method CTF-CHI. Then, features with higher ranks value are selected to construct the feature space. Finally, we lead experimental verification with parallel Naïve Bayes classifier on three datasets.

The rest of this paper is organized as follows: in Sect. 2, we briefly describe related work about FS techniques, then we introduce some preliminaries in Sect. 3; In Sect. 4, we propose our approach with category term frequency and chi-square; In Sect. 5, we report the experiments and conclude this paper with future work in Sect. 6.

2 Related Work

The aim of feature selection is to reduce dimensionality of the feature space and enhance the efficiency and performance of the classifiers by removing irrelevant and redundant features. The filter-based feature selection methods are widely used due to their efficiency and low computational complexity. Consequently, many scholars were focused on the research of this type of methods. This section presents some related works addressed for multi-label data.

In [14], authors focused on the feature importance calculation based on mutual information method and introduced a multi-label feature selection method. To assess the effectiveness of the proposed method five text data sets were used. In [5], authors designed a pruned problem transformation (PPT) method based on mutual information, called PPT-MI, converting multi-label data into single-label data. In [26], authors introduced a transformation method which uses the definition of ranking loss for multi-label feature selection. Four text datasets were used to evaluate the performance of the proposed method. In [29], authors proposed a feature selection for multi-label text based on feature importance. In this method, the label assignment method is used to transform the multi-label texts into single-label texts then category contribution (CC) is used to calculate the importance of each feature. In [3], authors presented a transformation method based on entropy and made the application of classical feature selection techniques to the multi-label text classification problem. In [13], authors introduced a feature selection approach for multilabel dataset based on kernelized fuzzy rough sets. To construct a robust multi-label kernelized fuzzy rough set model and achieve the lower approximation, they used a linear combination between kernelized information from the feature space and label space. In [8], authors presented a feature selection method for multi-label dataset called manifold based constraint Laplacian score (MCLS), which uses manifold learning to transform logical label space to Euclidean label space, where the corresponding numerical labels make the similarity between instances. In [21], authors presented four multi-label feature selection methods by combining two transformation methods and two feature importance calculation methods, and evaluated their performance on datasets of many fields, including the field of text. In [22], authors presented a multi-label feature selection method based on mutual information and label correlation. In [11], authors introduced a feature selection method for multi-label data based on the Pareto-dominance concept. They used non-dominating sorting to find the front number of each feature and then used a clustering approach to ponder the distribution of features. In [28], authors proposed a multi-label feature selection method with manifold regularization (MDFS). They evaluated the correlation of the features with labels locally and used objective function involving norm regularization. In [30], authors presented a multi-label feature selection based on label redundancy, called LRFS, which classified labels into independent labels and dependent labels and analyzed the differences between independent labels and dependent labels. In [6], authors proposed two different distributed feature selection methods for multi-label classification based on the vectorized form between a feature and a label set and study how to aggregate the mutual information of multiple labels.

Though many works, recently, were focused on feature selection for multi-label datasets, rare works were addressed for distributed computing environments such as Hadoop to manage large-scale data effectively and efficiently.

3   Preliminaries

This section introduces briefly the preliminaries which will be used throughout this work, including the Label Powerset method, feature selection methods, and the MapReduce paradigm programming.

In the following, let D denote a dataset composed of N instances (documents) $I_i = (d_i, L_i), i = 1..N$. Each instance I_i is associated with a feature space vector $d_i = (t_{i1}, t_{i2}, .., t_{iM})$ described by M features, and a subset of labels $L_i \subseteq L$, where $L = l_1, l_2, .., l_q$ is the set of q labels. In this scenario, the multi-label task consists in generating a classifier H which, given an unseen instance $I_x = (d_x, L_x)$, is capable of accurately predicting its subset of labels L_x.

3.1   Multi-label Learning

Multi-label learning methods are mainly organized into two main categories: algorithm adaptation and problem transformation [25]. The first category consists of methods which extend specific learning algorithms in order to handle multi-label data directly. The second category is algorithm independent, allowing the use of any state of the art single-label learning algorithm. It consists of methods which transform the multi-label classification problem into either several binary classification problems, such as the Binary Relevance approach, or one multi-class classification problem, such as the Label Powerset approach.

The simplest transformation method is the Binary Relevance (BR) whose idea is to learn a separate classification model for each label [15]. Said otherwise, there are as many prediction models as the maximum number of possible labels; each model decides whether or not a point belongs to a specific class independently of the result of the other classifiers. The final label set is obtained by combining the decisions of all classifiers. The BR approach does not take into account the possible dependence that could exist between the labels, since the decision for each class is made separately. To address this problem, Label Powerset (LP) approach considers each unique combination of labels in a training set as a label for a single-label classifier [4]. In this approach each distinct combination of labels present in training dataset is considered as different class then single label classification is performed on the transformed dataset [15]. Unlike BR, LP takes into account correlation between labels. In this work the LP method is used.

3.2 Chi-square

Text documents generally contains hundreds or thousands of features, however many of them are considered as noisy which influences negatively the performance of classifier. This makes the high dimensionality of feature space the major challenge of text classification, independently of any classifier. Therefore, feature selection must be used as a preprocessing phase to eliminate noisy and less informative features, so as to reduce the feature space to a manageable level and consequently improve the efficiency and accuracy of the classifiers used. Chi-square is one of the most efficient and widely used filter feature selection methods [20]. It is used to measure the degree of dependency between a feature t_i and a category labelled l_j. It is defined to be:

$$\chi^2(t_i, l_j) = \frac{N \times (ad - bc)^2}{(a + c) \times (b + d) \times (a + b) \times (c + d)} \tag{1}$$

where a is the number of documents such as t_i and l_j co-occurs, b is the number of documents such as t_i occurs without l_j, c is the number of documents such as l_j occurs without t_i, d is the number of documents such as neither t_i or l_j occurs, and N is the total number of documents and is the sum of a, b, c, and d.

3.3 MapReduce

MapReduce is a programming model for processing large datasets on a cluster of machines using a distributed and parallel algorithm [2]. It enables the specific application to run in parallel so that the task is accomplished in less period of time. A MapReduce program is achieved using two main phases, the map and reduce. The two phases operate on sets of key-value pairs (k,v). First, the input data are introduced to the Map phase which produces a set of records in the form of intermediate key-value pairs (k',v'). Then, the framework aggregate these intermediate key-value pairs by intermediate key k' and calls the reduce function for each group. Finally, the reduce phase produces another set of key-value pairs, as final output. In our approach, the implementation of the training phase using MapReduce includes the category term frequency and the chi-square method, and the implementation of the testing phase includes Naïve Bayes classifier.

4 Proposed Approach

In this section, we introduce our proposed approach for large dataset multi-label feature selection.

4.1 Description

First, the multi-label problem is transformed into single-label classification problem using the Label Powerset method introduced in Sect. 3. Then, the preprocessing step is applied including removing stop words, tokenization and stemming. Next, documents are represented using the vector space model (VSM)

[27], and documents associated to each one of the new categories generated by the transformation method are merged into one big document. Therefore, each new category will be represented using a single document. Thus, a new scheme of chi-square method is proposed and combined with category term frequency to select the most relevant features. Finally, the Multinomial Naïve Bayes (MNB) classifier is used to evaluate the efficiency of the selected subsets. To ensure the scalability and the efficiency of the proposed method, the proposal is implemented on Hadoop framework using MapReduce programming. Figure 1 presents a graphical abstract of the proposed system.

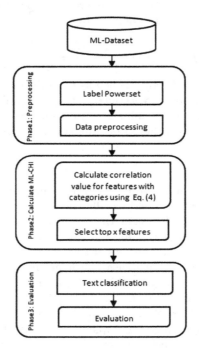

Fig. 1. Flowchart of the proposed method

4.2   CTF-CHI

The chi-square (CHI) method has two major drawbacks. First, it is a document frequency-based feature selection method. Effectively, it only focuses on the presence or absence of the term in the document and ignores the importance of the term frequency leading to exaggerate the role of the low-frequency term in a dataset. Second, CHI ignores the term distribution among documents. To deal with these drawbacks, in this work we propose to represent each category with only one documents. This can be applied in Hadoop environment because of its

HDFS system (Hadoop Distributed File System). Practically, all documents of each category will be merged in only one big document. Therefore, there is no document frequency to calculate, as well the frequencies of terms will be more important. Consequently, as each category l_k is represented using only one document, a term t_i can not be present and absent simultaneously in a specific category (document). Thus:

$if\ t_i \in l_k, then\ a = 1\ and\ c = 0$ and the chi-square value can be calculated as follows:

$$\chi^2(t_i, l_k) = \frac{N_y \times d}{(b+d) \times (1+b)} \tag{2}$$

$if\ t_i \notin l_k, then\ a = 0\ and\ c = 1$ and the chi-square value can be calculated as follows:

$$\chi^2(t_i, l_k) = \frac{N_y \times b}{(b+d) \times (1+d)} \tag{3}$$

where N_y is the number of categories generated after transformation method.

Finally, we give our approach based on the category term frequency to calculate the value in category l_k as follows:

$$CTF - CHI(t_i, l_k) = \log(1 + tf_i) \times \chi^2(t_i, l_k) \tag{4}$$

In the $CTF - CHI(t_i, l_k)$ we use logarithmic function to smooth the effect of the category term frequency tf_i then based on the basic theory of chi-square, the greater the value of CHI, the more category information the feature owns. In addition, since the higher value of a term in a special category, the more discriminative the term owns for this category, the proposed method gives high scores to most distinguishing features. Next, we rank features in descending order values of all terms and select x terms with maximum values.

5   Experiments and Results

The proposed CFT-CHI method was implemented manually on Hadoop framework using MapReduce programming model. The Label Powerset method is used to transform the multi-label classification problem into multiclass classification problem. All Documents of each new generated categories are merged into one big document.

5.1   Datasets

Three benchmark datasets were used to evaluate the performance of the proposed method. The first dataset is the top-10 categories of medical abstracts from U.S National Library of Medicine, named Ohsumed [10]. The second dataset is the top-10 categories of Reuters-21578 which consists of stories collected from the Reuters news [9]. The third dataset is Enron dataset which contains emails generated by employees of the Enron Corporation. In this work we use the top-20 categories from Enron as introduced by [18]. More detailed description of these datasets is presented in Table 1.

Table 1. Description of the datasets used in the experiments

Dataset	Domain	Num. of docs.	Num. of labels
Reuters 21578	News articles	9980	10
Ohsumed	Medical documents	16062	10
Enron	E-mails	18194	20

5.2   Evaluation Measures

In order to evaluate the performance for multi-label feature selection, two standard measures were used, namely the macro-F1 and micro-F1 [19]. In macro-F1, F-measure is calculated for each category within the dataset and then the average over all classes is obtained. Hence, the same weight is assigned to each category without regarding the class frequency. The macro-F1 can be formulated as:

$$Macro - F1 = \frac{\Sigma_{k=1}^{c} F_k}{C}, F_k = \frac{2 \times p_k \times r_k}{p_k + r_k}, \tag{5}$$

where couple of (p_k, r_k) corresponds to precision and recall values of class k, respectively. On the other hand, in micro-F1, F-measure is computed globally without class discrimination. In this way, all classification decisions in the whole dataset are considered. In case that the classes in a dataset are biased, large classes would dominate small ones in micro-averaging. The micro-F1 can be formulated as:

$$Micro - F1 = \frac{2 \times p \times r}{p + r}, \tag{6}$$

where pair of (p, r) represents the precision and recall values, respectively, over all the classification decisions within the whole dataset.

5.3   Results and Discussion

In this section, we perform experiments to investigate the influence of transforming individual documents into big documents, using Hadoop environment, on the performance. Also, we compare our method (CTF-CHI) with baseline filter methods including classical CHI, TFIDF, MI and IG using MNB classifier.

Table 2 presents the precision values for the fifth methods. The best performances are presented in bold. From the results it can be seen that generally, for the three datasets, the proposed method outperforms others when different numbers of features are selected. The results show that CTF-CHI obtains the highest precision value when 3500 features are selected from Reuters and Ohsumed datasets. In the case of Enron, the best result of precision is obtained for 3000 selected features. Moreover, it is shown that CTF-CHI results in the highest precision value for 83% of the trials. It can also be noted that the highest precision value (0,90) is performed when 3500 features are selected from Ohsumed dataset.

Table 2. The precision values of CTF-CHI compared to CHI, TFIDF, MI and IG methods using MNB classifier.

Dataset	Method	Number of features							
		500	1000	1500	2000	2500	3000	3500	4000
Reuters-12578	CTF-CHI	0.4167	0.5803	**0.7925**	**0.8025**	**0.8535**	**0.8652**	**0.8894**	**0.8652**
	CHI	0.4222	0.5401	0.7856	0.7364	0.8441	0.8377	0.8324	0.8494
	TFIDF	0.4382	0.5241	0.6681	0.7492	0.8164	0.8146	0.8125	0.8241
	MI	0.3634	0.5695	0.6329	0.7059	0.7881	0.8102	0.8109	0.8013
	IG	**0.4641**	**0.6487**	0.7108	0.7673	0.8110	0.8096	0.7963	0.7918
Ohsumed	CTF-CHI	0.4272	**0.7351**	**0.7693**	**0.8536**	**0.8691**	**0.8904**	**0.9042**	**0.8647**
	CHI	**0.5479**	0.6486	0.7517	0.7679	0.8150	0.8226	0.8425	0.8501
	TFIDF	0.4712	0.5776	0.6956	0.6862	0.7081	0.6989	0.7063	0.7127
	MI	0.4258	0.5003	0.5517	0.6045	0.6127	0.6224	0.6499	0.6743
	IG	0.3808	0.4772	0.5427	0.5880	0.6217	0.6289	0.6006	0.6034
Enron	CTF-CHI	0.2837	**0.5554**	**0.6302**	**0.6802**	**0.7347**	**0.7543**	**0.6983**	**0.6358**
	CHI	**0.2969**	0.4289	0.6227	0.6240	0.5901	0.6237	0.5771	0.5488
	TFIDF	0.2602	0.3571	0.5406	0.4776	0.5058	0.4760	0.5198	0.5460
	MI	0.2381	0.3282	0.4390	0.42985	0.4449	0.4309	0.4392	0.4765
	IG	0.2325	0.3448	0.3581	0.3684	0.4311	0.4498	0.3894	0.4249

The proposed CTF-CHI is also compared to other methods in term of recall measure as shown in Table 3.

Table 3. The recall values of CTF-CHI compared to CHI, TFIDF, MI and IG methods using MNB classifier.

Dataset	Method	Number of features							
		500	1000	1500	2000	2500	3000	3500	4000
Reuters-12578	CTF-CHI	0.3458	0.4273	**0.4821**	0.5387	**0.6218**	**0.6732**	**0.7423**	**0.7381**
	CHI	**0.3773**	**0.4466**	0.4763	**0.5452**	0.5940	0.6232	0.6533	0.7336
	TFIDF	0.3449	0.3723	0.4188	0.4580	0.5187	0.5251	0.5557	0.5734
	MI	0.3294	0.3399	0.3964	0.4393	0.4849	0.5109	0.5342	0.5370
	IG	0.3353	0.3449	0.3814	0.4243	0.4571	0.4904	0.5087	0.4950
Ohsumed	CTF-CHI	0.3692	**0.6738**	**0.7825**	**0.8352**	**0.8645**	**0.8821**	**0.8572**	0.8346
	CHI	**0.4592**	0.6322	0.7435	0.7633	0.7938	0.8050	0.8262	**0.8412**
	TFIDF	0.4066	0.5433	0.6740	0.6771	0.6928	0.6808	0.6874	0.7004
	MI	0.3553	0.4610	0.5227	0.5819	0.5994	0.6091	0.6216	0.6623
	IG	0.3322	0.4338	0.4971	0.5416	0.6068	0.5841	0.5950	0.5915
Enron	CTF-CHI	0.2407	**0.5304**	**0.5992**	**0.6582**	**0.6907**	**0.7213**	**0.6723**	**0.6188**
	CHI	**0.2629**	0.4119	0.5767	0.5780	0.5841	0.5997	0.5381	0.5228
	TFIDF	0.2452	0.3311	0.4996	0.4506	0.4818	0.4520	0.5038	0.5020
	MI	0.2181	0.2892	0.3900	0.4078	0.4329	0.4179	0.4122	0.4605
	IG	0.2095	0.2958	0.3421	0.3454	0.4201	0.3998	0.4434	0.4119

It can be seen that in most cases, CTF-CHI results in the highest recall values and outperforms baseline methods. The proposed method has the highest recall values for Ohsumed and Enron datasets with 3000 features, while its best performance is achieved for Reuters with 3500 features. Nevertheless, in the cases of 500 selected features, all methods present weak performance for all datasets, and CTF-CHI method underperforms the classical CHI. Up to 3500 selected features for Reuters and 3000 selected features for Ohsumed and Enron, the performance of CTF-CHI decreases. Also, it is shown that the results obtained for Reuters and Ohsumed are slightly better than those obtained for Enron. This difference might be related to the high number of labels, as well the transformation method used.

Figures 2, 3 and 4 show graphically the experimental results in terms of macro-F1 and micro-F1. It can be noted from these figures that CTF-CHI is the best filter selection method compared to CHI, TFIDF, MI, and IG. But, at the large number of selected features, the difference between CTF-CHI and classical CHI is rather small.

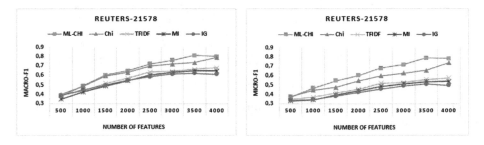

Fig. 2. F1-measure result on Reuters-21578 dataset

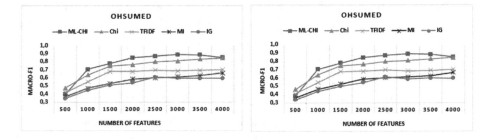

Fig. 3. F1-measure result on Ohsumed dataset

The goodness of CTF-CHI can be explained by the robustness of combining two aspects to evaluate the quality of the features, namely the global frequency of

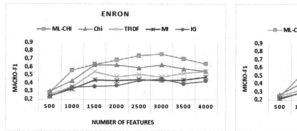
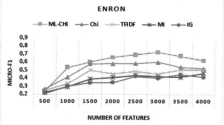

Fig. 4. F1-measure result on Enron dataset

terms as well their correlation to categories. Besides, due to the merging phase of documents, the category frequency of terms increases which affects the relevance of features.

Generally, the superiority of the proposed method is more noticeable when large number of features is used for classification, indicating that the number of selected features is an important factor in the performance of text classification methods. In the datasets, when the size of the feature set is fixed to a small value such as 500, all methods result in their worst performance. This is due to the fact that small number of features does not carry sufficient predictive information to allow an effective performance. Similarly, when the number of features is so huge, CTF-CHI do not performs well this can be due to the low frequency of terms.

6 Conclusion

This paper proposes a multi-label feature selection method designed upon MapReduce, intended to preprocess textual big datasets so that classification algorithms can perform better. Firstly, the Label Powerset method was used to transform multi-label texts into single-label texts. Then, a modified approach based on chi-square method is introduced. Finally, features with higher importance value were selected to construct the feature space. Besides its simplicity and scalability, the proposed algorithm has two advantages: (1) it selects features highly correlated with the category. (2) it can classify multi-label large textual datasets taking into account the correlation between categories. The algorithm has been implemented using Apache Hadoop and has been applied over three different large datasets with MNB classifier. We can observe that performances of our approach are better than the classical methods in most instances. In future work, we will consider some other methods which transform the multi-label dataset into single-label dataset and also will investigate how to choose the adequate amount of selected features according to the size of dataset.

References

1. Alelyani, S., Tang, J., Liu, H.: Feature selection for clustering: a review. In: Data Clustering, pp. 29–60. Chapman and Hall/CRC (2018)
2. Alshammari, S., Zolkepli, M.B., Abdullah, R.B.: Genetic algorithm based parallel k-means data clustering algorithm using mapreduce programming paradigm on hadoop environment (GAPKCA). In: Ghazali, R., Nawi, N., Deris, M., Abawajy, J. (eds.) SCDM 2020. AISC, vol. 978, pp. 98–108. Springer, Heidelberg (2020). https://doi.org/10.1007/978-3-030-36056-6_10
3. Chen, W., Yan, J., Zhang, B., Chen, Z., Yang, Q.: Document transformation for multi-label feature selection in text categorization. In: Seventh IEEE International Conference on Data Mining (ICDM 2007), pp. 451–456. IEEE (2007)
4. Chen, W., Liu, X., Guo, D., Lu, M.: Multi-label text classification based on sequence model. In: Tan, Y., Shi, Y. (eds.) DMBD 2019. CCIS, vol. 1071, pp. 201–210. Springer, Singapore (2019). https://doi.org/10.1007/978-981-32-9563-6_21
5. Doquire, G., Verleysen, M.: Feature selection for multi-label classification problems. In: Cabestany, J., Rojas, I., Joya, G. (eds.) IWANN 2011. LNCS, vol. 6691, pp. 9–16. Springer, Heidelberg (2011). https://doi.org/10.1007/978-3-642-21501-8_2
6. Gonzalez-Lopez, J., Ventura, S., Cano, A.: Distributed multi-label feature selection using individual mutual information measures. Knowl.-Based Syst. **188**, 105052 (2019)
7. Herrera, F., Charte, F., Rivera, A.J., del Jesus, M.J.: Multilabel classification. In: Herrera, F., Charte, F., Rivera, A.J., del Jesus, M.J. (eds.) Multilabel Classification, pp. 17–31. Springer, Cham (2016). https://doi.org/10.1007/978-3-319-41111-8_2
8. Huang, R., Jiang, W., Sun, G.: Manifold-based constraint laplacian score for multi-label feature selection. Pattern Recogn. Lett. **112**, 346–352 (2018)
9. Jia, L., Zhang, B.: Optimal document representation strategy for supervised term weighting schemes in automatic text categorization (2019)
10. Jiang, M., et al.: Text classification based on deep belief network and softmax regression. Neural Comput. Appl. **29**(1), 61–70 (2018)
11. Kashef, S., Nezamabadi-pour, H.: A label-specific multi-label feature selection algorithm based on the pareto dominance concept. Pattern Recogn. **88**, 654–667 (2019)
12. Labani, M., Moradi, P., Ahmadizar, F., Jalili, M.: A novel multivariate filter method for feature selection in text classification problems. Eng. Appl. Artif. Intell. **70**, 25–37 (2018)
13. Li, Y., Lin, Y., Liu, J., Weng, W., Shi, Z., Wu, S.: Feature selection for multi-label learning based on kernelized fuzzy rough sets. Neurocomputing **318**, 271–286 (2018)
14. Lin, Y., Hu, Q., Liu, J., Chen, J., Duan, J.: Multi-label feature selection based on neighborhood mutual information. Appl. Soft Comput. **38**, 244–256 (2016)
15. Pant, P., Sai Sabitha, A., Choudhury, T., Dhingra, P.: Multi-label classification trending challenges and approaches. In: Rathore, V.S., Worring, M., Mishra, D.K., Joshi, A., Maheshwari, S. (eds.) Emerging Trends in Expert Applications and Security. AISC, vol. 841, pp. 433–444. Springer, Singapore (2019). https://doi.org/10.1007/978-981-13-2285-3_51
16. Pereira, R.B., Plastino, A., Zadrozny, B., Merschmann, L.H.: Categorizing feature selection methods for multi-label classification. Artif. Intell. Rev. **49**(1), 57–78 (2018)
17. Ramesh, B., Sathiaseelan, J.: An advanced multi class instance selection based support vector machine for text classification. Procedia Comput. Sci. **57**, 1124–1130 (2015)

18. Rossi, R.G., Marcacini, R.M., Rezende, S.O., et al.: Benchmarking text collections for classification and clustering tasks (2013)
19. Schütze, H., Manning, C.D., Raghavan, P.: Introduction to information retrieval. In: Proceedings of the International Communication of Association for Computing Machinery Conference, vol. 4 (2008)
20. Singh, L., Singh, S., Aggarwal, N.: Two-stage text feature selection method for human emotion recognition. In: Krishna, C.R., Dutta, M., Kumar, R. (eds.) Proceedings of 2nd International Conference on Communication, Computing and Networking. LNNS, vol. 46, pp. 531–538. Springer, Singapore (2019). https://doi.org/10.1007/978-981-13-1217-5_51
21. SpolaôR, N., Cherman, E.A., Monard, M.C., Lee, H.D.: A comparison of multi-label feature selection methods using the problem transformation approach. Electron. Notes Theoret. Comput. Sci. **292**, 135–151 (2013)
22. Sun, Z., Zhang, J., Dai, L., Li, C., Zhou, C., Xin, J., Li, S.: Mutual information based multi-label feature selection via constrained convex optimization. Neurocomputing **329**, 447–456 (2019)
23. Thaseen, I.S., Kumar, C.A.: Intrusion detection model using fusion of chi-square feature selection and multi class SVM. J. King Saud Univ.-Comput. Inf. Sci. **29**(4), 462–472 (2017)
24. Trstenjak, B., Mikac, S., Donko, D.: KNN with TF-IDF based framework for text categorization. Procedia Eng. **69**, 1356–1364 (2014)
25. Tsoumakas, G., Katakis, I., Vlahavas, I.: Mining multi-label data. In: Maimon, O., Rokach, L. (eds.) Data Mining and Knowledge Discovery Handbook, pp. 667–685. Springer, Heidelberg (2009). https://doi.org/10.1007/978-0-387-09823-4_34
26. Xu, H., Xu, L.: Multi-label feature selection algorithm based on label pairwise ranking comparison transformation. In: 2017 International Joint Conference on Neural Networks (IJCNN), pp. 1210–1217. IEEE (2017)
27. Zhang, B.: Analysis and Research on Feature Selection Algorithm for Text Classification. University of Science and Technology of China, Anhui (2010)
28. Zhang, J., Luo, Z., Li, C., Zhou, C., Li, S.: Manifold regularized discriminative feature selection for multi-label learning. Pattern Recogn. **95**, 136–150 (2019)
29. Zhang, L., Duan, Q.: A feature selection method for multi-label text based on feature importance. Appl. Sci. **9**(4), 665 (2019)
30. Zhang, P., Liu, G., Gao, W.: Distinguishing two types of labels for multi-label feature selection. Pattern Recogn. **95**, 72–82 (2019)

Hardware Implementation of Roadway Classification System in FPGA Platform

Mohamed Atibi[1,2(✉)], Mohamed Boussaa[1], Issam Atouf[1],
Abdellatif Bennis[1], and Mohamed Tabaa[2]

[1] LTI Lab, Faculty of Science Ben M'sik, Hassan II University of Casablanca,
Casablanca, Morocco
m.atibi@yahoo.fr
[2] LPRI Lab, EMSI Casablanca, Casablanca, Morocco

Abstract. In this paper we present the implementation of a roadway classification system in the FPGA embedded platform. This system is based on the combination of an acoustic signal description algorithm (discrete wavelet transform) and an artificial intelligence algorithm (Artificial Neural Network ANN), in order to classify the different types of roadway (asphalt, gravel, snowy road, stone road). A hardware implementation of this system is done in order to equip the system with the functional autonomy of real-time systems. For this we have exploited the tools of this platform such as blocks Megafunctions. The results obtained in terms of execution time and hardware resources have shown that our implementation is a fast and optimal implementation.

Keywords: Roadway classification system · DWT · ANN · FPGA · Real time

1 Introduction

The roadway classification has become a highly requested task in driver assistance systems. It consists of estimating the state of the road surface [1]. There are several roadway classification methods, those based on vision sensors and those based on acoustic sensors.

Intelligent vision methods depend on the type of sensor used for vision and the algorithms used. This is a task that presents several difficulties due to the complexity of the scenes acquired by the vision sensors and the time allotted to this task. This requires the use and exploitation of powerful and fast algorithms for image processing and artificial intelligence [2].

As for the methods based on the acquisition of acoustic sound produced by tire-road interactions, their complexities depend on the signals acquired by the acoustic sensors and which are often drowned in the noise of the entourage (vehicle vibration, noise,...), which makes the task of roadway classification a little tricky [3].

For this, the developed system of driving assistance intended to indicate to the driver the roadway nature, must meet the parameters of road safety; namely the robustness which means that the system must classify or recognize the type of roadway with a very important rate and speed which means that the system should recognize the type of the road in real time.

© Springer Nature Switzerland AG 2020
M. Hamlich et al. (Eds.): SADASC 2020, CCIS 1207, pp. 200–208, 2020.
https://doi.org/10.1007/978-3-030-45183-7_15

To do this, the roadway classification system must exploit powerful algorithms in terms of signal description and classification. For the description phase, the system must represent the signals coming from the friction of the vehicle wheels with the roadway with a good quality and small quantity. However, during the classification phase, it must recognize the type of roadway with a high classification rate and in real time. This task must therefore make a compromise between the robustness and the classification time.

Different methods of roadway classification from acoustic sensors are presented in the literature. We can mention among others the Mel Frequency Cepstrum Coefficient algorithm [4] and the combination of MFCC, LPC and PSC algorithms [3] which are used for the feature of the signals acquired by the acoustic sensors. And artificial neural networks [3], the K-nearest neighbor [5] and the RBF classifieur [6] are used as classifiers.

This document presents a roadway classification system, which brings together two algorithms: the first is a signal processing algorithm and the second is an artificial intelligence algorithm. The signal processing algorithm aims at extracting the features of a road environment by using the discrete wavelet transform, and the artificial intelligence algorithm uses artificial neural networks to classify these roadways.

A hardware implementation is done in order to equip this system with a functional autonomy. This implementation benefits from megafunctions block performance in terms of computation speed.

2 Roadway Classification System Description

The roadway classification system is divided into two essential phases: the learning phase and the classification phase. The learning phase consists of learning the different types of roadway, but the classification phase consists in recognizing the new roadways.

During the learning phase, the signal descriptor based on the discrete wavelet transform DWT extracts, for each signal from the training base, a feature vector. This base contains a set of signals of different types of roadway (asphalt, gravel, snowy road, stone road). The vectors from the first phase form a training base for the Artificial Neural Network classifier.

In the classification phase, the same descriptor extracts a vector of features of the new signal to be processed, and which will then be classified by the same classifier, which is already trained in the first phase, in order to decide the nature of the roadway.

The Fig. 1 illustrates the overall system of Roadway classification.

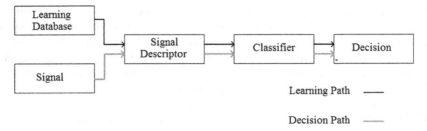

Fig. 1. Roadway classification system

3 Roadway Classification System Implementation

The properties of Roadway classification systems based on signal processing as well as the complexity of their processing chains require an efficient hardware implementation circuit [7].

The circuit that can satisfy these performances and requirements is the FPGA platform.

It is a digital programmable circuit that offers several perspectives for intelligent transportation systems. Among these advantages is parallel data processing, which allows the optimization of algorithms and hardware resources and therefore the execution of complex processes in a short and fast time [8].

With this in mind, an implementation in the FPGA platform is presented. This implementation will benefit from the performance of the Megafunctions blocks designed by the manufacturers of the FPGA platform; in terms of computing precision and speed.

This section describes in detail the implementation of our roadway classification system. This system requires the hardware implementation of 3 modules:

- DWT Module.
- ANN Module.
- Data and Commands Generating Module.

The implementation of our roadway classification system is illustrated in the Fig. 2:

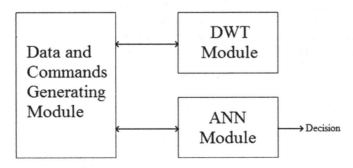

Fig. 2. The synoptic diagram of the roadway classification system

3.1 DWT Module

The hardware implementation of the DWT Module with the VHDL hardware description language makes use of very complicated mathematical functions and difficult to implement in the FPGA platform.

The solution proposed to implement this module is to use the megafunctions blocks.

The module consists of megafunction blocks of multiplication, addition and subtraction, multiplexers and demultiplexers.

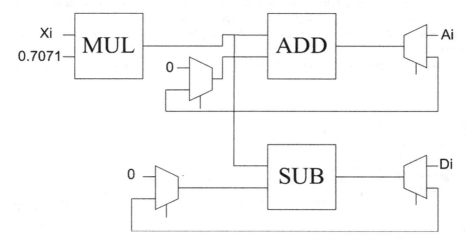

Fig. 3. Hardware implementation of DWT module

All of these blocks form the basis of the DWT algorithm implementation "Fig. 3", this algorithm receives as input a vector $X = (X1, X2, \ldots, Xn)$ which represents the signal to be processed, then the DWT will extract the features of this signal in several levels.

Indeed, the DWT algorithm decomposes the input signal Xi by calculating the approximations A1 and the details D1 of the 1st level, then it decomposes in the same way the A1 approximations of the 1st level by recalculating the approximations A2 and the details D2 of the 2nd level and this process will be repeated until the level of decomposition wanted.

This decomposition process is managed and synchronized by a set of signals from the Data and Commands Generating Module.

3.2 ANN Module

Among the problems of the implementation of this module in an FPGA platform with the VHDL language, it is that the real numbers are not synthesized in this language, the solution that proved this implementation is to design an architecture that manipulates these data in the floating point. This offers efficiency in terms of calculation accuracy.

To achieve this precision, we used blocks called megafunctions which are blocks offered by the FPGA manufacturers, these blocks are written in VHDL in order to implement complex arithmetic operations with a floating point representation (32 or 64 bits), these blocks are useful to guarantee the computational accuracy of the ANN module.

The implementation of artificial neuron networks MLP [9] type requires a set of formal neurons interconnected with each other according to a given architecture, this number of neurons increases progressively with the complexity of the task to be performed. This has an impact on the needed material resources.

To remedy this difficulty, our implementation is based on the exploitation of only one formal neuron, which will play all the neurons of the architecture. This neuron is composed of the megafunction blocks of multiplication, addition, exponential and division.

The Fig. 4 illustrates the different blocks of this formal neuron:

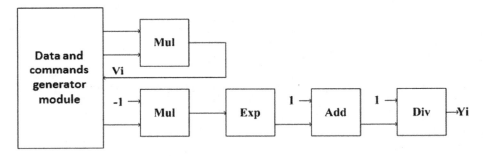

Fig. 4. The synoptic diagram of the formal neuron

The formal neuron receives as input an object vector $X = (X1, X2, \ldots, Xn)$ which represents the signal to be classified and a synaptic weight vector $W = (W1, W2, \ldots, Wn)$ which represents the connection between the neuron and its ith entry. The data and command generating module returns the Xi and Wi data to the megafunction multiplication block, the calculated product will be accumulated and stored in the internal memory of this module.

The Fig. 5 shows the implementation of this internal activation:

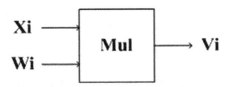

Fig. 5. Hardware implementation of the internal activation

The second block is a transfer function called activation function. It makes it possible to limit the exit of the neuron in an interval [0, 1]. The most used function is the sigmoid.

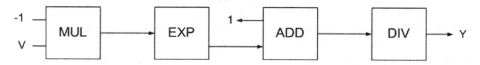

Fig. 6. Hardware implementation of the sigmoid function

The implementation of this function "Fig. 6" requires a number of complex operations such as division and exponential. It requires the use of megafunctions of exponential and division. The data and command generating module sends the data Vi to the megafunction blocks constituting the sigmoid function, in order to calculate the output Yi of each formal neuron.

The implementation of the artificial neuron network consists in implementing a single formal neuron controlled by the data and command generating module, in order to perform the work of an artificial neural network. This neuron calculates the output Y11 of the first neuron of the first layer and stores it in the internal memory of the data and command generating module. Then the same neuron calculates the Y12 output of the second neuron of the first layer and stores it in the same memory. This process is repeated until the last neuron of the output layer is calculated.

During this calculation process, the synchronization and data commands are generated by the data and command generating module.

3.3   Data and Commands Generating Module

This part reviews the different blocks needed for the implementation of the data and command generating module. This module consists of a processor that will take care of generating the data vectors that are previously stored in its internal memory and controls the DWT and ANN modules "Fig. 7".

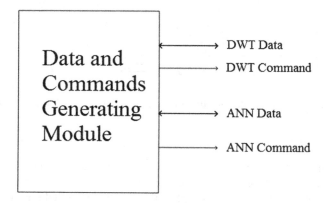

Fig. 7. Hardware implementation of the data and command generating module

The data and command generator module consists in generating a set of signals having the following functions:

- Generation of command and synchronization signals of the DWT module.
- Generation of data (signals to be processed) for the DWT module.
- Storage of the vectors provided by the DWT module.
- Generation of control and synchronization signals of the ANN module.
- Generation of data (vectors to be processed) for the ANN module.
- Storage of intermediate data (Y hidden layers) provided by the ANN module.

3.4   Roadway Classification System Implementation

The diagram "Fig. 8" shows how our implementation of the roadway classification system works. The first step is to generate the elements of the vector Xi from the internal memory. These elements go through the module that calculates the DWT features to create a feature vector. This vector, meanwhile, passes through the ANN module in order to be classified.

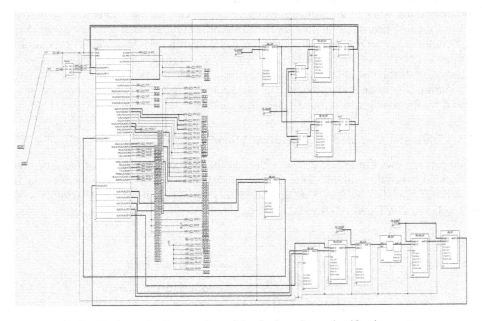

Fig. 8. Hardware implementation of the final roadway classification system

3.5   Results and Discussions

In this section, the hardware implementation of the roadway classification system proposed in the previous section will be simulated and tested in the FPGA DE2_70 version EP2C70F896C6. This paragraph will be devoted to taking two evaluation criteria of this implementation, which are the execution time and material resources consumed.

Regarding to hardware resources, the results obtained from the hardware implementation of the roadway classification system in the FPGA based on the megafunctions blocks and the Microprocessor, allow to show the performance of our system in terms of hardware capabilities.

The results are illustrated in the following figure "Fig. 9" and Table 1:

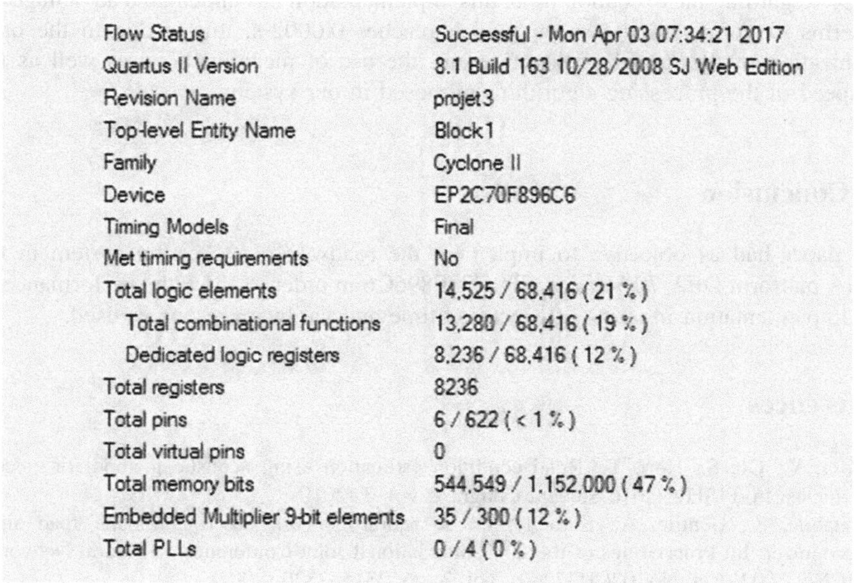

Flow Status	Successful - Mon Apr 03 07:34:21 2017
Quartus II Version	8.1 Build 163 10/28/2008 SJ Web Edition
Revision Name	projet3
Top-level Entity Name	Block1
Family	Cyclone II
Device	EP2C70F896C6
Timing Models	Final
Met timing requirements	No
Total logic elements	14,525 / 68,416 (21 %)
Total combinational functions	13,280 / 68,416 (19 %)
Dedicated logic registers	8,236 / 68,416 (12 %)
Total registers	8236
Total pins	6 / 622 (< 1 %)
Total virtual pins	0
Total memory bits	544,549 / 1,152,000 (47 %)
Embedded Multiplier 9-bit elements	35 / 300 (12 %)
Total PLLs	0 / 4 (0 %)

Fig. 9. Material consumption of our hardware implementation

Table 1. The material consumption of each part of our hardware implementation

	Logical elements (percentage)	Bit memory amount (percentage)
DWT	1923 (3%)	102 (1%)
ANN	8863 (13%)	848 (1%)
Microprocessor	3520 (5%)	543552 (47%)
Global system	**14525 (21%)**	**544549 (47%)**

The results can be divided into two parts:

- The number of logical elements (column 1):
  The Table 1 shows that the overall system consumed only 21% of total number of logic elements available in the FPGA as well as the processor for its creation requires a low number of logical elements. This makes it a very optimized system despite the use of megafunction blocks by the DWT and ANN, and which has had undeniable advantages in terms of optimization of hardware resources.

- The bit memory amount (column 2):

  From the results shown in the Table 1, megafunction blocks do not consume memory, on the other hand, the processor has requested an interesting amount of memory to store the program, but despite this interesting space the percentage remains average compared to other architecture (47%).

  Despite the use of these blocks megafunctions the system did not consume many registers and logical element. This is due to the use of this processor that manages and synchronizes blocks and calculations.

  Regarding the execution time, this implementation has undeniable advantages in terms of computational speed, which reaches 0.0002 s, this is due to the optimization of the neural architecture and the use of megafunctions as well as the speed of the processing algorithms proposed in our system.

4 Conclusion

Our paper had as objective to implement the roadway classification system in the FPGA platform DE2_70 Version EP2C70F896C6 in order to show the performance of this implementation in terms of execution time and hardware resources used.

References

1. Kim, Y., Oh, S., Hori, Y.: Road condition estimation using acoustic method for electric vehicles. In: FISITA 2010 Student Congress, vol. 3 (2010)
2. Vitabile, S., Gentile, A., Sorbello, F.: A neural network based automatic road signs recognizer. In: Proceedings of the 2002 International Joint Conference on Neural Networks, IJCNN 2002 (Cat. No. 02CH37290), vol. 3, pp. 2315–2320 (2002)
3. Boyraz, P.: Acoustic road-type estimation for intelligent vehicle safety applications. Iner. J. Veh. Saf. 7(2), 209 (2014)
4. Lakshmi Devasena, C., Hema Latha, M.: Automatic classification of audio data using gradient descent neural network based algorithm. J. Theor. Appl. Inf. Technol. 70(3), 375–389 (2014)
5. Duarte, M.F., Hu, Y.H.: Vehicle classification in distributed sensor networks. J. Parallel Distrib. Comput. 64(7), 826–838 (2004)
6. Qi, X.-X., Ji, J.-W., Han, X.-W.: Vehicle type classification by acoustic waves with dimension reduction technique. J. Comput. 8(3), 685–692 (2013)
7. Tisan, A., Cirstea, M.: SOM neural network design - a new Simulink library based approach targeting FPGA implementation. Math. Comput. Simul. 91, 134–149 (2013)
8. Aguirre-Dobernack, N., Guzmán-Miranda, H., Aguirre, M.A.: Implementation of a machine vision system for real-time traffic sign recognition on FPGA. In: IECON 2013, pp. 2283–2288 (2013)
9. Atibi, M., Boussaa, M., Bennis, A., Atouf, I.: Real-time implementation of artificial neural network in FPGA platform. In: Embedded Systems and Artificial Intelligence, pp. 3–13. Springer, Singapore (2020)

Optimization of LSTM Algorithm Through Outliers – Application to Financial Time Series Forecasting

Houda Benkerroum[1(✉)], Walid Cherif[2], and Mohamed Kissi[1]

[1] LIM Laboratory, Department of Computer Science,
Faculty of Sciences and Technology, University Hassan II Casablanca,
20650 Mohammedia, Morocco
houda.benkerroum@gmail.com, mohammed.kissi@univh2c.ma
[2] SI2M Laboratory, National Institute of Statistics and Applied Economics,
6217 Rabat, Morocco
chrf.walid@gmail.com

Abstract. The long short-term memory (LSTM) model is widely used in multiple areas, mainly for speech recognition, natural language processing and activity recognition. In the last few years, we started to see many variants of LSTM for recurrent neural networks since its inception in 1997. However, there weren't many studies that have addressed the LSTM's gating mechanism. In this paper, we propose a novel LSTM framework where we modify the architecture of the LSTM unit by adding a new layer that we call the "outlier gate". The latter controls the flow of information that goes into the LSTM cell. This added signal allows us to avoid both the carry-over effect that the outliers have on the forecasted point and a bias in the estimates of our LSTM model – caused by unusual or non-repetitive events. The proposed architecture led us to an end-to-end trainable model that we applied in this paper to a financial time-series forecasting problem. Our results demonstrate that the new proposed LSTM architecture achieves better performance than the state-of-the-art original LSTM model.

Keywords: LSTM · Time series · Forecasting · Outlier · Finance

1 Introduction

Recently, there has been an increased interest in time series analysis and forecasting. Time series analysis has the purpose of identifying trends, cycles and seasonal variances to aid in the forecasting of a future event. They are also used in multiple fields: medicine and pharmacotherapy [1], weather readings [2], financial time-series [3, 4] etc.

The latter are particularly complex to forecast or analyse as they are characteristically non-linear, non-stationary, and noisy [5] with high degree of uncertainty, in addition to showing some particular behaviours like the volatility clustering phenomenon [6]. Hence, traditional statistical models such GARCH (Generalized Autoregressive Conditional Heteroscedasticity), ARCH (Autoregressive Conditional

© Springer Nature Switzerland AG 2020
M. Hamlich et al. (Eds.): SADASC 2020, CCIS 1207, pp. 209–220, 2020.
https://doi.org/10.1007/978-3-030-45183-7_16

Heteroscedasticity), ARIMA (Autoregressive Integrated Moving Average) and AR (Autoregressive) models have usually failed to capture the complexity and behaviour of financial time-series.

Therefore, researchers are now using more sophisticated nonlinear techniques for time-series analysis, forecasting and classification. State of the art methods for handling these tasks often rely on both machine learning algorithms (like SVM (Support Vector Machine) [7] and K-nearest neighbours algorithm [8]) and deep learning techniques. The latter have been used successfully in multiple applications for time series data, and have radically changed many fields like computer vision [9] - through some new efficient architectures such as Residual and Convolutional Neural Networks [10].

Indeed, the automatic learning of temporal dependencies and handling of temporal structures like trends and seasonality that characterise deep learning algorithms make them a good framework for financial time series analysis and prediction.

Generally speaking, some of the most used deep learning methodologies for times series forecasting recently remain the stacked auto-encoders [11], Artificial Neural Networks and Recurrent Neural Networks.

Also, since causality constraint in time-series require that we respect the ordering in time, a network architecture that reflects this constraint would be relevant: this leads us to a recurrent network based on Long Short-Term Memory (LSTM) units [12, 13].

Long short-term memory recurrent neural networks are widely used recently and are considered as an improvement over the general recurrent neural networks, which have a vanishing gradient problem.

On one hand, LSTM networks are able to keep the contextual information of the inputs by integrating a loop that passes information from one step to the other, making any forecasting conditioned by the past states of the network's inputs, while being capable of learning long-term dependencies

On the other hand, the more time passes, the less likely it becomes for the next output to depend on a very old input. This time dependency distance itself is contextual information to be learned. LSTM networks manage this by learning when to remember and when to forget, through their forget gate weights (where a weight value of zero means that no information goes through and a value of one means that everything goes through).

One other advantage of LSTM RNNs (Long Short Term Memory Recurrent Neural Networks) is that it addresses the vanishing gradient problem, which is a problem commonly found in ordinary recurrent neural networks, as noted in Hochreiter and Schmidhuber [13]. LSTM addresses this limitation by including gating functions into their state dynamics through adding three gated units that efficiently control the memory of previous states: the "forget gate", the "input gate" and "the output gate". At every time step, the LSTM keeps both a hidden vector and a memory vector that is responsible for controlling state updates and outputs. However, as time series are often contaminated with outliers due to unusual or non-repetitive events, forecasting accuracy in such situations is reduced when these outliers are not handled correctly.

Therefore, this paper proposes a novel approach that extends the LSTM algorithm by handling the outliers of a financial time series dataset as a part of the model architecture.

The rest of this paper is structured as the following: the first section presents a brief summary of some of the main approaches that have been done to modify LSTM architecture. Then, the second section explains the proposed approach to improve LSTM forecasting efficiency. Finally, we use this novel model in a financial time series forecasting problem. The provided experimental results validate the proposed contributions and prove the effectiveness of our novel approach by achieving better performance over a vanilla LSTM.

2 Background and Related Work

Different works have been done recently trying to achieve a modified version of LSTM that gives a better accuracy to the model predictions. We present in the below the LSTM model first, then summarize some of the main approaches.

2.1 Long Short Term Memory Networks (LSTM)

LSTM networks are considered as a special type of Recurrent Neural Networks (RNN), and have been designed to avoid long-term dependency issue. In term of their architecture, the main difference between RNN and LSTM is that the former have only one hidden layer, whereas the latter contains four neural network layers that interact in a particular way that will be described in this section.

In order to implement an LSTM cell, we first need to calculate the values of the input gate i_t and he candidate value for the states of the memory cells at time t: $\tilde{C}_t$;

$$i_t = \sigma\left(W_f x_t + U_i h_{t-1} + b_i\right) \tag{1}$$

$$\tilde{C}_t = tanh(W_c x_t + U_c h_{t-1} + b_c) \tag{2}$$

Where $i_t \in \mathbb{R}^h$ represents the input gate activation vector, $x_t \in \mathbb{R}^d$ is the input vector at time t, $h_{t-1} \in \mathbb{R}^h$ *is the hidden state (which is also the output from the previous LSTM block at timestamp* t − 1), σ is the sigmoid activation function.

In all this sec, $W \in \mathbb{R}^{hxd}$, $U \in \mathbb{R}^{hxh}$ and $b \in \mathbb{R}^h$ refer respectively to the weight matrices and the bias vector parameters that need to be learned by LSTM during the training phase.

Then, as we need to decide what information the model will "forget" and what information it will keep, we calculate the value of f_t, which is the memory cells' forget gate at time t:

$$f_t = \sigma\left(W_f x_t + U_f h_{t-1} + b_f\right) \tag{3}$$

Now that we know the value of the input gate activation i_t, the forget gate activation f_t and the candidate state value $\tilde{C}_t$, we can calculate C_t, the memory cell' s updated state at time t:

$$C_t = \sigma\left(i_t * \tilde{C}_t + f_t * C_{t-1}\right) \tag{4}$$

Finally, given the new state of the memory cells, we can calculate the value of the output gates o_t and the hidden state h_t:

$$o_t = \sigma(W_o x_t + U_o h_{t-1} + V_o C_t + b_0) \tag{5}$$

$$h_t = o_t * tanh(C_t) \tag{6}$$

2.2   LSTM Additional Mean Layer

One of the popular LSTM variants that have been developed recently consists of adding both a Mean pooling layer and logistic regression to the initial LSTM layer [14]. The model used in this approach is composed of one single LSTM layer followed by mean pooling over time and a logistic regression layer. Hinton's dropout was used to prevent over-fitting and the sigmoid activation function has been applied to the output. Adam optimizer, proposed by Kingma and Lei Ba, has been used for stochastic optimization and binary cross entropy has been used as cost function.

The model architecture can be summarized in the Fig. 1 below.

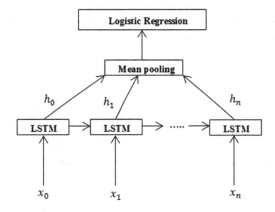

Fig. 1. LSTM model variant with mean pooling layer

2.3   LSTM Ensemble Forecasting

The ensemble forecasting consists of effectively combining multiple prediction results from a group of individual LSTM networks to produce the prediction output. As the simple averaging approach can be biased by outliers and not reliable for skewed distributions, this proposed averaging approach dynamically adjusts the weights used for combining multiple LSTM models [14]. Therefore, this approach updates the combining weights at each time step in a recursive and adaptive way by using both past prediction errors and forgetting weight factor. The weights are assigned to individual LSTM models, which improve the forecasting accuracy to a large extent.

This method is efficient when it comes to runtime performance because it does not require the complex optimization in the process of finding combining weights.

Assuming that a total of M LSTM models in a specific ensemble are provided, their ensemble forecast result for time series denoted as $(y^{(1)}, y^{(2)} \ldots, y^{(N)})$ for N observations, is given by:

$$\hat{y}^{(k)} = \sum_{m=1}^{M} w_m \hat{y}_m^{(k)} \; for \; k = 1, \ldots, N \tag{7}$$

Where $\hat{y}_m^{(k)}$ denotes the forecasted output (at the timestamp k) obtained using the LSTM model M and w_m is the associated combining weight, with $0 \leq w_m \leq 1$ and $\sum_{m=1}^{M} w_m = 1$ [14].

The weights are then computed recursively as per below:

$$w_m^{(k+1)} = w_m^{(k)} + \lambda \Delta w_m^{(k)} \; for \; m = 1, \ldots, M \tag{8}$$

Where it was suggested in the model that $\lambda = 0.3$ and that $\Delta w_m^{(k)}$ is calculated using the inverse prediction error of the respective LSTM base model as per below:

$$\Delta w_m^{(k)} = 1\varepsilon(k)1\varepsilon m(1) + 1\varepsilon m(2) + \ldots + 1\varepsilon m(k) \tag{9}$$

Where $\varepsilon_m^{(k)}$ is related to past prediction error measured up to the time step k as per below, $e_m^{(k)}$ being the prediction error at time t of the LSTM model m, such as:

$$\varepsilon(k) = \sum_{t=k-v+1}^{M} \gamma^{k-t} e_m^{(t)} \tag{10}$$

2.4   Gated Recurrent Unit Model (GRU)

The Gated Recurrent Unit (GRU) model, introduced by Cho et al. [15], is considered another variation of the LSTM. The GRU uses the hidden state to transfer information, while completely getting rid of the cell state. It is achieving so by combining both the input and forget gates into a single "update gate." It also merges the hidden state and cell state. The resulting model is much simpler than a standard LSTM model, and has been growing in popularity since it was built.

The "update gate" in the GRU makes the call on what information to throw away and what new information to add, whereas the "reset gate" is deciding on how much of the past information the model should forget.

Similar to LSTM and with same variables definitions detailed in *Eq. (1)* of the Sect. 2.1, the model unit needs to be updated by using the following equations, where r_t is the newly introduced "reset gate" vector and z_t is the "update gate" vector:

$$r_t = \sigma(W_r h_{t-1} + U_t x_t + b_r) \tag{11}$$

$$z_t = \sigma(W_z h_{t-1} + U_z x_t + b_z) \tag{12}$$

$$i_t = \sigma(W_i h_{t-1} + U_i x_t + b_i) \tag{13}$$

$$o_t = \sigma(W_t h_{t-1} + U_t x_t + b_t) \tag{14}$$

3 The Proposed Approach

3.1 Anomaly Detection

The anomaly detection for a time series refers to identifying the outlier data points present in our dataset, relatively to some "standard" or "usual" signal – i.e. extreme values that deviate a lot from other observations on data.

We will describe in this section three of the most popular methods commonly used for outlier detection.

Altman Z-Score (or "Standard Score"). The z-score of a specific observation is a parametric measure that calculates how many standard deviations a specific data point is from the sample's mean, assuming a Gaussian distribution of our data.

The z-score of a specific observation i is then defined as the following:

$$z_i = \frac{x_i - \bar{x}}{S} \tag{15}$$

Where x_i is the observation point, $\bar{x}$ is the sample mean of the dataset and S is the sample standard deviation.

One of the z-score methodology drawbacks is that it is only convenient to use it in a small to medium sized dataset and that the data distribution has to be parametric

Isolation Forests Algorithm. Isolation forests are an efficient method to identify novelties in the data. It "isolates" some observations by randomly selecting a feature and then randomly selecting a split value that falls between the minimum and the maximum values of the selected feature.

This recursive random partitioning generates considerably shorter paths for anomalies. Therefore, when a forest of random trees collectively produces shorter path lengths for some specific samples, it means that they are most likely to be anomalies. The Isolation tree algorithm can be summarized in the Fig. 2 below:

Isolation Tree Algorithm

Input:
X – matrix, $X \in \mathbb{R}^{nxp}$
Output:
Y – matrix of outliers, $Y \in \mathbb{R}^{mxk}$, with m<=n and k<=p (the matrix contains the outlier points)
1: t = ∅ (empty tree)
2: Randomly select x_i a feature of X
3: Randomly select a split point s ∈ (min(x_i), max(x_i))
4: Add the node $N_{x_i,p}$ to the tree t
5: Store in the matrix X_{left} all the samples of X where the observation x_i is larger than the split point s
6: Store in the matrix X_{right} all the samples of X where the observation x_i is lower than the split point s
7: Repeat the algorithm with $X = X_{left}$. Concatenate the obtained tree as the left child of the tree t.
8: Repeat the algorithm with $X = X_{right}$. Concatenate the obtained tree as the right child of the tree t.

Fig. 2. Pseudocode for the Isolation tree algorithm

However, although the Isolation Forests algorithm has proved to be efficient in many applications, its training can be very long and computationally expensive.

Interquartile Range Methodology (IQR). The IQR is a measure of variability of data that is based on dividing the data set into quartiles: the quartiles split a rank-ordered data set into four equal sections. The values that divide each part are called the first, second, and third quartiles (denoted by Q1, Q2, and Q3 respectively):

− Q1 is the "middle" value in the first half of the rank-ordered data set,
− Q2 is the median value,
− Q3 splits off the highest 25% of data from the lowest 75% and can also be seen as the "middle" value in the second half of the ordered data set.

The inter quartile range is then define the difference between the third and the first quartile, and hence can be used as a measure of how spread-out the values are. Using IQR definition, a data point is considered as an outlier if it lies more than 1.5 times (or other more conservative or non-conservative factor) further out from Q1 or Q3.

The IQR of a rank-ordered dataset K is defined by the equation below:

$$IQR_K = Q(0.75) - Q(0.25) \tag{16}$$

An observation x_i from the dataset K is considered an outlier if:

$$x_i \leq Q(0.25) - \lambda * IQR_K \tag{17}$$

$$or \ x_i \geq Q(0.75) + \lambda * IQR_K \tag{18}$$

Where $\lambda \in \mathbb{R}$ (in the rest of the paper, we consider $\lambda = 1.5$), $Q(0.25)$ is the first quartile of the dataset K and $Q(0.75)$ is its third quartile.

3.2   Optimization of LSTM Architecture

We propose in our paper a novel LSTM framework for time series forecasting, where we modify the architecture of the LSTM unit by adding a new layer called the "outlier gate", which controls the flow of information that goes into the LSTM cell. This added signal allows us to avoid the carry-over effect of the outlier on the forecasted point – caused by unusual or non-repetitive events – and a bias in the estimates of our LSTM model. The proposed architecture led us to an end-to-end trainable model that we applied in the next section to a financial time-series forecasting problem.

Before going through any of the conventional LSTM gates, the input x_t needs to go through the new "outlier gate" that we are introducing to the LSTM architecture (noted "OG" in the Fig. 3). We use the inter quartile range methodology for anomaly detection as it is efficient and doesn't consume lot of computation time.

$$OG_t = \sigma((1 - \lambda) * x_t) \tag{19}$$

Where:

$$\lambda = 0 \ if \ x_t \ \epsilon \ ] \ Q(0.25) - 1.5 * IQR_t; Q(0.75) + 1.5 * IQR_t [\tag{20}$$

At every timestamp t, the LSTM unit needs to be updated by using the equations below for a forward pass of an LSTM unit – using the same notations and variables definitions detailed in Eq. (1) of the Sect. 2.1:

$$i_t = \sigma\left(W_f x_t + U_i h_{t-1} + b_i\right) \tag{21}$$

$$\tilde{C}_t = tanh(W_c x_t + U_c h_{t-1} + b_c) \tag{22}$$

$$f_t = \sigma\left(W_f x_t + U_f h_{t-1} + b_f\right) \tag{23}$$

$$C_t = \sigma\left(i_t * \tilde{C}_t + f_t * C_{t-1}\right) \tag{24}$$

$$o_t = \sigma(W_o x_t + U_o h_{t-1} + V_o C_t + b_0) \tag{25}$$

$$h_t = o_t * tanh(C_t) \tag{26}$$

The cell's architecture of our novel model can be summarised in the Fig. 3 below, using the same notations as per the Sect. 2.1 of this paper – where "σ" is the sigmoid function, "f" the forget gate, "i" the input gate and "OG" the outlier gate.

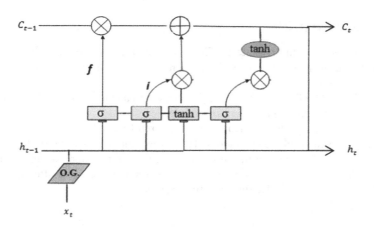

Fig. 3. Architecture of the proposed approach - optimization of LSTM

4   Results and Analysis

4.1   Dataset

The dataset used in this section to test our proposed approach consists of a financial time series of the Volatility Index (VIX) daily Open/Close prices and daily Highest/Lowest prices for the last fifteen years.

The VIX is a popular financial market index created by the Chicago Board Options Exchange (CBOE) to represent the market's expectation of volatility implied by the S&P 500 index. Hence, it is considered as a good measure of market risk and investors sentiments and can be used by investors either for hedging purposes or to express their outlook for broad market implied volatility.

4.2   Data Processing

We first standardize the data by scaling features to lie between 0 and 1: for each value of a given feature, we subtract the minimum value in the feature and divide it by the range (which is the difference between the maximum and the minimum of that feature).

Then, we transform the dataset into a multivariate supervised learning problem, where we forecast the close price of the VIX index of next day, using an input sequence having 5 time steps of all our features (open price, close price, High of the day, Low of the day and day of the week). In other words, the first five time steps of each feature are provided as an input to the model and the model associates these inputs with the value in the output series at the fifth time step and so on for the rest of the time steps.

We then split the data to a training set (80% of the dataset) and a testing set (remaining 20% of the dataset).

4.3   Training and Results

We train the modified multivariate LSTM model with fifty neurons in the first hidden layer and 1 neuron in the output layer (which is the VIX index closing price at the following day).

The model will be fit for 1000 training epochs with a batch size of 80. We use mean square error loss function and Adam optimizer.

The proposed approach has a Root Mean Squared Error of 1.5, which is 15% lower than using a conventional LSTM model. This shows that a modification to the LSTM architecture to include an outlier gate has proven to be more accurate than the Vanilla LSTM model. The Fig. 4 below shows the train and test loss after applying the proposed approach to the VIX financial time series.

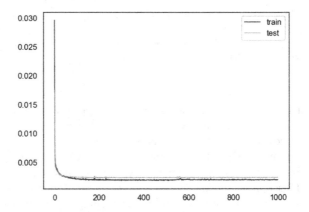

Fig. 4. Train and Test loss from our model during training

In the Fig. 5, we show a comparison between the actual values the VIX financial time series versus the predicted values using the approach.

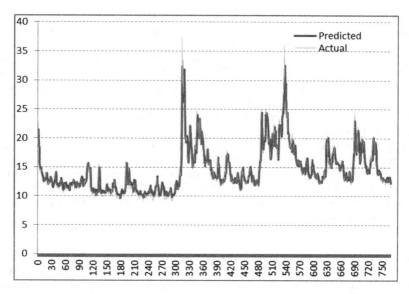

Fig. 5. Comparison between the actual values of our time series and the predicted values using our novel approach

4.4 Conclusion

In this paper, we have proposed a novel LSTM architecture where we add an "outlier gate", which controls the flow of information that goes into the LSTM cell. This added signal allows us to avoid the carry-over effect of the outlier on the forecasted point – caused by unusual or non-repetitive events – and a bias in the estimates of our LSTM model. We applied the proposed to a financial time-series forecasting problem.

The provided experimental results validate the proposed contributions by reducing the RMSE by 15%, and prove the effectiveness of our novel approach by achieving better performance over a vanilla LSTM.

References

1. Beard, E., et al.: Association between electronic cigarette use and changes in quit attempts, success of quit attempts, use of smoking cessation pharmacotherapy, and use of stop smoking services in England: time series analysis of population trends. BMJ **354** (2016). https://doi.org/10.1136/bmj.i4645
2. Gherboudj, I., Ghedira, H.: Assessment of solar energy potential over the United Arab Emirates using remote sensing and weather forecast data. Renew. Sustain. Energy Rev. **55**, 1210–1224 (2016)
3. Lahmiri, S.: A variational mode decomposition approach for analysis and forecasting of economic and financial time series. Expert Syst. Appl. **55**, 268–273 (2016)
4. Weigend, A.S.: Time Series Prediction: Forecasting the Future and Understanding the Past. Routledge, Abingdon (2018)

5. Chatfield, C.: The Analysis of Time Series: An Introduction. CRC Press, Boca Raton (2016)
6. Danielsson, J., Valenzuela, M., Zer, I.: Learning from history: volatility and financial crises. Rev. Financ. Stud. **31**(7), 2774–2805 (2018)
7. Zhou, C., et al.: Application of time series analysis and PSO–SVM model in predicting the Bazimen landslide in the Three Gorges Reservoir, China. Eng. Geol. **204**, 108–120 (2016)
8. Yu, B., et al.: k-nearest neighbor model for multiple-time-step prediction of short-term traffic condition. J. Transp. Eng. **142**(6), 04016018 (2016)
9. Litjens, G., et al.: A survey on deep learning in medical image analysis. Med. Image Anal. **42**, 60–88 (2017)
10. LeCun, Y., Bottou, L., Bengio, Y., Haffner, P.: Gradient-based learning applied to document recognition. Proc. IEEE **86**(11), 2278–2324 (1998)
11. Bao, W., Yue, J., Rao, Y.: A deep learning framework for financial time series using stacked autoencoders and long-short term memory. PLoS ONE **12**(7), e0180944 (2017)
12. Gers, F.A., Schmidhuber, J., Cummins, F.: Learning to forget: continual prediction with LSTM. Neural Comput. **12**(10), 2451–2471 (2000)
13. Hochreiter, S., Schmidhuber, J.: Long short-term memory. Neural Comput. **9**(8), 1735–1780 (1997)
14. Choi, J., Lee, B.: Combining LSTM network ensemble via adaptive weighting for improved time series forecasting. Math. Prob. Eng. 1–8 (2018). https://doi.org/10.1155/2018/2470171
15. Cho, K., van Merriënboer, B., Gulcehre, C., Bougares, F., Schwenk, H., Bengio, Y.: Learning phrase representations using RNN encoder-decoder for statistical machine translation (2014). https://doi.org/10.3115/v1/d14-1179

An Artificial Neural Network Combined to Object Oriented Method for Land Cover Classification of High Resolution RGB Remote Sensing Images

Sohaib Baroud[(✉)] , Soumia Chokri , Safa Belhaous , Zineb Hidila ,
and Mohammed Mestari

Laboratory SSDIA, ENSET Mohemmadia, University Hassan II Casablanca,
Casablanca, Morocco
sohaib.baroud89@gmail.com

Abstract. Land cover is the observed physical cover on the earth's surface. The complexity and similarity of the elements that occupy the earth's surface make the task of interpreting aerial and satellite images very tedious, especially when it comes to very high-resolution RGB images. A neural network can be used to learn from a large amount of imagery data and is useful at classifying semantic features of imagery data. Coupled with the object-oriented approach that enriches the characteristics of the images beyond the spectral data, the abilities of ANN can be significantly improved. This paper aims to evaluate the application of ANN combined to Object-Oriented Method for the classification of a high resolution (20 cm) RGB aerial images, we took the Moulay Bouselham Region in Morocco as example. First a quad-tree then multi-resolution algorithms are used to generate homogeneous objects. Second, a set of object's features is generated on the basis of segmentation results. Third, an Artificial neural network is tuned to rich the maximum classification performance. Finally, we discuss the results and elucidate perspective of this study.

Keywords: Remote sensing · Artificial neural network · Object
based · High resolution · Land cover · RGB

1 Introduction

Since ancient times, man has not stopped inventing new techniques to help him master his territory and this for different purposes: planning, development, security, expansion, preservation etc ...

The invention of air crafts was a major turning point in the history of cartography. From the first "hikes", the man started to take aerial photos which allowed him to better understand his territory.

Since that time and as the aerial and satellite images are more and more abundant, we have tried to find algorithms which will allow us to automate the

© Springer Nature Switzerland AG 2020
M. Hamlich et al. (Eds.): SADASC 2020, CCIS 1207, pp. 221–232, 2020.
https://doi.org/10.1007/978-3-030-45183-7_17

interpretation of these images, a new discipline then appeared that of aerial and space remote sensing. This multidisciplinary field of research has not ceased to experience progress both in terms of image acquisition sensors and in terms of analysis methods and its field of application. However, the complexity and similarity of the elements that occupy the earth's surface make the task of interpreting aerial and satellite images very tedious, especially when it comes to very high resolution RGB images. In morocco, urban planing administration has a big number of aerial images generally used to digitize land cover maps. The high availability of these images prompted us to think about an effective solution to exploit them to automatically generate land cover maps.

High resolution RGB images are easily readable by humans, but editing land cover maps using the manual digitization process is a repetitive task that requires a great deal of time and a lot of efforts. Contrariwise automatically classifying RGB images using pixel based approach and classical classification tools is nearly impossible. Therefore object base image analysis "OBIA" approach allows adding to RGB images other features beyond the spectral information, like texture, shape size, pattern, shadows... that gives large possibilities to better exploit those images and that mimics in a certain way the human vision process [1].

Many authors have demonstrated the advantages of using artificial neural network classifiers over conventional methods [2]. The ability of neural network to understand complex features, to generalize in noisy environment and to transfer knowledge justify the wide interest of remote sensing researchers (see Fig. 1). Another advantage of using ANN approach is that ANN supervised classifier use less training data to perform a classification [3].

This paper aims to explore the combination of ANN and object based image analysis to generate land cover maps from very high resolution RGB images (25 cm). Section 2 presents a summary of related works that raise the application of neural network techniques for remote sensing. Section 3 details the proposed approach for land cover mapping, including image segmentation, feature extraction, candidate selection, and training. Section 4 presents the results of experiments and performance evaluation. Finally, Sect. 5 provides some discussions and conclusions.

2   Related Works

The classification strategies of the remote sensed images can be distinguished between supervised or unsupervised classification and between pixel based and object based classification [4]. Whatever the strategies used, the traditional classification algorithms methods and about the same. These algorithms are based on statistical methods such as Minimum Distance [5], Maximum Likelihood [6], K means [7] and logistic regression [8].

2.1   Pixel and Object Based Classification

Blaschke et al. has shown that for low resolution images a range of sophisticated and well established techniques based on pixel have been developed [9]. However,

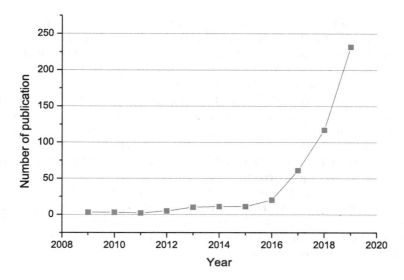

Fig. 1. Number of studies using neural network techniques in remote sensing analysis and published in MDPI remote sensing journal between 2009 and 2019

according to Wang et al. the current needs of the remote sensing community and their clients is not fully satisfied due to different characteristics in high resolution imagery and varying user needs [10]. The huge amount of details that figure in high resolution images decrease the accuracy of pixel based approach.

Image objects can be described as a set of adjacent pixels composed of similar data and construct a bunch of intrinsic characteristics such as size, shape and geographical relationships [12]. To generate objects from image we generally use segmentation algorithms. Blaschke et al. defined segmentation as the partitioning of an array of measurements on the basis of homogeneity. It divides an image into spatially continuous, disjoint and homogeneous regions referred to as 'segments' [10].

2.2   Neural Network Techniques for Remote Sensing

Mas et Flores indicate that the main tasks of applying ANN in remote sensing are land cover classification, unmixing and retrieval of biophysical parameters of cover. Applications of ANNs are also used in change detection, diachronic studies data, forecasting, and object recognition.

Lloyd et al. used an artificial neural network on Landsat thematic mapper imagery to generate land cover of Mediterranean region. He used in addition to spectral information, geostatistical structure function and texture measures extracted from occurrence matrix. This approach resulted in the highest overall classification accuracy [13].

Xie et al. used a multispectral, multitemporal and stereo data to classify land cover and tree species. This study compare the performance of six classification algorithms (ANN, KNN, MLC, SVM, DT, RF) under different data scenario. It concludes that if only spectral bands are used maximum likelihood algorithm (MLC) provides the best results (Land Cover classification accuracy 76.4% compared 72.9% for Machine learning algorithms). But when it comes to multi-source data Machine Learning classifier gives a way better results. This study also underlined that ANN has the lowest performance in this case [14].

Concerning Convolution neural network (CNN) Song et al. elucidated the advantages of using CNN for classifying remotely sensed data. The operation of convolution allows to extract abstract features directly from pixel data. CNN can rapidly extract feature from a massive amount of images, it usually used for scene classification, object detection and object extraction. Jin et al. proposed a land use classifier based on object-oriented method combined with CNN. The experimental data chosen for this study was an optical remote sensing image of 1 m resolution. The results of this study showed an accuracy of 96.2% with a convolution kernel size of 3*3 and mentioned that the accuracy can increase as we increase the depth of the CNN classifier [4].

3   Experiment Description

3.1   Experiment Data, Study Area and Environment

The image used for this study is an optical aerial image of low spectral resolution (Red, Green, Blue) and very high spatial resolution (25 cm) taken in September 2019 it's size is 28153*33756 pixels. The image covers the urban center of Moulay Bousselham and its peripheral rural area. Moulay Bouselham is a small urban center located 150 km north of the capital Rabat and which is administratively part of the province of Kenitra. This area is characterized by a variety of land use type where we can witness a large number of spectral confusions that make interpreting this image very difficult.

In this experiment we used Windows 10 operating system, with NVIDIA K2200 for GPU acceleration, Intel (R) Xeon(R) CPU E5-2620 composed of 24 cores and 32 Go of RAM. The segmentation and feature extraction tasks are processed using Ecognition Developer software and the ANN model is developed using the Keras open-source framework, Resulting maps are represented using QGIS (Fig. 3).

3.2   Methodology

On this section we will try to clarify the methodology adopted in this experiment. Figure 4 gives a general overview of the steps that guide to generate land cover of Moulay Bouselham Region using ANN combined to object based classification.

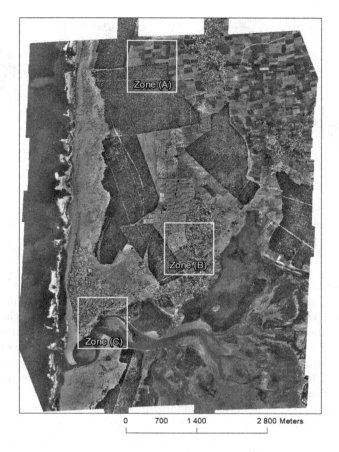

Fig. 2. Aerial RGB image of Moulay Bouselham Region spatial resolution: 25 cm

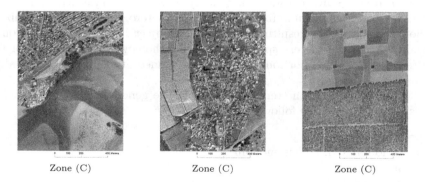

Zone (C)   Zone (C)   Zone (C)

Fig. 3. Different zoom on the Fig. 2 image that show the complexity and the variety of the components of the territory of Moulay Bouselham

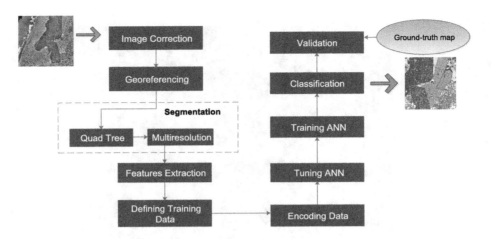

Fig. 4. Flowchart of the ANN object based classifier

Image Segmentation and Feature Extraction. The object-oriented app-roach is based on image segmentation by grouping the homogeneous pixels according to a threshold which depends on the scale chosen. The choice of the segmentation method and scale absurdly influences the classification result. The choice of these parameters is not formal depends on the experience of the user. Several segmentation algorithms exist such as chessboard, contrast split, spectral difference, multi threshold in this experiment we propose the combination of Quad tree Segmentation and multi-resolution segmentation.

The Quad-Tree Segmentation algorithm (QT) splits the pixel domain or an image object domain into a quad-tree grid formed by square objects. This algorithm allows to generate an object level formed with different size with a set of homogeneous square objects of different sizes depending on the homogeneity of the area that they represent.

The multi resolution algorithm (MR) consists on consecutively merging contiguous pixel while minimizing the average heterogeneity and maximizing the homogeneity of the resulting objects. The object homogeneity criterion is depends on two parameters spectral and shape homogeneity. The size of the objects generated is proportional to the scale defined at the input of this algo-rithm.

After the segmentation step we proceed to the generation objects features. In this study we used the following characteristics:

- Spectral features:
  - Ratio for Red, Green and Blue;
  - Brightness;
  - Standard deviation for Red, Green and Blue;
  - Maximum difference;

- Minimum pixel value for Red, Green and Blue
- Maximum pixel value for Red, Green and Blue
- Standard deviation to neighbor pixels
– Geometry features:
  - Area
  - Length
  - Border length
  - Length/Width
  - Asymmetry
  - Compactness
  - Density

Once we calculated this feature for all image objects we exported the results as a shape file where each objects has a proper ID for easily joining and exploiting it.

The Construction of the ANN Classifier. Figure 5 presents the ANN model constructed in this paper. This ANN has in its input layers 22 neurons that correspond to the feature extracted from the image fully connected to two hidden layers was defined with 25 neurons each. For the output layer the number of neurons correspond to the number of class in this study we defined 10 classes (see Fig. 5 and Fig. 6).

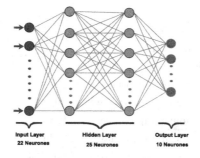

Fig. 5. Structure of the ANN constructed in this study

To Initialization of the network weights is accomplished using a normal distribution with a ratio of standard deviation/variance of 1 unit and a mean value of 0. Concerning the activation function we set the Relu activation function (1) for both the input and the hidden Layer and the Softmax activation function (2) for the output layer. The most adapted loss function for our ANN model is Categorical Crossentropy described in (3). Table 1 summarizes the most important parameter used to construct our model.

$$f(x) = max(0, x) \tag{1}$$

Fig. 6. A view of the 10 classes used in this study

Table 1.

Parameters	Value
Scale of Quad tree segmentation	100
Scale of multiresolution segmentation	150
Number of input features	22
Number of hidden layer	3
Number of neurones/hidden layer	22
Number of neurones in output layer	10
Activation function in input layer	Relu
Activation function in output layer	Relu
Activation function in hidden layer	SoftMax
Loss function	Categorical crossentropy
Kernel initializer	Uniform
Optimizer	adam

$$f(x)_i = \frac{exp(x_i)}{\sum_j exp(x_j))} \tag{2}$$

$$\frac{-1}{N} \sum_{i=1}^{N} \sum_{c=1}^{C} 1_y \, \epsilon \, C_c log P_{model} \, [y_i \epsilon C_y] \tag{3}$$

where, N is the number of observations, and C is the number of the classes. The P model is the probability predicted by the model for the 'i' th observation to belong to the 'c' th classes.

4   Experiment Results

In this experiment we used a set of training data of 2000 objects, nearly 200 objects per class, and a sample of 1200 objects as that we classified using the ANN and that we compared with ground truth. We observe a mean accuracy of 90,05 The accuracy of the classification differs from one class to another we have noticed a very good accuracy during the classification of cultivated land (accuracy = 98.36%), water (accuracy = 97.48%) and Wet Land (accuracy = 96.55%). While a poor precision was observed for roads (accuracy = 81.90%), hothouses (accuracy = 83.69%) and empty field (accuracy = 84.67%) the confusion matrix is presented in Table 2. The classification result is doubly impacted by the quality of the initial segmentation and by the accuracy of the ANN classifier. The presence of multi-scale objects (details of $50 \, m^2$ of surface area and others of several hectares) makes choosing the segmentation scale a very delicate task. Faced with these constraints, we estimate the result to be very satisfactory, provided that we improve the segmentation so that it adapts to multi-scale problems. The results obtained in this study are comparable to the results of these studies which used different methods based on neuronal network to produce land cover maps [4,15,16] (Fig. 7).

Fig. 7. Land cover map of Moulay Bouselham Region using image segmentation and ANN

Table 2. Confusion the ANN classifier

	Ground truth										Total	Accuracy
	Forest	Water	Construction	Wet Land	Hot-Houses	Sandy land	Roads	Empty Fields	Cultivated land	Waves		
Classification results												
Forest	119	0	0	7	0	2	2	0	3	0	133	89.47%
Water	0	116	0	0	0	0	0	0	0	3	119	97.48%
Construction	0	0	109	0	2	0	2	1	0	9	123	88.62%
Wet Land	3	0	0	112	0	0	0	0	1	0	116	96.55%
HotHouses	0	2	3	0	118	0	3	0	0	15	141	83.69%
Sandy land	0	0	0	1	0	100	2	5	0	0	108	92.59%
Roads	0	0	2	0	0	0	95	0	0	0	116	81.90%
Empty Fields	0	0	0	4	0	11	6	116	0	0	137	84.67%
Cultivated land	0	0	0	0	2	0	0	0	120	0	122	98.36%
Waves	0	4	0	0	7	0	0	0	0	90	101	89.11%
Total	122	122	126	124	129	115	110	127	124	117	1216	90.05%

5 Conclusion

The method proposed to produce land use maps by combining the object-oriented approach and artificial neural networks looks very promising given the size of the training set used in this experiment (2000, ie 3% of the number of objects classified). We notice that to improve the accuracy of these method we should review the segmentation phase and increase the size of the training set to reach at least 10%. As perspective we suggest to apply the trained ANN to classify other sets of images and evaluate how can we transfer the knowledge between classifier.

Acknowledgement. This project has received funding from the European Union's Horizon 2020 research and innovation programme under the Marie Skłodowska-Curie grant agreement No. 777720.

References

1. Olson Jr., C.E.: Elements of photographic interpretation common to several sensors. Photogram. Eng. **26**(4), 651–656 (1960)
2. Mas, J.F., Flores, J.J.: The application of artificial neural networks to the analysis of remotely sensed data. Int. J. Remote Sens. **29**(3), 617–663 (2008). https://doi.org/10.1080/01431160701352154
3. Paola, J.D., Schowengerdt, R.A.: A detailed comparison of backpropagation neural network and maximum-likelihood classifiers for urban land use classification. IEEE Trans. Geosci. Remote Sens. **33**, 981–996 (1995). https://doi.org/10.1109/36.406684

4. Jin, B., Ye, P., Zhang, X., Song, W., Li, S.: Object-oriented method combined with deep convolutional neural networks for land-use-type classification of remote sensing images. J. Indian Soc. Remote Sens. **47**(6), 951–965 (2019). https://doi.org/10.1007/s12524-019-00945-3
5. Wacker, A.G., Landgrebe, D.A.: Minimum distance classification in remote sensing (1972)
6. Settle, J.J., Briggs, S.A.: Fast maximum likelihood classification of remotely-sensed imagery. Int. J. Remote Sens. **8**(5), 723–734 (1987). https://doi.org/10.1080/01431168708948683
7. Lv, Z., Hu, Y., Zhong, H., Wu, J., Li, B., Zhao, H.: Parallel K-means clustering of remote sensing images based on MapReduce. In: Wang, F.L., Gong, Z., Luo, X., Lei, J. (eds.) WISM 2010. LNCS, vol. 6318, pp. 162–170. Springer, Heidelberg (2010). https://doi.org/10.1007/978-3-642-16515-3_21
8. Lee, S.: Application of logistic regression model and its validationd for landslide susceptibility mapping using GIS and remote sensing data. Int. J. Remote Sens. **26**(7), 1477–1491 (2005). https://doi.org/10.1080/01431160412331331012
9. Blaschke, T., et al.: Geographic object-based image analysis - towards a new paradigm. ISPRS J. Photogram. Remote Sens. **87**, 180–191 (2014). https://doi.org/10.1016/j.isprsjprs.2013.09.014
10. Wang, K., Franklin, S.E., Guo, X., He, Y., McDermid, G.Y.: Problems in remote sensing of landscapes and habitats (2009). https://doi.org/10.1177/0309133309350121
11. Hay, G.J., Niemann, K.O., McLean, G.F.: An object-specific image-texture analysis of H-resolution forest imagery. Remote Sens. Environ. **55**(2), 108–122 (1996). https://doi.org/10.1016/0034-4257(95)00189-1
12. Hay, G.J., Marceau, D.J., Dube, P., Bouchard, A.: A multiscale framework for landscape analysis: object-specific analysis and upscaling. Landscape Ecol. **16**, 471–490 (2001). https://doi.org/10.1023/A:1013101931793
13. Lloyd, C.D., Berberoglu, S., Curran, P.J., Atkinson, P.M.: A comparison of texture measures for the per-field classification of Mediterranean land cover. Int. J. Remote Sens. **25**(19), 3943–65 (2004). https://doi.org/10.1080/0143116042000192321
14. Xie, Z., Chen, Y., Lu, D., Li, G., Chen, E.: Classification of land cover, forest, and tree species classes with ZiYuan-3 multispectral and stereo data. Remote Sens. **11**(2), 164 (2019). https://doi.org/10.3390/rs11020164
15. Chen, Y., Dou, P., Yang, X.: Improving land use/cover classification with a multiple classifier system using AdaBoost integration technique. Remote Sens. **9**(10), 1055 (2017). https://doi.org/10.3390/rs9101055
16. Li, X., Chen, W., Cheng, X., Wang, L.: A comparison of machine learning algorithms for mapping of complex surface-mined and agricultural landscapes using ZiYuan-3 stereo satellite imagery. Remote Sens. **8**(6), 514 (2016). https://doi.org/10.3390/rs8060514

Implementing an ANN Model to Predict the Notch Band Frequency of an UWB Antenna

Lahcen Aguni[1]([✉]), Samira Chabaa[1,2], Saida Ibnyaich[1],
and Abdelouhab Zeroual[1]

[1] Department of Physics, Faculty of Sciences, Cadi Ayyad University,
Semlalia Marrakesh, Morocco
agunilahcen@gmail.com
[2] Industrial Engineering Department, National School of Applied Sciences,
Ibn Zohr University, Agadir, Morocco

Abstract. In this study, an artificial neural network (ANN) model has been implemented to predict the notch band frequency of an Ultra Wide Band (UWB) antenna. The structure of the proposed ANN model is obtained by varying the ANN parameters such as number of layers, number of neurons, and training algorithm and also by observing the statistical criteria Root Mean Squared Error (RMSE). In term of the regression coefficient R, the obtained value is about 0.98, which indicates that the predicted notch band frequency is good either in the training phase or in the test phase. The reflection coefficient result of the proposed UWB antenna indicates a notch band from 5.1 GHz to 6 GHz with a simulated notch frequency similar to the predicted one.

Keywords: ANN · UWB antenna · Notch band frequency

1 Introduction

The microstrip patch antennas are designed recently with huge amount, because nowadays many applications need a small device to send and receive the information such as Bluetooth, WLAN/WIMAX, ultra-wideband networks, Wi-Fi, and satellite applications. This patch antenna should satisfy some criteria like, low cost, good gain, good radiation pattern etc....

Since the Federal Communication Commission (FCC) recommended the use of the band 3–10 GHz for UWB applications, many topics in the literature have focused on the design of UWB antennas [1]. As revealed, as the UWB uses a large spectrum, the main challenge in designing an UWB antenna is to notch bands used by other systems like WLAN, WIMAX to avoid interferences with these applications.

In the article [2], a dual notch band (5G and WLAN) antenna is achieved by inserting a V-shaped slit and a spilt ring-shaped slit in the patch. In [3], an inverted U-shaped slot was etched on the patch to avoid IEEE 802.11a and HIPERLAN/2 signals. The UWB characteristics of the proposed antenna in the paper [4] is achieved by adding a rectangular parasitic ground plane with circles in the ground plane and circles at the edge and

© Springer Nature Switzerland AG 2020
M. Hamlich et al. (Eds.): SADASC 2020, CCIS 1207, pp. 233–240, 2020.
https://doi.org/10.1007/978-3-030-45183-7_18

vertex of the square patch. With insertion of a T-Shaped slot, an UWB antenna with dual band-notched characteristic is attained [5]. To minimize the potential interferences between the UWB system and the narrowband systems, a compact CPW-fed planar UWB antenna with dual rejection bands at WiMAX/WLAN frequencies is proposed [6].

The ANN have used widely in the design of microstrip patch antennas [7–10]. The principal contribution of this paper is the implementation of an ANN model in order to predict the notch band frequency generated by the slit ring printed in the circular patch of the proposed UWB antenna. The built ANN technique predict efficiently the desired output.

2 Proposed Technique

In order to enhance the performance of the proposed UWB antenna and to make the antenna suitable for avoiding interferences with other applications using a band in the large spectrum of the UWB antenna 3–10 GHz, we have applied the ANN model to predict the notch band frequency. To establish the ANN model, we followed the steps described in the flowchart as shown in Fig. 1.

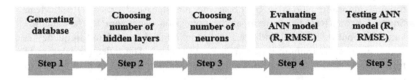

Fig. 1. ANN creation steps.

To establish the ANN structure, we generated a database of 360 samples forming our network input and output. The input components are the dimensions of the slit ring (r, R, g) printed in the circular patch of the proposed UWB antenna (Fig. 2), and the dielectric permittivity ε_r which describes the dielectric substrate material.

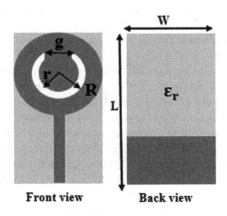

Fig. 2. Proposed antenna.

The choice of these inputs are based on the effect of these parameters on the notch band frequency [11], formulated by the given equation:

$$f = \frac{c}{2(2\pi r + 2(R - r) - g)\sqrt{\varepsilon_{eff}}} \quad (1)$$

Where c is the speed of light (c = 3 × 108 m/s) and ε_{eff} the effective dielectric:

$$\varepsilon_{eff} = \frac{\varepsilon_r + 1}{2} \quad (2)$$

The dimensions r, R, and g represent respectively the inner radius, the outer radius, and the gap of the slit ring (Fig. 2).

The 360 datasets are collected by varying the dimensions of the slit ring (r, R, g) and observing the notch band frequency which corresponds to a voltage standing wave ratio of VSWR > 2. The task is achieved by employing a visual basic (VB) script which controls the High Frequency Structure Simulator (HFSS) from MATLAB, each iteration on MATLAB corresponds to a design on HFSS. After each iteration the VB script recovers the input with its corresponding simulated notch band frequency which is the desired output. The input and output data of the ANN network are grouped respectively in Table 1 and Fig. 3.

Table 1. ANN inputs.

Number of samples	r	R	g	ε_r
120	2, 3, 4, 5	2.5, 3.5, 4.5, 5.5	1, 2, 3, 4	2.2, 4.3, 6.15
120	2.5, 3.5, 4.5, 5.5	3, 4, 5, 6	1, 2, 3, 4	2.2, 4.3, 6.15
120	2, 3, 4, 5	2.3, 3.3, 4.3, 5.3	1.5, 2.5, 3.5, 4.5	2.2, 4.3, 6.15

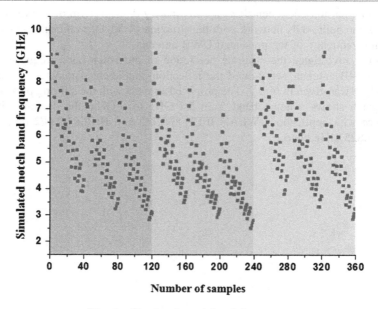

Fig. 3. Simulated notch band frequency.

After collecting the datasets, we have determined the suitable number of hidden layers, the number of neurons in each layer, and the appropriate training algorithm among Resilient Back Propagation (RP), Polak-Ribiere Conjugate Gradient (CGP), One Step Secant (OSS), Scaled Conjugate Gradient (SCG), Bayesian Regulation (BR), Conjugate Gradient with Fletcher-Peeves (CGF), and Levenberg-Marquardt (LM). These parameters were chosen accurately by calculating the root-mean-square error (RMSE) (formula 3), this statistical criterion measures the differences between the target data (simulated notch band frequency) and the output data (predicted notch band frequency by ANN), more RMSE close to zero high accuracy is attained.

Root Mean Squared Error (RMSE):

$$\text{RMSE} = \sqrt{\left(\frac{1}{N}\right) \sum_{i=1}^{N} (t_i - \alpha_i)^2} \tag{3}$$

Where: N is the total number of samples, t_i and α_i represent respectively target and output data.

3   Results and Discussions

The RMSE of different number of hidden layers, number of neurons, and training algorithms during the training and testing phase is depicted in Fig. 4. As given, the accurate ANN structure consists of 1 hidden layer, the hidden layer consists of 30 neurons, while the appropriate training algorithm is LM (Fig. 5).

Another parameter is used to evaluate the performance of the established model, we presented in Fig. 6, the regression coefficient R for our ANN network which describes the relationship between the predicted ANN values and the simulated ones. We obtained a regression coefficient R of approximately 0.98. In term of the value of this coefficient, the built ANN network with the structure (4-30-1) is efficient to predict the notch band frequency of the presented UWB antenna.

To better investigate the accurate prediction of the notch band frequency of the proposed UWB antenna, we plotted the reflection coefficient parameter simulated in HFSS and CST as given in Fig. 7. The proposed antenna with the slit ring printed in the circular patch shows a notch band from 5.1 GHz to 6 GHz, this feature will limit interference with applications WLAN IEEE 802.11a and HIPERLAN/2 operating in the 5.15–5.825 GHz band.

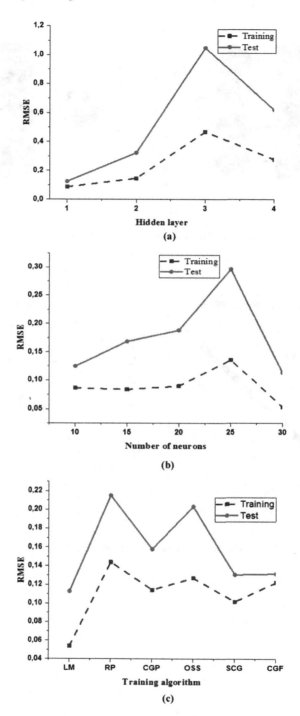

Fig. 4. ANN parameters: (a) number of hidden layer (b) number of neurons (c) training algorithm.

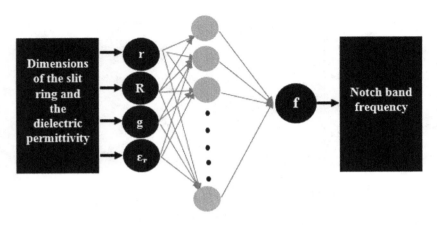

Fig. 5. Structure of the proposed ANN.

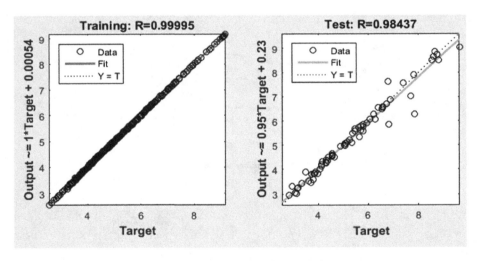

Fig. 6. Regression coefficient result.

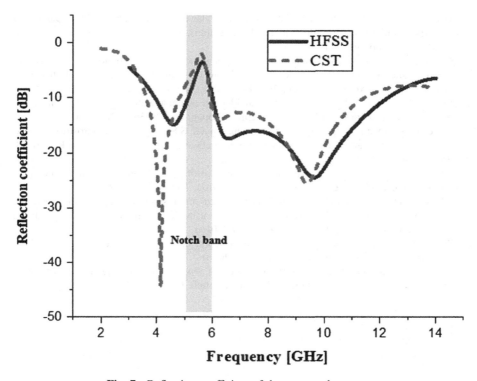

Fig. 7. Reflection coefficient of the presented antenna.

4 Conclusion

In this study, we applied the ANN technique to predict the notch band frequency of an UWB antenna. The structure 4-30-1 established with the appropriate parameters in terms of number of hidden layers, number of neurons in each layer, and training algorithm, helped us to better predict a crucial parameter to notch the band from 5.1 GHz to 6 GHz. This characteristic prevents interferences with applications such as WLAN IEEE 802.11a and HIPERLAN/2 using a part of the UWB spectrum.

References

1. Oppermann, I., Hämäläinen, M., Iinatti, J.: UWB: Theory and Applications. Wiley, Hoboken (2005)
2. Bong, H-U., Hussain, N., Rhee, S-Y., Gil, S-K., Kim, N.: Design of an UWB antenna with two slits for 5G/WLAN-notched bands. Microwave Opt. Technol. Lett. 1–6 (2019). https://doi.org/10.1002/mop.31670
3. Hussain, N., Jeong, M., Park, J., Rhee, S., Kim, P., Kim, N.: A compact size 2.9–23.5 GHz microstrip patch antenna with WLAN band-rejection. Microwave Opt. Technol. Lett. 1–7 (2019). https://doi.org/10.1002/mop.31708

4. Baudha, S., Yadav, M.V.: A novel design of a planar antenna with modified patch and defective ground plane for ultra-wideband applications. Microwave Opt. Technol. Lett. 1–8 (2019). https://doi.org/10.1002/mop.31716

5. Ojaroudi, N., Ojaroudi, M., Ghadimi, N.: Dual band-notched small monopole antenna with novel W-shaped conductor backed-plane and novel T-shaped slot for UWB applications. IET Microwaves Antennas Propag. 7(1), 8–14 (2013)

6. Chu, Q.X., Yang, Y.Y.: A compact ultrawideband antenna with 3.4/5.5 GHz dual band-notched characteristics. IEEE Trans. Antennas Propag. 56(12), 3637–3644 (2008)

7. Aneesh, M., Ansari, J.A., Singh, A., Kamakshi, Saiyed, S.S.: Analysis of microstrip line feed slot loaded patch antenna using artificial neural network. Prog. Electromagnet. Res. B **58**, 35–46 (2014)

8. Akdagli, A., Kayabasi, A., Develi, I.: Computing resonant frequency of C-shaped compact microstrip antennas by using ANFIS. Int. J. Electron. **102**, 407–417 (2015)

9. Khan, T., De, A., Uddin, M.: Prediction of slot-size and inserted air-gap for improving the performance of rectangular microstrip antennas using artificial neural networks. IEEE Antennas Wirel. Propag. Lett. **12**, 1367–1371 (2013)

10. Turker, N., Gunes, F., Yildirim, T.: Artificial neural design of microstrip antennas. Turk. J. Electr. Eng. Comput. Sci. **14**(3), 445–453 (2006)

11. Syed, A., Aldhaheri, R.W.: A very compact and low profile UWB planar antenna with WLAN band rejection. Sci. World J. 7 (2016), Article ID 3560938

Combinatorial Optimization

Optimization of Truck-Shovel Allocation Problem in Open-Pit Mines

Sanaa Benlaajili[1,2,3](✉), Fouad Moutaouakkil[2], Ahmed Chebak[3],
Hicham Medromi[1,2], Laurent Deshayes[3], and Salma Mourad[2]

[1] Research Foundation for Development and Innovation
in Science and Engineering, Casablanca, Morocco
benlaajili.sanaa@gmail.com, hmedromi@yahoo.fr

[2] Engineering Research Laboratory, National Higher School of Electricity
and Mechanics, Hassan II University, Casablanca, Morocco
fmoutaouakkil@hotmail.com, mouradsalma95@gmail.com

[3] Innovation Lab for Operations, Mohammed VI Polytechnic University,
Benguerir, Morocco
{Ahmed.CHEBAK, Laurent.DESHAYES}@um6p.ma

Abstract. The use of an optimized dispatching system for the haul trucks in an open-pit mine plays a crucial role to increase the production, especially with the introduction of autonomous trucks into the mine. This involves managing the entire transport system in order to reduce the mine's operating costs and enhance the mine efficiency. This paper presents a trucks-shovel dispatching model that performs the first phase of a mining fleet management system (production optimization and allocation planning) and which is developed in two main steps. The first step proposes a modeling of the allocation of shovels problem as a vehicle routing problem. In the second step, a mixed integer linear programming model is proposed to determine the optimal number of trips required to transport the quantity of ore from each loading point to each dumping site, this model is used to dispatch available trucks to the appropriate shovel. The feature of the proposed models is that they include the assignment of shovels which is generally ignored and left to the task's dispatcher. The second specificity is that they take into account a heterogeneous fleet of trucks and shovels with different capacities. For validation, a case study using the developed models in a Moroccan mining company is presented and discussed.

Keywords: Fleet management system · Truck-shovel allocation problem · Mixed integer linear programming · Vehicle routing problem · Autonomous trucks

1 Introduction

The truck-shovel allocation problem is a major problem in open-pit mines. It was a research topic of several researchers and significant efforts were made to solve this problem. Ore transport costs represent 50% to 60% of the mine's operating costs and

© Springer Nature Switzerland AG 2020
M. Hamlich et al. (Eds.): SADASC 2020, CCIS 1207, pp. 243–255, 2020.
https://doi.org/10.1007/978-3-030-45183-7_19

reducing them is an active research field [1]. A modest reduction in these costs will significantly contribute to increase the productivity of the mine operation.

To monitor the transport system in the mine, a fleet management system (FMS) is required. The main objective of this system is to allocate transport trucks to shovels while optimizing the production and efficiency of the mine based on real-time data. The mining fleet management system model must find the best allocation of equipment in order to satisfy production requirements and minimize truck operating costs. The literature show that the majority of approaches used for the allocation of trucks and shovels can be classified into two categories: single-stage and multi-stage approaches [2, 3]. The common approach is a multi-stage optimization, where the problem is divided into two or three parts and the solution from each step is used in the next step [3]. In the fixed allocation approach, a number of trucks dedicated to specific shovel are fixed and will never be changed during a shift.

In this paper, we present a modeling of the upper-stage of the truck-shovel allocation problem. First, we establish a model for the assignment of shovels to each available ore loading point. Then we develop a modeling of the allocation of trucks to shovels. A case study based on the Moroccan mining company's Data is also presented and discussed in order to validate the developed models.

2 State of the Art of Truck-Shovel Allocation Problem in Open-Pit Mines

2.1 Allocation System of Transport Trucks in Open-Pit Mine

A fleet management system allow to identify in real-time the location and direction of movement of each truck in the fleet and automatically transmits this information to the dispatchers [3]. The objectives of an allocation system are essentially to make a certain number of trucks to accomplish tasks while maintaining specific objectives. These objectives may be in terms of economic or time factors, or both. In some cases, these different objectives are contradictory, and a compromise must then be found. Therefore, an important step in developing an allocation system is to determine the relative importance of the various parameters that must be taken into account [4, 5].

2.2 Models Behind a Mining Fleet Management System

In the mining fleet management systems used in open-pit mines, a truck allocation model includes two types of allocation: fixed allocation and dynamic allocation.

Fixed Allocation
In this method, a group of trucks are assigned to a fixed transport route (special shovel) and this condition will remain unchanged until the end of the shift. The routes to which the trucks have been assigned will not change until a shovel breaks down or a critical event occurs. In other words, it can be said that a fixed allocation method is a static method [6, 7]. The classic methods in which the principles of queuing theory and mathematical programming are among the different methods used in the fixed allocation of trucks. All these methods are designed to determine the optimal number of

trucks allocated to each shovel during a shift [8]. Despite these drawbacks, the fixed allocation method can be used to validate simulation models and serve as a 'reference' to compare the effectiveness of other heuristics methods [9].

Dynamic Allocation
Research results in the literature show that a fixed allocation method is not appropriate and efficient for scheduling transport in large mines [8], and the dynamic allocation method can be a good alternative. In the dynamic allocation, a number of trucks available in the fleet are assigned to a specific shovel at the beginning of the shift. However, instead of serving a single shovel or road during the shift, these trucks will receive a new assignment from the dispatching system each time after loading and unloading [3]. Therefore, these trucks can be used for a several shovels or roads throughout the shift.

2.3   Trucks Allocation Approaches

Single-Stage Approach
In the single-stage approach, trucks are allocated without considering any constraints or production targets, generally following empirical rules [2]. When the single-stage approach is used, trucks are allocated among the shovels based on available experience, without taking into account specific needs or operating conditions. In fact, it is a heuristic approach, which is purely empirical in nature [10].

Multi-stage Approach
It was demonstrated that the multi-stage approach is better than the single-stage approach because it takes into account the production objective. The multi-stage approach generally divides the dispatching problem into two sub-problems, including production optimization and allocation planning with setting the production target in an upper stage and allocating trucks to shovels in real-time in a lower stage with the objective of achieving the production targets set by the upper stage [7]. This paper discusses the upper stage of the multi-stage dispatching system.

In generally, the best allocation of trucks is that which maximizes the satisfaction of one or more dispatching objectives, called criteria. Various criteria are used to allocate trucks and they try, directly or indirectly, to maximize ore production or minimize equipment inactivity such as truck waiting time in front of shovels and shovel idle time. Authors in [10] provide a detailed description of these criteria and also the different methods proposed in the literature for the dispatching of transport trucks in open-pit mines.

3   Methodology

The dispatching system to be developed should be based on the multi-stage approach because it has a great advantage over the single-stage approach [2]. This article is the subject of the first phase (production optimization and allocation planning) of the global model for the truck-shovel system in the mine. Most of the models proposed in the literature and especially in the allocation planning stage do not provide information for shovel assignments, which are still entirely the task of the dispatcher [3]. The problem of transport and loading are closely linked, solving one without taking into account the other remains a flawed task since the loading of ore is the most expensive phase after that of haulage in the mining industry. The model proposed in [7] determines the number of trips that a truck must make to achieve the production objective. However, the model does not provide information about the allocation of shovels in to different ore points. In the model that was developed in [11], the upper stage was performed in two phases. First, they determine the assignment of shovels with the objective of maximizing production while respecting quality constraints. Then, as the second step, they represent the truck's travel plan between the shovels and the dumping sites. Besides the advantages of the model, the authors assume that all the trucks in the fleet have the same capacity, a homogeneous fleet of trucks. The second disadvantage of the model of [11] is the assumption of a fixed content material in each size front. However, the stochastic nature of ore quality, even in a single block, is not negligible [3].

In this paper, the problem is divided in two main steps. In the first phase, the assignment of shovels to the different ore points is accomplished by solving a vehicle routing problem. It is a question of determining the routing of a fleet of shovels from each ore points in order to minimize the global loading costs. In the second hand, we determine the number of trips required to transport the quantity of ore from each shovel to each dumping site during a full shift while taking into account time and availability constraints. The results of this study are used as input data for the real-time truck allocation phase.

4   Modeling of the Shovel Assignment Problem

The allocation planning stage in the majority of models in the literature does not provide information for the task of assigning shovels to different ore points in order to optimize the overall transport system, which is still entirely the dispatcher's task. A mathematical formulation and modeling of the problem remains imperative in order to manage the entire transport system and satisfy customer demands with reduced operating costs. The problem is part of an operational research problem class called the vehicle routing problem. The aim is to determine the routing of a fleet of shovels with different capacities in order to load all the available quantity in the different ore points.

The variants of the vehicle routing problem (VRP) are different depending on the addition and/or elimination of the constraints of the traditional VRP [12]. In the following, we present the problem of the VRP related to the heterogeneous fleet. The aim of vehicle routing problem is to find a set of minimum total cost routes for a fleet of vehicles based at a single depot (shovels), to serve a set of customers (ore points) under the following constraints: (i) Each route begins and ends at the depot, (ii) Each customer is visited exactly once [13].

Before formulating the problem, we first introduce some notations:

C^{kr}: Facturation rate of shovel type kr

V^{kr}: Shovel speed

D_{ij}: Distance between the ore point i and the point j

t_c^{hkr}: Loading time of the truck type h by the shovel kr type r

D^i: Distance between the ore point i and the dumping site

V_r^h: Truck's return speed type h

N_i^h: Number of trips made by the truck type h to move from ore point i and the dumping site

T_s^{kr}: Operating time of the shovel kr

n: Number of ore points

R: Number of types of shovels

H: Number of types of trucks

mr: Number of shovels type r

Decision Variables:

The Boolean decision variable x_{ij}^{kr} is defined to indicate if the shovel kr traverses an arc $(i; j)$ in an optimal solution.

x_{ij}^{kr} : Boolean: If point i is served after point j by the shovel kr type r

Objective Function:

The objective function (1) minimizes the total travel cost of shovels.

$$\sum_{k=1}^{mr}\sum_{r=1}^{R}\sum_{i=1}^{n}\sum_{\substack{j=1\\j\neq i}}^{n}\frac{C^{kr}}{V^{kr}}\times D_{ij}\times x_{ij}^{kr} \tag{1}$$

Constraints:

In order to correctly model the problem, it is essential to consider all constraints that govern the use of the different shovels. All considered constraints are as follow:

$$\sum_{\substack{i=1\\j\neq i}}^{n}\sum_{k=1}^{mr}\sum_{r=1}^{R}x_{ij}^{kr}=1 \quad \forall j\in\{1,\ldots,n\} \tag{2}$$

$$\sum_{\substack{j=1\\j\neq i}}^{n}\sum_{k=1}^{mr}\sum_{r=1}^{R}x_{ij}^{kr}=1 \quad \forall i\in\{1,\ldots,n\} \tag{3}$$

Constraint (2) and (3) indicate that each point j will be served after each point i, only one time and by a unique shovel.

$$\sum_{i=0}^{n}\sum_{k=1}^{mr}\sum_{r=1}^{R}x_{il}^{kr}=\sum_{j=1}^{n}\sum_{k=1}^{mr}x_{lj}^{kr} \quad \forall l\in\{1,\ldots,n\} \tag{4}$$

The constraint (4) ensures that the flow is conserved. A visited point must be left imperatively.

$$\sum_{j=1}^{n} x_{0j}^{kr} = 1 \quad \forall k \in \{1,\ldots,mr\} \quad \forall r \in \{1,\ldots,R\} \tag{5}$$

$$\sum_{i=1}^{n} x_{i0}^{kr} = 1 \quad \forall k \in \{1,\ldots,mr\} \quad \forall r \in \{1,\ldots,R\} \tag{6}$$

Constraints (5) and (6) ensure that the shovel fleet indicated by index 0 is the starting and arrival point of all shovels.

$$\sum_{i=1}^{n} \sum_{h=1}^{H} \left(t_c^{hkr} + \frac{D^i}{V_r^h} \times N_i^h \right) \times x_{ij}^{kr} \leq T_s^{kr}$$

$$\forall k \in \{1,\ldots,mr\} \quad \forall r \in \{1,\ldots,R\} \quad \forall j \in \{1,\ldots,n\} \tag{7}$$

The constraint (7) ensures that the demand of each point i in time does not exceed the capacity of the shovel in time.

$$x_{ii}^{kr} = 0 \quad \forall j \in \{1,\ldots,n\} \quad \forall k \in \{1,\ldots,mr\} \quad \forall r \in \{1,\ldots,R\} \tag{8}$$

$$x_{ij}^{kr} + x_{ji}^{kr} \leq 1$$

$$\forall i \in \{1,\ldots,n\} \quad \forall j \in \{1,\ldots,n\} \quad \forall k \in \{1,\ldots,mr\} \quad \forall r \in \{1,\ldots,R\} \tag{9}$$

Constraints (8) and (9) ensure that there is no loop.

Resolution Approach

The VRP is belongs the category of NP hard problems that can be exactly solved only for small instances of the problem [12]. In fact, in its symmetrical version, i.e. in the case where the associated graph is not oriented, the total number of possible solutions is $(n - 1)/2$ where n is the number of points. With such factorial complexity, efficient VRP resolution requires the use of specialized heuristics or even Meta-heuristics. Indeed, the exact methods remain limited to small problems. Therefore, researchers [14, 15] have concentrated on developing heuristic algorithms to solve this kind of problem. Even though the heuristic algorithms are adapted to our problem, but they are usually trapped by a local optimum and therefore fail to obtain the global optimal solution [16]. For that reason, our choice of algorithm is "Simulated Annealing"; this choice is due to the facility of its implementation. A generalized simulated annealing method has been developed and applied to the optimization of functions (possibly constrained) having many local extrema [17]. The main feature of simulated annealing is that it provides a mechanism to escape the local optimum by allowing upward movements in the hope of finding a global optimum [14].

5 Formulation and Modeling of the Transport Problem

The transport problem is modeled as a mixed integer linear program (MILP) that aims to find the optimal number of trips to transport a specific quantity of ore by truck type from shovel j to the dumping site i.

Before formulating the problem, we introduce some notations:

Q_j: Quantity of ore available in front of each shovel j

d_{ij}: Distance from shovel j to dumping site i

C^h: Truck capacity type h

α^h: Transport cost of the loaded truck type h per kilometer

β^h: Transport cost of the empty truck type h per kilometer

R_d: Stripping ratio according to the production planning

K_i: Demand for dumping site i

V_p^j: Average loading speed of the shovel j

V_T^i: Average unloading speed of dump site I of the type h truck

V_{vi}^h: Average travel speed of the empty truck

V_c^h: Average speed of the loaded

t_{mt}: Average truck maneuvering time in the unloading area

t_{ms}: Average truck maneuvering time in the unloading area

M_i: Quantity of desired ore in each dumping site

Decision Variables:

x_{ij}^h: Number of loaded trips of the truck type h required from the shovel j to the dumping site i.

y_{ij}^h: Number of unloaded trips of the truck type h required from the dumping site i to the shovel j.

Objective Function:

The objective function (10) consists in minimizing the number of trips required to transport the ore during a work shift.

$$F = \sum_{h=1}^{H} \sum_{i=1}^{m} \sum_{j=1}^{n} d_{ij} \times (\alpha^h x_{ij}^h + \beta^h y_{ij}^h) \tag{10}$$

Constraints:

In order to correctly model the problem, it is essential to take into consideration all the constraints that govern the use of the different trucks. The problem also requires taking into account the various constraints of the site, which are described below:

$$\sum_{h=1}^{H} \sum_{i=1}^{m} C^h x_{ij}^h \leq Q_j \quad \forall j \in [1, n] \tag{11}$$

The constraint (11) provides that the quantity of ore transported must not exceed the available quantity at each shovel j.

$$\sum_{h=1}^{H} \sum_{j=1}^{n} C^h x_{ij}^h \leq K_i \quad \forall i \in [1, m] \tag{12}$$

The constraint (12) ensures that trucks must be dispatched in such a way that the desired production volume in the mine is achieved and optimized in the best possible way without exceeding the demand in each dumping site i.

$$\sum_{h=1}^{H} \sum_{i=1}^{m} \sum_{j=1}^{n} x_{ij}^h \times \left[\frac{C^h}{V_p^j} + \frac{d_{ij}}{V_{vi}^h} + t_{ms} \right] + y_{ij}^h \times \left[\frac{C^h}{V_T^i} + \frac{d_{ij}}{V_c^h} + t_{mt} \right] \leq H \times T \tag{13}$$

The constraint (13) ensures that the real total travel time of trucks does not exceed their average operating time in a work shift.

$$\sum_{h=1}^{H} \sum_{j=1}^{n} C^h x_{ij}^h \geq R_d \times M_i \quad \forall i \in [1, m] \tag{14}$$

The constraint (14) ensures that the stripping ratio is adjusted according to the production planning.

$$\sum_{i=1}^{m} x_{ij}^h = \sum_{i=1}^{m} y_{ij}^h \quad \forall j \in [1, n] \tag{15}$$

The constraint (15) ensures the continuity of the loading and transport flow, the number of each trips truck type h arriving at the loading point must be equal to the number of trips trucks type h leaving the dumping sites.

$$\forall i \in [1, \ldots, m]; \forall j \in [1, \ldots, n] x_{ij} \in N^+ \tag{16}$$

The constraint (16) ensures that the solution is physically significant, i.e. the number of trips is an integer number.

Resolution Approach
The present transport problem is modeled using a mixed integer linear program (MILP). However, looking for a feasible solution for MILP is equivalent to looking for a point in the polynomial of feasible solutions with all its full coordinates. Deciding whether a MILP has feasible solutions is an example of a NP-complete problem. The methods for solving optimization problems NP-difficult are classified into two categories: exact methods and heuristic methods. The exact methods are designed to find an optimal solution to the problem. However, their calculation times tend to increase exponentially with the size of the instances of the NP-difficult problems [18]. On the other hand, heuristic methods are algorithms designed to produce a feasible solution to

the problem, but not necessarily optimal, without requiring significant computation time [14]. For the present problem, all the solutions are enumerable. Rather than listing all these solutions, we can try to use the classic computer paradigm of dividing the problem. Branch and Bound methods (B&B) try to avoid exploring the entire solution space by using the characteristics of optimal solutions and solution cost estimates.

6 Case Study

To validate the effectiveness of the proposed model, we illustrate a real case based on the Moroccan mining company's data. The allocation in the mine of Benguerir is made at the beginning of each shift. A number of trucks are assigned to serve a single shovel. Due to the confidentiality of the data, we used virtual data based on the actual mine situation. The fixed allocation strategy adopted for the allocation of trucks to the different shovels in the mine is used as a reference to illustrate the benefits of the proposed approach.

The proposed models for two types of trucks of different capacities are tested. We have four 136T capacity trucks and three 190T capacity trucks. We suppose two 36T capacity shovels (F1, F2) and another one F3 with 28T capacity. Table 1 presents the collected data to solve the truck-shovel allocation problem.

Table 1. Data required for solving the allocation truck shovel problem

Ore point	Distance	Dumping site demand	Available quantity	Longitude of the ore point	Latitude of the ore point
1	6.6	3240	4077	32.2592	−7.8856
2	5.3	2256	5245	32.2639	−7.8851
3	5.9	2146	6402	32.2430	−7.0207
4	3.7	828	3672	32.2265	−7.8515
5	6.7	3740	4822	32.1952	−7.8659
6	5.7	3220	4220	32.1410	−7.8638
7	4.7	1542	2755	32.0663	−7.8083

The proposed models with the collected data are simulated using MATLAB. In the loading phase, we load the longitude and latitude of the ore points, the program uses the simulated annealing algorithm for the resolution of our VRP. The obtained results are presented in Table 2 and the solution of VRP for the allocation of shovels to each ore point is illustrated on the Fig. 1. The first figure on the left shows the positioning of the ore points expressed in geocentric Cartesian coordinates, and the evolution of the shovel turns during the search for the optimum. Each shovel is presented in a different color. The second figure on the right shows the evolution of the cost while searching the optimum.

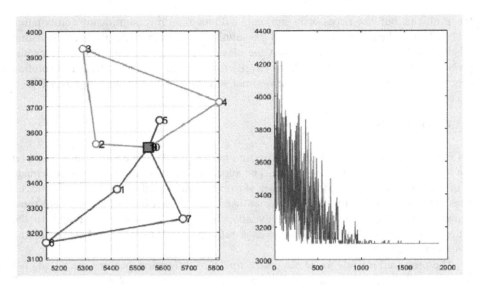

Fig. 1. Resolution of the VRP problem for the allocation of shovels

Figure 1 shows that the cost trend fluctuates with a negative slope. This shows that the proposed model provides a low loading cost compared to the classic approach. The fluctuation ensures that the program does not get bogged down in local optimizations.

To check the effectiveness of the proposed model in the loading phase, we have calculated the cost per kilometer of loading at each ore point according to the method adopted by the company and after implementing the proposed loader allocation model. The result of this comparison is shown in Fig. 2.

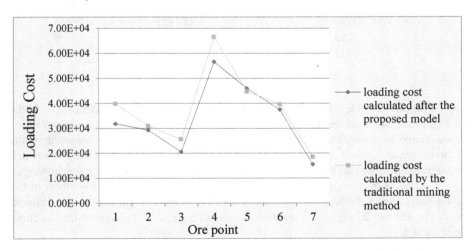

Fig. 2. Comparison of the loading cost between the proposed model and the traditional method in loading phase

In the transport phase, we have introduced the data concerning the distance between the ore points and the dumping sites, the requested quantity from each ore point as well as the quantity available at each point. The program uses the Branch and Bound algorithm to determine the optimal number of trips for each type of truck. Our transportation problem was solved in a time of 0.7903 s for a number of points equal to 10 in MATLAB. However, as soon as the size of the data increases, an approximate method is required.

Before launching the resolution, it is essential to introduce the number of trucks available in the fleet in order to distribute the trucks in an equitable way on the shovels and their demands instead of being at the service of only one shovel loader during the work shift.

Table 2. Solution for the allocation truck shovel problem following the proposed models

Ore point	Trips 136T	Trips 190T	Shovel working time	Shovel F1	Shovel F2	Shovel F3	Dumping site demand	Transported quantity
1	3	15	5.3			✗	3240	3258
2	11	4	2.7167	✗			2256	2256
3	13	2	2.6833	✗			2146	2148
4	2	3	0.8167	✗			828	842
5	22	4	5.3		✗		3740	3752
6	14	7	4.2			✗	3220	3234
7	10	1	1.5333			✗	1542	1550

Table 2 shows that the proposed models provide an optimal allocation of the truck-shovel system based on a scientific method that takes into account the objective in production and the constraints of the exploitation.

The proposed models achieved good results while satisfying the demand for transporting the quantities available at each ore point to each dumping site with a minimum global transport cost compared to the costs generated by the previous transport activity. They are used to dispatch available trucks to the appropriate shovel while taking into account the availability of trucks in the fleet, the heterogeneity of truck capacities, and all constraints that govern the use of the different shovels and trucks in the mine environment.

7 Conclusion

This paper presents a trucks-shovel dispatching model in open-pit mines. One of the features of this model of the first phase of truck-shovel allocation problem is its ability to optimize the planning phase of truck allocation in the mine while optimizing the assignment of shovels to different ore points through a VRP problem resolution and seeking the number of trips necessary to transport the quantity of ore from each point. Simplicity and precision are the two major merits of such a model. The model also has other advantages such as the possibility of using several types of trucks of different capacities within the transport fleet and shovels in a heterogeneous fleet.

The application of autonomous truck technology in the mining sector has recently received a lot of attention. Mining sites using autonomous technology in their haulage system have also benefited from other advantages, including increased productivity, better equipment utilization rates and reduced damage to manual trucks. Autonomous trucks homogenize cycle times, while ensuring that equipment operates according to predefined parameters [19]. However, mines focus more on the purely technical development of completely autonomous transport trucks and do not highlight fleet management system, which is a necessary and an essential element for managing the fleet of autonomous trucks and allowing this new technology to be combined with manual trucks. As a perspective to this work, we will develop the second phase model that will allow us to assign trucks in real-time and we will develop a truck dispatching system in a manual environment and in a completely autonomous environment.

Acknowledgments. The authors would like to thank Mohammed VI Polytechnic University, OCP Group for their valuable support throughout this study and for providing the necessary data. We would like to thank all the members of the research team who contributed greatly to this work.

References

1. Kennedy, B.A.: Surface Mining, 2nd edn. SME, Littleton (1990)
2. Alarie, S., Gamache, M.: Overview of solution strategies used in truck dispatching systems for open pit mines. Int. J. Surf. Min. Reclam. Environ. **16**, 59–76 (2002)
3. Moradi Afrapoli, A, Askari-Nasab, H: Mining fleet management systems: a review of models and algorithms. Int. J. Min. Reclam. Environ. 1–19 (2017)
4. Dindarloo, S.R., Osanloo, M., Frimpong, S.: A stochastic simulation framework for truck and shovel selection and sizing in open pit mines. J. South Afr. Inst. Min. Metall. **115**, 209–219 (2015)
5. Moradi Afrapoli, A., Tabesh, M., Askari-Nasab, H.: A multiple objective transportation problem approach to dynamic truck dispatching in surface mines. Eur. J. Oper. Res. **276**, 331–342 (2019)
6. Munirathinam, M., Yingling, J.C.: A review of computer-based truck dispatching strategies for surface mining operations. Int. J. Surf. Min. Reclam. Environ. **8**, 1–15 (1994)
7. Zhang, L., Xia, X.: An integer programming approach for truck-shovel dispatching problem in open-pit mines. Energy Proc. **75**, 1779–1784 (2015)
8. Ahangaran, D.K., Yasrebi, A.B., Wetherelt, A., Foster, P.: Real-time dispatching modelling for trucks with different capacities in open pit mines. Arch. Min. Sci. **57**, 39–52 (2012)
9. Subtil, R.F., Silva, D.M., Alves, J.C.: A practical approach to truck dispatch for open pit mines, vol. 14 (2011)
10. Koryagin, M., Voronov, A.: Improving the organization of the shovel-truck systems in open-pit coal mines. Transp. Probl. **12**(2), 113–122 (2017)
11. Soumis, F., Ethier, J., Elbrond, J.: Evaluation of the new truck dispatching in the Mount Wright mine. In: 21st APCOM, Littleton, CO, (1989)
12. Ralphs, T.K., Kopman, L., Pulleyblank, W.R., Trotter, L.E.: On the capacitated vehicle routing problem. Math. Program. Ser. B **94**, 343–359 (2003)

13. Borčinova, Z.: Two models of the capacitated vehicle routing problem. Croat. Oper. Res. Rev. **8**, 463–469 (2017)

14. Gendreau, M., Potvin, J.-Y.: Handbook of Metaheuristics, 2nd edn. Springer, Boston (2010). https://doi.org/10.1007/978-1-4419-1665-5

15. Laporte, G., Ropke, S., Vidal, T.: Vehicle Routing: Problems, Methods and Applications, 2nd edn. SIAM, Philadelphia (2014)

16. Gendreau, M., Potvin, J.Y., Bräumlaysy, O., Hasle, G., Løkketangen, A.: Metaheuristics for the vehicle routing problem and its extensions: a categorized bibliography. In: Golden, B., Raghavan, S., Wasil, E. (eds.) The Vehicle Routing Problem: Latest Advances and New Challenges. ORCS, vol. 43, pp. 143–169. Springer, Boston (2008). https://doi.org/10.1007/978-0-387-77778-8_7

17. Bohachevsky, I.O., Johnson, M.E., Stein, M.L.: Generalized simulated annealing for function optimization. Technometrics **28**, 209–217 (1986)

18. Puchinger, J., Raidl, G.R.: Combining metaheuristics and exact algorithms in combinatorial optimization: a survey and classification. In: Mira, J., Álvarez, J.R. (eds.) Artificial Intelligence and Knowledge Engineering Applications: A Bioinspired Approach. LNCS, vol. 3562, pp. 41–53. Springer, Heidelberg (2005). https://doi.org/10.1007/11499305_5

19. Autonomous mining: Improving safety and increasing productivity. https://www.cat.com/fr_US/support/operations/technology/cat-minestar/minestar-in-action/auto-mining-safe-productivity.html

Multi-objective Optimization of Heterogeneous Vehicles Routing in the Case of Medical Waste Using Genetic Algorithm

Mustapha Ahlaqqach[1,2(✉)], Jamal Benhra[1], Salma Mouatassim[1], and Safia Lamrani[1]

[1] ENSEM, LRI Laboratory, OSIL ENSEM, Hassan II University of Casablanca, Casablanca, Morocco
ahlaqqach@gmail.com, jamalbenhra@gmail.com,
mouatassimsalma@gmail.com, safialamrani@gmail.com
[2] CELOG-ESITH, Casablanca, Morocco

Abstract. Medical waste in Morocco, classified as a time bomb, imposes on the authorities and professionals the obligation to provide an economic and sustainable solution. Through this article, the authors propose a model for optimizing the incineration of hospital waste on behalf of healthcare facilities. This model of a multi-objective vehicles routing problem, expressed as a linear program, takes into account the heterogeneity of the fleet, the hazardous nature of waste collected and the respect of time windows. The complexity of the model leads the researchers to opt for the genetic algorithm to process an instance of 80 nodes. The appropriate choice of parameters of the genetic algorithm allowed the model to be tested and to show how it can contribute to seek trade-off between the main objectives related to the supply of medical waste.

Keywords: Multi-objective optimization · Reverse logistic · Genetic algorithm

1 Introduction

The medical waste (MW) are defined as those generated by medical care activities. According to the World Health Organization (WHO), they include infectious waste, anatomical waste, pointed and sharp objects, chemicals, genotoxic waste, and radioactive waste [1]. Hospitals, health care facilities, laboratories and research centers are the main sources of these wastes. The seriousness of the potential risks stemming from poor management of these wastes has made management of solid wastes in general, and medical in particular, one of the pillars of the United Nations program for sustainable development [2]. Morocco is no exception to this international trend. As an important component in the climate system, the management of MW has caused a great deal of ink from civil society and the local press. Consequently, the Moroccan Kingdom has reinforced the legal framework by several decrees [3], and has made technical effort to improve the management of MW. However, the current situation reveals a dramatic gap between regulation and practice in the field [4]. The technical capacity of the current waste disposal process is sufficient to treat all medical and pharmaceutical

M. Hamlich et al. (Eds.): SADASC 2020, CCIS 1207, pp. 256–269, 2020.
https://doi.org/10.1007/978-3-030-45183-7_20

wastes estimated at 21,000 T per year according to a report published by GIZ [5], however measures need to be taken to improve the collection, sorting and transport. A considerable amount of recommendations has been cited in the GIZ report. Among these recommendations one can find the standardization of waste sorting in hospitals, the outsourcing of collection and transport to professionals according to the specifications complying with the laws in force and the treatment according to European standards.

The objective of this work is to adhere to these recommendations to guarantee to Morocco a real stepping stone towards sustainable development. To do this, this paper begins by proposing a model to improve the current waste disposal process. It will then go on to present the mathematical model that governs the proposed model. The third part will carry out the experimentation of the genetic algorithm parameters. The last part will perform a series of experiments to test the robustness of the model and the tuning of weighting parameters.

2 Proposed Management Model

In order to professionalize the treatment of hospital waste in Morocco, the researchers propose a model where medical waste from hospitals will be centralized in a central warehouse belonging to a professional provider. The authors assume that the medical waste is sorted at the hospital level before being transported to the central warehouse as shown in Fig. 1. The use of this centralization is motivated by the results of the study of Ahlaqqach et al. [6]. The waste will, therefore, be distributed via a heterogeneous fleet to incinerators. The proposed model is part of the Vehicle Routing Problem (VRP), which is defined as a class of problems in which customer's demand is satisfied with products from a depot and transported using a fleet of vehicles in such a way that the total traveling cost of all vehicles is minimized [7]. The VRP was first formulated by Dantzig and Ramser [8], as the generalized form of the well-known Traveling Salesman Problem. The VRP plays a central role in the fields of physical distribution and logistics [9] and a considerable amount of literature has been published on this class of problems. In the context of this paper, the researchers aim to incorporate real-life constraints of the model described above, so they assume that incinerators are going to be served in a certain time interval. These problems are called the Vehicle Routing Problem with Time Windows (VRPTW). For recent research work in the area of the VRP and its variants see [10–12], which represent a taxonomic review of the VRP literature published between 2009 and 2016. The work of [13] and [14] are part of work related to the VRPTW, they assumed that the deliveries to the customers can be done outside the TW (Soft TW), but on the other hand they induced penalties of delay in the objective function. However, Agra et al. [15] and Vidal et al. [16] have adopted a strict system (Hard TW) wherein it is not allowed to deliver outside the TW. Another particularity is linked to our model, namely the nature of products collected from clinics which is classified, by the United Nations Economic Commission for Europe [17], as Hazardous Materials (HazMat). More than a few studies have considered the problem of waste collection and distribution. Pradhananga et al. [18] have presented a Pareto-based bi-objective optimization of hazardous materials vehicle routing and scheduling problem with TW and have showed its application to a realistic hazardous material logistics instance. Ahlaqqach et al. [19] have proposed a model of collectors' management and optimization of the incineration of hospital waste, on behalf of the University and Hospital Centers (CHU) and other medical centers. They optimized vehicle routing in upstream and downstream of the central warehouse. This study is followed by a particular case of MW [20], in which the authors proposed a new design to collect the used healthcare textile. In another study, the authors were able to integrate the medical waste routing management into the design of a sustainable closed-loop supply chain network [21].

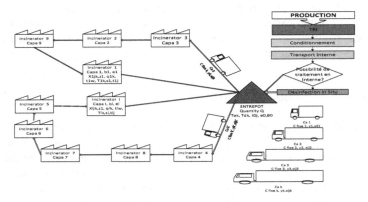

Fig. 1. The proposed scheme for the waste disposal management

The present study fills a gap in the literature by adding some particularities compared to the existing models:

Multi-objective model;
Heterogeneous fleet;
Single Depot;
Strict Time Windows;
Hazardous Materials (MW).

Then, the authors can name the model studied a Multi-objective HazMat Heterogeneous Fleet Vehicle Routing Problem with Time Windows (HHFVRPTW). The reader should bear in mind that the study is based on a model where sorting takes place in-house. The distances, the probability of a HazMat accident and the exposure population on each road are symmetrical.

3   Model Formulation

3.1   Problem Definition

The previous discussion ruled on the specifications related to this study. This paper, therefore, set out to assess the tradeoff between the cost and risk related of using a heterogeneous fleet of vehicles. All vehicles must start and end their routes at a single depot and have to deliver each incinerator within time windows.

3.2 Risk Calculation

Several studies have sought to determine the best risk models, in this study the authors will focus on risk calculation presented by Pradhananga [18], as it fits our case of Hazmat transportation and also because of its simplicity. The risk is expressed as follows:

$$R_{ij} = \delta_{(i,j)} * \phi_{(i,j)} \tag{1}$$

$\delta_{(i,j)}$ Probability of a HazMat accident on the road (i, j)

$\phi_{(i,j)}$ Population exposed to contamination during the accident on the road (i, j).

3.3 Mathematical Formulation

The parameters of our model are the following:
Parameters:

Al_i: Allocated waste to the incinerator i; i $\in$ I

s_i: Unloading time in vertex i; (= 0; for i = 0)

b_i: Start of time window at the vertex i; i $\in$ {0,..,I}

e_i: End of time window at the vertex i; i $\in$ {0,..,I}

K: Set of vehicles at depot

Ca_k: Capacity of vehicle k; k $\in$ K

Z_1: Total cost of the routes (variable cost + fixed vehicle cost)

Z_2: Total risk exposure associated with the transportation process

c_{ij}: Service travel time for arc (i, j) = s_i + t_{ij}

$Cfixe_k$: The fixed cost if the vehicle k is used

$Cvar_k$: The variable cost of transport (proportional to distance)

Alpha: Weighting of cost function

Beta: Weighting of Risk

Variables:

x_{ijk}: = 1; if vehicle k uses arc (i, j) = 0; otherwise

y_k: = 1 if vehicle k is used = 0; otherwise

t_{wi}: Waiting time at customer i; i $\in$ I

T_{ik}: Time at which vehicle k begins servicing at customer i; i $\in$ {0,..,I}

q_{ik}: Quantity of medical waste served at incinerator i by vehicle k

T_{ak}: Arrival time of vehicle k at depot

T_{dk}: Departure time of vehicle k from depot

In the following, mathematical formulation to the HHFVRPTW is provided:

$$\text{Minimize Alpha} * Z1 + \text{Beta} * Z2 \tag{2}$$

$$Z_1 = \sum_{k=0}^{K} y_k * Cfixe_k + \sum_{i=0}^{n} \sum_{j=0}^{n} \sum_{k=1}^{K} Cvar_k x_{ijk} C_{ij} \tag{3}$$

$$Z_2 = \sum_{i=0}^{n} \sum_{i=0}^{n} \sum_{k=1}^{K} x_{ijk} R_{ij} \tag{4}$$

Subject to:

$$\sum_{i=0}^{n} \sum_{k=1}^{K} x_{ijk} = 1 \qquad\qquad ; j \in I \tag{5}$$

$$\sum_{i=0}^{n} x_{ipk} = \sum_{j=0}^{n} x_{ipk} \qquad\qquad p \in I, k \in K \tag{6}$$

$$\sum_{j=0}^{n} \sum_{k=1}^{K} x_{ijk} = 1 \qquad\qquad ; i \in I \tag{7}$$

$$q_{jk} = \sum_{i=1}^{n} x_{ijk} * Al_j \qquad\qquad j \in I, k \in K \tag{8}$$

$$\sum_{i=1}^{n} q_{ik} \leqslant ca_k * y_k \qquad\qquad k \in K \tag{9}$$

$$\sum_{j=1}^{n} x_{0jk} = y_k \qquad\qquad k \in K \tag{10}$$

$$\sum_{i=1}^{n} x_{i0k} = y_k \qquad\qquad k \in K \tag{11}$$

$$x_{iik} = 0 \qquad\qquad i \in I, j \in J, k \in K \tag{12}$$

$$T_{ik} + s_i + t_{ij} + tw_j - T_{jk} \leqslant (1 - x_{ijk}) * M \qquad\qquad i, j \in I, k \in K \tag{13}$$

$$T_{ik} + s_i + t_{i0} - Ta_k \leqslant (1 - x_{i0k}) * M \qquad\qquad i \in I, k \in K \tag{14}$$

$$T_{dk} + t_{0j} - T_{jk} \leq (1 - x_{i0k}) * M \qquad\qquad j \in I, k \in K \tag{15}$$

$$b_i * y_k \leq T_{ik} \leq e_i * y_k \qquad\qquad i \in I, k \in K \tag{16}$$

$$b_0 * y_k \leqslant Ta_k \leqslant e_0 * y_k \qquad\qquad k \in K \tag{17}$$

$$b_0 * y_k \leqslant Td_k \leqslant e_0 * y_k \qquad\qquad k \in K \tag{18}$$

$$\text{Alpha} + \text{Beta} = 1 \tag{19}$$

$$x_{ijk}, \ z_i, y_k, N, M, P \in \{0,1\} tw_i, \ T_{ik}, q_{ik}, Ta_k, Td_k \in \mathbb{R}^+ i, j \in \{0..n\}, k \in K \tag{20}$$

Equation (2) to (4) express the multi-objective function to optimize, taking into account the total cost and the total risk of the transportation process. Equations (5) and

(6) enforce each incinerator to be serviced once by a unique truck and a unique arc. Equation (7), (10) and (11) guarantee flow conservation and Eqs. (8) and (9) ensure the distributed quantity to incinerators and the respect of trucks. Equation (12) deals with the elimination of loops, while Eqs. (13)–(18) compute the time variables and ensure that the TW are respected, also they avoid sub-tours. The sum of the weights, equal to 1, is expressed in Eq. (19) and Eq. (20) specifies the nature of the variables. Instead of using the absolutes values of Z1 and Z2, respectively, we normalize them so they become comparable. We use normalization in Bronfman et al. [22], where Yi is the normalized objective function. Zimax, Zimin and Zi represent the maximum, minimum and actual value of each objective before normalization.

$$\text{Yi} = \left[\frac{Z_i - Z_{imin}}{Z_{imax} - Z_{imin}} \right] \tag{21}$$

4 Heuristic Approach

4.1 Genetic Algorithm (GA)

The GA is one of the best known evolutionary optimization techniques [23]. This meta-heuristic, which is based on the genetic method of the human body and the "elite of the strongest" in Darwin's theory, was initially developed by Holland [24] at the University of Michigan. Subsequently, its scope is broadened to cover several optimization problems, among which one can find the VRP. Thangiah et al. [25] were the first to apply a GA to VRPTW on order find good coalition of customers. This work is followed by numerous articles that have opted for the hybridization of GAs with meta-heuristics such as Ant Colony Systems [26], Game theory [27] and Ridesharing [28].

The GA is initiated by starting a set of chromosomes, called population. In most cases, the basic population is generated randomly since the final solution is independent of initial solutions [23]. The initialization stage of the population is followed by a number of iterations that give birth to a new generation composed of the best solutions. The performance of each solution is evaluated by a quality function (fitness) that illustrates the quality of the genes that make up the individual. The selection stage is automatically triggered, generally individuals with a better quality are more likely to be selected than those with poor quality [29]. Afterwards, the crossover and the mutation of the operators are applied. The main search operator in Genetic algorithms (GA) is the crossover operator which equally as significant as mutation, selection and coding in GA [30]. The crossover combines blocks from parents to produce their children. On the other hand, the mutation makes small local changes to ensure diversity in the population for a greater exploration of possible solutions. Several papers focus on crossover and mutation parameters for VRPTW [31] and others have worked on the improvement and comparison of crossover operators [32, 33] and [34]. Potvin and Bengio [31] proposed a GA called GENEROUS (The Genetic Routing System) where two cross-overs operators RBX (Route-Based Crossover) and SBX (Sequence-Based Crossover), and two mutation operators, namely One-Level Exchange and one Two-level exchange are applied directly to the solutions. The RBX crossover operator is based on the routes; it ensures an exchange between two different mother solutions (roads) to form the child. However, for the crossover operator, SBX, the end portions of two parent solutions are exchanged using the 2-opt* exchanges [35]. In both cases, a repair operator is applied to produce feasible solutions. This repair involves eliminating duplicate customers and inserting missing customers using the low-cost insertion heuristic. Crossover operators RBX and SBX can improve the total journey time, but they cannot reduce the number of routes. Therefore, the two mutation operators were designed to eliminate routes containing a reduced number of customers, inserting these customers one by one in the other tours. The "One-Level Exchange" mutation operator selects a route and then tries to move customers to that route. However, it can be difficult to add a new customer in the second road, due to the constraints of the capacity and time windows. As a result, a Two-Level Exchange is trying to insert the new customer by moving another customer to a second route. The interesting results from the operators of the Generous GA and the availability of those operators on the HeuristicLab platform will guide our choice towards the Potvin's operators.

The steps of the algorithm proposed in our case are presented as follows:

1. Make an initial random population as starting solutions;
2. Assess the quality for all solutions according to the objective function of the model;
3. Use the Crossover RBX and SBX operator to generate the children and set the crossover probability (CP);
4. Use the mutation operator one Level and two Level Exchange operator and set the mutation probability (MP);
5. Calculate the quality for all solutions;
6. Choose the best solutions, according to the population size, between all new children and parents to constitute the next generation;
7. Repeat the procedure from line 3.

In order to develop our model (HHFCVRPTW) on the HeuristicLab platform, the researchers extend the CVRPTW. So, they have incorporated into the platform the parameters specific to the model studied. Then, they re-adapted the case on the assumption that the fleet is heterogeneous. After that, they coded the evaluator of the model HHFCVRPTW. Finally, they customized the GA to the context studied. It remains to define the other parameters namely: Maximum generation, CP and MP. As mentioned above the choice of these parameters will be made based on the experimentation which will be the subject of the following section.

The validation of the GA is done on the platform HeuristicLab 3.3.12.12751 and experiments are carried out on an Intel® CORE Duo CPU working with a processor of 2,53 Ghz and 3 GB of installed memory RAM.

4.2   GA Parameters

Maximum Generations. To perform this test the authors varied the number of iterations according to the values 100, 300, 500, 1000, 1500 and 2000. Then they carried out 10 tests for each value and then they calculated the average values of the results for the objective function (Best Quality in the graph) and execution time. The results are shown in the graph below. The researchers find that starting from a maximum generations of 500, the objective function does not improve, while the execution time grows in a spectacular way. Thus, one will opt for a maximum generations of 500 (Fig. 2).

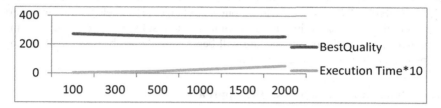

Fig. 2. The evolution of the objective function and the time of execution according to maximum generations

Mutation Probability - Crossover Probability. The experimentation of these parameters was carried out by setting the maximum iteration at the best value obtained in the previous section, then several pairs (MP – CP) were launched. The CP was varied according to the following values: 20%, 30%, 50%, 60% and 80% and the MP was varied according to the following values: 5%, 10%, 20%, 30%, 50% and 60%. For a better analysis of the results, the GAP for the two performances: Execution Time and Quality was calculated according to the following formulas: GAP Performance = (Performance-Best Performance)/ Best Performance. The scatter plot that represents the GAP of the two performances for each couple tested was presented on Fig. 3. The reading of this Pareto frontier shows several points around the frontier, based on the vehicle utilization and the fact that the execution time is negligible in terms of scale, we chose the green circular point. Therefore, the authors can conclude that the best pair is (MP20% - CP80%).

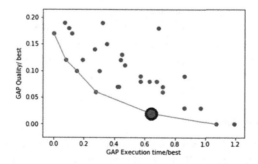

Fig. 3. Pareto front of the couples tested according to the GAP of their performance

Summary. Based on the results of the above experiment, the parameters chosen for the launch of the GA in this case are as follows: Maximum number of iterations = 500, Population size = 200, MP = 20%, CP = 80%.

The next step is to follow the full validation process at the base of our model. The benchmarking is the best way to validate the meta-heuristic proposed in the case of Multi-Objective HHFVRPTW. However, this is the first time that a problem of Multi-Objective HHFVRPTW is dealt with in our knowledge. Nonetheless, we can generate our proposed GA for small instances to compare the results with the global optimum. Consequently, our validation procedure will begin with the analysis of small instances and then we will work on large instances.

4.3   Validation and Analysis of the Approach

Small Instance Analysis. The proposed routings by the GA are relevant, any loops or sub-tours weren't recorded and all constraints are respected. The best objective function resulting from the ten instances is of the order of 55.7, so a difference of 5% compared to the global optimum (GO) given by CPLEX. However, the resolution time of the GA is much more interesting compared to the exact approach. To complete this analysis, we generate an experiment of 10 tests for each size. Based on the results presented in Table 1, the following points are concluded:

- The low difference between the GO and the results of the proposed GA is permitted to justify the acceptability of a proposed algorithm's performance.
- The resolution time of the GA is significantly better than that of the GO.

As a result, the performance of the proposed GA has passed the first validation step compared to the GO. The next section is devoted to large instances.

Table 1. Results of the different instances tested

Instance size	Objective function			Execution time	
	GO	GA	GAP	GO	GA
5	27.1	27.4	1%	00:03.4	00:13.3
10	54.1	57.2	5%	0:10:12	00:18.9
15	73.9	81.6	9%	18:7.12	00:29.3

Large Instance Analysis

Instance Size Variation. In this section, the authors will launch large sizes instance experimentation, where they will choose the instances of the following sizes: 20, 40, 60, 80 and 100. They carried out 10 tests for each instance. The values shown in Table 2 show the average of the performances from the experimental tests of each size.

Table 2. Average performance from large instance experimentation

Instance size	Vehicle utilization	Cost	Risk	Travel time	Objective-function	Execution time
20	6	57.0	114.6	498.1	171.6	**00:42.5**
40	10.7	109.6	142.9	224.7	252.5	**02:19.4**
60	13.8	160.5	173.4	1944.1	334.5	**02:24.2**
80	15.2	204.7	237.1	8723.9	441.8	**03:56.5**
100	17.1	234.28	294.93	8075.5	529.22	**05:15.1**

The results show that the different instances gave the best solutions within a reasonable time. The results of this experiment confirm the validation of the chosen GA.

Variation in the Weighting of the Objective Function. The results coming from the tuning of the value of Alpha, for the instance of size 80, are presented in the Fig. 4. As expected, the normalized cost function decreases with the reinforcement of the Alpha value. An inverse behavior is observed for the normalized risk function. However, the normalized cost function experiment a spectacular decrease in the range where alpha varies from 0 to 0.4. Whereas the strong variation in the normalized risk function is located for Alpha included between 0 and 0.4 and Alpha from 0.7 to 1. Thus, any compromise between cost and risk can be located in the interval 0.4 to 0.6 where both functions seem to be stationary and close to each.

Population Size Experiments. To carry out this experiment the size of the population was varied according to the following values 200, 400 and 600. The analysis of the results, presented in Fig. 5, reveals a difference between the quality of the instances GA (200), GA (400) and GA (600). However, this difference, of the order of 3%, remains negligible, whereas the resolution time in the GA (200) is better than the GA (400) or GA (600). These negligible differences in quality lead us to conclude on the stability of the proposed GA, the accuracy of the parameterization procedure and the effectiveness of the results of the present study.

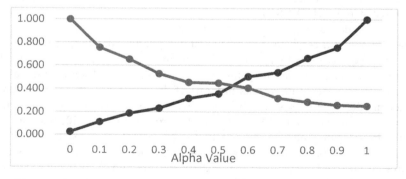

Fig. 4. Evolution of normalized cost and normalized risk according to Alpha

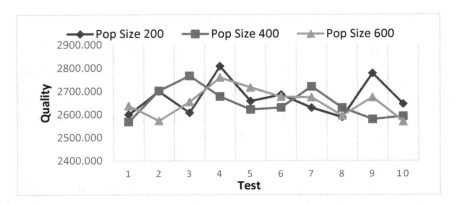

Fig. 5. Result of large scale population size analysis

The results of these experiments confirm the validation of the selected GA. Indeed, the performance of the GA is highly acceptable in both small and large scale cases. For the large scale the GA gave the best solutions within a reasonable time and showed its stability.

5   Conclusion

This research sheds new light on reverse logistics in the case of MW, by proposing a multi-objective mathematical model with a heuristic resolution of a very complicated case of VRPTW. The aim of researches was to find a solution to a problem that humanity is experiencing. This problem takes part in sustainable development program led by WHO all over the world. To this end, they have taken into consideration several realistic characteristics of the problem in order to make the model solid and close to reality.

The hazardous nature of the waste has led us to integrate the risk associated with the transport of these materials. The heterogeneity of the fleet and the use of vehicles as required are the main distinctions of this model in a framework of optimization of the hazardous materials (HTWVRP).

To better understand the phenomenon of the problem size, the authors proposed a GA and performed a complete computational analysis to validate the GA and set its parameters. They started with a parameterization procedure, which is done on the basis of the operator's analysis and the parameters experimentation. Then they ran a small-sized instance to validate the results in terms of the pertinence of routings obtained, after they did the same for several small sizes in order to compare GA's results with the global optimum found by CPLEX. The results proved just 9% difference to global optimum. In order to cope with large-scale instances, firstly they experiment different size from 20 to 100, secondly they launch experimentation where they vary the weighting of cost and risk, finally they experiment the impact of population size on large instance. The first experimentation with large-scale instances gave a good result in a reasonable time. The second experiment allowed them to conclude that thanks to this model, they can seek a compromise between the different stakeholders in the project of medical waste treatment professionalization. The third experiment shows a difference of just 2% between different population sizes. The results prove the constancy of the proposed GA and its applicability in real-size situations. GA performance is highly acceptable in both small and large scale cases. In fact, the authors can trust GAs in the multi-objective optimization of vehicle routing carrying hazardous materials with time windows and a heterogeneous fleet.

The reader should bear in mind that the study is based on assumptions, such as data related to the routes, which is supposed to be static. Except in reality, roads are subject to traffic that varies over time. Thus, for a better contribution in the framework of our scientific research, there is some guidance for future research. The authors will create an interface between the model and a geographical map, taking into consideration the dynamics of the information concerning the itineraries. This information will enable them to generate, in real time, changes in the routing of vehicles. Due to practical constraints, this paper didn't experiment other meta-heuristic to challenge the proposed GA. For this reason, the future contribution will focus on other meta-heuristic such ACO or PSO to compare it with the GA proposed.

References

1. OMS: Organisation mondiale de la Santé—Les déchets liés aux soins de santé. WHO (2015). http://www.who.int/mediacentre/factsheets/fs253/fr/. Accessed 28 Feb 2016
2. UNDP: Chemicals and waste management—United Nations Development Programme (2016). http://www.undp.org/content/undp/en/home/ourwork/sustainable-development/natural-capital-and-the-environment/chemicals-and-waste-management.html. Accessed 28 Feb 2016
3. Morocco, K.: Décret n° 2.09.538 du 5 rabii II 1431 (22 mars 2010) fixant les modalités d'élaboration du plan directeur national de gestion des déchets dangereux. Bulletin Officiel **5830**, 1268 (2010)
4. Mbarki, A., Kabbachi, B., Ezaidi, A., Benssaou, M.: Medical waste management: a case study of the Souss-Massa-Drâa region, Morocco. J. Environ. Prot. (Irvine, Calif.) **4**(2), 914–919 (2013)
5. SWEEPNET: Country report on the solid waste management in Kingdom of Morocco (2014)
6. Ahlaqqach, M., Benhra, J., Mouatassim, S., Lamrani, S.: Ruin & recreate approach applied to multi-objective optimization of HHCVRPTW in the case of medical waste collection. Indian J. Sci. Technol. **12**(28), 1–11 (2019)
7. Abdulkader, M.M.S., Gajpal, Y., Elmekkawy, T.Y.: Hybridized ant colony algorithm for the multi compartment vehicle routing problem. Appl. Soft Comput. J. **37**, 196–203 (2015)
8. Dantzing, G.B., Ramser, J.H.: The truck dispatching problem. Manag. Sci. **6**(1), 80–91 (1959)
9. Mulloorakam, A.T., Mathew Nidhiry, N.: Combined objective optimization for vehicle routing using genetic algorithm. Mater. Today: Proc. **11**, 891–902 (2019)
10. Braekers, K., Ramaekers, K., Van Nieuwenhuyse, I.: The vehicle routing problem: state of the art classification and review. Comput. Ind. Eng. **99**, 300–313 (2016)

11. Leyerer, M., Sonneberg, M.-O., Heumann, M., Kammann, T., Breitner, M.H.: Individually optimized commercial road transport: a decision support system for customizable routing problems. Sustainability **11**(20), 5544 (2019)
12. Han, M., Wang, Y.: A survey for vehicle routing problems and its derivatives. In: IOP Conference Series: Materials Science and Engineering, vol. 452, no. 4 (2018)
13. Tas, D., Dellaert, N., Van Woensel, T., De Kok, T.: Vehicle routing problem with stochastic travel times including soft time windows and service costs. Comput. Oper. Res. **40**(1), 214–224 (2013)
14. Figliozzi, M.A.: An iterative route construction and improvement algorithm for the vehicle routing problem with soft time windows. Transp. Res. Part C Emerg. Technol. **18**(5), 668–679 (2010)
15. Agra, A., Christiansen, M., Figueiredo, R., Hvattum, L.M., Poss, M., Requejo, C.: The robust vehicle routing problem with time windows. Comput. Oper. Res. **40**(3), 856–866 (2013)
16. Vidal, T., Crainic, T.G., Gendreau, M., Prins, C.: A hybrid genetic algorithm with adaptive diversity management for a large class of vehicle routing problems with time-windows. Comput. Oper. Res. **40**(1), 475–489 (2013)
17. United Nations Economic Commission for Europe (UNECE): ADR European Agreement Concerning the International Carriage of Dangerous Goods by Road, New York and Geneva, vol. 1 (2014)
18. Pradhananga, R., Taniguchi, E., Yamada, T., Qureshi, A.G.: Bi-objective decision support system for routing and scheduling of hazardous materials. Socioecon. Plann. Sci. **48**(2), 135–148 (2014)
19. Ahlaqqach, M., Benhra, J., Mouatassim, S.: Optimization of routing for the collection and delivery of medical waste passing through a common warehouse. Logistique Manag. **25**(1), 25–33 (2017)
20. Mustapha, A., Jamal, B., Salma, M., Safia, L.: Smart city through the control of the healthcare textiles transport. In: Smart Application and Data Analysis for Smart Cities (SADASC 2018), 28 May 2018. https://doi.org/10.2139/ssrn.3186336
21. Ahlaqqach, M., Benhra, J., Mouatassim, S., Lamrani, S.: Closed loop location routing supply chain network design in the end of life pharmaceutical products. Supply Chain Forum: Int. J. (2020). https://doi.org/10.1080/16258312.2020.1752112
22. Bronfman, A., Marianov, V., Paredes-Belmar, G., Lüer-Villagra, A.: The maxisum and maximin-maxisum HAZMAT routing problems. Transp. Res. Part E Logist. Transp. Rev. **93**, 316–333 (2016)
23. Soleimani, H., Seyyed-Esfahani, M., Shirazi, M.A.: Designing and planning a multi-echelon multi-period multi-product closed-loop supply chain utilizing genetic algorithm. Int. J. Adv. Manuf. Technol. **68**(1–4), 917–931 (2013)
24. Holland, J.H.: Adaptation in Natural and Artificial Systems. University of Michigan Press, Ann Arbor (1975)
25. Thangiah, S.R., Nygard, K.E., Juell, P.L.: GIDEON: a genetic algorithm system for vehicle routing with time windows. In: The Seventh IEEE Conference on Artificial Intelligence Application, vol. 1, pp. 322–328 (1991)
26. Bräysy, O., Berger, J., Barkaoui, M.: A route-directed hybrid genetic approach for the vehicle routing problem with time windows. Inform. Syst. Oper. Res. **41**, 131–154 (2003)
27. Mouatassim, S., Ahlaqqach, M., Benhra, J., Eloualidi, M.: Model based on hybridized game theory to optimize logistics case of blood supply chain. Int. J. Comput. Appl. **145**(15), 37–48 (2016)

28. Ahlaqqach, M., Benhra, J., Mouatassim, S., Lamrani, S.: Modeling and optimization of a multi-objective ridesharing problem in the case of medical waste. Int. J. Recent Technol. Eng. **8**(2S8), 1911–1918 (2019)

29. Vaira, G., Kurasova, O.: Genetic algorithms and VRP: the behaviour of a crossover operator. Baltic J. Mod. Comput. **1**(3), 161–185 (2013)

30. Lim, S.M., Sultan, A.B.M., Sulaiman, M.N., Mustapha, A., Leong, K.Y.: Crossover and mutation operators of genetic algorithms. Int. J. Mach. Learn. Comput. **7**(1), 9–12 (2017)

31. Potvin, J.-Y., Bengio, S.: The vehicle routing problem with time windows - Part II: genetic search Jean-Yves Potvin. Informs J. Comput. **8**(2), 1–21 (1996)

32. Misevičius, A., Kilda, B.: Comparison of crossover operators for the quadratic assignment problem. Inf. Technol. Control **34**(2), 109–119 (2005)

33. Kumar, R., Kumar, N., Karambir: A comparative analysis of PMX, CX and OX crossover operators for solving travelling salesman problem. Int. J. Latest Res. Sci. Technol. **1**(2), 98–101 (2012)

34. El Hassani, H., Benkachcha, S., Benhra, J.: New genetic operator (jump crossover) for the traveling salesman problem. Int. J. Appl. Metaheuristic Comput. **6**(2), 33–44 (2015)

35. Potvin, J.-Y., Rousseau, J.-M.: An exchange heuristic for routeing problems with time windows. J. Oper. Res. Soc. **46**(12), 1433–1446 (1995)

Safe and Optimal Path Planning for Autonomous UAV Using a Decomposition-Coordination Method

Imane Nizar[1,2]([✉]) [iD], Youssef Illoussamen[1,2], El Hossein Illoussamen[1,2], and Mohammed Mestari[1,2]

[1] Laboratory of Signals, Distributed Systems and Artificial Intelligence (SSDIA), ENSET Mohammedia, Av Hassan II, 28830 Mohammedia, Morocco
`imane.nizar@gmail.com`
[2] University Hassan II Casablanca-Mohammedia, Casablanca, Morocco

Abstract. In this paper, we propose a new Decomposition-Coordination Method (DCM) to solve the nonlinear problem of optimal path planning, for autonomous Unmanned Aerial Vehicle (UAV) in a dynamic environment. The main objective of this work is to enable safe autonomous navigation to the UAV. Our algorithm of decomposition-coordination computes initially an optimal path leading to the desired position, and according to the information supplied by a deciding unit, the UAV can predict the potential collisions, and avoid them by computing new collision-free paths if needed, allowing more reactivity to the UAV. This approach consists of first, choosing a suitable mathematical model that depicts the dynamics of the UAV, to which we associate the objective functions to end up with a multi-objective optimization problem. We proceed then to the resolution of the nonlinear system, by subdividing it into a set of smaller interconnected subsystems. The DCM is then used to achieve a local treatment of the non-linearity and reduce the processing time, where each subsystem is split between two levels for parallel processing, and the coordination is ensured after the resolution of the system using the method of Lagrange multipliers. We study as well the convergence and the stability of the algorithm, then we present the results of our simulation on Matlab to corroborate the potential of this theoretical method.

Keywords: Decomposition-Coordination Method · Optimal control · Non-linear system · Autonomous navigation · Unmanned Aerial Vehicle

1 Introduction

Optimal path planning and obstacles avoidance are the key factors to advance autonomous machines. Over the last decades, scientists have been more interested in this area of research, given the great advantages that autonomous

Supported by the European Union's Horizon 2020 research and innovation program under the Marie Skłodowska-Curie grant agreement No 777720.

reactive robots can offer, and their capability for improving the quality of our daily life. The autonomous Unmanned Aerial Vehicles (UAVs), called also aerial robots [1], are becoming more intelligent and convenient for military, industrial and entertainment applications [2–4]. However, most of the revolutionary technologies are still expressive, and generally limited to military usage, while most of the existing UAVs available to the large public are still underdeveloped. In this study, we aim to solve the non-linear problem of safe and optimal navigation for autonomous UAVs, using a Decomposition-Coordination Method (DCM) [5] that allows us to reduce the processing time, and consequently increases the reactivity of the UAV, using a minimum of energy, through the optimal control. Perusing modern literature, we noted that scientists are trying to solve non-linear problems using various mathematical methods, most of them are metaheuristic evolutionary algorithms, such as Genetic Algorithms (GA) [6,7], or Ant Colony Optimization (ACO) algorithm [8,9]. Indeed, these approaches can provide interesting results. However, for real-time implementation they are not the best choice for problems of large size and high complexity, given the difficulty of their convergence to the Pareto front. The principal of our approach, relies mainly on overall planning of the path. We consider a deciding unit that supervises the whole indoor environment. Initially, we compute an optimal path using the DCM method, then the deciding unit has to run an obstacle avoidance algorithm to make sure that the path is collision-free, and if not send the required instructions to the autonomous UAV that has to compute a new safe path, taking into consideration the size, the orientation and the speed of the moving obstacle, to find the right state p_k that shall be used as an intermediate state to escape the collision, and compute the optimal path from the initial state p_i to p_k, and then from the intermediate point p_k to another, until it reaches the desired state p_d. To apply this method, we first choose a mathematical model that describes the behavior and the dynamics of a regular UAV quad-copter [10–12] to which we associate a multi-objective optimization problem, with several objective functions that have to be simultaneously satisfied in a conflicting situation. We proceed after that to the resolution of the multi-objective optimization problem, starting by decomposing the system into smaller interconnected subsystems. Making use of a decomposition-coordination method, we splits each system between two levels to process the equations in parallel in real-time, as for the coordination we use the Lagrange multipliers to provide the overall resolution. This method allows a local treatment of the non-linearity and reduces enormously the processing time. The multi-objective optimization problem is changed into an equivalent scalar optimization problem that we can solve by mapping the differential equations into corresponding difference equations in discrete-time. In the upcoming sections we present the principal of this method in detail [13–15]. This paper in organized as follow: Sect. 2 presents the mathematical model of the quad-copter. In Sect. 3 we introduce the obstacle avoidance principal, the Sect. 4 is devoted to the statement of the problem, then the analysis of the problem in Sect. 5. To affirm the effectiveness of the method and we present a simulation results in the Sect. 6. The last section is a brief conclusion.

2   The Model of the Quad-Copter UAV

For this study we use a mathematical model of a regular quad-copter UAV, taking into consideration the following assumptions:

– The UAV is a symmetric and rigid body,
– The quad-copter's center of mass coincides with the origin of the body frame,
– The rotation directions of the four rotors is fixed,
– The effects of the translation lift are neglected.

In the Fig. 1 we represent the configuration of a fixed arms quad-copter, with the forces created by each rotor, and the corresponding angular velocities.

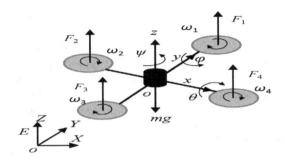

Fig. 1. The quad-copter's structure

The Newton and Euler equations for a rigid body dynamics [11,12] allows as to mathematically model the dynamics of translation and rotation of the quad-copter UAV as follows:

$$\dot{p} = a\,(p, u)\,p + b\,(p)\,u + c \tag{1}$$

The state vector is: $p = \left(x, y, z, \dot{x}, \dot{y}, \dot{z}, \theta, \phi, \psi, \dot{\theta}, \dot{\phi}, \dot{\psi}\right)^T$, (x, y, z) represents the position in the earth frame E, and $(\dot{x}, \dot{y}, \dot{z})$ is the linear velocity vector, (θ, ϕ, ψ) are called Euler angles of rotation, and finally the angular velocity $(\dot{\theta}, \dot{\phi}, \dot{\psi})$.

The control vector is: $u = (F_{th}, u_\theta, u_\phi, u_\psi)^T$, where $F_{th} = bl \sum_{i=1}^{n} \omega_i^2$ is the total thrust, and $u_\theta = \dfrac{\Gamma_\theta}{bl}\omega_2^2 - \omega_2^2$, $u_\phi = \dfrac{\Gamma_\phi}{bl} = -\omega_1^2 + \omega_3^2$, and $u_\psi = \dfrac{\Gamma_\psi}{d} = \omega_1^2 - \omega_2^2 + \omega_3^2 - \omega_4^2$.

Where Γ_θ, Γ_ϕ and Γ_ψ are respectively the roll, pitch and yaw torques, while ω_i are the rotation velocities of the four rotors, for $i = 1, 2, 3, 4$. b is the thrust constant, d is the drag constant, and l the length of the quad-copter arm.

The state matrix $a(p, u)$, the control matrix $b(p)$ are described as bellow:

$$a(p,u) = \begin{pmatrix} 0_{3\times3} & I_{3\times3} & 0_{3\times3} & 0_{3\times3} \\ 0_{3\times3} & 0_{3\times3} & 0_{3\times3} & 0_{3\times3} \\ 0_{3\times3} & 0_{3\times3} & 0_{3\times3} & a_{11} \\ 0_{3\times3} & 0_{3\times3} & 0_{3\times3} & a_{22} \end{pmatrix}$$

Where : $a_{11} = \begin{pmatrix} 1 & s\phi t\theta & c\psi t\theta \\ 0 & cos\phi & -sin\phi \\ 0 & sins\phi sin\theta & ccos\phi sin\phi \end{pmatrix}$, $a_{22} = \begin{pmatrix} 0 & -I_r\frac{\tau\psi}{I_y} & \dot{\phi}\frac{I_z-I_x}{I_y} \\ -I_r\frac{\tau\psi}{I_x} & 0 & \dot{\theta}\frac{I_y-I_z}{I_x} \\ 0 & \dot{\theta}\frac{I_x-I_y}{I_z} & 0 \end{pmatrix}$

$$b(p) = \begin{pmatrix} 0_{3\times1} & 0_{3\times3} \\ b_{11} & 0_{3\times3} \\ 0_{3\times1} & 0_{3\times3} \\ 0_{3\times1} & b_{22} \end{pmatrix}$$

with: $b_{11} = \begin{pmatrix} \frac{1}{m}(cos\psi sin\theta cos\phi - sin\psi sin\phi) \\ \frac{1}{m}(sin\psi sin\theta cos\phi - cos\psi sin\phi) \\ \frac{1}{m}cos\theta cos\psi \end{pmatrix}$ and $b_{22} = \begin{pmatrix} 0 & \frac{bl}{I_y} & 0 \\ \frac{bl}{I_x} & 0 & 0 \\ 0 & 0 & \frac{d}{I_z} \end{pmatrix}$

The constant matrix is: $c = \begin{pmatrix} 0_{3\times1} \\ 0_{2\times1} \\ -g_a \\ 0_{3\times1} \\ 0_{3\times1} \end{pmatrix}$

Where g_a is the gravitational acceleration, I_r is the rotor's inertia, I_x, I_y, I_z are respectively the roll, pitch, and yaw moments of inertia, the constant m is the mass of the quad-copter.

3   The Obstacle Avoidance Principal

In this approach, we consider a deciding unit that supervises the indoor environment and manages the traffic of the autonomous UAV. Initially, the quad-copter computes an optimal path Fig. 2, from its position p_i towards the desired position p_d, then the deciding unit has to make sure that this optimal path is safe. Otherwise, it provides an intermediate point $p_{k,1}$ for which the optimal path is safe, so that the UAV can escape the collisions whenever an obstacle or more are located. This point is accurately chosen, taking into consideration the orientation, the speed and the size of the obstacle to efficiently prevent the collision as the figure Fig. 3 shows, and if needed another intermediate point $p_{k+1,2}$ could be provided (see Fig. 4), these operations continue until the autonomous UAV reaches the desired point p_d safely as shown in Fig. 5.

4   The Problem Statement

We consider the following non-linear discrete-time optimization problem:

$$\begin{cases} p_{k+1} = f(p_k, p_k) & k \in [|0, N-1|] \\ p_0 = p_i \, given \\ p_N = p_d \, given \end{cases} \quad (2)$$

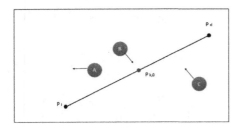

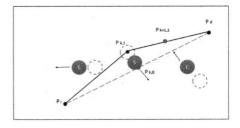

Fig. 2. The initial optimal path computed by the UAV.

Fig. 3. The safe path to avoid the first obstacle

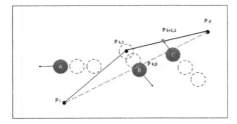

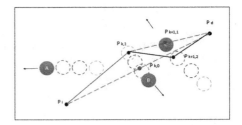

Fig. 4. The detection of a second obstacle

Fig. 5. The final path collision-free leading the p_d

With p_k the state vector and u_k the input control of the system at t_k. Our objective is to find the optimal control that makes the UAV reach the desired state. For this sake we associate to this system an optimization problem, using several objective functions that have to be satisfied in a conflicting situation, thus we need to find an optimal compromise solution that satisfies, our objective function $J_1(y^*) \geq J_1(y)$, $J_2(y^*) \geq J_2(y)$,..., $J_n(y^*) \geq J_n(y)$, using the Minimax method that computes the smallest value of the maximum values of all the objective functions J_i. We put w_i the weight of the i objective function, where $\sum_{i=0}^{n} w_i = 1$, and we define the objective function below:

$$E(p,u) = max_{1 \leq i \leq n} \{w_i J_i(p,u)\} \tag{3}$$

The following system describe our multi-objective optimization problem:

$$\begin{cases} min_{(u_i^*/0 \leq i \leq N-1)} E(p,u) \\ p_{k+1} = f(p_k, u_k) \\ p_0, given \\ k \in [|0, N-1|] \end{cases} \tag{4}$$

5   The Problem Analysis

This section is devoted to the mathematical approach we are applying to solve the problem (4), defined in the previous section. To proceed with our method, we decompose the system into N subsystems, interconnected (see the figure Fig. 6), and we define a new variable z_k:

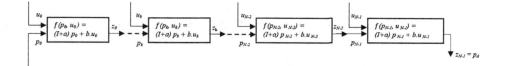

Fig. 6. Decomposition into N subsystems in serial structure

$$z_k = f(p_k, u_k) \quad k \in [|0, N-2|] \tag{5}$$

$$p_k = z_{k-1} \quad k \in [|1, N-1|] \tag{6}$$

Which allows us to write the optimization problem as:

$$\begin{cases} min_{(u_k^*/0 \leq k \leq N-1)} E(p, u) \\ z_k = f(p_k, u_k) & k \in [|0, N-1|] \\ p_k = z_{k-1} & k \in [|1, N|] \\ p_0 = p_i \ given \\ p_N = p_f \ given \end{cases} \tag{7}$$

After the decomposition we construct the ordinary Lagrange function.

$$L_0 = \frac{1}{N} E(p_0, u_0) + \mu_0^T \left(f(p_0, u_0) - z_0 \right) \tag{8}$$

$$L_k = \frac{1}{N} E(p_k, u_k) + \mu_k^T \left(f(p_k, u_k) - z_k \right) + \beta_k^T \left(p_k - z_{k-1} \right) \qquad for \ k \in [|1, N-2|] \tag{9}$$

$$L_{N-1} = \frac{1}{N} E(p_{N-1}, u_{N-1}) + \mu_{N-1}^T \left(f(p_{N-1}, u_{N-1}) - p_f \right) + \beta_{N-1}^T \left(p_{N-1} - z_{N-2} \right) \tag{10}$$

The Lagrange multipliers μ_k and β_k allow us to take into consideration the system constraints, and by the derivation of the ordinary Lagrange function according to KKT conditions, we transform the equality-constrained optimization problem (7) into differential equations, considering an equilibrium point $(Q_k^*, U_k^*, \mu_k^*, \beta_k^*, T_k^*)$ that satisfies the following equations:

$$\nabla_{p_k} L = \frac{1}{N} \frac{\partial E}{\partial p_k} (p_k^*, u_k^*) + \mu_k^{*T} \frac{\partial f}{\partial p_k} (p_k^*, u_k^*) + \beta_k^{*T} = 0, \quad for \ k \in [|1, N-1|] \tag{11}$$

$$\nabla_{u_k} L = \frac{1}{N}\frac{\partial E}{\partial u_k}(p_k^*, u_k^*) + \mu_k^{*T}\frac{\partial f}{\partial p_k}(p_k^*, u_k^*) = 0, \quad for\ k \in [|0, N-1|]$$
(12)

$$\nabla_{\mu_k} L = f(p_k^*, u_k^*) - z_k^* = 0 \quad for\ k \in [|0, N-1|]$$
(13)

$$\nabla_{z_k} L = -\mu_k^{*T} - \beta_{k+1}^{*T} = 0 \quad for\ k \in [|0, N-2|]$$
(14)

$$\nabla_{\beta_k} L = p_k^* - z_{k-1}^* = 0 \quad for\ k \in [|1, N-1|]$$
(15)

Solving the system of differential equations (11)-(15), is now equivalent to solving the equality constrained optimization problem (7).

5.1   The Principal of the DCM Method

The DCM method has been introduced previously in [5]. In this section, we describe again its principal which consists of splitting the system of differential Eqs. (11)–(15)between an upper level and a lower level, the first one handles the two Eqs. (15) and (14). Initially it fixes the values of z_k, and β_k for the first iteration, and proposes these values to the second level which solves the remaining Eqs. (11), (12) and (13). We obtain the optimal solution for the problem (7), after all the Eqss. (11)–(15) are locally satisfied. The resolution of every subsystem k comes to the resolution of the Eqs. (11)–(15), for each β_k $(k = 1...N-1)$ and z_k $(k = 0...N-2)$.

By applying the gradient method we can write the differential equations:

$$\frac{dp_k}{dt} = -\lambda_p \nabla_{p_k} L$$
(16)

$$\frac{du_k}{dt} = -\lambda_u \nabla_{u_k} L$$
(17)

$$\frac{d\mu_k}{dt} = -\lambda_\mu \nabla_{\mu_k} L$$
(18)

With $\lambda_p > 0$, $\lambda_u > 0$, and $\lambda_\mu > 0$. Using Forward Euler method we convert the differential equations into equation in discrete time:

$$p_k^{(i+1)} = p_k^{(i)} - \lambda_p \nabla_{p_k} L, \qquad k \in [|1, N-1|]$$
(19)

$$u_k^{(i+1)} = u_k^{(i)} - \lambda_u \nabla_{u_k} L, \qquad k \in [|0, N-1|]$$
(20)

$$\mu_k^{(i+1)} = \mu_k^{(i)} - \lambda_\mu \nabla_{\mu_k} L, \qquad k \in [|0, N-1|]$$
(21)

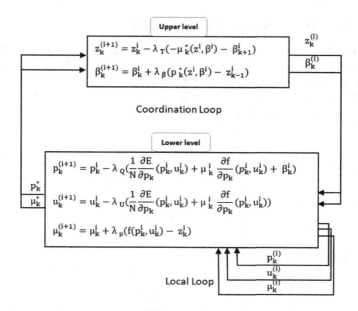

Fig. 7. Coordination between the upper and the lower level.

To insure the coordination, the upper level works simultaneously on the coordination parameters β_k^i, and z_k^i which are known within the lower level, to enable a local resolution of the system of difference Eqs. (19)–(21) and find the values of $p_k^*\left(z_k^i, \beta_k^i\right)$, $u_k^*\left(z_k^i, \beta_k^i\right)$ and $\mu_k^*\left(T_k^i, \beta_k^i\right)$ that satisfy the Eqs. (19)–(21), $p_k^*\left(z_k^i, \beta_k^i\right)$ and $\mu_k^*\left(_k^i, \beta_k^i\right)$ the computed values are then forwarded to the upper level to solve the system and check the previous values of z_k^i and β_k^i and correct them if necessary.

z_k^i and β_k^i given by:

$$z_k^{(i+1)} = z_k^{(i)} - \lambda_z \nabla_{z_k} L, \qquad k \in [|0, N-2|] \tag{22}$$

$$\beta_k^{(i+1)} = \beta_k^{(i)} + \lambda_\beta \nabla_{\beta_k} L, \qquad k \in [|1, N-1|] \tag{23}$$

With $\lambda_T > 0$, $\lambda_\beta > 0$.

The loop of the algorithm is repeated until coordination is obtained, i.e. satisfaction of coordination equations.

The figure Fig. 7 describes this processing.

5.2   The Stability and Convergence of the Method

In this section we answer the question of stability and convergence of the DCM method,for this end we will prov that the convergence of the algorithm comes to the convergence of the coordinating level.

To Simplify we use the variable $V_k = (p_k, u_k)^T$, with $V_k^*(z_k^*, \beta_k^*)$.

Our problem can be presented in a compact form as below:

$$Lower\ level\ equations \begin{cases} X_k\left(V_k, \mu_k, \beta_k\right) = \begin{pmatrix} \nabla_{p_k} L \\ \nabla_{u_k} L \end{pmatrix} \\ P_k\left(V_k, z_k\right) = \nabla_{\mu_k} L \end{cases}$$

$$Upper\ level\ equations \begin{cases} R_k\left(V_k, z_{k-1}\right) = \nabla_{\beta_k} L \\ S_k\left(\mu_k, \beta_{k+1}\right) = \nabla_{z_k} L \end{cases}$$

For the solution sought we have:

$$\begin{cases} X_k^* = \begin{pmatrix} \frac{1}{N}\frac{\partial E}{\partial p_k} + \beta_k^* + \mu_k^*\frac{\partial f}{\partial p_k} \\ \frac{1}{N}\frac{\partial E}{\partial p_k} + \mu_k^*\frac{\partial f}{\partial p_k} \end{pmatrix} = 0 \\ P_k^* = f(p_k^*, u_k^*) - z_k^* = 0 \\ R_k^* = p_k^* - z_{k-1}^* = 0 \\ S_k^* = -\mu_k^* - \beta_{k+1}^* = 0 \end{cases}$$

The errors at each iteration i are defined as:

$$\begin{cases} e_{V_k}^{(i)} = V_k^*(z_k^{(i)}, \beta_k^{(i)}) - V_k^*(z_k^*, \beta_k^*) \\ e_{\mu_k}^{(i)} = \mu_k^*(z_k^{(i)}, \beta_k^{(i)}) - \mu_k^*(z_k^*, \beta_k^*) \\ e_{T_k}^{(i)} = z_k^{(i)} - z_k^* \\ e_{\beta_k}^{(i)} = \beta_k^{(i)} - \beta_k^* \end{cases}$$

We construct the following Lyapunov function, to proof the convergence of the errors at each iteration i:

$$\Phi(i) = \sum_{k=0}^{N-1} \left(e_{\beta_k}^{(i)T} e_{\beta_k}^{(i)} + e_{z_k}^{(i)T} e_{z_k}^{(i)} \right) \tag{24}$$

We define as well:

$$\Delta e_{z_k}^{(i)} = e_{z_k}^{(i+1)} - e_{z_k}^{(i)} = -\lambda S_k^{(i)} \tag{25}$$

$$\Delta e_{\beta_k}^{(i)} = e_{\beta_k}^{(i+1)} - e_{\beta_k}^{(i)} = -\lambda R_k^{(i)} \tag{26}$$

Where $\lambda = \lambda_z = \lambda_\beta$

By linearizing the upper level equations in the neighborhood of the solution we obtain:

$$S_k^{(i)} \simeq S_k^* + \frac{\partial S_k^*}{\partial \mu_k} e_{\mu_k}^{(i)} + \frac{\partial S_k^*}{\partial \beta_{k+1}} e_{\beta_{k+1}}^{(i)} \tag{27}$$

$$R_k^{(i)} \simeq R_k^* + \frac{\partial R_k^*}{\partial V_k} e_{V_k}^{(i)} + \frac{\partial R_k^*}{\partial z_{k-1}} e_{z_{k-1}}^{(i)} \tag{28}$$

Then we have:

$$\Delta e_{z_k}^{(i)} = -\lambda(-e_{\mu_k}^{(i)} + \frac{\partial S_k^*}{\partial \beta_{k+1}} e_{\beta_{k+1}}^{(i)}) \tag{29}$$

$$\Delta e_{\beta_k}^{(i)} = -\lambda(\frac{\partial R_k^*}{\partial V_k} e_{V_k}^{(i)} - e_{z_{k-1}}^{(i)}) \tag{30}$$

So the Lyapunov function becomes:

$$\Delta\Phi = \Phi(i+1) - \Phi(i) = A(i)\lambda^2 + C(j)\lambda \tag{31}$$

Where

$$\begin{cases} A(i) = \sum_{k=0}^{N-1} \Delta e_{\beta_k}^{(i)T} \Delta e_{\beta_k}^{(i)} + \Delta e_{z_k}^{(i)T} \Delta e_{z_k}^{(i)} \geq 0 \\ C(i) = \sum_{k=0}^{N-1} e_{\beta_k}^{(i)T} \Delta e_{\beta_k}^{(i)} + e_{z_k}^{(i)T} \Delta e_{z_k}^{(i)} \end{cases}$$

The following theorems, allow us to prov the satability and the convergence of the method in :

Theorem 1. *Let us note $e_{V_k}^{(i)}$, $e_{\mu_k}^{(i)}$, $e_{z_k}^{(i)}$ and $e_{\beta_k}^{(i)}$ the errors at the iteration i of the coordination loop. if $e_{V_k}^{(i)}$ and $e_{\mu_k}^{(i)}$ converge to zero, then $e_{z_k}^{(i)}$ and $e_{\beta_k}^{(i)}$ will converge to zero as well.*

Theorem 2. *Let λ be the adaptive coefficient for the coordination loop. The convergence is guaranteed if one of the matrices $(\frac{\partial X_k^*}{\partial V_k})^T$ $(k = 0, 1, ..., N-1)$ is positive definite and the others are positive semi-definite and if $A(i) \neq 0$, λ is defined as: $0 < \lambda < |\frac{C(i)}{A(i)}|$.*

The proof of the two algorithms is previously published in [5].

6 Simulation Results

In this section we present the results of our simulation on Matlab. The inputs of our algorithm are the initial position p_i, and the arrival position p_d. For this application we choose $p_i = (0,0,0)$, and $p_d = (15, 14, 6)$, while the outputs are the optimal trajectory that consist of intermediate states p_k computed at each $k\delta t$, along with the associated sequence of control u_k.

For this simulation we consider the numerical parameters of the UAV presented in Table 1.

Table 1. Numerical parameters used in the simulation

Parameter	Symbol	Value
Drag factor	d	1.31
Lift constant	b	3,74
Length of the UAV's arm	l	0,2 m
The mass of the UAV	m	0,5 kg
Gravitational acceleration	g	9,8 m/s^2
Inertia in X axis	I_x	$2e^3$ kgm^2
Inertia in Y axis	I_y	$2,9e^3$ kgm^2
Inertia in Z axis	I_z	$4,8e^3$ kgm^2
Rotor's inertia	I_{rotor}	$2,02e^5$ kgm^2

In this example, we suppose that the initial optimal path is not safe. To avoid the collisions, the deciding unit provides two states $p_{k,1}$ and $p_{k+1,2}$ to the autonomous UAV which are considered as intermediate targets. The UAV will then compute the optimal trajectory from the initial position p_i to $p_{k,1}$ in order to escape the first potential obstacle, and again from $p_{k,1}$ to $p_{k+1,2}$, to avoid the second collision, and continues from $p_{k+1,2}$ to the desired state p_d. In the Fig. 8 we represent the first optimal path beside the second path computed according the instructions received from the deciding unit. The Figs. 10 and 11 illustrate the variation of the control for both trajectories. The control $u_k = (F_{th,k}, u_{\theta,k}, u_{\phi,k}, u_{\psi,k})$ is noted on the figures: $u_k = (u_{1,k}, u_{2,k}, u_{3,k}, u_{4,k})$.

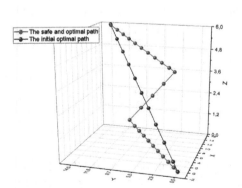

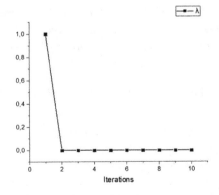

Fig. 8. The initial optimal path and the collision-free path computed according the DU instructions.

Fig. 9. The convergence coefficient lambda at the second etiration.

The Fig. 9 shows the converges of the parameter λ at the second iteration, which proves that the algorithm converges and processing time is optimal.

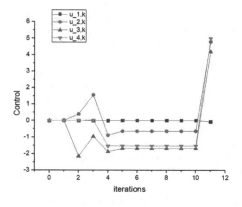

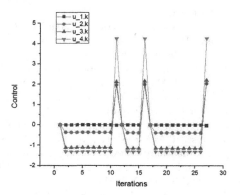

Fig. 10. The variation of the control for the initial optimal path.

Fig. 11. The variation of the control for the collision-free optimal path.

7 Conclusion

In this work, we propose a novel method to solve the path planning problem for quad-rotor UAV, we suppose that the environment is dynamic, and we make use of the method of DCM to solve the non-linear multi-objective optimization problem. We suppose in our approach that the UAV is autonomous, and we consider a deciding unit that gives instructions to this UAV, to make it reach its goal while avoiding the dynamic obstacles. The method we are using herein relies on the idea of breaking down the complex system into several interconnected subsystems in a serial structure, after that we proceed to the resolution of these subsystems using the DCM approach that consists of splitting the computation between two levels, to reduce considerably the processing time, and provide the optimal control that satisfies the problem's constraints.

In the last section we present the results of our simulation on Matlab, to demonstrate the efficiency of the method, where we consider intermediate positions that the UAV should reach to avoid collisions. This approach gives enough flexibility to the UAV and allows it to fly safely towards the final destination.

References

1. Rakha, T., Gorodetsky, A.: Review of Unmanned Aerial System (UAS) applications in the built environment: towards automated building inspection procedures using drones. Autom. Constr. **93**, 252–264 (2018). https://doi.org/10.1016/j.autcon.2018.05.002
2. Tseng, F.H., Liang, T.T., Lee, C.H., Chou, L.D., Chao, H.C.: A star search algorithm for civil UAV path planning with 3G Communication. In: 2014 Tenth International Conference on Intelligent Information Hiding and Multimedia Signal Processing, pp. 942–945 (2014). https://doi.org/10.1109/IIH-MSP.2014.236

3. Dujoncquoy, E., et al.: UAV-based 3D outcrop analog models for oil and gas exploration and production. In: 2019 IGARSS 2019–2019 IEEE International Geoscience and Remote Sensing Symposium, pp. 6791–6794 (2019). https://doi.org/10.1109/IGARSS.2019.8900176

4. Gunchenko, Y.A., Shvorov, S.A., Zagrebnyuk, V.I., Kumysh, V.U., Lenkov, E.S.: Using UAV for unmanned agricultural harvesting equipment route planning and harvest volume measuring. In: 2017 IEEE 4th International Conference Actual Problems of Unmanned Aerial Vehicles Developments (APUAVD), pp. 262–265 (2017). https://doi.org/10.1109/APUAVD.2017.8308825

5. Mestari, M., Benzirar, M., Saber, N., Khouil, M.: Solving nonlinear equality constrained multiobjective optimization problems using neural networks. IEEE Trans. Neural Netw. Learn. Syst. **26**(10), 2500–2520 (2015). https://doi.org/10.1109/TNNLS.2015.2388511

6. Galvez, R.L., Dadios, E.P., Bandala, A.A.: Path planning for quadrotor UAV using genetic algorithm. In: 2014 International Conference on Humanoid, Nanotechnology, Information Technology, Communication and Control, Environment and Management (HNICEM), pp. 1–6 (2014). https://doi.org/10.1109/HNICEM.2014.7016260

7. Al-Oqaily, A.T., Shakah, G.: Solving non-linear optimization problems using parallel genetic algorithm. In: 2018 8th International Conference on Computer Science and Information Technology (CSIT), pp. 103–106 (2018). https://doi.org/10.1109/CSIT.2018.8486176

8. Zhao, T., Pan, X., He, Q.: Application of dynamic ant colony algorithm in route planning for UAV. In: 2017 Seventh International Conference on Information Science and Technology (ICIST), pp. 433–437 (2017). https://doi.org/10.1109/ICIST.2017.7926799

9. Zhang, C., Zhen, Z., Wang, D., Li, M.: UAV path planning method based on ant colony optimization. In: 2010 Chinese Control and Decision Conference, pp. 3790–3792 (2010). https://doi.org/10.1109/CCDC.2010.5498477

10. Nizar, I., Illoussamen, Y., Bentaleb, K., Ouarrak, H.E., Illoussamen, E.H., Mestari, M.: Aerial traffic planning for autonomous multi-rotor in a dynamic known environment based on a Decomposition-Coordination method. In: 2019 Third International Conference on Intelligent Computing in Data Sciences (ICDS), pp. 1–8 (2019)

11. Luukkonen, T.: Modelling and control of quadcopter, p. 26 (2011)

12. Altamash, S., Adnan, S., Aamir, P.: Kinematic, dynamic modeling and simulation of quadcopter, p. 73 (2016)

13. Jihane, C., El Ouarrak, H., Mestari, M., Rachik, M.: Autonomous navigation for an unmanned aerial vehicle by the decomposition coordination method, pp. 1–6 (2017). https://doi.org/10.1109/EECSI.2017.8239170

14. Nizar, I., Illoussamen, Y., El Ouarrak, H., Illoussamen, E.H., Mestari, M.: Traffic optimization for UAV using a method of decomposition-Coordination. In: 2019 Third World Conference on Smart Trends in Systems Security and Sustainablity (WorldS4), pp. 199–206 (2019). https://doi.org/10.1109/WorldS4.2019.8903968

15. El Ouarrak, H., Bouaine, A., Rachik, M., Mestari, M.: Trajectory planning for a four-wheel robot using decomposition-coordination principle, pp. 1–6 (2015). https://doi.org/10.1109/ICoCS.2015.7483265

An Execution Time Comparison
of Parallel Computing Algorithms
for Solving Heat Equation

Safa Belhaous$^{(\boxtimes)}$ ⓘ, Zineb Hidila ⓘ, Sohaib Baroud ⓘ, Soumia Chokri ⓘ,
and Mohammed Mestari$^{(\boxtimes)}$ ⓘ

SSDIA Laboratory, ENSET, Hassan II University, Mohammedia, Morocco
`safaabelhaous@gmail.com`, `mestari@enset-media.ac.ma`

Abstract. Parallel Computing contributes significantly to most disciplines for solving several scientific problems such as partial differential equations (PDEs), load balancing, and deep learning. The primary characteristic of parallelism is its ability to ameliorate performance on many different sets of computers. Consequently, many researchers are continually expending their efforts to produce efficient parallel solutions for various problems such as heat equation. Heat equation is a natural phenomenon used in many fields like mathematics and physics. Usually, its associated model is defined by a set of partial differential equations (PDEs). This paper is primarily aimed at showing two parallel programs for solving the heat equation which has been discrete-sized using the finite difference method (FDM). These programs have been implemented through different parallel platforms such as SkelGIS and Compute Unified Device Architecture (CUDA).

Keywords: Parallel computing · Parallel programming · Heat equation · CUDA · SkelGIS library · GPU · Finite difference method

1 Introduction

Parallel computing has gone forth as a new solution to deal with the intensive computational time when dealing with large datasets. This is mainly due to the drop of hardware costs, which has been fruitfully applied to speed up the recent advances of parallelism. Parallelism [1] is achieved with numerous ways, for example, we can use supercomputers, workstations, grid computing and clusters. In the literature, parallel computing [3] is a type of computation that permits performing calculations simultaneously, basically when dealing with a large size problem that is often separated into smaller ones which are solved at the same time by assuming that we dispose of hardware capable of executing the computation in parallel. The main strong point of parallel is the fact of providing computational power by incorporating multiple CPUs on the same process ship, in other words speeding up the process of computation. Parallelism manifest itself in many hardware structures:

© Springer Nature Switzerland AG 2020
M. Hamlich et al. (Eds.): SADASC 2020, CCIS 1207, pp. 283–295, 2020.
https://doi.org/10.1007/978-3-030-45183-7_22

- multi-core processors
- symmetric multiprocessors
- general purpose graphics processing unit
- field-programmable gate arrays
- computer clusters

Parallel programming [18] is the hardest phase of parallelism, since the complexity is much greater compared to sequential programming, this is why in this work we are going to explore the use of two libraries(CUDA, SkelGis) for a comparison concerning the heat equation simulation. The organization of this paper is as follows: Sect. 2 is devoted to an examination of the state of the art concerning the scientific simulations and the heat equation. Section 3 is consecrated to the CUDA and SkelGIS model to describe the parallel architecture used in each approach. Section 4 focuses on the implementation of parallel algorithms to solve the heat equation. The result of the real execution of these algorithms is presented in Sect. 5. Finally, the last section contains the conclusion.

2   Related Work

This section presents a constructive review of the state of the art concerning the relevant role of parallelism in solving scientific simulations in general, and heat equation in particular.

2.1   Parallelism for Scientific Simulation

Stevanski et al. presented, in their paper [14], the performance and efficiency evaluation of Open Computing Language (OpenCL) used to implement the Finite Difference Time Domain (FDTD) method. The contribution of authors only focused on portability and performance of tests on multi-core CPU machine supported by a single GPU. Therefore, the advantage of OpenCL FDTD code was that can be executed on multi-core CPUs, but the best performance was only obtained after specific code optimization. Although, the OpenCL FDTD simulations was more effective at a lower speed than native CUDA or OpenMP versions. The evaluation presented in this paper deducted that, despite current performance drawbacks, the future ability of OpenCL will be important thanks to its flexibility and portability to different architectures.

Jinghui et al. proposed in [2] a parallel computing paradigm based on a generalized fusion model for pan-sharpening algorithms. The paradigm can be applied to most pan-sharpening algorithms. The image processing adopted the Master-Slave parallel Model in order that the structural and textural details of the lower resolution multispectral image are enhanced by adopting the higher resolution panchromatic image corresponding to the multispectral image. The slave processors read the necessary data from the block, execute re-sampling and fusion operations subsequently, and then send the results to the master. The master receives the results sent from all processors and writes them in the output image.

The experimental results showed that an algorithm using the paradigm is 32.6 times faster than the corresponding version in the ERDAS IMAGINE software. The shortest time to complete the processing of pan-sharpening is only 64.71 (s) in an experiment where the file sizes of the input and resulting images are 973 MB and 3.02 GB, respectively.

2.2   Parallelism for Heat Equation

Vinaya Sivanandan et al. in [6] developed a three dimensional code based on the finite difference method for solving the heat equation. The code consists in calculating the temperature values on the whole nodes in the Cartesian mesh. The results got by the proposed code are compared with general purpose CFD software. The authors implemented the code using three frameworks. These implementations have been made in parallel using Message passing interface (MPI), Open Multi-Processing (OpenMP), and Compute Unified Device Architecture (CUDA). The main result of this work describes the relationship between the grid size and the execution time. As the mesh size increases, the execution time progressively increments. The authors have been observed that the execution time on GPU of the CUDA implementation is the least relative to the OpenMP and MPI programs.

Hélène Coullon and Sébastien Limet [5] proposed an implicit parallelism model, called Structured Implicit Parallelism on scientific Simulations (SIPSim). The implementation, done with C++, of the proposed model is called SkelGis. This solution was dedicated to two different cases of simulations: simulations on Cartesian meshes especially heat equation and network simulations which also called multiphysics simulation. For each case, the implementation of the SIPSim components is described with a simple example.

In order to evaluate the performance of SkelGIS, the authors made some experiments using 8 to 2048 cores, applied on the shallow water equations to compare the execution time with MPI version. As a result, performance and programming efforts of both implementations have been experimented and validated by a set of convincing results.

Yogesh D. Bhadke et al. in [9] proposed a heat conduction code on CUDA platform, which will solve the system of discrete equations using the Graphics processing unit (GPU). This work shown that regardless of the grid size the execution times for Alternative Direction Implicit (ADI) is way greater than the execution on ADI-CUDA except for the initial grid size.

3   CUDA and Sipsim Model

The principle of parallel computing is to enhance an application's performance through its execution on multiple processors. An algorithm model describes the structure of a parallel algorithm by selecting decomposition and mapping technique and applying the appropriate strategy to minimize interactions. This paper adopts two different models:

3.1   CUDA

In CUDA model, a kernel corresponds to a C++ function that is executed N times in parallel by N different CUDA threads. As indicated by fundamental structure of CUDA programming, before calling CUDA kernel, some pre-processing are performed where firstly memory allocation is performed for GPU devices equivalent number of variables used at host side. Moreover, data is transmitted from host to GPU devices, according to many particular methods provided by CUDA. Once we have confirmed the data transformation, CUDA kernel is called for GPU computation. At this level, we can use multiple CUDA kernels to run over multiple accelerated NVIDIA GPU devices. A detailed overview has been displayed in Fig. 1. The execution of kernel can be done by multiple equally-shaped thread blocks, so that the total number of threads is equal to the number of threads per block times the number of blocks. We also have three possibilities of blocks organization: one-dimensional, two-dimensional, or three-dimensional grid of thread blocks as shown in Fig. 2. The number of thread blocks in a grid is

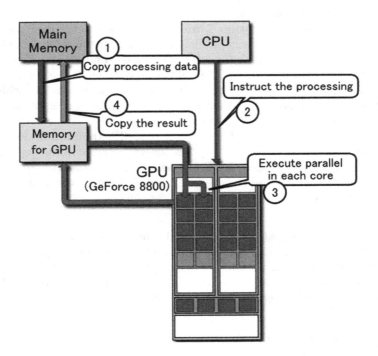

Fig. 1. Processing flow on CUDA [15].

normally ordered by the size of the data being processed, which typically exceeds the number of processors in the system [17].

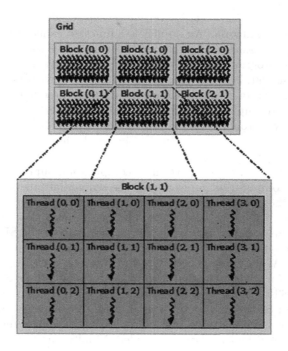

Fig. 2. Grid of thread blocks [17].

3.2 Sipsim [5]

Sipsim is an implicit parallell model that corresponds to the SkelGIS library. The main objective of this model is to give to users a simple development environment that resembles to sequential programming with algorithm and data structure. However, Sipsim generates parallel programs. SIPSim dissociates four classes of components to hide parallelization of programs:

Distributed Data Structure (DDS) represents a data structure, the mesh and its connectivity, to offer an efficient access to the elements of the mesh and to the needed neighborhood for the computation. It proceeds a partitioning of the mesh among processors. This partitioning is hidden from the user and has to solve automatically domain decomposition problems. The most important point to obtain a good efficiency is to have a good load balancing of data among processors. The load-balancing [11] problem have been a subject of many theses.

Distributed Property Map (DPMap). When at least one DDS is available, the model is looking for away to map data on it. Data mapped on DDS represent the quantities to simulate.

Appliers and Operations. An applier is a function called for following interchanges among processors and afterward calls the sequential code of the user. Hence, a parallel program written with a solution based on SIPSim follows the Bulk Synchronous Parallel (BSP) model [13]. In a BSP program, every processor uses the values stored in its own local memory; along these lines, the BSP model is widely utilized to implement SPMD programs. Furthermore, a BSP program is organized in asynchronous computation super steps and communication super steps that synchronize processors. In SIPSim, each time an applier is called, a communication super step synchronizes processors and proceeds exchanges of information, and afterward we perform a computation super step. In the SIPSim model, the computation super step is the sequential function that the user writes and it is then called by the applier. We denote the sequential function as an operation. Yet, to obtain an efficient solution, an overlap of communications with computations is performed in the implementation of the SIPSim model.

Interfaces offer sequential interfaces and tools for manipulating distributed data structures. We identify Three types of interfaces: iterators, get/set, and neighborhoods. An iterator in the SIPSim model is nearly as equivalent as an iterator in the STL of C++. An iterator is an object that traverse through a container, and in SIPSim, an iterator is an item that traverse through a DDS. Once the iterator is instantiated and moves through a set of mesh elements, a way to get and set values to data are needed. Finally, the last type of interface needed to code an operation is a way to access neighborhood values at the current position of an iterator.

4   Implementation

The goal of this section consists to discretize the two-dimensional heat equation using the explicit scheme or forward time centered space (FTCS) [4] of the finite difference method (FDM) [7]. The FTCS is considered as the least complex method based on the mathematical discretization for solving PDE through algebraic equations [6].

The two-dimensional heat equation is as follows:

$$\frac{\partial U}{\partial t} = \frac{\partial^2 U}{\partial x^2} + \frac{\partial^2 U}{\partial y^2} \qquad (1)$$

The Cartesian mesh [12] (see Fig. 3) is characterized by two parameters which are Δx, the local distance between a neighborhood in space, and Δt, the local distance between a neighborhood in time. In this chapter, the both parameters Δx and Δt are uniform throughout the mesh. Both the time and space derivatives are replaced by finite differences, we are using $U(x_i, y_j, t_n) = U_{i,j}^n$ to simplify the writing. At that point, The Eq. (1) is discritized by supposing that $\Delta x = \Delta y$, we obtain the final equation as follows:

$$U_{i,j}^{n+1} = (1 - 4\lambda)U_{i,j}^n + \lambda(U_{i+1,j}^n + U_{i-1,j}^n + U_{i,j+1}^n + U_{i,j-1}^n) \qquad (2)$$

where $\lambda = \frac{\Delta t}{\Delta x^2} \leq 0.5$.

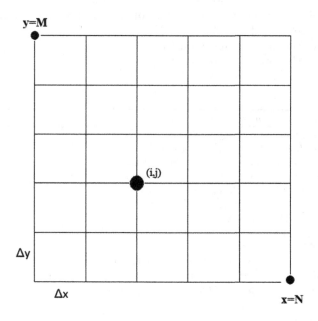

Fig. 3. Cartesian mesh.

4.1   CUDA Implementation

CUDA is a programming model and software environment developed by NVIDIA to let developers write adaptable parallel programs through these different levels of parallelism [8]. The CUDA programming model helps the software engineer to develop adequate, scalable and efficient programs for using massively multithreaded GPUs. The majority of scientists and programmers consider it as a convenient environment for parallel programming. Because it furnishes a simple syntax, minimalist abstraction of parallelism and inherits all the well-known semantics of C language.

The corresponding code in CUDA [16] for solving numerically (2) is implemented as follows [10]:

- Identify global variables as mesh size(along with x and y) and a number of Jacobi iterations.
- Initialize the condition of temperature.

- Declaration of the pointer to Host (CPU) memory and pointers to Device (GPU) memory.
- Allocate and initialize an array on the host for pre-computation.
- Allocate Memory on Device.
- Copy data from CPU memory to GPU memory.
- Assign a 2D distribution of CUDA "threads" within each CUDA "block".
- Calculate the number of blocks in CUDA "grid".
- Begin Jacobi iteration and call Laplace operation (see Algorithm 1).
- Copy the final array from Device to Host.
- Release the Allocated Memory on Device.
- Release the Allocated Memory on Host.

Algorithm 1 : function laplace in CUDA

1: **function** LAPLACE($^*Temp_{old}$, $^*Temp_{new}$)
2:     $i = blockIdx.x * blockDim.x + threadIdx.x$;
3:     $j = blockIdx.y * blockDim.y + threadIdx.y$;
4:     $current = i + j * NX$;
5:     $north = i + (j + 1) * NX$;
6:     $south = i + (j - 1) * NX$;
7:     $east = (i + 1) + j * NX$;
8:     $west = (i - 1) + j * NX$;
9:     $\lambda = 0.05$;
10:     **if** $i \langle 0 \&\& i \langle NX - 1 \&\& j \langle 0 \&\& j \langle NY - 1$ **then**
11:         $Temp_{new}[current] = (1 - 4 * \lambda) * Temp_{old}[current] + \lambda * (Temp_{old}[east] + Temp_{old}[west] + Temp_{old}[north] + Temp_{old}[south])$
12:     **end if**
13: **end function**

A CUDA program is sorted out into a host program, comprising of at least one successive threads running on the host CPU, and at least one parallel kernel that are appropriate for execution on a parallel processing device as the GPU.

A kernel runs a scalar consecutive program on the whole of parallel threads. The software engineer arranges these threads into a grid of threads blocks. The threads of a solitary thread square are permitted to synchronize with one another by means of boundaries and have access to a fast, per-block shared on-chip memory for inter-thread communication. Threads from various blocks in a similar grid can coordinate just via operations in a shared global memory space obvious to all threads. CUDA necessitates that thread blocks must be independent, implying that a kernel should execute effectively regardless of the order in which blocks are run, regardless of whether all blocks are executed successively in discretionary order without preemption.

4.2   SkelGIS Implementation

SkelGIS library is implemented following the SIPSim model (see CUDA and SkelGIS model section), and it proposed an implicit parallelism solution to solve PDEs. SkelGIS has been implemented for two different kinds of numerical simulations, those applied on a Cartesian, two-dimensional, mesh and those applied on a network of two different meshes (multiphysics simulations) [5]. The parallelism model SIPSim can be used for various simulations, from regular to irregular data structures. This flexibility is due to a pragmatic of the numerical simulation domain. The experiments have been executed on two different large clusters to better test the scalability of the proposed interface. Algorithm 2 shows the corresponding SkelGIS code to solve the heat equation. According to Eq. (2),

---

Algorithm 2 : Main function in SkelGIS to solve heat equation

---

```
1:  include skelgis library.
2:  function MAIN(int argc, char** argv)
3:      Initialisation of the library by INITSKELGIS;
4:      Declaration of the head with HEAD type;
5:      Initialisation of the head;
6:      DMatrix < double, 1 > m(head, 0);
7:      m.setGlobalMiddleValue(1);
8:      DMatrix < double, 1 > m2(head, 0);
9:      for <i=0;i<100;i++> do
10:         Called Laplacien function;
11:         DMatrix < double, 1 > m3(head, 0);
12:         m = m2;
13:         m2 = m3;
14:     end for
15:     ENDSKELGIS;
16: end function
```

---

there is an important dependence between the computation at time n+1 and at time n, that's why two distributed Matrices are instantiated (lines 6 and 8) to manage the input and output of the scheme. The main loop (lines 9 to 14) consists to call the laplacian function in order to compute for each time iteration the numerical scheme of Eq. (2).

5   Results

In our experiments presented in Table 1, we executed the parallel CUDA program of the heat equation in different domain sizes to study its efficiency; firstly, with the problem size 5120 * 5120 and 5000 iterations, the execution time of the

program was just 8.85 (s). Second, in the two lines following, we remarked that
we have almost the same time execution in both experiments. Finally, from the
two last lines, we concluded that the increment of domain size has more effect
on the result than the increment of time iterations.

Table 1. Execution time of CUDA

Experiments	Time iterations	Domain size	Time (seconds)
EXP1	5000	5120*5120	8.85
EXP2	20000	5120*5120	35.24
EXP3	5000	10.000*10.000	34.62
EXP4	5000	20.000*20.000	141.11

For a real execution of the CUDA program, the computer hardware used
in the experiments contains an Intel CPU i7-4770k with 4 cores at a speed of
3.50 GHz and 8 threads; a RAM memory of 16.00 GB and the operating system
used is Windows 7. The GPU hardware is a NVIDIA GeForce GTX 10606 GB
with 1280 of Cuda cores.

According to Table 2, which is based on results of [5], the difference between
execution time of the CUDA version and SkelGIS version is very vast because
the CUDA architecture is characterized by several blocks which execute the
algorithm in parallel as shown in Fig. 5.

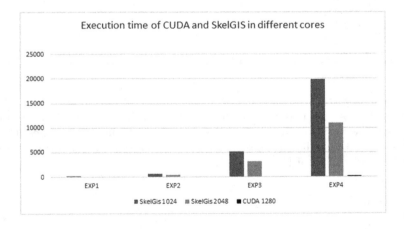

Fig. 4. Execution time of CUDA and SkelGIS.

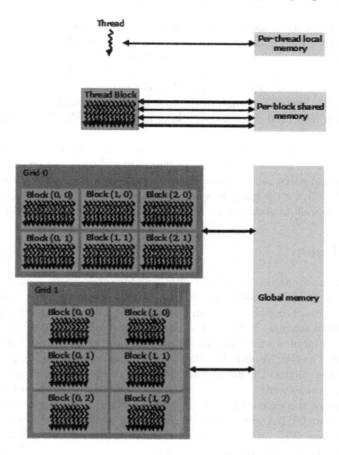

Fig. 5. GPU memory architecture [17].

Table 2. Comparison between execution time CUDA and SkelGIS

	SkelGIS library (s) [5]		CUDA (s)
	Cores = 1024	Cores = 2048	Cores = 1280
EXP1	155.85	103.363	8.85
EXP2	602.66	407.73	35.24
EXP3	5127.93	3196.71	34.62
EXP4	19821.3	10986.8	141.11

A CUDA kernel executes an algorithm in an important number of threads in parallel. The block contains a set of threads which work together effectively by exchanging data via a local shared memory.

The experiments presented in Table 1 consist to evaluate the efficiency of both algorithms with a variation of time iterations and the size of mesh. From Fig. 4, we can concluded some important results.

First, the performances of CUDA, compared with SkelGIS, are very convincing. Always, The execution time of CUDA is the fastest (see Fig. 4). Second, it is clear that the SkelGIS version in the first experiment with 2048 cores, CUDA executed with just 1280 cores, takes a long time almost the CUDA time is multiplied by 12.

Finally, from the real execution and theoretical evaluation, we can deduct that Halstead metrics wasn't efficient to compare algorithms. Because, it showed that CUDA language is the more difficult with a long code. While, the real execution proved, for the same language, that is the best parallel language due to the performance of its architecture and its quickness to execute parallel program.

6 Conclusion

In this work, we focused on parallel computing for solving heat equation through a comparative study between two parallel models. To implement these models, we began by identifying the equation that should be discretized with the explicit finite difference scheme. Then, in the rest of the paper we focused on the approach to implement numerically the heat equation using parallel development languages such as CUDA and SkelGIS Library. As a result, we observed that each language is way different from another. In order to evaluate the two algorithms, we used the real execution because it is more efficient to compare the results. Finally, through the execution time of the algorithms in several experiments, we can deduce that CUDA gives effective results with a GPU architecture.

In conclusion, The implementation of the heat equation in particular or scientific simulation in general, is not limited to those languages. There are also other parallel languages such as Python, MPI, OpenCL and PCN. Each language of these is useful according to the necessity of the program.

Acknowledgment. This project has received funding from:

- The European Union's Horizon 2020 research and innovation program under the Marie Skłodowska-Curie grant agreement No. 777720.
- The National Center for Scientific and Technical Research (NCSTR - Morocco) grant agreement No. 10UH2C2017.

References

1. Pacheco, P.: An Introduction to Parallel Programming, 1st edn. Elsevier/Morgan Kaufmann, Massachusetts (2011)
2. Jinghui, Y., Jixian, Z., Guoman, H.: A parallel computing paradigm for pansharpening algorithms of remotely sensed images on a multi-core computer. Remote Sens. J. **6**(7), 6039–6063 (2014)

3. Lucquin, B., Pironneau, O.: Introduction to Scientific Computing. Wiley, New York (1997)
4. Recktenwald, G.W.: Finite-Difference Approximations to the Heat Equation. http://www.nada.kth.se/~jjalap/numme/FDheat.pdf. Accessed 13 Jan 2020
5. Coullon, H., Limet, S.: The SIPSim implicit parallelism model and the SkelGIS library. Concurr. Comput.: Pract. Exp. **28**, 2120–2144 (2015)
6. Sivanandan, V., Kumar, V., Meher, S.: Designing a parallel algorithm for Heat Conduction using MPI, OpenMP and CUDA (2015)
7. Cerovský, A., Dulce, A., Ferreira, A.: Application of the finite difference method and the finite element method to solve a thermal problem, Porto, March 2014
8. Garland M., et al.: Parallel Computing Experiences with CUDA. IEEE Computer Society (2008)
9. Bhadke, Y.D., Kawale, M.R., Inamdar, V.: Development of 3D-CFD code for heat conduction process using CUDA. In: IEEE International Conference on Advances in Engineering and Technology Research (ICAETR - 2014), Unnao, India, 01–02 August 2014 (2014)
10. Belhaous, S., Chokri, S., Bentaleb, M., Naji, A., Mestari, M.: Implementation of a parallel algorithm for Heat Equation using SkelGIS library, CUDA and SISAL. In: IEEE 4th International Conference in Optimization and application, Morocco (2018)
11. Chokri, S., Baroud, S., Belhaous, S., Bentaleb, M., El Youssfi, M., Mestari, M.: Heuristics for dynamic load balancing in parallel computing. In: IEEE 4th International Conference in Optimization and Application, Morocco (2018)
12. He, G., Zhao, R., Qin, J., Jiang, L., Wang, H., Tang, Y.: Research on temperature gradient model of SiC smelting furnace based on finite difference method. In: 9th International Congress on Image and Signal Processing, BioMedical Engineering and Informatics (CISP-BMEI 2016), pp. 1900–1904 (2016)
13. Valiant, L.G.: A bridging model for parallel computation. Commun. ACM **33**(8), 103–111 (1990)
14. Stefański, T.P., Benkler, S., Chavannes, N., Kuster, N.: Parallel implementation of the finite-difference TimeDomain method in open computing language. In: IEEE International Conference, Switzerland (2010)
15. Ashraf, U., Alburaei Eassa, F., Albeshri, A.A., Algarni, A.: Performance and power efficient massive parallel computational model for HPC heterogeneous exascale systems. IEEE Access J. **6**, 23095–2310 (2018)
16. Solution of the 2D heat equation in CUDA. http://www.joshiscorner.com/2013/12/2d-heat-conduction-solving-laplaces-equation-on-the-cpu-and-the-gpu/. Accessed 8 Jan 2020
17. CUDA Programming Guide. https://docs.nvidia.com/cuda/cuda-c-programming-guide/index.html. Accessed 8 Jan 2020
18. Bousselham, A.: J. Therm. Biol. (2017). https://doi.org/10.1016/j.jtherbio.2017.10.014

Simulations and Deep Learning

Automatic Microservices Identification from a Set of Business Processes

Mohamed Daoud[1(✉)], Asmae El Mezouari[2], Noura Faci[1],
Djamal Benslimane[1(✉)], Zakaria Maamar[3], and Aziz El Fazziki[2]

[1] Claude Bernard Lyon 1 University, Lyon, France
{Mohamed-taoufik.daoud,djamal.benslimane}@univ-lyon1.fr
[2] Caddi Ayyad University, Marrakesh, Morocco
[3] Zayed University, Dubai, United Arab Emirates

Abstract. All organizations engage in ongoing maintenance of their information systems due to constant changes in users' needs and governments' regulations. However these systems are monolithic making this maintenance a nightmare. To address this monolithic nature different technologies like commercial-of-the-shelf, service-oriented architecture, and lately microservices are proposed. This paper focuses on microservices by discussing their automatic identification from a set of business processes. Thanks to business processes, control and data dependencies between their activities are extracted and then clustered together. Each cluster constitutes a candidate microservice. To illustrate and demonstrate microservice automatic identification, a case study about renting bikes in the city of Barcelona is adopted and then implemented. In term of precision, the results show how business processes as inputs permit to generate better microservices compared to other approaches discussed in the paper, as well.

Keywords: Business process · Control dependencies · Data dependencies · Microservice

1 Introduction

Modern organizations' information systems (systems for short) are continuously subject to functional and architectural changes so these organizations can address users' new requirements and tap into the latest developments in Information and Communication Technologies (ICT). An example of functional change is when organizations deploy mobile services for users-on-the-move. And, an example of architectural change is when organizations adopt cloud for its elasticity and pay-as-you-go benefits. Although functional and architectural changes are a must, many organizations continue running their existing (legacy) systems despite the high maintenance cost along with missing the opportunities of improving their competitiveness posture. Many reasons justify this resisting

© Springer Nature Switzerland AG 2020
M. Hamlich et al. (Eds.): SADASC 2020, CCIS 1207, pp. 299–315, 2020.
https://doi.org/10.1007/978-3-030-45183-7_23

"attitude" with focus in this paper on the **monolithic** nature of systems. Monolithic means one block that encompasses strongly-coupled components and that is sometimes "sealed" preventing its analysis for the sake of improvement.

Over the years many technologies were put forward to address monolithic systems including Commercial-Of-The-Shelf (COTS) [19], Component-Based Software Engineering (CBSE) [17], and lately Service-Oriented Architecture (SOA) [5]. Unfortunately many of these technologies did not live up to their expectations due to many reasons such as making organizations change to accommodate technologies, lack of capturing organizations' unique features, and complexity of adoption amplified with resistance to change. A recent trend referred to as microservices seems surging from the "ashes" of SOA [13].

Although microservices could be confused to SOA-based Web services and/or Restful services, Cerny et al. shed light on these 2 architectural styles' strengths and weaknesses in [3]. Both μServices with reference to Microservice Architecture and SOA have the same objective that is service cooperation through their integration across many independent platforms, but adopt different ways of achieving this cooperation. These architectures' strengths and weaknesses are related to 18 concerns that range from deployment and scalability to versioning and administration till business-rules location. While the 18 concerns provide a comprehensive coverage of how ICT practitioners could adopt either architecture, the identification of microservices and SOA services does not seem to be a concern. SOA is a well-established discipline so μServices could have benefited from its best practices when it comes to service identification, but this is not the case until now. In this paper we address this gap with a collaborative clustering-based approach to identify microservices from a set of Business Processes (BPs).

For a successful adoption of microservices, guidelines for identifying them are deemed necessary. The objective is to avoid system designers' disappointments in microservices, which could put them at risk of no-adoption like other technologies. The literature refers to different works on microservices identification using log files [8], source codes [9], UML class diagram [2], and legacy databases [4] as inputs to the identification exercise. While all these works have the same objective, automatic identification of microservices, none of them considers BPs as input. Referred to as organizations' main assets, BPs could constitute an important source for identifying microservices. According to Weske, "... *A business process consists of a set of activities that are performed in coordination in an organizational and technical environment. These activities jointly realize a business goal. Each business process is enacted by a single organization, but it may interact with business processes performed by other organizations*" [24]. Despite being a rich reservoir of many details like who does what, when, where, and why, BPs seem overlooked during the exercise of identifying microservices. To the best of our knowledge, Amiri is the only one who adopted BPs in this exercise [1].

Although the pioneering nature of Amiri's work, it suffers from many limitations. First, structural activity dependencies model is not defined to show how dependencies are formally obtained with respect to business process modeling languages' operators. Secondly, the data dependencies model is very simple and limited to read and write operations. Thirdly, only structural and data dependencies are considered while other dependencies like semantics between activities are overlooked. Fourthly, aggregating all dependency types into a single data structure (matrix in our case) to be used for clustering needs will lead to data quality degradation in the sense that strengths and/or weaknesses of each dependency type are potentially hidden.

In this paper, we design and develop a collaborative clustering-based approach to automatically identify microservices. At the core of our approach is the idea of extracting microservices from BPs' activities by using first, a set of separate models that individually identify different kinds of information related to these activities and their dependencies and second, a collaborative clustering technique instead of a classical clustering technique to avoid aggregating extracted data that could lead to losing some implicit details. Our approach is multi-models in the sense that it combines independent models to represent a BP's structural dependencies, data dependencies, semantic dependencies, and so on. It is also based on collaborative clustering in the sense that all data that could be extracted from the different models are kept independent instead of aggregating them. Each data set is then handled by a separate clustering algorithm. At the end, the collaborative clustering allows to each clustering component algorithm to benefit from the work done by other clustering components [6].

The rest of the paper is organized as follows. Section 2 describes related work. Section 3 presents a case study, gives an overview of our approach to automatically identify microservices from existing BPs, and formalizes the structural and data dependencies models. Section 4 details the collaborative clustering in this approach and then, the system implementing this approach along with some experiments' results. Section 5 concludes the paper.

2   Related Work

There exist a good number of works that discuss monolithic systems' limitations and how microservices could address them. These systems are known for incurring significant development, maintenance, and evolution cost [22].

In [11], a service-cutter system is presented allowing to decompose monolithic systems into small services. The decomposition uses the systems' functions and considers three criteria that are between entities at the property level, coherence between data of each microservice, and communication cost between services. In [4], an approach to identify microservices is proposed. The approach uses the semantic similarity of functionalities that are described in openAPI[1] and a reference vocabulary. Microservices are identified as a cohesive cluster of operations extracted from an UML diagram class. The semantic similarity is based

---

[1] www.openapis.org.

on the pre-computed database DISCO (DIStributionally related words using CO-occurences)[2].

In [18], modernizing a monolithic system using microservices is proposed. This system is described using three types of objects: interfaces, business functions, and database tables. These objects are then linked in a dependency graph by means of calls from interfaces to business functions, calls between business functions themselves, and accesses from business functions to database tables. Candidate microservices correspond to the business rules that depend on database tables, and correspond to the facades connected to the database tables.

In [16], clustering techniques are used to optimize the performance and scalability of an existing microservice architecture. Given this architecture as an input, its current deployment, workload, features (a check of functionalities that deliver a business value) model that describes properties and their dependencies, an automatic approach is proposed to recommend a new deployment that optimizes the performance and scalability of the architecture. Some features can then be moved from one microservice to another. The results of experimenting the approach highlight the importance of considering performance metrics when generating a microservice architecture. A study that analyses microservices architectures with detailed performance profile data is also presented in [23].

In [14], a functionality-oriented microservice extraction by clustering execution traces of programs collected at run-time is described. These traces are collected by using techniques of program execution monitoring and are used to collect implicit and explicit program functional behavior. They also reveal which entities are used for which business logic. The approach clusters source code entities that are related to the same functionalities. Even if the work in [14] is interesting, it suffers from its strong dependence on the quality of the generated execution traces, and consequently on the quality of the test cases.

3   Our Approach for Identifying Microservices

This section consists of 4 parts. The first part presents a case study that refers to Barcelona's bike sharing system known as Bicing. The second and third parts discuss our approach's foundations in terms of dependencies between BPs' activities and collaborative clustering. Finally, the last part formalizes these dependencies.

3.1   Bicing Case-Study

Bicing includes more than 400 bike anchor-stations spread across Barcelona and about 6000 bikes that users rent for a fee. Bicing's monolithic system is described in [10] along with the managerial and technical challenges that undermine its operations. For the needs of our work, we suggest in Fig. 1 a high-level representation of Bicing from a BP perspective. We resorted to the standard Business

---

[2] www.commonspaces.eu/en/oer/disco-extracting-distributionally-related-words-us.

Process Model and Notation (BPMN) to illustrate this representation. We have identified different activities (a_1: request bike and a_9: dismantle bike), different dependencies (between a_1 and a_2), different logical operators (XOR between a_6 and a_{10} and OR between a_2 and a_3), and, finally, different artefacts (bike and user) and their respective attributes (e.g., ID and status). In the rest of this paper the discussion about Bicing is not restricted to renting bikes but includes other aspects like reporting and fixing bikes' defects and disposing bikes, if necessary. It all starts when a user requests a bike (a_1) at a certain anchor station. After checking the user's credentials (a_2) and any late fee payment (a_3), the Bicing system updates the user's records (a_4) and then, approves the user's request (a_5). If it turns out that the bike is defective, the user puts it back (a_6) and eventually requests another one. Otherwise, the user starts his journey (a_{10}). Regularly all bikes are serviced (a_7) leading to either putting them back for rent (a_8) or disposing them (a_9). When the user arrives to destination, he returns the bike at a certain anchor point (a_{11}). Otherwise, the Bicing system blacklists the user (a_{14}) due to bike inappropriate return and geo-locates the bike (a_{12}) so that it is collected by the competent services and then made available to other users (a_{13}).

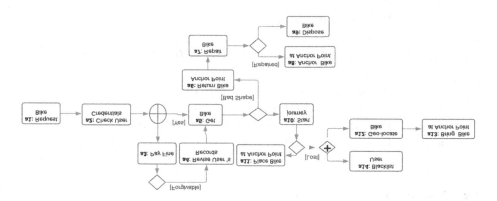

Fig. 1. An illustrative BPMN-based representation of the Bicing system

From a specification perspective, activities ($\{a_i\}$) may require inputs ($\{i_i\}$) and produce outputs ($\{o_i\}$) that both correspond to specific artefacts' attributes. An activity acts upon an attribute through 2 operations that are *read* (r) and/or *write* (w), which could lead to *updating* (u), *creating* (c), and/or *deleting* (d) artefacts. Table 1 lists activities, artefacts, attributes of artefacts, and also the operations that artefacts/attributes are subject to.

Table 1. Bicing's BPs as a set of activities, artefacts, attributes, and operations

Activity	Artefacts	Attributes
a_1	Bike (u)	Anchor_Point (r), Bike_ID (r), Bike_Status (w)
	User (u)	User_ID (r), User_Destination (r)
a_2	User (u)	User_ID (r), User_Credit (r), User_Destination (r)
a_3	User (u)	User_ID (r), User_History (r), User_Validity (r)
a_4	User (u)	User_ID (r), User_History (w)
a_5	Bike (u)	Bike_ID (r), Bike_Status (w)
	User (u)	User_ID (r), User_Status (w)
	Rental (c)	User_Destination (w), Rent_Date (w)
a_6	Bike (u)	Anchor_Point (r), Bike_ID (r), Bike_Status (w)
	User (u)	User_ID (r), User_Status (w)
	Rental (d)	Rent_ID (r)
a_7	Bike (u)	Bike_Status (w)
	Repair (c)	estimated_Repair_Cost (w), agree_Repair (w)
a_8	Bike (u)	Anchor_Point (r), Bike_Status (w)
a_9	Bike (d)	Bike_ID (r)
a_{10}	User (u)	User_ID (r), User_Status (w)
a_{11}	Bike (u)	Anchor_Point (r), Bike_ID (r), Bike_Status (w)
	User (u)	User_ID (r)
	Rental (u)	Rent_ID (r), Rent_Cost (w), User_History (w)
a_{12}	Bike (u)	Bike_ID (r), Bike_Location (w)
a_{13}	Bike (u)	Bike_ID (r), Anchor_Point (r), Bike_Status (w)
a_{14}	User (u)	User_ID (r), User_Status (w), User_History (w)

3.2 Foundations

It is largely known that BP automation helps organizations track events, assign activities, manage resources, etc. In this work we adopt the definition of BP given in [7] stating that a BP is a set of logically related activities that are performed to achieve goals. "Logically related" refers to dependencies between activities such as *control* (with respect to an execution order), data (with respect to information sharing), and *functional* (with respect to horizontal- and vertical-business operations). By using BPs as an input to identifying microservices, we would like to ensure that these microservices are fine-grained, strongly cohesive (i.e., degree to which activities in a microservice belong together), and loosely-coupled (i.e., degree to which microservices can be easily replaced). These 3 dependencies are illustrated below.

- *Control dependency* refers to both the execution order (e.g., finish-to-start and start-to-start) between activities and the logical operators (e.g., XOR and AND) between activities as well. Should 2 activities be directly connected through a control dependency, then most probably they would form a highly-cohesive microservice to which they will belong. Contrarily, they would most probably be used to form separate microservices to which each will belong.

– *Data dependency* refers to associating activities' outputs/inputs in a way that permits to illustrate data flowing from one activity to another. These inputs/outputs correspond to artefacts' attributes. Data dependency sheds light on both artefacts and artefacts' attributes that could be subject to operations illustrated in Table 1 like *create* (c) and *write* (w). In addition to input/output association, data dependency could indicate to what extent artefacts and/or artefacts' attributes are either mandatory or optional for BP execution. We advocate that activities that exchange mandatory artefacts' attributes should be part of the same microservice allowing to avoid delaying this exchange, for example.

– *Functional dependency* refers to horizontal (cross) and vertical (silo) business operations. The former denotes activities whose execution would cross multiple departments in the same organization. The latter denotes activities whose execution would be confined into the same department. We advocate that activities that would take part in horizontal interactions would less likely be part of the same microservices.

We focus on *control* and *data dependencies*, only. Upon establishing such dependencies, we quantify them using specific metrics. The objective is to evaluate cohesion and coupling among activities so that they are gathered in either same or separate microservices. To measure a *control dependency* between 2 activities (a_i, a_j), we consider a_j's occurrence probability after executing a_i. This probability depends on the execution order and/or logical operators between a_i and a_j. Let us consider the *control dependency* between a_5 and a_{10} that is connected with a_6 through XOR (Fig. 1). After executing a_5, a_{10}'s occurrence probability depends on the decision made at XOR (i.e., either a_6 or a_{10}). We note that any activity's occurrence probability is calculated over time by using BP's execution logs. To measure a *data dependency* between 2 activities (a_i, a_j), we consider an artefact's and attribute's criticality level that would reflect the importance of information shared between these activities. This level denotes the impact of artefact/attribute unavailability on the continuity of business operations. More details are given in the next sections.

Based on dependencies among activities, we gather activities into microservices by using clustering techniques. In the literature, clustering is either centralized or collaborative [12]. In the former, a single component manages the clustering by utilizing all individuals' features[3] as inputs. In the latter, multiple components, each in charge of one type of features, exchange some details during clustering so that appropriate clusters are jointly built. Performance and appropriateness of clustering techniques are thoroughly discussed in the literature [6] and [25]. Many works like [6] and [12] advocate for collaborative clustering to

---

[3] In our work, individuals are activities and features are control and data dependencies.

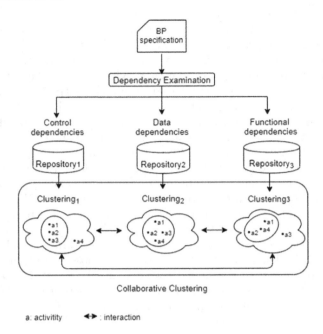

Fig. 2. General representation of our microservice identification approach

identify microservices. It provides fine-grained and accurate results contrarily to centralized clustering where individuals' features need to be aggregated before initiating any clustering.

Figure 2 depicts our approach for microservices identification. It relies on the aforementioned dependencies and collaborative clustering to group activities that would form fine-grained, highly-cohesive, and loosely-coupled microservices. Our approach consists of the following steps. After examining activity dependencies, their details are stored in dedicated repositories. Then, these repositories' contents are submitted for collaborative clustering where different clustering techniques (one per dependency) are used to obtain consensual clustering solutions. More details are given in Sect. 4.1.

3.3   Control Dependency Analysis

Let $CD(a_i, a_j[\text{Operator } \{a_k\}])_{\text{ExecOrder}}$ be a a direct *control dependency* referring to a certain execution order between a_i and a_j that is connected to other activities $\{a_k\}$ through a certain Operator. An execution order between 2 activities could be exemplified with either *finish-to-start* (our focus and denoted by SEQ)), *finish-to-finish*, *start-to-start*, or *start-to-finish*.

Let us start with the *control dependency* $CD(a_i, a_j)_{\text{SEQ}}$ (i.e., $\{a_k\} = \emptyset)$). Since SEQ between a_i and a_j means that a_j starts only after a_i has successfully completed, $CD(a_i, a_j)_{\text{SEQ}}$ denotes a_j's occurrence probability (p) after a_i's completion as per Eq. 1:

$$CD(a_i, a_j)_{\text{SEQ}} = p \qquad (1)$$

where $p \in\,]0, 1]$.

We now examine the *control dependency* $CD(a_i, a_j \text{ Operator } \{a_k\})_{\text{SEQ}}$ (i.e., $\{a_k\} \neq \emptyset$). According to Operator's semantics, we assume that some r activities in $\{a_k\} \cup a_j$ will be selected for execution. Eq. 2 defines the number of activities that will be selected for execution as a combination $C(n, r)$ where n corresponds to $card(\{a_k\} \cup a_j)$.

$$C(n, r) = \frac{n!}{r! \times (n - r)!} \qquad (2)$$

Depending on the semantics of Operator whether AND, XOR, or OR, $CD(a_i, a_j \text{ Operator } \{a_k\})_{\text{SEQ}}$ is calculated as follows:

1. $CD(a_i, a_j \text{ AND } \{a_k\})_{\text{SEQ}}$. This dependency means that a_j will start only after a_i has successfully completed regardless of $\{a_k\}$. Formally, Eq. 3 computes $CD(a_i, a_j \text{ AND } \{a_k\})_{\text{SEQ}}$ as follows:

$$CD(a_i, a_j \text{ AND } \{a_k\})_{\text{SEQ}} = C(n, n) * CD(a_i, a_j)_{\text{SEQ}} \qquad (3)$$

   where $p \in\,]0, 1]$ & $C(n, n) = 1$, as per Eq. 2.

2. $CD(a_i, a_j \text{ XOR } \{a_k\})_{\text{SEQ}}$. This dependency means that one activity from $\{a_k\} \cup a_j$ will be selected after a_i has successfully completed. Formally, Eq. 4 computes $CD(a_i, a_j \text{ XOR } \{a_k\})_{\text{SEQ}}$ as follows:

$$CD(a_i, a_j \text{ XOR } \{a_k\})_{\text{SEQ}} = \frac{1}{C(n, 1)} * CD(a_i, a_j)_{\text{SEQ}} \qquad (4)$$

   where $C(n, 1)$ is the number of possibilities to select one activity from $\{a_k\} \cup a_j$. As per Eq. 2, $C(n, 1)$ is equal to n.

3. $CD(a_i, a_j \text{ OR } \{a_k\})_{\text{SEQ}}$. This dependency means that a set of r activities from $2^{\{a_k\} \cup a_j}$ (i.e., all possible multiple choices) will be selected after a_i has successfully completed. For the sake of simplicity, we assume that any activity in $\{a_k\} \cup a_j$ has the same occurrence probability over $2^{\{a_k\} \cup a_j}$, that is equal to $\frac{r}{n}$ where r varies from 1 to n. Formally, Eq. 5 computes $CD(a_i, a_j \text{ OR } \{a_k\})_{\text{SEQ}}$ as follows.

$$CD(a_i, a_j \text{ OR } \{a_k\})_{\text{SEQ}} = \frac{\sum_{r=1,n}(\frac{r}{n} \times C(n, r))}{\sum_{r=1,n} C(n, r)} * CD(a_i, a_j)_{\text{SEQ}} \qquad (5)$$

   where
   - $\sum_{r=1,n}(\frac{r}{n} \times C(n, r))$ represents the number of a_j's occurrences among possible combinations of activities[4].
   - $\sum_{r=1,n} C(n, r)$ corresponds to the total number of possible combinations of activities[5].

---

[4] Let n be 3, $\sum_{r=1,n}(\frac{r}{n} \times C(n, r))$ has the following value: $(\frac{1}{3} \times 3 + \frac{2}{3} \times 3 + \frac{3}{3} \times 1 {=} 4)$.
[5] Let n be 3, $\sum_{r=1,n} C(n, r)$ has the following value: $(3 {+} 3 {+} 1) {=} 7$.

We now look into indirect *control dependency* between a_i and a_j where there is a set of other peers connected with operators. This dependency, denoted as $CD(a_i, a_j)_{path^1_{i,j}}$, refers to a certain execution path $(path^1_{i,j})$ and is computed as per Eq. 6:

$$CD(a_i, a_j)_{path^1_{i,j}} = \prod_{a_l, a_m \in path^1_{i,j}} CD(a_l, a_m \text{ Operator } \{a_{k_m}\})_{\mathsf{SEQ}} \qquad (6)$$

When multiple execution paths exist between a_i and a_j, we refer to this *control dependency* as $CD(a_i, a_j)_{paths_{i,j}}$ and is computed as per Eq. 7:

$$CD(a_i, a_j)_{paths_{i,j}} = \max_{q=1,\ldots} (CD(a_i, a_j)_{path^q_{i,j}}) \qquad (7)$$

where $path^q_{i,j}$ represents the qth possible execution path between a_i and a_j. Table 2 depicts an excerpt of *control dependencies* in the Bicing system.

Table 2. Control dependencies with $p = 0.5$

Activity	a_1	a_2	a_3	a_4	a_5
a_1	-	1/2	5/6	11/12	17/12
a_2	1/2	-	1/3	7/12	11 /12
a_3	5/6	1/3	-	1/4	3/4
a_4	11/12	7/12	1/4	-	1/2
a_5	7/12	11/12	3/4	1/2	-

3.4 Data Dependency Analysis

As mentioned in Sect. 3.2, we consider artefact's and attribute's *criticality* as a metric for measuring *data dependency* between 2 activities. In [21], Paulsen et al. describe a comprehensive criticality analysis for helping organizations identify and prioritize assets (e.g., artefacts and processes) that are vital for the success of organizational goals. Based on this analysis, we distinguish 2 types of criticality: *functional* and *non-functional*. The former refers to artefact/attribute's unavailability that would hinder the BP's proper execution while the latter refers to artefact/attribute's corruption would undermine the BP's QoS. On the one hand, we rely on the traditional 3 information levels (i.e., *strategic, tactical,* and *operational*) to define artefact's and attribute's *functional-criticality* level. A *strategic* attribute's criticality should be higher than an *operational* attribute. On the other hand, we rely on security, privacy, and safety levels to define artefact's and attribute's *non-functional-criticality* level. Table 3 depicts certain attributes per type of criticality for the Bicing case-study.

Table 3. Attribute examples per criticality type

Type	Level	Example
Functional	Operational	Decision-making data
	Tactical	Concurrency data
	Strategic	Customer experience data
Non-functional	Privacy	Protected personal data
		Stakeholder's identity
	Confidentiality	Financial data

We define 3 criticality degrees, *high* (H), *medium* (M), and *low* (L) that have, respectively, k, $k' < k$, and $k'' < k'$ as quantitative value. Note that the BP designer specifies artefact's and attribute's criticality level with respect to Table 3. Since artefacts and attributes can be associated with both types of criticality (i.e., *functional* and *non-functional*), we define 2 strategies for calculating an artefact (ar)'s and attribute (at)'s criticality $(\mathcal{C}(ar|at))$. The first strategy computes $\mathcal{C}(ar|at)$ as a weighted sum (Eq. 10).

$$\mathcal{C}(ar|at) = w_1 \times \mathcal{C}^F(ar|at) + w_2 \times \mathcal{C}^{NF}(ar|at), \quad w_1 + w_2 = 1 \qquad (8)$$

where:

- $\mathcal{C}^F(ar|at) \mid \mathcal{C}^{NF}(ar|at)$ corresponds to $ar|at$'s *functional/non-functional criticality* degree, and
- $w_1 \mid w_2$ is the weight (i.e., importance) the BP designer associates with $\mathcal{C}^F(ar|at) \mid \mathcal{C}^{NF}(ar|at)$.

Considering k, k', and k'' as parameters gives more flexibility and generality to our approach. Some simulations will show how k's and k'''s values impact the cohesion among activities within the identified microservices and fine-coupling among those microservices.

Once $ar|at$'s criticality is established, we specify *data dependencies* $(\mathcal{DD})$ between a_i and a_j as follows:

$$\mathcal{DD}(a_i, a_j) = \sum_{d_p \in DATA_{i,j}} pair(d_p)_{i,j} \times \mathcal{C}(d_p) \qquad (9)$$

where

- $DATA_{i,j}$ indicates the set of artefacts/attributes exchanged between a_i and a_j,
- d_p represents the artefact/attribute exchanged between a_i and a_j,
- $pair(d_p)_{i,j}$ denotes the value associated with the operation pair (e.g., r/w and w/w) between a_i and a_j, proposed by Amiri [1].

Table 4. Artefact/Attribute criticality for Bicing case-study

Artefact	Attributes	$\mathcal{C}^F$
Bicycle	Anchor_Point	M (k'$_1$)
	Bike_Status	H (k$_1$)
User	User_Status	H (k$_2$)
	User_Destination	L (k"$_2$)
	User_History	H (k$_2$)
Rental	Rent_ID	H (k$_3$)
	Rent_Cost	M (k'$_3$)
Repair	agree_Repair	M (k'$_4$)

Artefact	Attributes	$\mathcal{C}^{NF}$
Bicycle	Bike_ID	H (k$_1$)
User	User_ID	H (k$_2$)
	User_Validity	M (k'$_2$)
Repair	estimated_Repair_Cost	H (k$_4$)

The second strategy considers $\mathcal{C}(ar|at)$ as a tuple $< \mathcal{C}^F(ar|at), \mathcal{C}^{NF}(ar|at) >$. We, thus, specify *data dependencies* ($\mathcal{DD}$) between a_i and a_j as follows:

$$\mathcal{DD}(a_i, a_j) = \sum_{d_p \in DATA_{i,j}} \mathcal{F}(pair(d_p)_{i,j}, \mathcal{C}^F(d_p), \mathcal{C}^{NF}(d_p)) \tag{10}$$

where $\mathcal{F}$ returns the *data dependency* value specified by the BP designer for the tuple $< pair(d_p)_{i,j}, \mathcal{C}^F(d_p), \mathcal{C}^{NF}(d_p) >$.

Table 5. Excerpt of data dependencies for the 1st strategy

Activity	a_1	a_2	a_3	a_4	a_5
a_1	-	1/2	5/6	11/12	17/12
a_2	1/2	-	1/3	7/12	11 /12
a_3	5/6	1/3	-	1/4	3/4
a_4	11/12	7/12	1/4	-	1/2
a_5	7/12	11/12	3/4	1/2	-

4   Experimenting the Collaborative Clustering

In this section we detail the collaborative clustering approach and then present how it was implemented and evaluated.

4.1   Collaborative Clustering

Clustering is about partitioning a set of objects into groups called clusters. Each cluster regroups similar objects in the sense that objects of a group are more similar to each other than objects of other groups. In our approach, objects represent activities "expecting" that activities of the same group would form a highly-cohesive candidate mircoservice. Contrarily, activities in different groups would form loosely-coupled microservices.

We extended the classical Hierarchical agglomerative algorithm (HAC) [20] to design our collaborative clustering algorithm (cHAC). cHAC runs over n clustering nodes $(CN_1, CN_2,\ldots, CN_n)$, where a CN partitions the whole set of activities into clusters of activities by using one given dependency matrix. The chosen number k of clusters at each CN is not necessary the same; it can be different from one CN to another. cHAC fosters collaboration between CN since each CN will have its own dependency matrix along with "keeping an eye" on what other CNs are doing by sharing some dependencies scores of activities, if deemed necessary. Thus, prior to each new HAC clustering iteration, a CN uses both a Local Score Matrix (LSM) that stores dependency scores between couple of activities and a Shared Score Matrix (SSM) that stores a global dependency score between each couple of activities (Tables 4 and 5).

- cHAC's first iteration: creation of the local dependence score matrix. It corresponds to the dependency matrix used as input. An empty shared dependence matrix is also created to store the shared dependency score of activities. Each activity constitutes a cluster.
- cHAC's p^{th} iteration: the nearest pair of clusters C_u and C_v is computed by using both LDSM and SDSM. C_u and C_v are merged if and only if[6] $[distance(C_u, C_v)]^p_{LDSM} >= [distance(C_u, C_v)]^{p-1}_{SDSM}$.
  To foster similarities between couples of activities (t_i, t_j), the shared score matrix is also updated as follows: $[LDSM(t_i, t_j)]_p = Max([LDSM(t_i, t_j)]_p, [MSP(t_i, t_j)]_{p-1})$

Once the different clustering results are produced by the different CNs, the distance metrics are applied to them to choose the best one that fosters both cohesion and loose-coupling of groups. It is important to note that our cHAC algorithm can work either in a uniform collaboration strategy whereh each CN collaborates with other $CNss$, or in diverse collaboration strategy where each CN node has its own collaborators. For the latter case, different shred matrices are needed, one by CN node.

Our cHAC is different from the distributed HAC (dHAC) [15]. dHAC consists of 2 phases. In the first phase, the entire collection of objects is divided into n disjoint segments and distributed over n HAC processes. Each HAC process generates a separate clustering. In the second phase, the previous generated clusters are merged into one final cluster result. In our cHAC, and contrarily to dHAC, the collaboration between the different HAC nodes is realized between two successive iterations by sharing intermediate clustering results.

4.2   Experiments

We implemented the collaborative clustering approach in Java. To this end, different modules have been developed. Some of these modules permitted to extract

---

[6] $distance[distance(C_u, C_v)]^p_M$ computes any distance between 2 clusters C_u and C_v by using the score Matrix M of the iteration p.

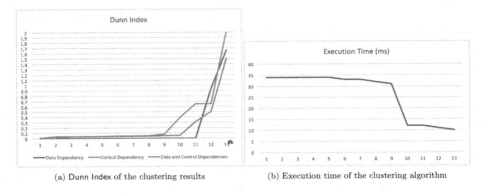

(a) Dunn Index of the clustering results   (b) Execution time of the clustering algorithm

Fig. 3. Bicing system's 14 activities analysis

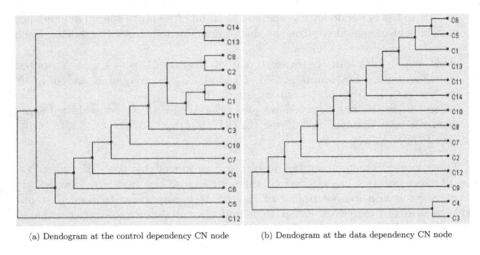

(a) Dendogram at the control dependency CN node   (b) Dendogram at the data dependency CN node

Fig. 4. Dendograms at CN nodes

control dependencies and data dependencies from BPs and to run the collaborative clustering algorithm that took the number of clusters and dependency matrices as inputs. Bicing system's 14 activities were initially used to test the algorithm. Then, more activities were randomly generated to capture the complexity of real BPs.

For evaluation needs we considered the internal validation metric Dunn index that measures the quality of clustered results by identifying the clusters that are compact (minor variance between activities of the same cluster) and separate (clusters are enough far apart). A higher Dunn index indicates better clustering.

In the first experiment, we measured the Dunn index of the clustering algorithm with respect to the "Control Dependencies" CN node (CDCN) and the "Data Dependencies" CN node (DDCN). Figure 3a illustrates the obtained results clearly showing that the Dunn index that results from the CDCN node is almost always better than the Dunn index that results from the DDCN node. This means that for a given BP, the control dependency model is richer and more informative than the data dependency model. We also computed the Dunn index of the clustering result by aggregating both control and data dependencies in one matrix.

Figure 3b illustrates the obtained results showing that the clustering quality of the CDCN node is often better than the one obtained by merging control and data dependencies. It confirms that aggregating different dependency matrices degrades the quality of the final microservice generation and the collaboration between nodes is the appropriate option. Figure 4 illustrates the obtained dendograms at both control and data dependency nodes. C_i refers to teh activity a_i.

5   Conclusion

To address monolithic systems' limitations, this paper examined microservices as a novel way for breaking down these systems into "small" manageable units. We shed light on how to identify necessary microservices from a set of BPs. Compared to other approaches that adopt log files, source codes, among others as inputs to identifying microservices, BPs constitute a better alternative to these inputs. Indeed, referred to as organizations' know how, BPs' activities allow to define who does what, when, where, and why. We firstly capture these details into different kinds of separate dependencies known as control and data. We then process these dependencies using our designed collaborative clustering algorithm. Each cluster of activities constitutes a microservice candidate.

The technical doability of our work has been verified using the Bicing system that allows users to rent bikes in the city of Barcelona. The results are promising showing how our collaborative clustering algorithm outperforms in term of precision the cooperative clustering algorithm. In term of future work we would like to consider a larger dataset for testing the collaborative clustering algorithm, examine other forms of dependencies like semantics dependencies between activities, benchmark our identified microservices to other approaches that do not use BPs, and finally recommend clustering techniques with respect to the nature of these dependencies.

References

1. Amiri, M.J.: Object-aware identification of microservices. In: 2018 IEEE International Conference on Services Computing (SCC), pp. 253–256. IEEE (2018)
2. Baresi, L., Garriga, M., De Renzis, A.: Microservices identification through interface analysis. In: De Paoli, F., Schulte, S., Broch Johnsen, E. (eds.) ESOCC 2017. LNCS, vol. 10465, pp. 19–33. Springer, Cham (2017). https://doi.org/10.1007/978-3-319-67262-5_2
3. Cerný, T., Donahoo, M.J., Pechanec, J.: Disambiguation and comparison of SOA, microservices and self-contained systems. In: Proceedings of the International Conference on Research in Adaptive and Convergent Systems, RACS 2017, Krakow, Poland, 20–23 September 2017, pp. 228–235 (2017)

4. Chen, R., Li, S., Li, Z.: From monolith to microservices: a dataflow-driven approach. In: 2017 24th Asia-Pacific Software Engineering Conference (APSEC), pp. 466–475. IEEE, December 2017
5. Chung, J., Chao, K.: A view on service-oriented architecture. Servi. Oriented Comput. Appl. 1(2), 93–95 (2007). https://doi.org/10.1007/s11761-007-0011-2
6. Cornuéjols, A., Wemmert, C., Gançarski, P., Bennani, Y.: Collaborative clustering: why, when, what and how. Inform. Fusion 39, 81–95 (2018). https://doi.org/10.1016/j.inffus.2017.04.008
7. Davenport, T., Short, J.: The new industrial engineering: information technology and business process redesign. Sloan Manag. Rev. (1990)
8. Djogic, E., Ribic, S., Donko, D.: Monolithic to microservices redesign of event driven integration platform. In: 41st International Convention on Information and Communication Technology, Electronics and Microelectronics, MIPRO 2018, Opatija, Croatia, 21–25 May 2018, pp. 1411–1414 (2018). https://doi.org/10.23919/MIPRO.2018.8400254
9. Escobar, D., et al.: Towards the understanding and evolution of monolithic applications as microservices. In: XLII Latin American Computing Conference, CLEI 2016, Valparaíso, Chile, 10–14 October 2016, pp. 1–11 (2016). https://doi.org/10.1109/CLEI.2016.7833410
10. Estañol, M.: Artefact-centric business process models in UML: specification and reasoning. Ph.D. thesis, Universitat Politècnica de Catalunya (2016)
11. Gysel, M., Kölbener, L., Giersche, W., Zimmermann, O.: Service cutter: a systematic approach to service decomposition. In: Aiello, M., Johnsen, E.B., Dustdar, S., Georgievski, I. (eds.) ESOCC 2016. LNCS, vol. 9846, pp. 185–200. Springer, Cham (2016). https://doi.org/10.1007/978-3-319-44482-6_12
12. Hammouda, K., Kamel, M.: Collaborative document clustering. In: SIAM International Conference on Data Mining (2006)
13. Hassan, S., Bahsoon, R.: Microservices and their design trade-offs: a self-adaptive roadmap. In: IEEE International Conference on Services Computing, SCC 2016, San Francisco, CA, USA, June 27–July 2 2016, pp. 813–818 (2016). https://doi.org/10.1109/SCC.2016.113
14. Jin, W., Liu, T., Zheng, Q., Cui, D., Cai, Y.: Functionality-oriented microservice extraction based on execution trace clustering. In: 2018 IEEE International Conference on Web Services, ICWS 2018, San Francisco, CA, USA, 2–7 July 2018, pp. 211–218 (2018). https://doi.org/10.1109/ICWS.2018.00034
15. Ke, W., Gong, X.: Collaborative hierarchical clustering in the browser for scatter/gather on the web. In: Information, Interaction, Innovation: Celebrating the Past, Constructing the Present and Creating the Future - Proceedings of the 75th ASIS&T Annual Meeting, ASIST 2012, Baltimore, MD, USA, 26–30 October 2012, pp. 1–8 (2012). https://doi.org/10.1002/meet.14504901139
16. Klock, S., van der Werf, J.M.E.M., Guelen, J.P., Jansen, S.: Workload-based clustering of coherent feature sets in microservice architectures. In: 2017 IEEE International Conference on Software Architecture, ICSA 2017, Gothenburg, Sweden, 3–7 April 2017, pp. 11–20 (2017). https://doi.org/10.1109/ICSA.2017.38
17. Kouroshfar, E., Shahir, H.Y., Ramsin, R.: Process patterns for component-based software development. In: Proceedings of the Component-Based Software Engineering, 12th International Symposium, CBSE 2009, East Stroudsburg, PA, USA, 24–26 June 2009, pp. 54–68 (2009). https://doi.org/10.1007/978-3-642-02414-6_4
18. Levcovitz, A., Terra, R., Valente, M.T.: Towards a technique for extracting microservices from monolithic enterprise systems. arXiv preprint arXiv:1605.03175 (2016)

19. Mendez-Bonilla, O., Franch, X., Quer, C.: Requirements patterns for COTS systems. In: Proceedings of the Seventh International Conference on Composition-Based Software Systems (ICCBSS 2008), Madrid, Spain, 25–29 February 2008, pp. 232–234 (2008). https://doi.org/10.1109/ICCBSS.2008.34

20. Murtagh, F., Legendre, P.: Ward's hierarchical clustering method: clustering criterion and agglomerative algorithm. CoRR abs/1111.6285 (2011). http://arxiv.org/abs/1111.6285

21. Paulsen, C., J.M., B., Bartol, Winkler, N.: Criticality analysis process model. Technical report (2018)

22. Singh, V., Peddoju, S.K.: Container-based microservice architecture for cloud applications. In: 2017 International Conference on Computing, Communication and Automation (ICCCA), pp. 847–852. IEEE (2017)

23. Ueda, T., Nakaike, T., Ohara, M.: Workload characterization for microservices. In: 2016 IEEE International Symposium on Workload Characterization (IISWC), pp. 1–10. IEEE (2016)

24. Weske, M.: Business Process Management – Concepts, Languages, Architectures, 2nd edn. Springer, Heidelberg (2012). https://doi.org/10.1007/978-3-642-28616-2

25. Wilkin, G., H., X.: A practical comparison of two k-means clustering algorithms. BMC Bioinform. **9** (2008)

Numerical Study of Damaged, Failure and Cracking of Concrete Beam Reinforced by Honeycomb Sandwich Panel Structures

K. Essaadaoui[1,2], M. Ait El Fqih[1(✉)], M. Idiri[2], and B. Boubeker[2]

[1] Laboratoire d'Ingénierie des Structures, Systèmes Intelligents Energie Electrique (LI2SI2E), ENSAM, Hassan II University of Casablanca, Casablanca, Morocco
m.aitelfqih@gmail.com
[2] Laboratoire d'Ingénierie et Matériaux (LIMAT), Hassan II University of Casablanca, Casablanca, Morocco

Abstract. In this work, we present experimental and simulation study of damaged, failure and cracking of concrete beam in the absence and in the presence of reinforced honeycomb sandwich panel structures. The experimental program included three beam specimens. Two of the beams were reinforced with different thicknesses of honeycomb panel structures. Flexural test was performed. The material model was simulated in Abaqus finite element package and is capable of developing the stress-strain curves, stress max principal versus tensile damage and load displacement. The beam was loaded in three-points. The mechanical properties of the used materials in our simulation are obtained from the data of the literature. The results obtained are discussed. By this study, we intend to contribute to a better understanding tensile damage-strain by using reinforcement in concrete beam. The main goal is to predict what extent a reinforced concrete structure can resist.

Keywords: Concrete beam · Finite element · Honeycomb panel structures · Strengthening · Tensile damage · Cracking

1 Introduction

Composite materials in general and sandwich panels (honeycomb) in particular, due to their mechanical performance, now offer new perspectives for civil engineering. Why all the excitement? It is clear that the sandwich solution offers a much more interesting compromise in terms of lightness and stiffness compared to so-called traditional materials. Indeed, sandwich structures have long been recognized as one of the materials that best combines lightness and flexural strength in particular. The aerospace industry, with its low weight requirement, has used sandwich constructions that largely use aluminum honeycomb cores [1]. However, their performance is greatly affected by the buckling that characterizes the walls of honeycomb cells as a result of compressive or impact loads.

© Springer Nature Switzerland AG 2020
M. Hamlich et al. (Eds.): SADASC 2020, CCIS 1207, pp. 316–325, 2020.
https://doi.org/10.1007/978-3-030-45183-7_24

The characterization of the mechanical properties of sandwich structures poses particular challenges due to their heterogeneity and the considerable disparities in the properties between core and skin [2]. The need for effective numerical modeling to predict the mechanical behavior of sandwich structures is still an open field of research. Various works [3], were carried out on the development of numerical models to study the response of sandwich panels in an attempt to make their use more widespread. Today, numerical simulations based on the finite element method (FE) have become a standard tool in the development process of the aviation industry. In this context, Kaoua et al. [4] describe a numerical procedure based on the finite elements to predict the mechanical bending behavior of sandwich panels. The numerical characterization of the sandwich structure is confronted with both experimental results and the homogenization technique.

A finite element simulation followed by an experimental study is presented by Sadighi and Hosseini [5] to study the mechanical behavior of composites. The comparison between finite element predictions and experimental results showed a good agreement that finite element simulation can be used instead of experimental procedures to study the effect of different parameters on the mechanical properties of sandwich composites.

The article by Gaiotti and Rizzo [6] discusses the buckling behavior of sandwich composites under compression loading. Finite element modeling strategies are discussed in order to test a suitable and cost-effective solution for evaluating the buckling behavior of sandwiches.

Virtual tests using finite element dynamic simulations are an effective way to study the mechanical behavior of small and large scale structures in order to reduce the time and cost of prototyping. In addition, numerical models allow parametric studies or optimizations. The method for determining the mechanical properties of cell core sandwich structures of different geometries subjected to dynamic compression, tension and shear is discussed in reference [7], covering a number of important aspects of modeling: modeling of cell wall material, influence of mesh size and number of unit cells, consideration of imperfections.

Therefore, these models allow not only the complete mechanical characterization of cellular structures, but also for a detailed examination of cell wall strain modes and failure modes to obtain a better understanding of structural behavior, which may be difficult to obtain from observations that are solely experimental in nature.

Thus, numerical models allow the study or optimization of efficient parameters. In this work, a numerical model is used to examine the behavior of concrete beams reinforced with honeycomb sandwich panels structures subjected to flexural three-point bending.

2   Materials and Methods

2.1   Finite Element Analysis

Finite element method the RC beam is created by Abaqus software (CAE 6.14-1). Is able to investigate the physical and mechanical behavior of the beams. Moreover, The FEM is applied widely in the calculation of structures with reliable results such as reinforcing structures with honeycomb sandwiches panel one. Concrete beam and reinforcing honeycomb sandwich panel were modeled with C3D8R solid element and S4R shell element respectively (see Fig. 1). In this study, C3D8R element that is used in more accurate finite element model dominated by inelastic behavior. In FEM Analysis, C3D8R finite element was preferred. Because this element shows accurate results nonlinear behavior of structure systems. Concrete beam model that was created by using the combination of C3D8R and S4R element are shown in Fig. 1.

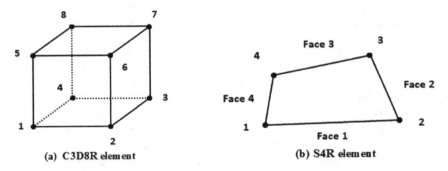

(a) C3D8R element   (b) S4R element

Fig. 1. Finite element used in modeling of RC beam.

2.2   Concrete Damaged Plasticity (CDP) Model

The reinforced concrete (RC) beams that were used for the finite element models have the strength class of concrete C30 (the compressive strength of concrete is 30 MPa). It is necessary to know the concrete that defined the use of modeling of reinforced concrete beams that are exposed to impact loads, changes in compressive strength and tensile strength due to the deformation rate. The coefficient of increase was taken as 1.30 corresponding to the deformation rate 1.0 1/s of the Ammann and Nussbaumer (1995) [8] scale. The stress-strain curves that, under the effect of uniaxial compression and concrete tensile strength, were used for the modeling of the reinforced concrete beam are given in Fig. 2.

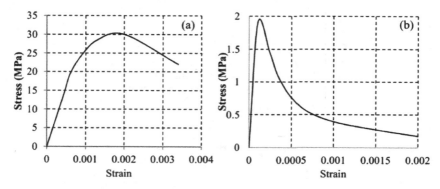

Fig. 2. Stress-strain curves of concrete under uniaxial compressive (a) and tensile [8].

The CDP model is used for the Abaqus software to model plain or RC beams. This model has been proposed by Lubliner et al. (1989) [9], for static charges and then improved by Lee and Fenves (1998) [10] for dynamic and cyclic loading conditions. In addition, the degradation of the material's stiffness was taken into account in the CDP model under compression and tension behaviors. Lee and Fenves (1998) [10] defined two different scalar variables (d_c,d_t)In accordance with this change in the modulus of elasticity of concrete is defined as:

$$E = (1 - d_{t,c})E_0 \tag{1}$$

Were d_t and d_c are the degradation parameters of compressive and tensile stiffness and E_0 is the initial young's modulus.

As can be seen from Eq. (1), two damage parameters vary between $0 < d < 1$ interval. When it is equal to $d = 0$, this condition shows that the material is not damaged. Under another condition $d = 1$, the degradation of stiffness cannot be controlled. Under these two conditions, it is not possible to define the behavior of the concrete (Fig. 3). In these variables, dc controls the degradation of uniaxial compression stiffness and d_t controls the degradation of uniaxial tension stiffness.

Behavior of the concrete under the uniaxial loading in CDP model, ε_c^{in} for uniaxial compression and ε_t^{ck} for uniaxial tension for strain values are defined Eqs. (2) and (3). These strains are respectively as inelastic and cracking strains. They were calculated by following equations according to Hibbit et al. (2011) [11]. In the Abaqus software, the uniaxial stress-strain relations of concrete are converted into stress-plastic strain relations with damage parameters ($d_{t,c}$) and inelastic and cracking strains automatically. These strains are given in Eqs. (4) and (5).

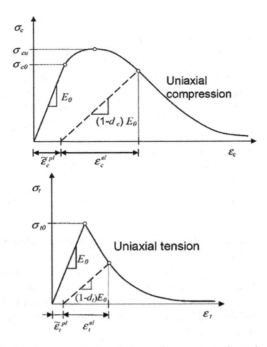

Fig. 3. CDP model with the stress-strain relations of concrete under uniaxial compression and tension [10].

$$\varepsilon_c^{in} = \varepsilon_c - \frac{\sigma_c}{E_0} \tag{2}$$

$$\varepsilon_t^{ck} = \varepsilon_t - \frac{\sigma_t}{E_0} \tag{3}$$

$$\varepsilon_c^{pl} = \varepsilon_c^{ck} - \frac{d_c}{1 - d_c} \cdot \frac{\sigma_c}{E_0} \tag{4}$$

$$\varepsilon_t^{pl} = \varepsilon_t^{ck} - \frac{d_t}{1 - d_t} \cdot \frac{\sigma_t}{E_0} \tag{5}$$

The mechanical and materials properties used in the simulation for concrete and honeycomb sandwich panel structures were depicted respectively in the Table 1 and Table 2.

Table 1 Material properties and parameters of the concrete.

Initial modulus of elasticity, E_0 (MPa)	32000
Poisson's ratio, ν	0.2
Density, ρ (kg/m^3)	2400
Compressive strength, f_{ck} (MPa)	30
Peak strain of compressive, ε	0.0021
Ultimate strain, ε_u	0.0034
Tensile strength, f_{ctk} (MPa)	1.9
Dilation angle, ψ	36
Eccentricity, e (Abaqus, 2014)	0.01
Viscosity parameter, μ	0.0001
Max damage parameter of tensile, d_t	0.99
Ratio of the second stress invariant on the tensile meridian to that on the compressive meridian, K_c	0.6667
Ratio of initial equibiaxial compressive yield stress to initial uniaxial compressive yield stress, σ_{b0}/σ_{c0}	1.16

The modeling of structures in honeycomb is too long and tiring. The homogenization of the honeycomb allows acquiring solid homogeneous one identical and its modules of stretch to accomplish very efficient simulation: diminish broadly the time of preparation of geometries and mesh sizes, as well as the time CPU.

The classical models of homogenization of honeycomb were systematically represented by Gibson et al. [12].

For the homogenization of the honeycomb, we will use mindlin's theory with an orthotropic material, to perform homogenization; we need to define a Representative Volume Elementary (RVE) of the material as show in the Fig. 4.

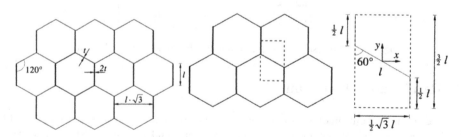

Fig. 4. RVE and Geometry of a cell of cardboard honeycomb [13].

From the geometry of a honeycomb cell (Fig. 4 and Table 2) and mechanical properties of cardboard paper, we use our homogenization models for calculating the properties of the equivalent homogenized solid (Table 3).

Table 2. Geometric parameters of a cell of cardboard honeycomb.

Φ (mm)	θ (°)	l = h (mm)	t (mm)
8	60	4.62	0.19

Table 3. Properties of homogenized solid equivalent to honeycomb.

E_1 (MPa)	E_2 (MPa)	E_3 (MPa)	G_{12} (MPa)	G_{13} (MPa)	G_{23} (MPa)
14.42	17.58	226.61	1.09	19.99	24.71
v_{12}	v_{13}	v_{23}	v_{21}	v_{31}	v_{32}
0.6474	0.0255	0.0310	0.789	0.4	0.4

2.3   Materials

The numerical study was carried out by preparing test beams of the same dimensions as well as honeycomb sandwich panel structures of different thicknesses (Fig. (5-a). The beams were supported by rollers. All samples used had a length of 400 mm and a width of 100 mm with a height of 100 mm as shown in Fig. 5-b.

An unreinforced specimen (S-Ref). Two specimens were reinforced with honey-comb sandwich panel structures respectively (S-HCt1) and (S-HCt2) with two different thicknesses of 3.22 (HCt$_1$) and 5.76 mm (HCt2).

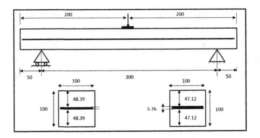

Fig. 5. a: Cross section of the beams b: FE model of the RC beam.

3   Results and Discussion

The FE model of reinforced concrete beam consists of two types of materials, concrete in the absence and in the presence of honeycomb sandwich panel structures. The numerical results on beam loaded in three-points in the absence (S-REF) and in the presence on reinforced by composite with the different thickness (HC$_{t1}$, HC$_{t2}$) are presented in Fig. 6 (a), Fig. 6 (b) and Fig. 6 (c) (Tensile damage), and Fig. 7 (a), Fig. 7 (b) and Fig. 7 (c) (Magnitude of plastic strain). The comparison of FEM results on flexing shows that the reinforced beam less damaged.

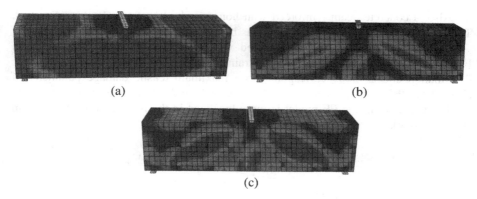

Fig. 6. a: Tensile damage of beam not reinforced (S-Ref), b: Tensile damage of beam not reinforced $(S - HC_{t1})$, c: Tensile damage of beam not reinforced (S-HC$_{t2}$)

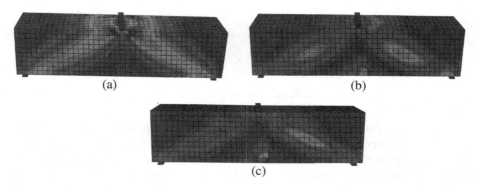

Fig. 7. a: Magnitude of plastic strain (S-Ref), b: Magnitude of plastic strain $(S - HC_{t1})$, c: Magnitude of plastic strain $(S - HC_{t1})$ (Color figure online)

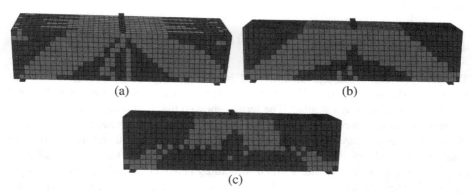

Fig. 8. a: Active yield flag (S-Ref), b: Active yield flag (S-HC$_{t1}$), c: Active yield flag (S-HC$_{t2}$)

Also, a concrete beam reinforced with honeycomb slabs under load was studied. The results showed that reinforcement was better in the presence of reinforcement.

Positive plastic strain can be mapped with color-coded contours as shown in Fig. (7-a, b, c), the maximum plastic strain occurs in "red" regions where plastic deformation equals 0.005 corresponds to a maximum tensile damage parameter of about 0.89. "Blue" regions correspond to areas where there is no tension damage.

The Cracking in the FE model is more localized in the middle third of the beam (Fig. 8-a, b, c).

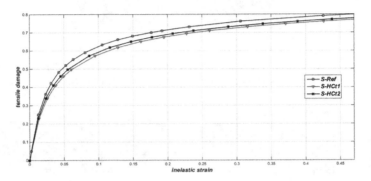

Fig. 9. Tensile damage-inelastic strain of plastic curves.

Figure 9 presents the tensile damage – inelastic strain of plastic curves for the used specimens, based on both numerical approaches. It can be seen that there is a limitation of the damage, in particular between the unreinforced specimen (S-Ref) and the honeycomb reinforced specimens (S-HCt₁) and (S-HCt₂). In another part there is also a small limitation of the damping between the specimen reinforced by the honeycomb thickness 1 (S-HCt₁) and the honeycomb thickness 2 (S-HCt₂), which shows that the specimen becomes more resistant and the overshoot increases the thickness of the reinforcement.

4 Concluding Remarks

This study of reinforced and unreinforced beams by finite elements was carried out using the Abaqus software. A concrete beam reinforced with a honeycomb panel structures under load was studied. The results showed that reinforcement was better in the presence of reinforcement. The location of the honeycomb insertion is in the center of the concrete and may limit damage to the bending stress. It is therefore proposed to continue the study of the shear behavior and failure modes of fiber-reinforced honeycomb composite beams due to their structures and mechanical properties, which remain significantly superior. In addition, it is envisaged to improve the database on shear reinforcement and then to validate the approach of the model proposed in the literature by using a new simulation using different fibers as reinforcement and to carry out an experimental study using the same reinforcement materials.

References

1. Palazotto, A.N., Herup, E.J., Gummadi, L.N.B.: Finite element analysis of low-velocity impact on composite sandwich plates. Compos. Struct. **49**, 209–227 (2000)
2. Ravichandran, G., Rajapakse, Y.D.S.: Sandwich structures. Exp. Mech. **52**, 1–2 (2012)
3. Rahman, H., Jamshed, R., Hameed, H., Raza, S.: Finite Element Analysis (FEA) of honeycomb sandwich panel for continuum properties evaluation and core height influence on the dynamic behavior. In: Advanced Materials Research, vol. 326, pp. 1–10 (2011)
4. Kaoua, S.A., Mesbah, A., Boutaleb, S., Azouaoui, K.: Finite element prediction of mechanical behaviour under bending of honeycomb sandwich panels. In: Advanced Materials Research, vol. 980, pp. 81–85 (2014)
5. Sadighi, M., Hosseini, S.A.: Finite element simulation and experimental study on mechanical behavior of 3D woven glass fiber composite sandwich panels. Compos. Part B: Eng. **55**, 158–166 (2013)
6. Gaiotti, M., Rizzo, C.M.: Finite element modeling strategies for sandwich composite laminates under compressive loading. Ocean Eng. **63**, 44–51 (2013)
7. Heimbs, S.: Virtual testing of sandwich core structures using dynamic finite element simulations. Comput. Mater. Sci. **45**(2), 205–216 (2009)
8. Ammann, H., Nussbaumer, H.: Behavior of Concrete and Steel Under Dynamic Actions. Vibrations Problems in Structures: Practical Guide. Springer, Berlin (1995)
9. Lubliner, J., Oliver, J., Oller, S., Onate, E.: A plastic-damage model for concrete. Solid. Struct. **25**(3), 299–326 (1989)
10. Lee, J., Fenves, G.: Plastic-damage model for cyclic loading of concrete structure. Eng. Mech. **124**(8), 892–900 (1998)
11. Hibbitt, H., Karlsson, B., Sorensen, P.: ABAQUS Analysis User's Manual Version 6.11. Dassault Systèmes Simulia Corp., Providence (2011)
12. Gibson, L., Ashby, M.: Cellular Solids: Structure and Properties, 2nd édn. Cambridge Solid State Science Series, Cambridge (1999)
13. Becker, W.: Closed form analysis of the thickness effect of regular honeycomb core material. Compos. Struct. **48**, 67–70 (2000)

Workshop Session

Convolutional Neural Networks for Multimodal Brain MRI Images Segmentation: A Comparative Study

Hicham Moujahid[1], Bouchaib Cherradi[1,2(✉)], and Lhoussain Bahatti[1]

[1] SSDIA Laboratory, ENSET of Mohammedia,
Hassan II University of Casablanca, B.P 159 Mohammedia, Morocco
hicham88moujahid@gmail.com,
bouchaib.cherradi@gmail.com
[2] STIE Team, CRMEF Casablanca-Settat, Provincial Section of El Jadida,
El Jadida, Morocco

Abstract. Manual segmentation of brain tumors from MRI images is very frustrating and time consuming for medical doctors, and relies on accurate segmentation of regions of interests. Convolutional Neural Networks (CNN) based segmentation has gained a huge amount of attention over the last few years due to its speed and automated aspect. As the CNN models are becoming more efficient for image analysis and processing, they increasingly defeat previous state-of-the-art classical machine learning algorithms. Through this study, we provide an overview of CNN-based segmentation models for quantitative brain MRI images segmentation. As this has become a fast expanding field, we will not survey the entire existing landscape of methods but we will focus on the three best outperforming algorithms according to evaluation parameters. Firstly, we review the current conventional methods and deep learning architectures used for segmentation of brain lesions. Next, we perform deep performance comparison based on accuracy and loss function of some relevant selected CNN methods. Finally, a critical analysis of the current study is made to identify all pertinent issues and limitations to work on.

Keywords: Convolutional neural network · Machine learning · Brain tumor segmentation · MRI images

1 Introduction

Malignant Brain tumors still the second biggest cause of death in the world for patients between 15 and 34 years old. Therefore, the early and accurate diagnosis is very important to get an efficient treatment. This task requires a deep analysis of MRI brain images to achieve an accurate segmentation by medical experts [1].

The goal of brain image segmentation is to separate the different cerebral tissues. The main tissues in normal MRI brain images contain White Matter (WM), Gray Matter (GM), and Cerebrospinal Fluid (CSF). Pathological images are detected based on the examination of tumor tissues according to their density, shape, location, size and edge (Fig. 1).

© Springer Nature Switzerland AG 2020
M. Hamlich et al. (Eds.): SADASC 2020, CCIS 1207, pp. 329–338, 2020.
https://doi.org/10.1007/978-3-030-45183-7_25

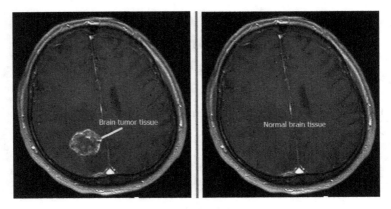

Fig. 1. Density in normal brain tissue and brain tumor tissue.

The malignant brain tumor has a higher density, an irregular shape and a blurred boundary, while benign tumors are not very dense and have lucent-centered lesions.

Manual method of brain tumor segmentation stills the most efficient approach and usually used by radiology experts. The main inconvenient of this method is that it's very linked to human mistakes and it's a laborious time-consuming task.

Automatic methods of brain medical images segmentation are still a challenging problem for scientists.

Recently many researchers become interested in artificial neural networks (ANN), especially convolutional neural networks (CNN) to achieve medical image segmentation tasks [2]. It enables machines to solve complicated pattern recognition problems and extract objects from 2D or 3D images by classification process using the ability of CNN models to learn from large data sets.

Several visual recognition challenges are organized each year over the world in purpose to improve the performance of existing related models retrieving the best accuracy rate on the image classification and object extraction tasks [3].

Conventional medical image segmentation methods are still attracting researchers. In [3], authors proposed a brief study about a survey of MRI Based Brain Tumor Segmentation methods and grouping them to three subcategories: conventional methods (Threshold-based and Region-based), clustering methods and Deformable model methods, they also make a deep and detailed description of some for each category. In [4], authors have made a comparative Study for three MRI segmentation methods: thresholding, region based segmentation and watershed segmentation.

In this paper, we propose a comparative study of some CNN methods that presents a high accuracy on brain tumor segmentation task; especially the models which are proposed by the teams obtained the first position on some famous challenges.

The rest of this paper is organized as follows: In Sect. 2, we introduce an introduction to artificial neural network concept and we cover the structure of convolutional neural networks and its mean processes in Sect. 3. In the Sect. 4, we make a detailed comparison for three best CNN models. Then we will make a brief discussion about results of the comparison in Sect. 5.

2 Methods

2.1 Artificial Neural Networks

Artificial neural network (ANN) is a system with a concept that is inspired from the biological brain which is the most complicated smart system that processes data received from the five senses in the body. The processing ability is obtained from synapses in the form of a connection between large amounts of biological neurons, forming a huge neural network able to process a lot of complicated operation. ANN consists of connecting multitude artificial neurons [5].

The single-layer ANN, also called as a perceptron is the elementary learnable ANN model (Fig. 2).

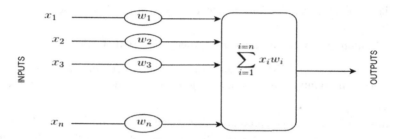

Fig. 2. Single-layer neural network architecture.

The perceptron gets inputs from its input layer as a vector $\{x_i\}$, has a predefined weights vector $\{w_i\}$ and a bias almost equal to zero. The output $\{y_i\}$ is a weighted summation of inputs.

$$yi = \sum_{i=1}^{i=n} wi.xi = w1.x1 + w2.x2 + \ldots + wn.xn \qquad (1)$$

2.2 Convolutional Neural Networks

In deep learning context, a convolutional neural network is a subclass of the ANN network, most commonly applied to analyze image and video contents. As its name indicates, a CNN is an ANN network containing at least one convolution layer.

The idea of CNN is relatively old. This model had been proved to work better for hand written characters recognition as early as 1998 [6]. However, due to the failure of these networks to process too much larger images, they become slowly rejected. This was because of memory and graphic processing constraints, and the lack of large brain datasets (MRI images as a Collection of raw data from various sources distributed and formatted according to the same characteristics). With the increase in computational power thanks to wide availability of GPUs, CPU, RAM and the introduction of large scale datasets, it was possible to train complex CNN models.

2.3   Building CNN Blocks

CNNs have architectural constraints to reduce the processing complexity and ensure patterns detection disregarding the translational aspect of objects. A CNN consists of two principal constraints.

Shared Weights: A convolution unit receives its input from multiple neurons from the previous layer, the input neurons share their weights creating proximity, every shared weight set is known as a kernel (convolution kernel) and is propagated through the network layers.

Local Connectivity: layer neurons are connected only to neurons in the next layer. This design reduces the number of connections between successive layers.

Building a model require adding a convolution layers to the CNN classifier, then defining a pooling operation by choosing the adequate activation function. Flattening is the fact of converting all the resultant arrays into a single linear vector which is a primordial step before adding fully connected layers to a CNN model [5].

2.4   Methodology for Brain Tumor Segmentation with CNN

The principle stages for MRI segmentation are: pre-processing, features extraction, features selection, training, validation, testing, CNN classification and post-processing.

Pre-processing
During this step dataset is prepared and regularized to feed the network. The result of this process can be saved under a specific extension and used again for training or testing step later. The mean sub-processes of this step are normalization, standardization and whitening [3]. The outputs of data preprocessing can be utilized to feed various neural network models.

Features Extraction
This step consists of extracting and converting original raw data to useful features expected to be irredundant and useful. This is necessary for the future learning steps.

Features Selection
This process consists of selecting top ranked features forming a subset of original features according to predefined criteria. This is an important and usually used to reduce dimensionality in deep learning. Recently, many researchers have created a lot of feature selection methods designed for different goals and have some advantages and inconvenient [5].

Training
Learning is achieved through this step by minimizing as much as possible the loss function over iterations. CNN based models usually use the soft-max loss function or the sigmoid cross-entropy function [5].

CNN networks are generally trained using the back-propagation algorithms by using the chain concept to implement and execute the gradient descent (GD) algorithm. However, for datasets with a huge amount of images, using GD is not recommended. A model called stochastic gradient descent (SGD) must be used to compute gradients according to individual image or sub-dataset rather than the whole dataset [6, 7].

There are four important factors used to estimate the performance of the network during training step:

True positives (TP): Images containing the tumor that the neural network judge matching the ground truth.

Negative positives (NP): Images not containing the tumor and the neural network identify properly matching the ground truth.

False positives (FP): CNN classifies images as containing tumor but that actually do not contain any tumor in the ground truth.

False negatives (FN): CNN classifies images as not containing any tumor but are actually containing a tumor in the ground truth, which is very important parameter in case of MRI tumor detection [5].

For quantitative analysis, we define the ground-truth areas as circular regions (ROI). Based on the above definitions, we can compute the precision (P), recall (R) and F1 score as:

$$P = \frac{TP}{TP + FP} \tag{2}$$

$$R = \frac{TP}{TP + FN} \tag{3}$$

$$F1 = \frac{2 * P * R}{P + R} \tag{4}$$

F1 combines (Eq. 2) and (Eq. 3) to get a specific parameter; it can be interpreted as a weighted average of the P and R, and its value is between 0 and 1.

Precision tells us that quantity of the time we have been able to identify the object correctly, but the recall tells us how many objects are found in the dataset. In other words, the neural network has not been able to recognize all of the objects, but it is very sure of its judgment once it has identifies one.

Validation and Testing

This step lets us measure the network performance by calculating the minimal error function using a different dataset of that used in the training stage. Usually networks are trained with huge dataset to minimize error function. The comparison of that minimal error function of networks and the error function of the network in the validation set step lets us determine the performance of the network.

Test set is used to make unbiased evaluation of the model fit in the training dataset, however, test dataset must be independent of the training dataset, but that represents the same probability distribution as the training dataset. If a model fit to the training dataset as well as the test dataset, then we get a minimal over-fitting [8].

Classification

Consists of classifying and affecting labels to detected objects by the network, this task is the mean goal of the network and depends on multiple parameters and processes through the network:

Initialization. Initializing the network with accurate weights is very important for proper functioning of the neural network. The weights must be in a reasonable range before training the network. The most utilized method for initialization method for CNN is called Xavier initialization [3].

Activation Function. It's a function used to get the output of a node. Also known as Transfer Function. There is a linear and a non-linear function according to the distribution of the outputs. Most used activation function for CNN is Rectified Linear Unit (Re-LU) [5].

Pooling. It compresses spatially features in the feature maps by combining redundant features which makes the representation more stable to small image changes. It also reduces the calculation complexity for the next stages to join features. Usually max-pooling or average-pooling is used [3].

Regularization. Used for minimizing over-fitting in order to improve the model's performance. We use mostly dropout technique in the full connected layers. Dropout can be seen as different network and a form of bagging, since each network is trained with a part of the data. Randomly selected nodes from the full connected layer are removed. The result is seen on the network becoming capable of better generalization and independent to the missing nodes [3, 5].

Loss Function. It's essential in CNN networks, used to calculate the inconsistency between predicted value, and real label. It's non-negative value, where the power of the model increases as the loss function decreases. Loss function is the significant component of risk function. The widely used loss functions are squared error (MSE) or quadratic error [5].

Post-processing
This step is the last step of generating over-segmented regions, like super-pixels, for obtaining the final segmentation result.

However, post-processing method is used for simplifying the network in order to improve the output without losing much in terms of prediction accuracy. At each hidden layer of the network, this method tries to find a small subset of features/nodes that can be used to reconstruct the entire layer approximately [5].

3   Comparison of Some CNN Models

Many CNN architectures have shown interesting results in recent publications. They differ in depth of the network and the number of used. Many organizations organize events to increase competitiveness of teams to improve as much as possible their CNN models. Multimodal Brain Tumor Segmentation Challenge (BRATS[1]) has the goal of evaluating the state-of-the-art methods for brain tumors segmentation by providing a 3D MRI dataset with ground truth tumor segmentation labels approved by experts of the field [9].

---

[1] https://www.med.upenn.edu/sbia/.

3.1   Model 1: Ensembles of Multiple Models and Architectures (EMMA)

EMMA is a deep learning model which can be run with excellent performance. It gets the first position in the BRATS 2017 competition among more than 50 teams. This algorithm is combining multiple configured and trained CNN models. The system won the competition by achieving the overall best performance in the testing phase, based on Dice score.

Traditional CNN architectures if not regularized can over-fit noise in the training data, which leads to mistakes when they are used for generalization. Emma proceeds of averaging the bias infused by individual model configurations [8, 10].

The first employed architecture is Deep-Medic. It is a fully 3D and multi-scale CNN, designed for processing efficiently 3D-images. Two Deep-Medic models are used in this experiment. The first is the residual version previously presented in the BRATS 2016 and the other is a wider variant doubling the number of feature maps at each layer. The models are trained using a cross-entropy loss function conserving their original parameters.

This model include also three different 3D-FCN models where layers ReLU and zero padding to ensure batch normalization. EMMA model also integrates two versions of 3D-Unet model with a few modifications.

Included models are trained separately and differently. At testing step, every model segments image and outputs its class-confidence maps. Models are then joined into EMMA model. For each voxel, the final model calculates the average confidence of the individual models for the voxel. Final segmentation is performed by classifying each voxel as according to its probability to be in a class.

The model wins the first position by obtaining the dice coefficient scores as below: 73.8 for enhancing tumor, 90.1 in the whole and 79.7 in core. The next two models in position are ULC-TIG and MIC_DKFZ [10].

3.2   Model 2: CNN-Based Segmentation of Medical Imaging Data

The proposed model is first ranked in BRATS 2015 and ISLES[2]. This CNN-based method consists of combining segmentation maps created at different points in the network. The work is similar to U-Net CNN architecture with two modifications [11]:

- Combining multiple segmentation maps created at different scales.
- Using element-wise summation to forward feature maps from one stage of the network to another.

The architecture consists of contracting and expanding stages found in other works using similar networks, where feature maps from the first stage are combined with feature maps from the second stage via long skip connections [11].

Element-wise summation directly inserts local details found in the feature maps of the contracting stage to the feature maps of the expanding stage.

---

[2] http://www.isles-challenge.org/.

3.3   Model 3: Auto Encoder Regularization Based

This algorithm is the most ranked one for BRATS 18 challenge named NVDLMED method introduced by ANDRIY MYRONENKO.

BRATS 2018 training dataset included 285 cases (210 HGG and 75 LGG), each with four 3D MRI modalities (T1, T1c, T2 and FLAIR) rigidly aligned.

The proposed approach follows encoder-decoder based CNN architecture with an asymmetrically larger encoder to extract image features and a smaller decoder to reconstruct the segmentation mask. To better cluster the features of the encoder end-point it follows the variational auto-encoder (VAE) approach [9].

The RESNET [12] blocks are used in the encoder part, but each block contain two convolutions including normalization (Group Normalization) and ReLU, followed by additive identity skip connection [9].

The decoder architecture is the same as the encoder with just the difference of just one block per each special level. The special size of the end of the decoder is the same as the original size.

VAE consist of reducing the result of the encoder output to lower dimensional space and then reconstruct it following the same structure as the decoder.

The loss function is defined as follow:

$$L = \mathrm{L}_{dice} + 0.1 * L_{L2} + 0.1 * L_{KL} \tag{5}$$

With:

- L_{dice} is a soft Dice loss off the decoder output to match the segmentation mask [13]
- L_{L2} is an L2 loss on the VAE branch output to match the input image
- L_{KL} is standard VAE penalty term [14]

This method was implemented in TENSORFLOW and trained on NVIDIA Tesla V100 32 GB using BRATS 2018 dataset (285 cases, 300 epochs) in three days with the speed of 9 min/epoch [9].

4   Discussion

This paper presents an overview of several methods for the automatic brain tumor segmentation task, using 3D convolutional neural networks [15]. There is a large-scale of methods but we propose to compare and analyze some methods including the three best ranked architecture implementations in BRATS challenges over the last three years according to dice coefficient.

Table 1. Competition positions with Dice score (%) obtained on different models.

Method	Enhanced tumor	Whole tumor	Tumor core	Challenge
EMMA [10] (Kamnitsas et al.)	73.8	**90.1**	79.7	BRATS 2017
CNN-based Segmentation of Medical Imaging Data [11] (Baris et al.)	61	85	72	BRATS 2015
U-net based CNN [16] (Dong et al.)	74	88	76	BRATS 2018
S3D-UNet [17] (Chen et al.)	73	88	80	BRATS 2018
NVDLMED [9] (Myronenko)	**76**	88	**81.5**	BRATS 2018

CNN-based Segmentation of Medical Imaging Data gets the best performance (Dice score) on BRATS 2015 challenge, showing the results of: 61% for enhancing tumor, 85% in the whole and 72% in core. The model performance for EMMA in the validation and testing stage of BRATS 2017 dataset are on the top of the list with dice score: 73.8% for enhancing tumor, 90.1% in the whole and 79.7% in core. NVDLMED gets the best performance on BRATS 2018 challenge, showing the results of: 76% for enhancing tumor, 88% in the whole and 81.5% in core.

The other models in (Table 1) are included just for comparison. All methods are presenting a significant calculation complexity, which leads to the necessity of developing new challenging mechanisms to improve processing task and be able to train a huge datasets easily in order to obtain better precisions and reduce errors.

5   Conclusion and Perspectives

Brain tumor segmentation presents a very challenging task for researchers all over the world. Many laboratories propose each year new methods for automatic segmentation of brain tumors to surpass the limitations presented in the previous methods. However, the mean blocks that faces those methods and needs a lot of development is, processing capacities due to the constraint of training neural networks with an extensive number of datasets to improve predictions and reduce errors, especially when classifying and segmenting the 3D MRI images of brain tumors.

Time consuming is another big limitation for the training stage that lies to the processing complexity too and needs to be minimized as much as possible over the future research.

References

1. Dubey, R.B., Hanmandlu, M., Vasikarla, S.: Evaluation of three methods for MRI brain tumor segmentation. In: 2011 Eighth International Conference on Information Technology: New Generations (2011). https://doi.org/10.1109/itng.2011.92
2. Parihar, A.S.: A study on brain tumor segmentation using convolution neural network. In: 2017 International Conference on Inventive Computing and Informatics (ICICI) (2017). https://doi.org/10.1109/icici.2017.8365336

3. Pereira, S., Pinto, A., Alves, V., Silva, C.A.: Brain tumor segmentation using convolutional neural networks in MRI images. IEEE Trans. Med. Imaging **35**(5), 1240–1251 (2016). https://doi.org/10.1109/tmi.2016.2538465

4. Pham, D.L., Xu, C., Prince, J.L.: Current methods in medical image segmentation. Ann. Rev. Biomed. Eng. **2**(1), 315–337 (2000). https://doi.org/10.1146/annurev.bioeng.2.1.315

5. Zhou, S.K., Greenspan, H., Shen, D.: Deep learning for medical image analysis (2018). https://doi.org/10.4103/jpi.jpi_27_18

6. Lecun, Y., Bottou, L., Bengio, Y., Haffner, P.: Gradient-based learning applied to document recognition. Proc. IEEE **86**(11), 2278–2324 (1998). https://doi.org/10.1109/5.726791

7. Rumelhart, D.E., Hinton, G.E., Williams, R.J.: Learning representations by back-propagating errors. Nature **323**(6088), 533–536 (1986). https://doi.org/10.1038/323533a0

8. Srivastava, N., Hinton, G., Krizhevsky, A., Sutskever, I., Salakhutdinov, R.: Dropout: a simple way to prevent neural networks from overfitting. J. Mach. Learn. Res. **15**, 1929–1958 (2014)

9. Myronenko, A.: 3D MRI brain tumor segmentation using autoencoder regularization. In: Crimi, A., Bakas, S., Kuijf, H., Keyvan, F., Reyes, M., van Walsum, T. (eds.) BrainLes 2018. LNCS, vol. 11384, pp. 311–320. Springer, Cham (2019). https://doi.org/10.1007/978-3-030-11726-9_28

10. Kamnitsas, K., et al.: Ensembles of multiple models and architectures for robust brain tumour segmentation. In: Crimi, A., Bakas, S., Kuijf, H., Menze, B., Reyes, M. (eds.) BrainLes 2017. LNCS, vol. 10670, pp. 450–462. Springer, Cham (2018). https://doi.org/10.1007/978-3-319-75238-9_38

11. Kayalibay, B., Jensen, G., van der Smagt, P.: CNN-based segmentation of medical imaging data (2017)

12. He, K., Zhang, X., Ren, S., Sun, J.: Identity mappings in deep residual networks. In: Leibe, B., Matas, J., Sebe, N., Welling, M. (eds.) ECCV 2016. LNCS, vol. 9908, pp. 630–645. Springer, Cham (2016). https://doi.org/10.1007/978-3-319-46493-0_38

13. Milletari, F., Navab, N., Ahmadi, S.-A.: V-Net: fully convolutional neural networks for volumetric medical image segmentation. In: 2016 Fourth International Conference on 3D Vision (3DV) (2016). https://doi.org/10.1109/3dv.2016.79

14. Kingma, D.P., Welling, M.: Auto-encoding variational Bayes. In: The International Conference on Learning Representations (ICLR) (2014)

15. Işın, A., Direkoğlu, C., Şah, M.: Review of MRI-based brain tumor image segmentation using deep learning methods. Procedia Comput. Sci. **102**, 317–324 (2016). https://doi.org/10.1016/j.procs.2016.09.407

16. Dong, H., Yang, G., Liu, F., Mo, Y., Guo, Y.: Automatic brain tumor detection and segmentation using U-Net based fully convolutional networks. In: Valdés Hernández, M., González-Castro, V. (eds.) MIUA 2017. CCIS, vol. 723, pp. 506–517. Springer, Cham (2017). https://doi.org/10.1007/978-3-319-60964-5_44

17. Chen, W., Liu, B., Peng, S., Sun, J., Qiao, X.: S3D-UNet: separable 3D U-Net for brain tumor segmentation. In: Crimi, A., Bakas, S., Kuijf, H., Keyvan, F., Reyes, M., van Walsum, T. (eds.) BrainLes 2018. LNCS, vol. 11384, pp. 358–368. Springer, Cham (2019). https://doi.org/10.1007/978-3-030-11726-9_32

Towards a New ICT Competency Framework Using Open Linked Data

Meriem Hnida[1(✉)], Mohammed Khalidi Idrissi[2], and Samir Bennani[2]

[1] Information Sciences School, Rabat, Morocco
mhnida@esi.ac.ma
[2] Mohammadia School of Engineers, Mohammed V University in Rabat,
Rabat, Morocco
{khalidi,sbennani}@emi.ac.ma

Abstract. Competency framework are widely used by human resources managers in their recruitment process and by educators to design training plans aligned to labor market demand. However, data available in competency frameworks are structured and stored in website or published as pdf files. For instance, computer processing of these information remains difficult. To this end, this paper presents and discusses a methodology for developing ICT frameworks according to W3C technologies and standards. As result, a competency framework has been developed for ICT (Information and Communications Technology). The purpose is to make data available on the web as Open Linked Data for both human and software agents.

Keywords: Ontology · Open Linked Data · Competency frameworks · OWL · RDF

1 Introduction

Competency frameworks are widely used in competency-based education and in many professions as a reference guide from describing competencies and standard of performance. In educational settings, a competency framework help institutions identify labor market demand and identify the most relevant learning needs. It can also be used for measuring evidence-based knowledge.

The implementation of a competency framework is often considered as a long and complicated process [1]. It's a task that might take many iterations to come up with a model and requires consensus among practitioners. It also requires complex knowledge and skills drawn from many disciplines [2]. Still, most available frameworks aim to define competencies using text. These frameworks are not intended to be operated directly by computers or used as knowledge base in intelligent e-learning platforms.

The purpose of this paper is to describe the main steps for designing and developing a competency framework. An example of ICT competency framework is presented and discussed in order to illustrate the potential use of Open Linked Data. For instance, when exposed on the web, the framework is available for human and software agents. It can also be extensible and reducible according to needs.

M. Hamlich et al. (Eds.): SADASC 2020, CCIS 1207, pp. 339–348, 2020.
https://doi.org/10.1007/978-3-030-45183-7_26

The reminder of this article is organized as following: in the second section, related works are presented and discussed. Some challenges regarding the process of creating and publishing linked open data on the web are highlighted. We also present some research works, tools and technologies used in the field as well *as 5-star deployment scheme* of Open Linked Data proposed by the W3C Group. In the third section, two competency frameworks are presented. The purpose is to present examples of popular competency frameworks used by managers and institutions. In the fourth section, the methodology for creation a framework from existing competency frameworks using open linked data principles and related web technologies is explained. Finally, we came up with some conclusions, then we announce some future works.

2   Related Works

Linked Open Data (LOD) refers to a set of data available on the world wild web as semantic network. Data is structured in an oriented graph with nodes connected by semantic links. The "Open" is justified by the need for unrestricted access and reuse of data. The growing popularity of Open Linked Data in the literature is related to the growing need of interoperability and data integration from legacy data sources. For instance, data are stored on heterogeneous and distributed data sources [3]. Yusniel Hidalgo-Delgado [3] proposes to use linked data-based semantic interoperability framework for digital libraries. The purpose is to enable access and reuse of metadata by computers. To this end, the authors published library data according to linked data principals and web standards such as Resource Description Framework (RDF) and SPARQL (SPARQL Protocol and RDF Query Language). Another work [4] discusses technologies to access semantic referential called "Onto-Amazon-Timber" based on JENA API (Application Programming Interface) and SPARQL query language. Still, one of the main issues in the field is the lack of methodologies and guidelines to create and publish data on the web. Many standards, tools and technologies are proposed in the literature and there is no consensus among researchers and practitioners. To this end, [5] Proposes an integrated framework for knowledge representation and reasoning. The framework intend to gather all web technologies tools related to web of data in a unified environment for creating, exploring, visualizing and querying data. [6] Created a web application using techniques from web scrapping, Linked Data and Open Data technology. The application enables access to dashboard to visualize up-to-date and relevant information about education and job vacancy in Jakarta [6].

T. Berners-Lee proposed a 5-star deployment scheme [7] to identify costs and benefits of creating Open Linked Data for both consumers and publishers. Another work [8], provides a 5 star system to guide Public Administrations in setting up an Open Data Portal. According to T. Berners-Lee, one of the key points of linked Open Data is to provide users and application with quick access to relevant and structured data under an open license. The first star means that data should be available on the web under an Open License. The file format and structure is not important at this stage. The purpose is to make data available on the web in files and documents rather than using a scrapper to get data out of files. The first star recommends also the use of an Open License. The second star postulates that the data should be structured and machine readable. This enables computer and intelligent agents to process data inside documents. It also enables users to navigate between different nodes in the web of data. However, the main drawback at this level is that data may be structured, machine readable and available on the web but might depend on a proprietary software. To this end, the third star suggests to use an open format to store and publish data. Users and services could easily manipulate data when based on Open Format without the need for a specific software. The four star advocates the use of Uniform Resource Identifier (URI) to identify concepts on the web. Data could be structured and queried using W3C standards such as RDF and SPARQL. Finally, the five stars proposes to link data with exiting datasets on the web. The purpose is to enhance reuse of existing datasets and avoid reinventing the wheel. 5-star deployment scheme is depicted on table below (Table 1).

Table 1. 5-star deployment scheme of Open Linked Data

*	Data is available on the web under an Open License
**	Data is structured and machine readable
***	Using an open format
****	use URLs to identify things on the web
*****	Enhance Reuse of existing vocabularies to create new datasets

To sum up, Open Linked Data is useful to build and publish data over the web. Many technologies, standards and tools are presented in the literature to enhance interoperability among existing systems and to publish data as semantic graphs on the web. In the following section we present and discuss example of ICT competency frameworks which represents relevant data that inspired us to develop a new model of ICT frameworks.

3   ICT Competency Frameworks

Competency framework defines knowledge, skills, and abilities needed for employers within an organization. It is also used by institutions to match Curricula with Labour Market Needs and by HR managers in their recruitment process. Fernández-Sanz highlighted that there is linkable parts of the existing frameworks and proposed a framework that provides a useful system for job candidates and employers [9]. Still, data is stored on distributed and heterogeneous data sources. Some of data isn't explicitly machine-readable. In this section, two frameworks are presented namely e-CF and SFIA before we dive in the methodology we adopted to create an ICT framework based on web technologies.

3.1 Framework e-CF

The e-CF (European e-Competence Framework) [10] focuses on IT and communication technology skills. The framework is used by IT employees who want to improve their ICT skills, human resources managers, educational stakeholders, etc. The framework is also used in educational settings to prepare educational programs based on labor market demand or adjust existing ones responding to labor market changes.

The competencies described in e-CF framework are oriented towards performance in the workplace. The purpose is to improve the recruitment process based on a document that explains all the skills required to perform a given task or a job. It is also a reference for students who want to understand the requirements of the IT job market and to identify potential opportunities. The purpose of the e-CF framework is to offer a common definition that can be used by several European countries and reduce the gap between competences developed at school that are subject to qualifications and those required by the European job market referring to as professional competencies. For instance, the framework proposes an association between professional competencies and learning outcomes described by the EQF (European Qualification Framework).

According to e-CF framework, a competency can be defined as the ability to apply acquired knowledge as well as soft skills to demonstrate an observable results. Each competency is related to a proficiency level which integrates 3 main aspects: autonomy, context and behavior. It is also divided into five levels of performance: e-1, e-2, e-3, e-4 and e-5.

Actually, the framework is in its version 3.0 and structured in 4 dimensions:

- **Dimension 1:** Specifies the areas of competence that are described from the job profile.
- **Dimension 2:** Identifies the key competencies for each area of dimension 1.
- **Dimension 3:** Specifies the level of mastery of the competences for each key competence identified in dimension 2.
- **Dimension 4:** Provides examples of knowledge and skills for the competencies identified and described in dimensions 2 and 3.

3.2 SFIA Framework (Skills Framework for the Information Age)

The SFIA framework (SFIA V6) [11] is a framework for defining competencies and skills intended for IT professions. [12] It is a two-dimensional model displaying the professions on one axis and the levels of responsibility on the other. The SFIA framework is constantly updated in order to follow the job market demand. Especially for the IT field given the speed of its evolution. The SFIA standard has several objectives. First of all, it is open to public for consultation. Therefore, the first potential use of the repository would be to compare one's skills with those required for of a given profession. In this case, anyone will be able to highlight strengths and weaknesses and plan for improvements. HR managers use it in their recruitment process and educators can also use it to design training plans aligned with the IT (Information Technology) domain requirements.

SFIA framework is designed as following:

- IT professions are organized into categories and sub-categories. Each sub-category is described as a set of skills.
- Each skill is described by a name, a code, a description and a desired level of mastery.
- Each level is defined by the autonomy, influence, complexity and business skills involved: autonomy is defined as the ability of a person to work alone or ask for help when needed. Influence defines whether the person can work alone or must interact with colleagues to accomplish a task. Complexity describes the level of difficulty of the task. Finally, business skills refer to key competencies defined as action verbs that express what the person is capable of doing. The SFIA framework specifies for each category of jobs, the competencies involved and the desired degree of mastery.

For example, software development is an example of a competency identified by id "PROG". This competency belongs to the category "development and implementation", which includes everything related to modelling, developing, testing and documentation of computer software. The PROG competency belongs to the sub-category "system development". In order to be competent in programming, it is necessary to have mastery of levels N2, N3, N4, N5 as described in the table below (Table 2).

Table 2. Example of competency according to SFIA framework

Category	Sub-category	Competencies	Proficiency level
Development and implementation	System development	Programmation/Software development (PROG)	N2- N3- N4- N5

Although these frameworks hold relevant information. However, the computer processing of these information remains difficult. Most of the available information is in the form of web pages or PDF files. One potential solution could be to redesign those frameworks. For instance, we propose to use Linked Open data and ontologies to create a new model of ICT framework that can be used by human agents as well as software agents.

4 Methodology

In order to design a new ICT Competency Framework we proceeded as following:

- Design of competency framework as a domain ontology using a knowledge description language.
- Development of the ontology using the Protégé Editor.
- Publication of the ontology to be available on the web as Linked Open Data.

4.1 Ontology Design

In order to conceive an ontology. We first extracted relevant concepts from the literature and existing frameworks using natural language. Then, these fundamental concepts were structured in a domain ontology.

This step consists of creating the concepts, their properties, and semantic relationships. To this end we used the OWL knowledge representation language of the Protégé tool following these steps:

1. Creating classes: a class defines a group of individuals (instances of a class) with similar characteristics. Every class is a subclass of Owl:Thing. Classes are depicted in figure bellow with yellow color.
2. Creation of relations between classes: a relation takes the form of a triplet (Subject, Predicate, Object).
3. Creation of individuals: an individual is an instance of a class. For example in the following figure, "DeveOps" is an instance of the class "Competency"

Data is structured according the rdf serialization format. The purpose is to use an Open Format which is a fundamental aspect of Linked Open Data.

The figure below illustrates an overview of the ICT Framework ontology design using the OWL knowledge definition language using Protégé Tool. In this example, a competency is described by a name (rdfs: label), and has a definition. Each competency requires the acquisition of several skills with a level of performance (Fig. 1).

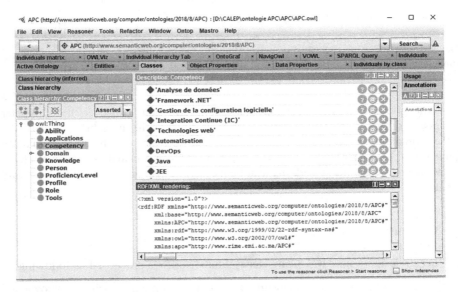

Fig. 1. Overview of the ICT Framework ontology using Protégé Tool (Color figure online)

In the sidebar, several instances are declared that represent competencies related to ICT domain. It is also possible to navigate in the knowledge base (ontology) to visualize its structure and its content using more sophisticated editors like the "Onto-dia". The Fig. 2, depicts a fragment of the ICT framework design.

- In order to develop a competency, one needs to acquire "Knowledge and "Abili-ties". Each of them is related to a proficiency level.
- A competency has a definition belongs to a domain.
- A profile has a definition, a context in which it is applied and includes one or many competencies.
- A person is identified by many information and acquires one or many competencies.
- A competency is applied in one or many domains.

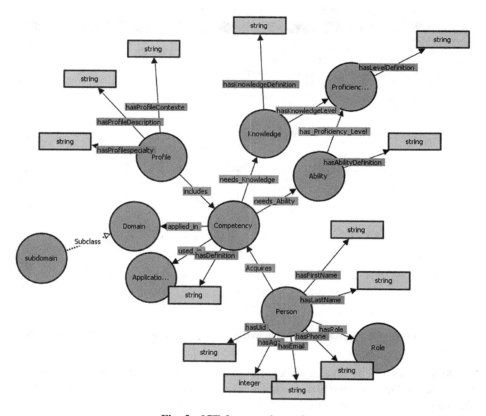

Fig. 2. ICT framework ontology

Once ontology design is created, and instances are added, it is considered as a knowledge base and can be used locally or published in a remote server. The ontology can be queried using an SQL Like query language called SPARQL language and can also be used in applications using APIs depending on the programming language the application uses. SPARQL is the acronym for SPARQL Protocol and RDF Query

Language and represents both a protocol and a query language. It allows to query RDF graphs: search, add, modify and delete RDF triplets. It is the equivalent of SQL for Linked Data and is a standard developed by the DAWG (Data Access Working Group) of the W3C.

The following figure (Fig. 3) describes an example of a SPARQL query. The first part contains a set of Prefixes used to define the ontology. This prevents the URIs from being repeated several times in the same query. Followed by the SELECT clause which specifies the variables that will be returned by the query. The WHERE clause specifies a set of conditions to be satisfied. For example, the query depicted in Fig. 3 return the list of ICT competencies stored in the ontology.

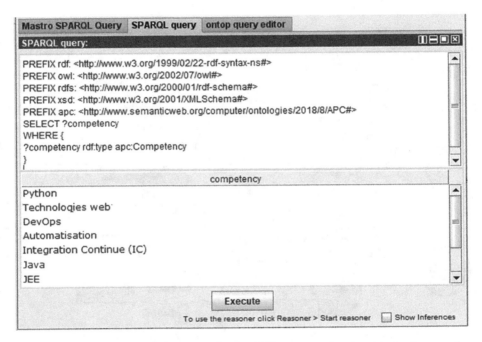

Fig. 3. Example of a SPARQL query showing ICT competencies stored in the framework

At this stage, the ICT framework is designed as a domain ontology, and stored in a local system. The next step is to make data available for all users and applications over the web as Open Linked Data. The next section provides an overview of the step of publishing data on a remote server.

4.2   Publish the ICT Framework

To make our data available on the web we used the Fuseki server [13]. The ontology is published as Linked Open Data. It is accessible via the http protocol from any application and from any web browser. The server allows also remote access data and provides SPARQL End-point to query the content of the framework using a web form. Content returned by the server may be JSON, XML or CSV file format. For example, in the following figure (Fig. 4), the user asks for a description of a Profile named "Full Stack Java Developer", the language of the response should be in French (@fr). Figure 5 shows an example response provided by Fuseki Server as JSON file format. The purpose of using JSON as output format is to enable external service consuming Open Linked Data such as REST Web Services or Multi-agents Systems, etc.

Fig. 4. Example of SPARQL query related to Linked Open Data

Fig. 5. Example of response of Fuseki Server as JSON format

5 Conclusion

This paper discusses a new linked data-based approach for building online ICT frameworks from scratch. The proposed method is based on web technologies, standards and emerging tools to ensure interoperability with existing systems. OWL language definition is used to create a model of ICT Framework based on existing ones in the literature. As result, data from multiples frameworks was aggregated and added to the model using RDF technology. RDF ensures easy information processing by computers. After that, data was published on the web as Open Linked Data using Fuseki Server. The purpose is to provide both educators and intelligent systems with a knowledge base holding relevant data about competencies and their requirements. For future work, we intend to create a web application for visualizing and exploring data of ICT framework.

References

1. Koster, A., Schalekamp, T., Meijerman, I.: Implementation of Competency-Based Pharmacy Education (CBPE). Pharmacy **5**(4), 10 (2017)
2. Fleiner, R.: Linking of open government data. In: SACI 2018 - IEEE 12th International Symposium on Applied Computational Intelligence and Informatics, Proceedings, pp. 479–483 (2018)
3. Hidalgo-Delgado, Y., Xu, B., Mariño-Molerio, A.J., Febles-Rodríguez, J.P., Leiva-Mederos, A.A.: A linked data-based semantic interoperability framework for digital libraries. Revista Cubana de Ciencias Informáticas **13**(1), 14–30 (2019)

4. da Ponte, M.J.M., Figueiras, P.A., Jardim-Gonçalves, R., Lima, C.P.: Ontological interaction using JENA and SPARQL applied to Onto-AmazonTimber ontology. In: C-M, L.M., Falcão, A.J., Vafaei, N., Najdi, S. (eds.) DoCEIS 2016. IAICT, vol. 470, pp. 54–61. Springer, Cham (2016). https://doi.org/10.1007/978-3-319-31165-4_6
5. Mishra, S., Jain, S.: A unified approach for OWL ontologies (2016)
6. Hosen, A., Alfina, I.: Aggregation of open data information using linked data: case study education and job vacancy data in Jakarta. In: 2016 International Conference on Advanced Computer Science and Information Systems, ICACSIS 2016, pp. 579–584 (2017)
7. Tim, B.-L.: 5-star open data (2006). https://5stardata.info/en/. Accessed 06 Feb 2020
8. Colpaert, P., Joye, S.: The 5 stars of open data portals. In: Proceedings of the 7th International Conference on Methodologies, Technologies and Tools Enabling E-Government, pp. 61–67 (2013)
9. Fernández-Sanz, L., Gómez-Pérez, J., Castillo-Martínez, A.: e-Skills match: a framework for mapping and integrating the main skills, knowledge and competence standards and models for ICT occupations. Comput. Stand. Interfaces 51, 30–42 (2017)
10. Breyer, J.: European e-competence framework. Framework (2007)
11. SFIA: Skills framework for the information age (2012). https://www.sfia-online.org/en/framework/sfia-6/reference-guide. Accessed 04 Feb 2020
12. Costa, C., Santos, M.Y.: The data scientist profile and its representativeness in the European e-Competence framework and the skills framework for the information age. Int. J. Inf. Manag. 37(6), 726–734 (2017)
13. Apache_Jena_Fuseki: Apache Jena - Apache Jena Fuseki (2018). https://jena.apache.org/documentation/fuseki2/. Accessed 02 Feb 2020

An Overview of Gradient Descent Algorithm Optimization in Machine Learning: Application in the Ophthalmology Field

Aatila Mustapha[(⊠)], Lachgar Mohamed[(⊠)], and Kartit Ali[(⊠)]

LTI Laboratory, ENSA, Chouaib Doukkali University, El Jadida, Morocco
mu.aatila@gmail.com, lachgar.m@gmail.com,
alikartit@gmail.com

Abstract. Maximizing or minimizing a function is a problem in several areas. In computer science and for systems based on Machine Learning (ML), a panoply of optimization algorithms makes it possible to grasp the main learning bases, particularly in terms of features number, and this by reducing the volume of data to be kept in memory while producing satisfactory results. Among these algorithms, the different variants of the gradient descent algorithm which is widely used in ML. This paper presents a comparative study of batch, stochastic and mini-batch gradient descent algorithms as well as the normal equation algorithm of optimization, this study will facilitate the choice of the appropriate optimization algorithm to adopt when building a system based on ML. The case study implemented in this work is based on the keratoconus dataset of Harvard Dataverse. The obtained results show that stochastic and mini-batch gradient descent algorithms represent the best performances than the other algorithms, particularly for systems based on ML involving a high number of variables.

Keywords: Optimization · Batch gradient descent · Stochastic gradient descent · Mini-batch gradient descent · Normal equation

1 Introduction

Artificial intelligence (AI) based on ML has drawn tremendous attention in recent years. ML integrates several fields such as recognition of objects in images or video scenes, planning of robot movements to do a given task, vehicle automatic driving or text recognition.

AI has also revolutionized the field of health, systems based on ML make it possible to detect certain diseases, such as cancer and many other diseases, and to predict their evolution. In ophthalmology [1], research works have helped ophthalmologists to diagnose the eye [2], they also allow the classification of some diseases such as age-related macular degeneration, glaucoma, diabetic retinopathy and keratoconus [3, 4].

These systems must analyze a very large volume of data (thousands or millions of images) to be able to classify the different diseases during the diagnoses. The processing of such large data is costly and requires high material resources, hence the usefulness of optimization algorithms.

© Springer Nature Switzerland AG 2020
M. Hamlich et al. (Eds.): SADASC 2020, CCIS 1207, pp. 349–359, 2020.
https://doi.org/10.1007/978-3-030-45183-7_27

The present paper is organized in five sections: Sect. 2 presents the normal equation algorithm, the batch, stochastic and mini-batch gradient descent algorithms. Section 3 flies over some related works. Simulation and experimental results are given in the Sect. 4. The Sect. 5 contains obtained results discussion and analysis. Finally, conclusions derived are presented in Sect. 6.

2 Context

Several ML techniques have been implemented, namely: decision trees, vector machine support (SVM) and different types of neural networks [5].

In ophthalmology, ML systems have demonstrated good distinction between the normal eye and the sick one [6]. These systems are based on the analysis of the eye topographic images and manipulate a very large number of features, hence the importance of optimization algorithms to reduce the volume of processed data.

2.1 Normal Equation Algorithm

The normal equation is an analytical (non-iterative) method of calculating the global minimum, or the weight that minimize the cost function. This approach is very effective and reduces time when using datasets with small features [7]. The mathematical equation of this algorithm is described as following:

$$\theta = \left(X^T \cdot X\right)^{-1} \cdot X^T \cdot y \tag{1}$$

Where θ is the cost function minimization value, y is the target values vector and X is the features matrix.

For the used features matrix X, the normal equation algorithm is the following:

- Add an additional column (bias x_0)
- Build a matrix which contains all the features of the training data
- Construct the target values vector y
- Use the following equation: $\theta = \left(X^T \cdot X\right)^{-1} \cdot X^T \cdot y$

However, as the features number increases, the performances of the normal equation gradually decrease. This is due to the costly matrix computations since it is necessary to keep all the data in memory for the calculations.

2.2 Gradient Descent Algorithms

The resolution of the optimization problems using the analytical method is not always obvious given the great number of parameters or the very expensive calculations. One of the most popular optimization algorithms used to optimize features in ML is gradient descent [5]. The gradient descent algorithm provides a solution using an iterative approach which gradually corrects the parameters in order to minimize the cost function [8]. The three variants of gradient descent algorithm studied in this work differ in the amount of data used to calculate the gradient of the objective function [8].

Batch Gradient Descent Algorithm. The batch gradient descent algorithm implementation is carried out by calculating the gradient of the cost function with respect to each parameter θ_i of the model, i.e. the modification of the cost function when we modify a little θ_i, to do this, partial derivatives are calculated. The partial derivative of the cost function (mean squared error MSE) with respect to θ_j denoted: $\frac{\partial}{\partial \theta_j} MSE(\theta)$ is calculated as follows [7]:

$$\frac{\partial}{\partial \theta_j} MSE(\theta) = \frac{2}{m} \sum_{i=1}^{m} \left(\theta^T \cdot X^{(i)} - y^{(i)} \right) x_j^{(i)} \tag{2}$$

It's possible to calculate the vector of partial derivatives all together instead of calculating them individually, the gradient vector $\nabla_\theta MSE(\theta)$ composed of all these partial derivatives of the cost function is the following [7]:

$$\nabla_\theta MSE(\theta) = \begin{pmatrix} \frac{\partial}{\partial \theta_0} MSE(\theta) \\ \frac{\partial}{\partial \theta_1} MSE(\theta) \\ \cdot \\ \cdot \\ \cdot \\ \frac{\partial}{\partial \theta_n} MSE(\theta) \end{pmatrix} = \frac{2}{m} X^T \cdot (X \cdot \theta - y) \tag{3}$$

The step of convergence towards the minimization solution is given by the following equation [8]:

$$\theta = \theta - \eta \times \nabla_\theta MSE(\theta) \tag{4}$$

The algorithm of minimization can be depicted as follows:

- Initialize θ_0 (randomly)
- Repeat
- $\theta_{t+1} = \theta_t - \eta \times \nabla_\theta MSE(\theta_t)$
- Until convergence

Where $\nabla_\theta MSE(\theta_t)$ is the gradient, generalization of the derivative at point θ_t, η is the learning rate and convergence is a fixed number of iterations. It's generally impossible to suggest good values for θ_0.

Stochastic Gradient Descent Algorithm (SGD). Batch gradient descent algorithm recomputes the gradients for similar examples before each parameters update [7], so it performs redundant calculations for large datasets. SGD avoid this redundancy by performing one update at a time. It is therefore generally much faster and can also be used for learning online. SGD performs frequent updates with a high variance, for that, the objective function changes strongly [7]. SGD chooses at each step only one observation, taken randomly, from the training set and calculates the gradients based just on this single observation. This makes the algorithm faster, because it has little data to manipulate at each iteration [7]. The mathematical equation of the stochastic gradient descent algorithm is structured as follows [8]:

$$\theta_{t+1} = \theta_t - \eta \times \nabla_\theta \text{MSE}(z_t, \theta_t) \tag{5}$$

Where z_t is the observation randomly selected at each iteration [9]. The algorithm of the stochastic gradient descent is as follows:

Input: initial vector θ, learning rate η
   Repeat until convergence and k ≤ maximum number of iterations
     mix the dataset
     For i = 1, 2, 3, . . ., n
       Select an observation randomly
       Calculate the step with the gradient from $\nabla_f(\theta)$, scores and η
       θ = θ + step
     Endfor
   EndRepeat

Mini-batch Gradient Descent Algorithm. The mini-batch gradient descent algorithm allows, at each iteration, to compute the gradients for small fixed size subsets of observations, those subsets are randomly selected and called mini-batches [7]. This algorithm is faster than the batch and the stochastic gradient algorithms. The mathematical equation of the mini-batch gradient descent algorithm is structured as follows [8]:

$$\theta_{t+1} = \theta_t - \eta \times \nabla_\theta MSE(z_t, \theta_t) \tag{6}$$

Where z_t is the mini-batch randomly picked at each iteration [7]. The mini-batch gradient descent algorithm is below:

Input: initial vector θ, mini-batch size j, learning rate η
Repeat until convergence and k ≤ maximum number of iterations
   mix the dataset
   For i = 1, 2, 3, . . ., n/j
      build a mini-batch with j individuals
      calculate the scores for each individual in the mini-batch
      calculate the step with the gradient from $\nabla_f(\theta)$, scores and η
      θ = θ + step
      i = i + j
   Endfor
EndRepeat

3   Related Works

The gradient descent algorithm is widely used in ML, particularly for optimizing neural networks. Several research works have focused on the comparison of different gradient descent algorithms. [9] presents an improved Adagrad gradient descent algorithm in order to provide optimization solutions with more stable convergence function in multiple epochs. In [10] authors propose an approach to guide SGD algorithm through inconsistency present in a dataset, this approach is compatible with all the popular variations of SGD such as Adagrad and Momentum. The authors in [11] presented a comparative study of the SGD algorithms, based on the alternate minimization, for the computations of matrices on a large scale. In [12] the authors provide useful recommendations to apply the SGD and explain the efficiency of this algorithm, used in large datasets. Authors in [13] propose a comparative study of the normal equation and the gradient descent algorithms in order to minimize the cost function for online prediction, using linear regression with several variables.

4   Case Study

Proposed case study is implemented in Python in order to compare the performances of the already cited algorithms. This implementation is based on the keratoconus dataset of Harvard Dataverse. The dataset used is composed of two columns and 96 rows. For the gradient descent algorithms, we maintained the same number of iterations and the same learning rate in all experiments.

4.1   Data Visualization

The visualization of the used dataset is presented in the figure below. The visualized data represent the correlation between steep corneal meridian (Ks) and flat corneal meridian (Kf) (Fig. 1).

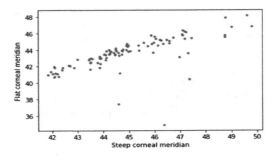

Fig. 1. Data visualization.

The visualization of data shows a linear correlation between the variables. As the value of the steep corneal meridian increases, so does the flat corneal meridian value.

4.2 Normal Equation

The normal equation makes it possible to find a predictive function F(X) which will take as input a steep corneal meridian and will produce as output an estimate of the expected flat corneal meridian. The idea is to have a prediction close to the observed value $F(X) \approx Y$.

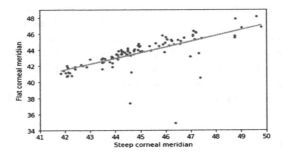

Fig. 2. Normal equation solution. (Color figure online)

The red line represents the normal equation solution, the solution approaches as much as possible all the points of the dataset.

4.3 Batch Gradient Descent

The application of the batch gradient descent algorithm to the same data with 250 iterations and a learning rate of 0.0001 provides the solution generated in the following graph.

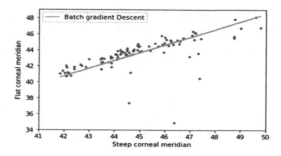

Fig. 3. Batch gradient descent solution.

The minimization solution generated by the batch gradient descent algorithm provides a curve close to the dataset with some difference compared to the curve of the normal equation. The convergence global cost error corresponding to the number of iterations is presented in the following graph.

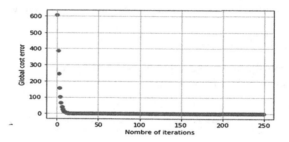

Fig. 4. Convergence global cost error of the batch gradient descent.

After a certain number of iterations, the global cost error function stabilizes, this stability indicates the convergence of the algorithm.

4.4 Stochastic Gradient Descent

The curve represented in the graph below illustrates the results of the stochastic gradient descent algorithm with a learning rate $\eta = 0.0001$ and 250 iterations.

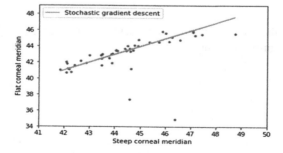

Fig. 5. Stochastic gradient descent solution.

The convergence global cost error compared to the number of iterations for the stochastic gradient solution is presented in the following graph.

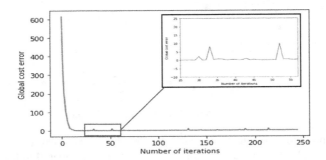

Fig. 6. Convergence global cost error of the stochastic gradient descent.

The global cost error function obtained fluctuates in the convergence.

4.5 Mini-batch Gradient Descent

The following graph illustrates the solution obtained by the application of the mini-batch gradient descent with a learning rate $\eta = 0.0001$ and 250 iterations.

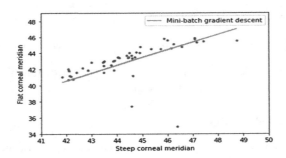

Fig. 7. Mini-batch gradient descent solution.

The curve in the following graph represents the convergence global cost error function for the mini-batch solution.

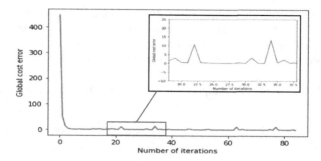

Fig. 8. Convergence global cost error for the mini-batch solution.

The mini-batch cost function generated represents an instability in the convergence.

4.6   Algorithms Comparison

The figure below illustrates the comparison of the solutions obtained by the application of different algorithms.

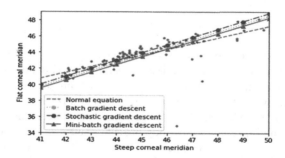

Fig. 9. Comparison of different algorithms solutions.

5   Discussion of Simulation Results

The solutions obtained by the application of normal equation, batch gradient, stochastic gradient and mini-batch gradient algorithms are presented respectively in Figs. 2, 3, 5 and 7. The mean absolute error (MAE) calculated for normal equation algorithm result is 0.754, the MAE provided by the batch gradient algorithm solution is 0.816, the solution found by the mini-batch gradient algorithm presents a MAE of 0.931 and the stochastic gradient algorithm solution MAE is 0.722.

For iterative algorithms, the batch gradient result presents a stabilization of the cost error function from a given point as illustrated in Fig. 4, this stability shows the convergence of the algorithm to an optimization solution. The cost error functions of stochastic gradient solution and mini-batch gradient minimization, generated respectively in Figs. 6 and 8, provide fluctuations in the convergence of the algorithms, this variance shows that algorithms continue to move around of the minimization solution and calculate an approximation close to the minimum [8]. The Fig. 9 illustrates the comparison of different solutions generated by all the algorithms already studied.

The table below illustrates the performances of the different studied algorithms.

Table 1. Performances of different algorithms studied.

Algorithms	Mean absolute error	High variables number	High iterations number
Normal equation	0.754	Slow	Rapid
Batch gradient	0.816	Slow	Slow
Stochastic gradient	0.722	Rapid	Rapid
Mini-batch gradient	0.931	Rapid	Rapid

The experiments of the different algorithms, accordingly to [7] and [8], show that increasing the number of iterations and the number of variables influences their performances as mentioned in the Table 1.

6 Conclusion

This work presented a comparative study of batch, stochastic mini-batch gradient descent algorithms, as well as the algorithm of the normal equation optimization. The main motivation for this comparative study is based on the large using of those algorithms in ML, particularly in neural networks optimization. Among the studied algorithms, stochastic and mini-batch algorithms are interesting considering the approximation of minimization which they provide, their speed and the possibility of using them for large datasets. The batch gradient and the normal equation algorithms provide good solutions, but the calculations become slower or impossible in the case of large datasets. This work was realized to compare these algorithms for a later use in an image classification work for the keratoconus detection and prediction.

References

1. Parampal, G., Faraz, O., et al.: Deep learning in ophthalmology: a review. Can. J. Ophthalmol. **53**(4), 309–313 (2018)
2. Ting, D., Pasquale, L., Peng, L., et al.: Artificial intelligence and deep learning in ophthalmology. Br. J. Ophthalmol. **103**(2), 167–175 (2019)
3. Alexandru, L., Popa, V.: KeratoDetect: keratoconus detection algorithm using convolutional neural networks. Hindawi Comput. Intell. Neurosci. **2019**, 1–9 (2019)
4. Qaisar, A.: Glaucoma-deep: detection of glaucoma eye disease on retinal fundus images using deep learning. (IJACSA) Int. J. Adv. Comput. Sci. Appl. **8**, 41–45 (2017)

5. Simon, S., Jason, D., Haochuan, L., Liwei, W., Xiyu, Z.: Gradient descent finds global minima of deep neural networks. In: 36 th International Conference on Machine Learning, PMLR 1997, Long Beach, California, pp. 1675–1685 (2019)
6. Ehsan, R.: Deep learning applications in ophthalmology. Curr. Opin. Ophthalmol. **29**(3), 254–260 (2018)
7. Aurélien, G.: Deep learning Avec TensorFlow, mise en œuvre et cas concrets, DUNOD (2017)
8. Sebastian, R.: An overview of gradient descent optimization algorithms (2016). https://arxiv. org/abs/1609.04747. Accessed 05 Feb 2020
9. Zhang, N., Lei, D., Zhao, J.F.: An improved Adagrad gradient descent optimization algorithm. In: 2018 Chinese Automation Congress (CAC), pp. 2359–2362. IEEE (2018)
10. Anuraganand, S.: Guided stochastic gradient descent algorithm for inconsistent datasets. Appl. Soft Comput. **73**, 1068–1080 (2018)
11. Faraz, M., Christina, T., et al.: Shared-memory and shared-nothing stochastic gradient descent algorithms for matrix completion. Knowl. Inf. Syst. **42**, 493–523 (2015)
12. Bottou, L.: Stochastic gradient descent tricks. In: Montavon, G., Orr, G.B., Müller, K.-R. (eds.) Neural Networks: Tricks of the Trade. LNCS, vol. 7700, pp. 421–436. Springer, Heidelberg (2012). https://doi.org/10.1007/978-3-642-35289-8_25
13. Fetty, F., et al.: Gradient descent and normal equations on cost function minimization for online predictive using linear regression with multiple variables. In: International Conference on ICT For Smart Society (ICISS), Bandung, Indonesia (2014)

Author Index

Printed in the United States
By Bookmasters